Shojo Beat

kimi ni todoke
From Me to You

Vol. 6

Story & Art by
Karuho Shiina

Volume 6

Contents

Story Thus Far

Sawako Kuronuma has always been a loner. Though not by choice, this optimistic 15-year-old can't seem to make any friends. Stuck with the unfortunate nickname "Sadako" after the haunting movie character, rumors about her summoning spirits have been greatly exaggerated. With her shy personality and scary looks, most of her classmates would barely talk to her, much less look into her eyes for more than three seconds lest they be cursed. Drawn out of her shell by her popular classmate Shota Kazehaya, Sawako is no longer an outcast in class. And with her new friends Ayane and Chizu, she's finally leading a more normal teenage life. Sawako helps Chizu shop for a birthday present for her childhood friend Ryu. Ryu told Sawako about his feelings for Chizu, but it turns out that Chizu likes Ryu's brother, Toru. Chizu is excited to show herself in a miniskirt to Toru when he comes home for New Year's. However, Toru comes home early with a surprise...

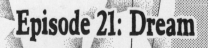

kimi ni todoke
From Me to You

Episode 21: Dream

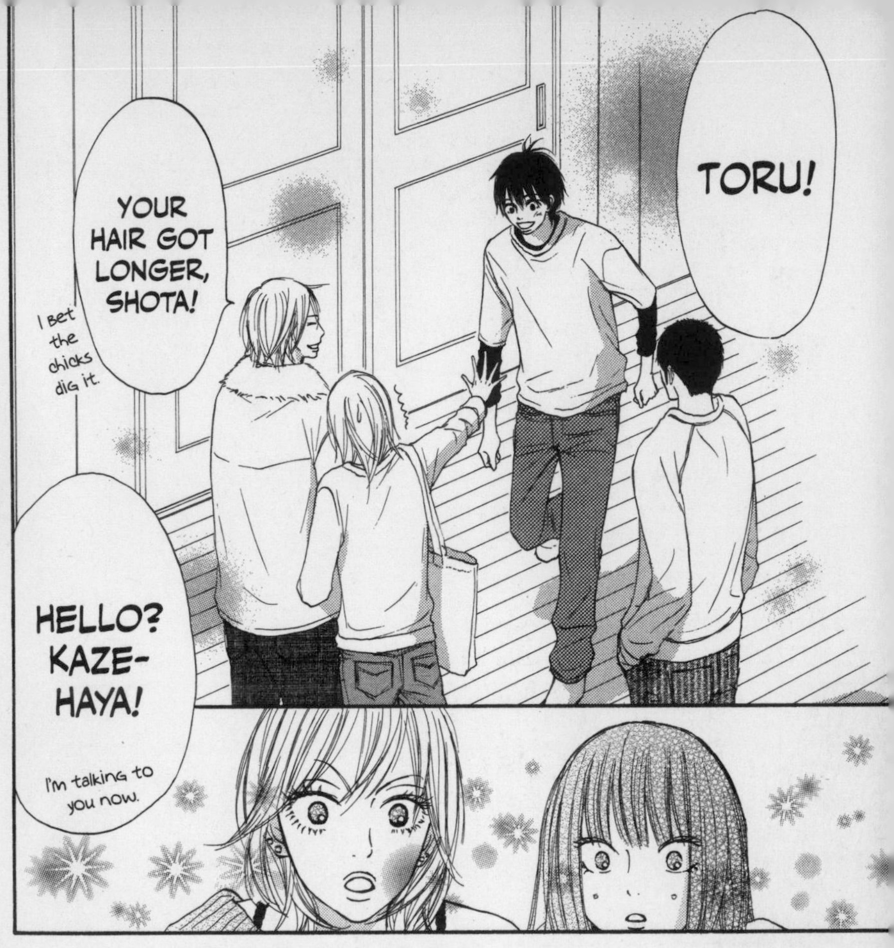
TORU!
YOUR HAIR GOT LONGER, SHOTA!
I bet the chicks dig it.
HELLO? KAZE-HAYA!
I'm talking to you now.

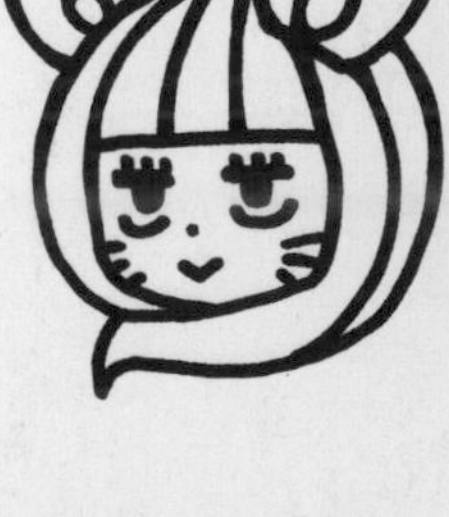

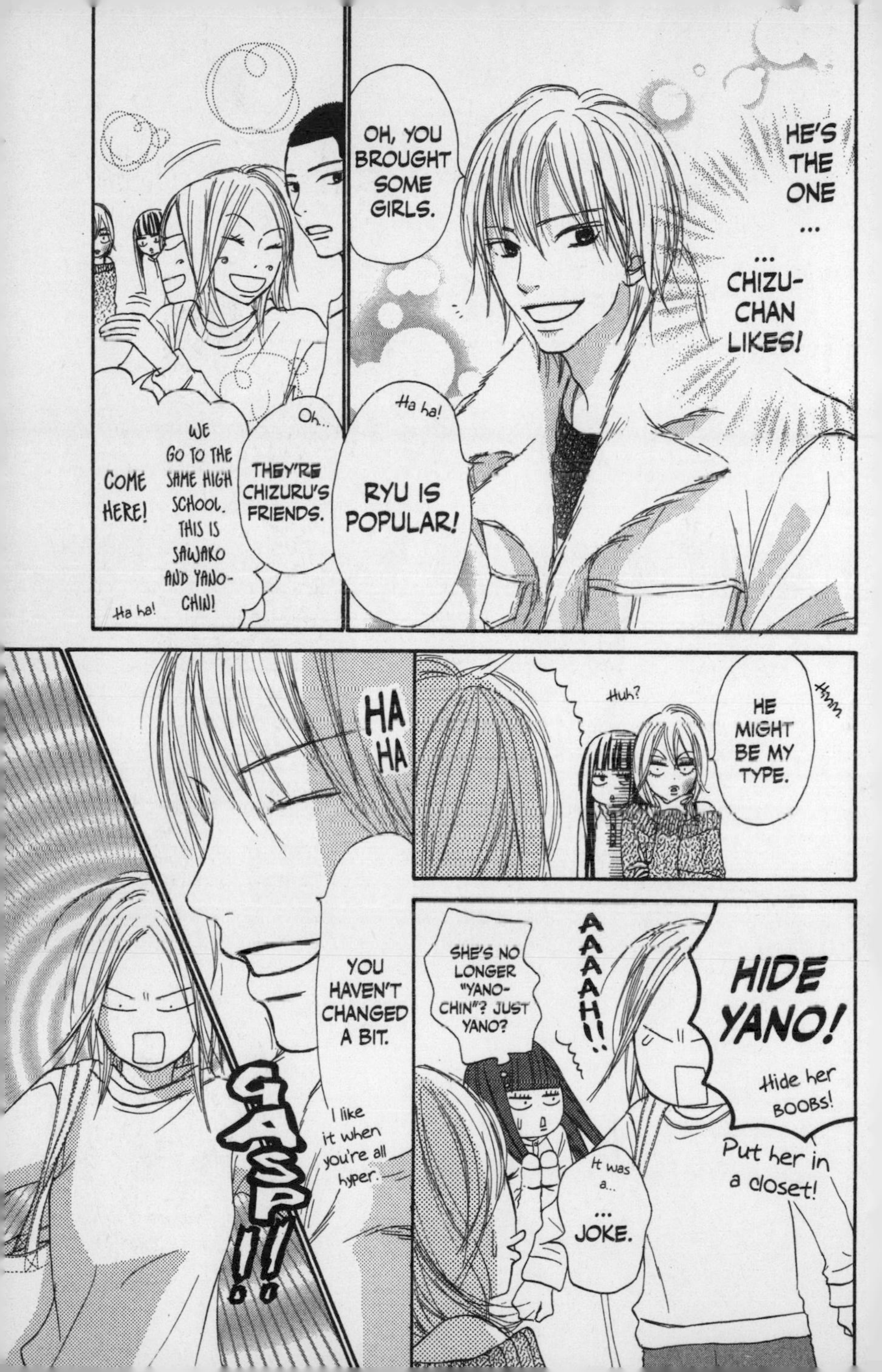
HE'S THE ONE ...
... CHIZU-CHAN LIKES!
OH, YOU BROUGHT SOME GIRLS.
Ha ha!
RYU IS POPULAR!
Oh...
THEY'RE CHIZURU'S FRIENDS.
WE GO TO THE SAME HIGH SCHOOL. THIS IS SAWAKO AND YANO-CHIN!
COME HERE!
Ha ha!
Hmm
HE MIGHT BE MY TYPE.
Huh?
HIDE YANO!
Hide her BOOBS!
Put her in a closet!
AAAAH!!
SHE'S NO LONGER "YANO-CHIN"? JUST YANO?
It was a...
... JOKE.
HA HA
YOU HAVEN'T CHANGED A BIT.
I like it when you're all hyper.
GASP!!

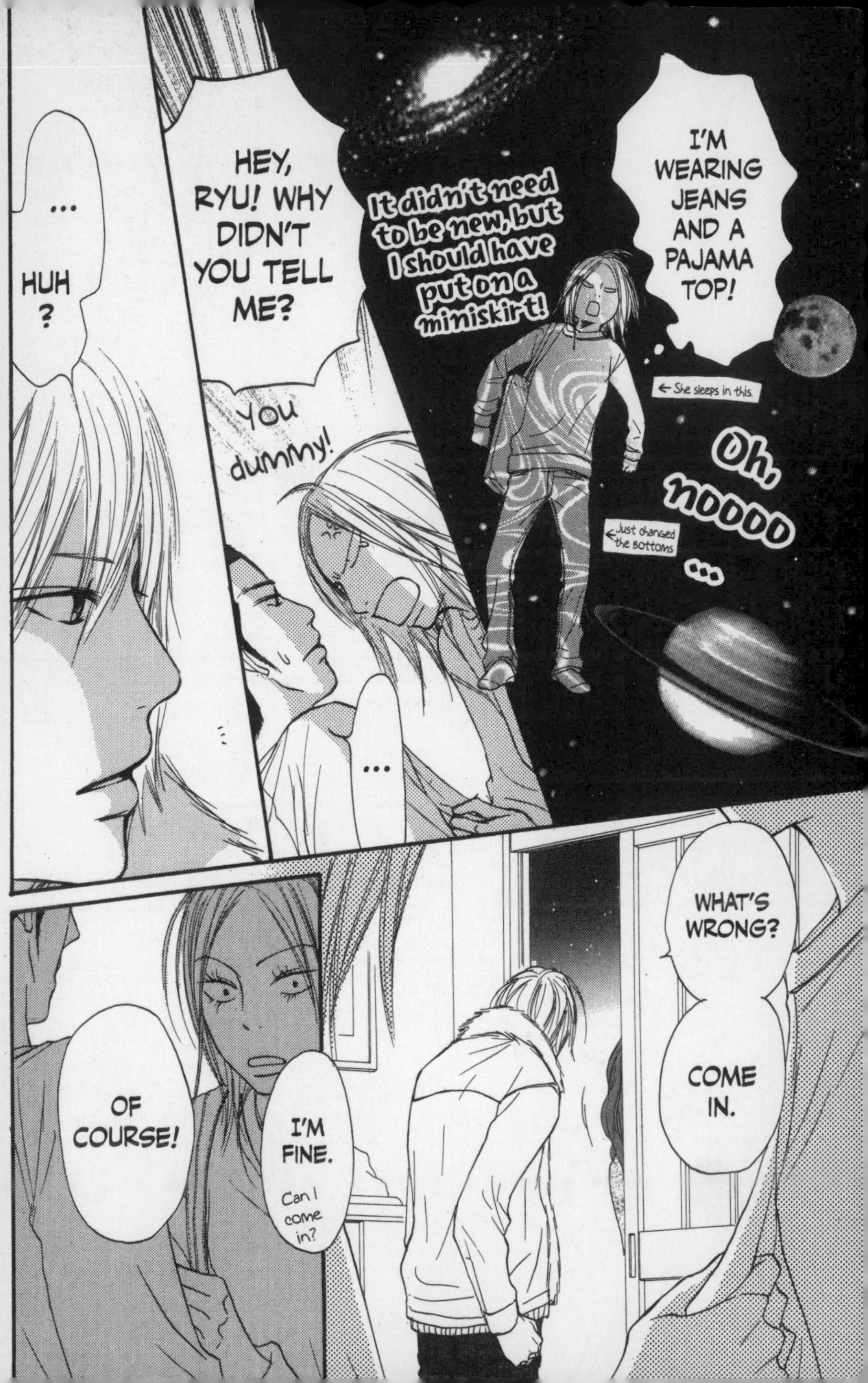
I'M WEARING JEANS AND A PAJAMA TOP!
It didn't need to be new, but I should have put on a miniskirt!
← She sleeps in this.
Oh, noooo ...
← Just changed the bottoms
HEY, RYU! WHY DIDN'T YOU TELL ME?
You dummy!
...
...
HUH?
WHAT'S WRONG?
COME IN.
I'M FINE.
Can I come in?
OF COURSE!

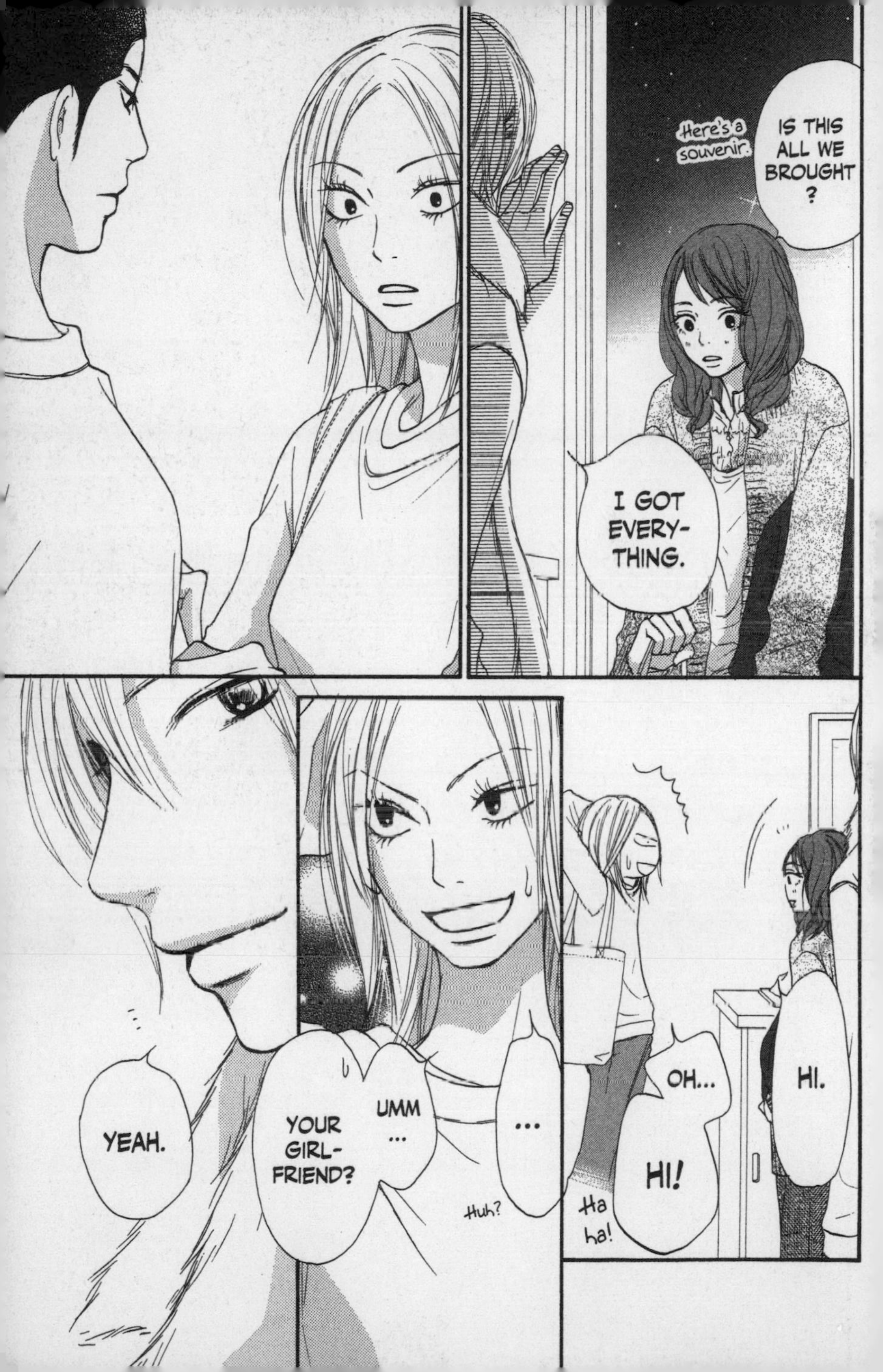
IS THIS ALL WE BROUGHT?
Here's a souvenir.
I GOT EVERY-THING.
HI.
OH...
HI!
Ha ha!
...
Huh?
UMM ...
YOUR GIRL-FRIEND?
YEAH.

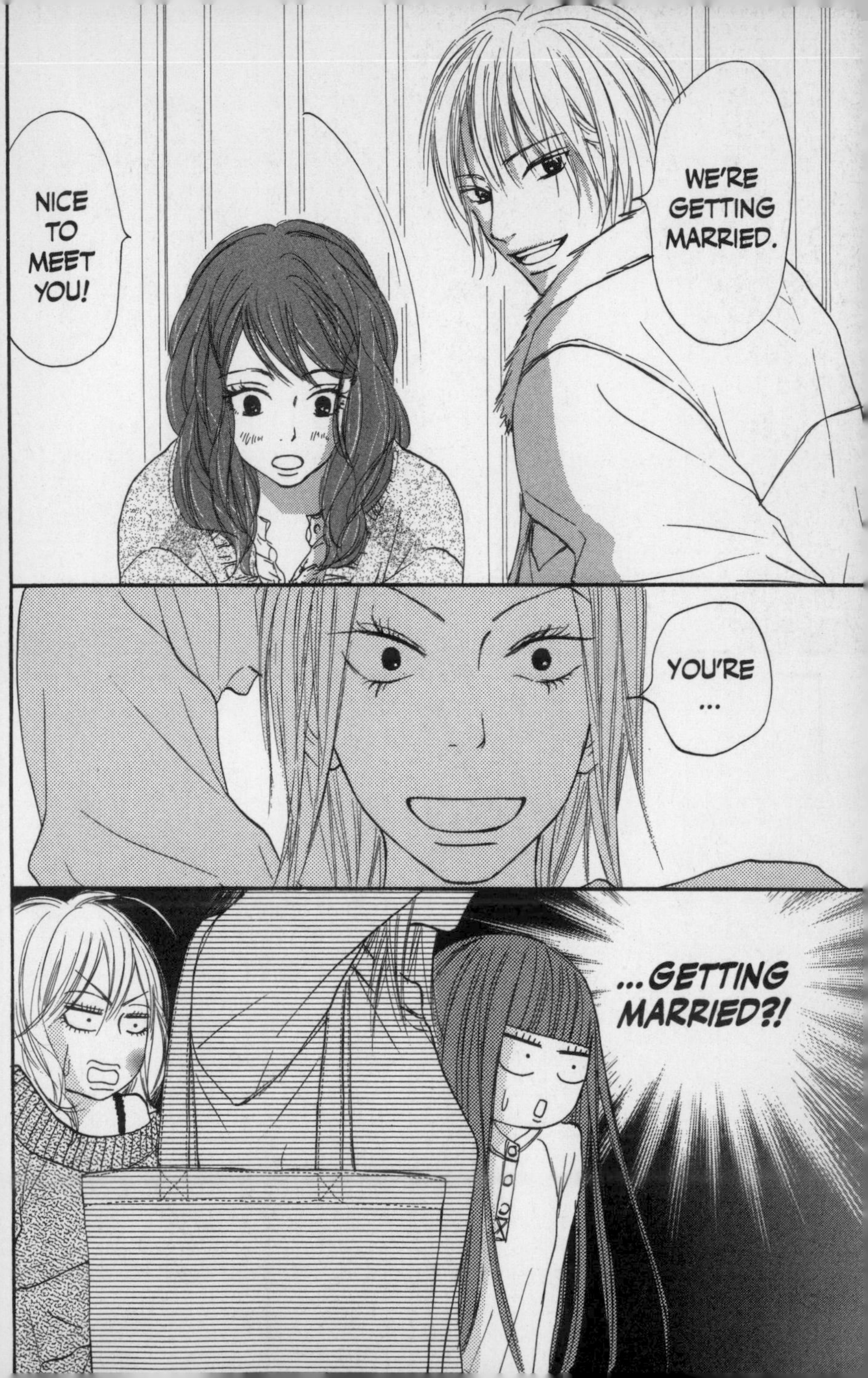
WE'RE GETTING MARRIED.
NICE TO MEET YOU!
YOU'RE ...
...GETTING MARRIED?!

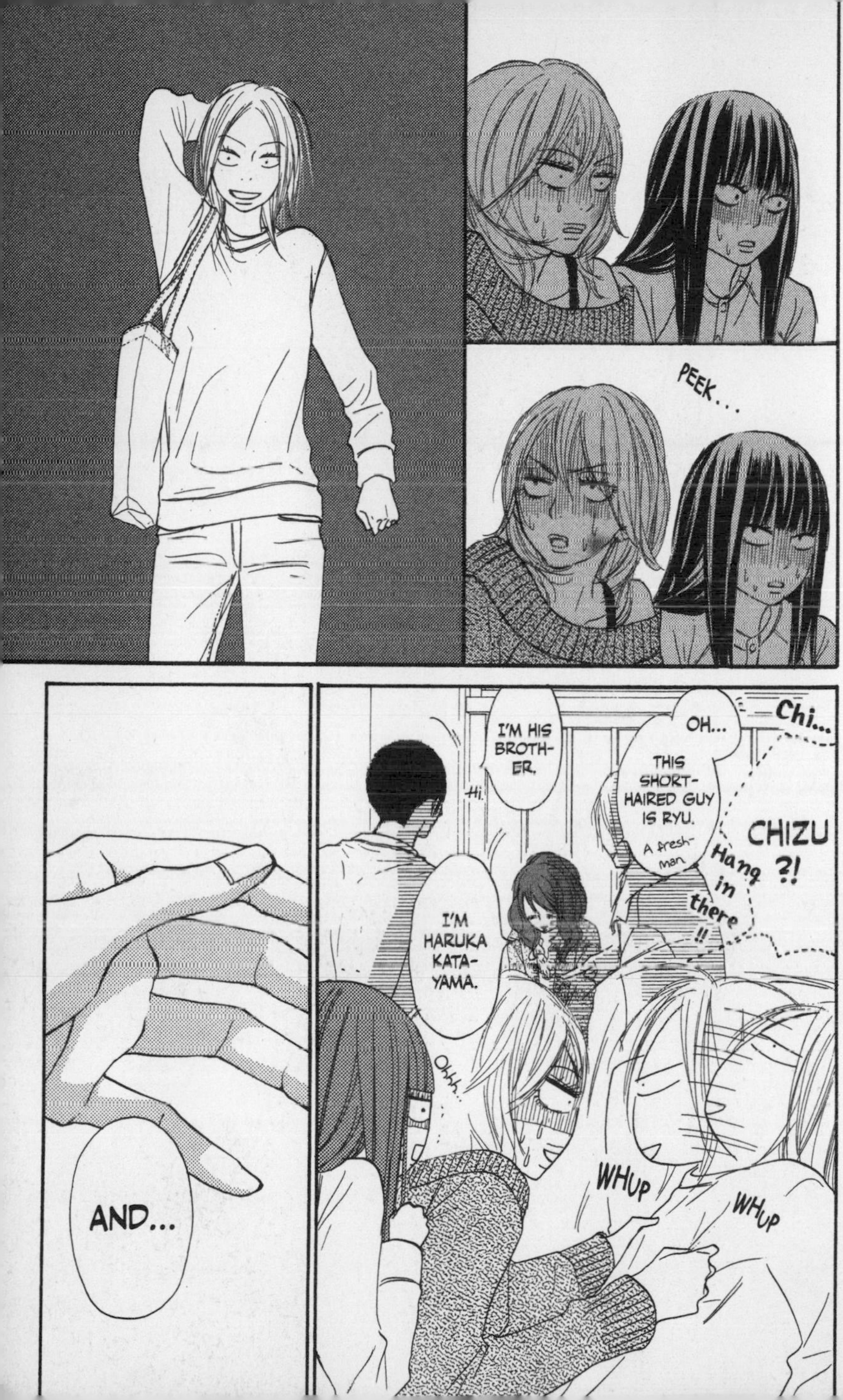
PEEK...
Chi...
CHIZU ?!
Hang in there!!
OH... THIS SHORT-HAIRED GUY IS RYU.
A fresh-man.
I'M HIS BROTH-ER.
Hi.
I'M HARUKA KATA-YAMA.
Ohhh...
WHUP
WHUP
AND...

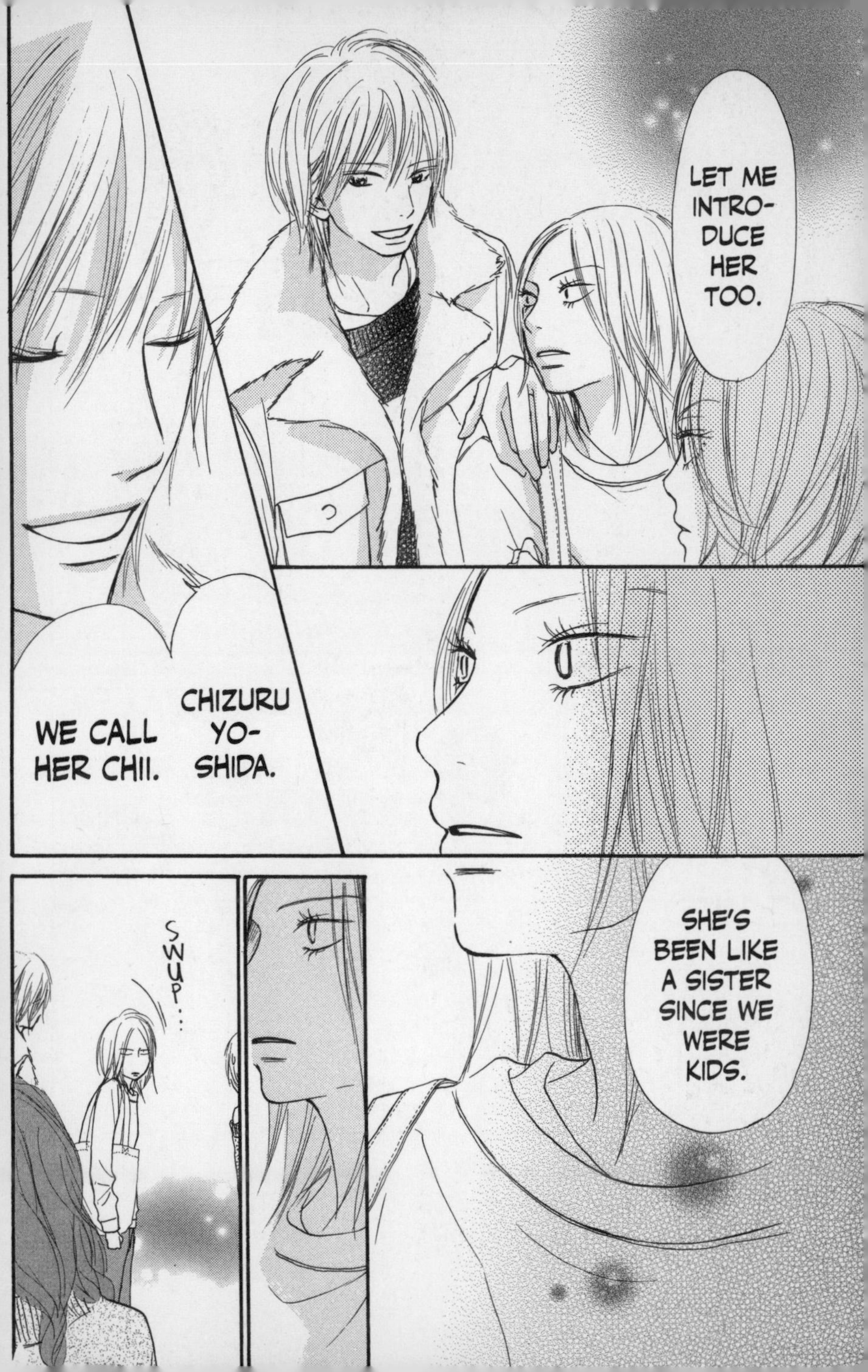
LET ME INTRO-DUCE HER TOO.
CHIZURU YO-SHIDA.
WE CALL HER CHII.
SHE'S BEEN LIKE A SISTER SINCE WE WERE KIDS.
SWUP...

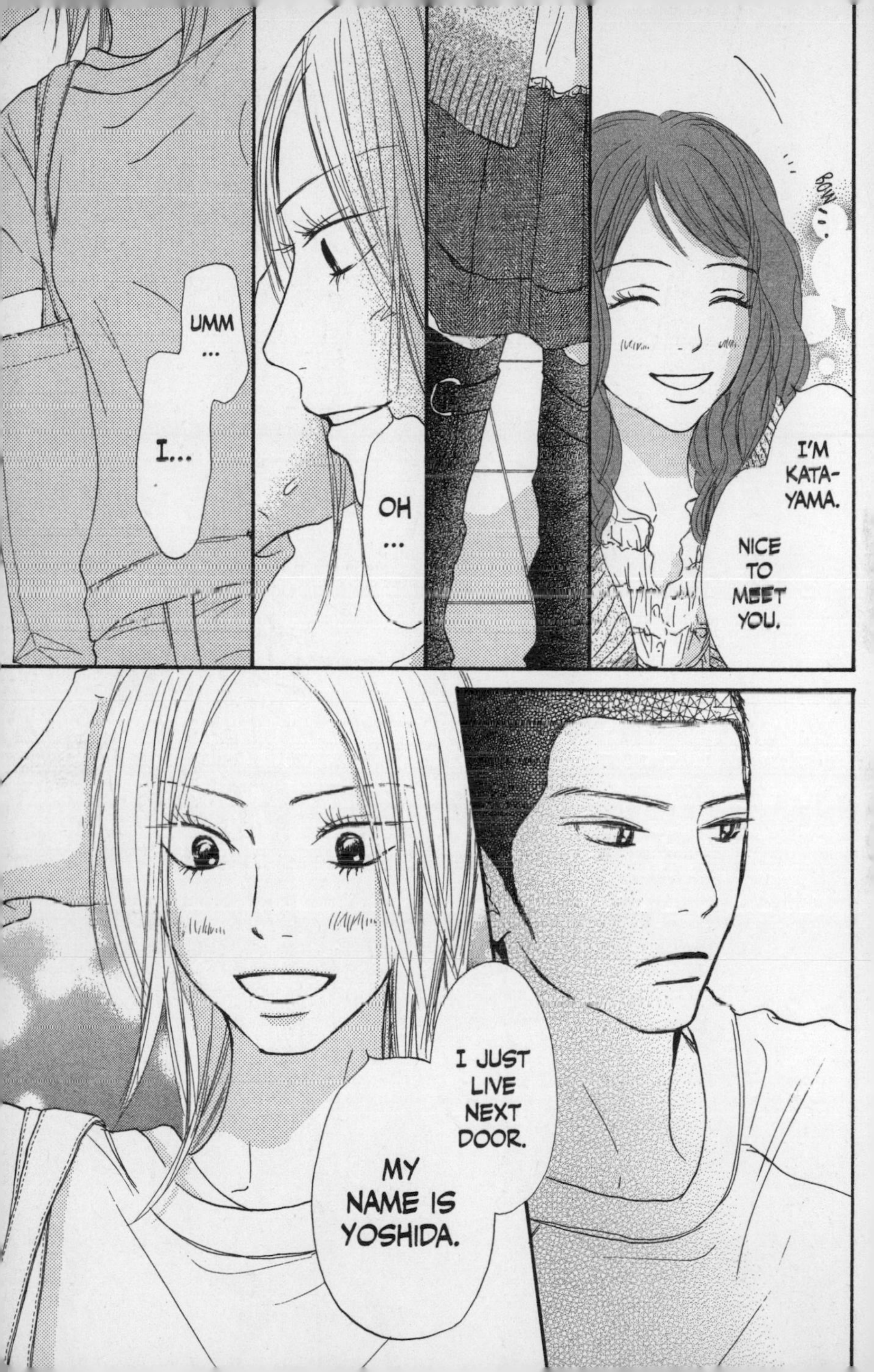
BOW...
I'M KATA-YAMA.
NICE TO MEET YOU.
OH ...
UMM ...
I...
I JUST LIVE NEXT DOOR.
MY NAME IS YOSHIDA.

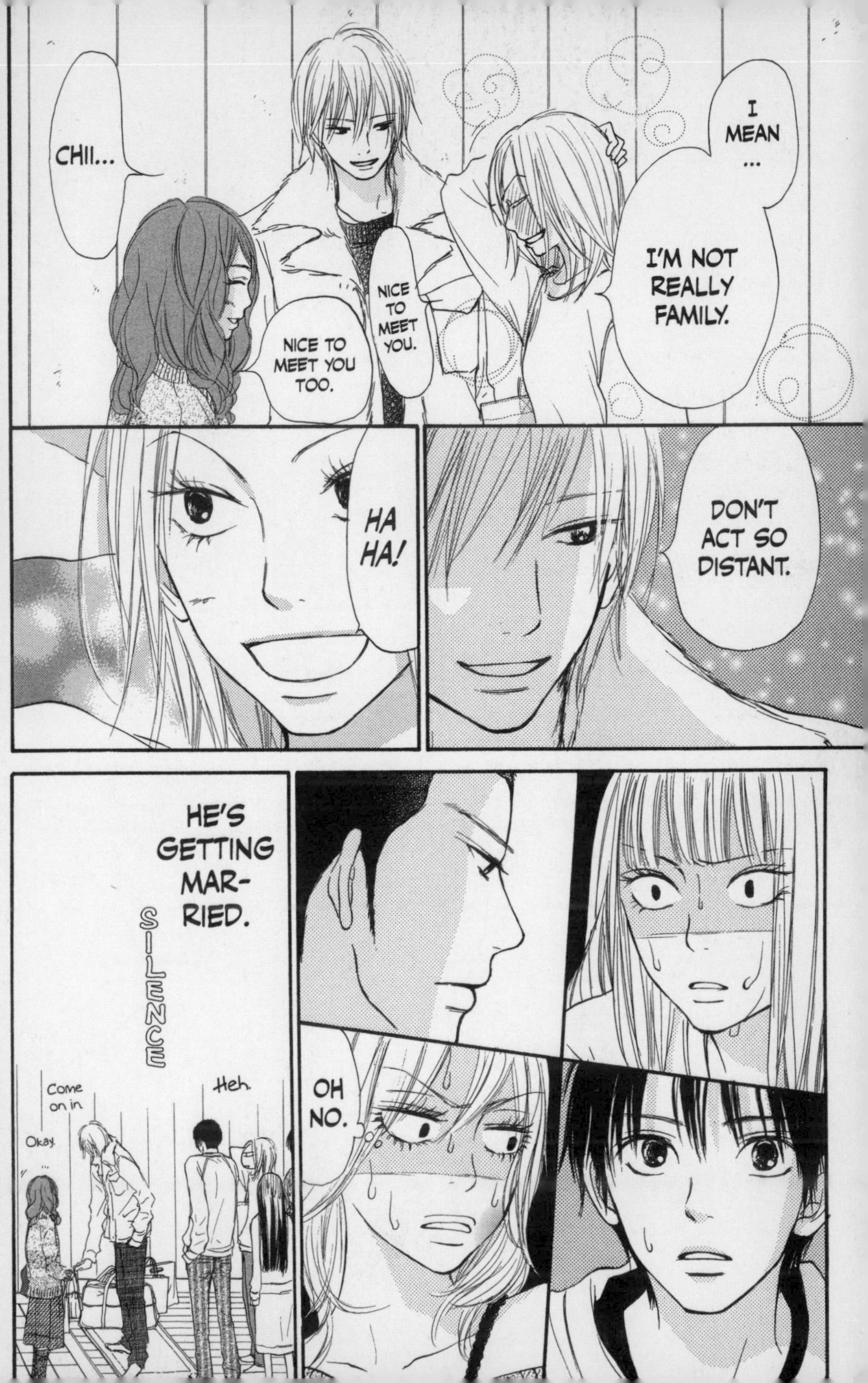
I MEAN ...
I'M NOT REALLY FAMILY.
NICE TO MEET YOU.
NICE TO MEET YOU TOO.
CHII...
DON'T ACT SO DISTANT.
HA HA!
OH NO.
HE'S GETTING MAR-RIED.
SILENCE
Heh.
Come on in.
Okay.
...

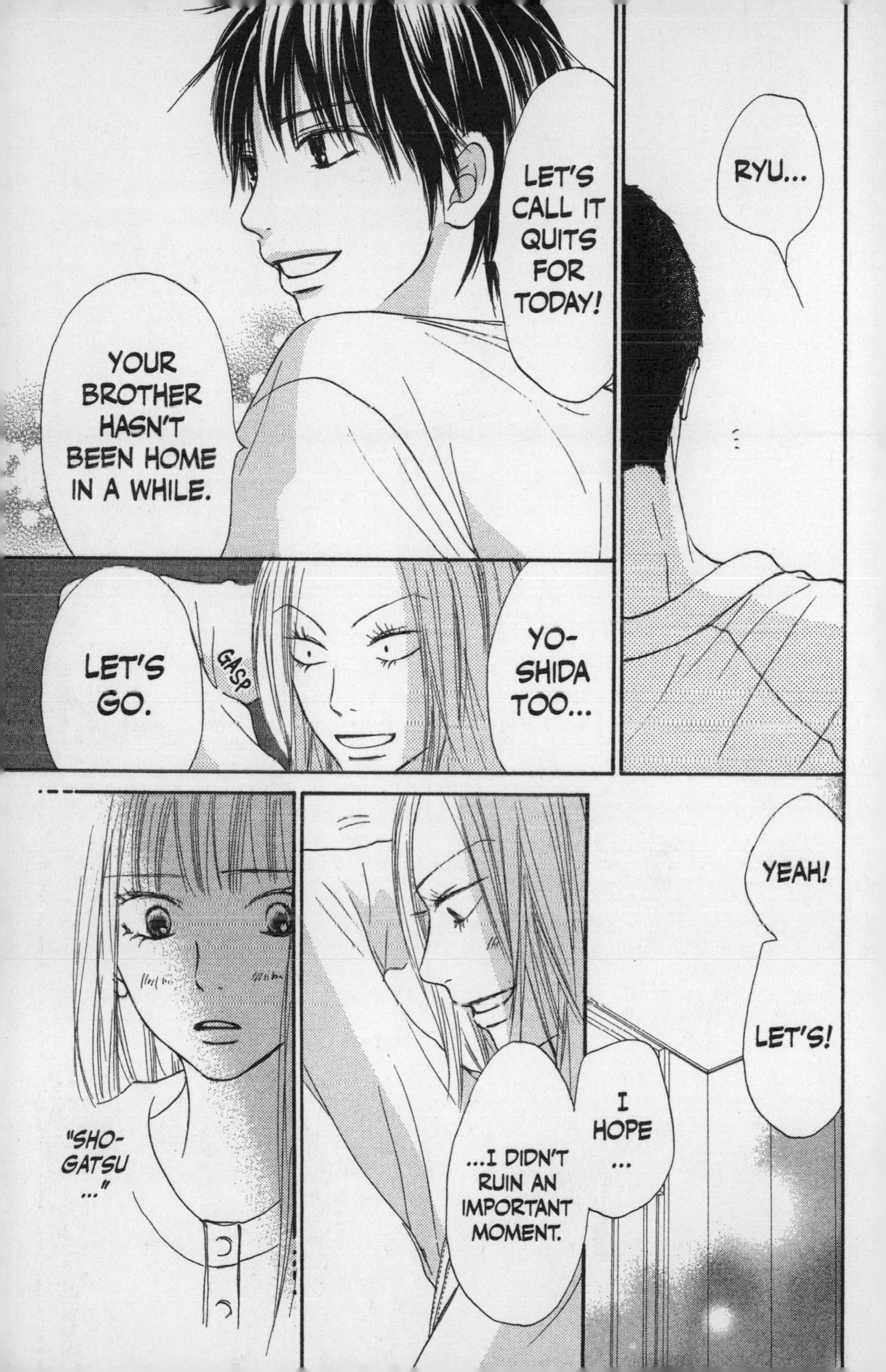
RYU...
LET'S CALL IT QUITS FOR TODAY!
YOUR BROTHER HASN'T BEEN HOME IN A WHILE.
YO-SHIDA TOO...
GASP
LET'S GO.
YEAH!
LET'S!
I HOPE ...
...I DIDN'T RUIN AN IMPORTANT MOMENT.
"SHO-GATSU ..."

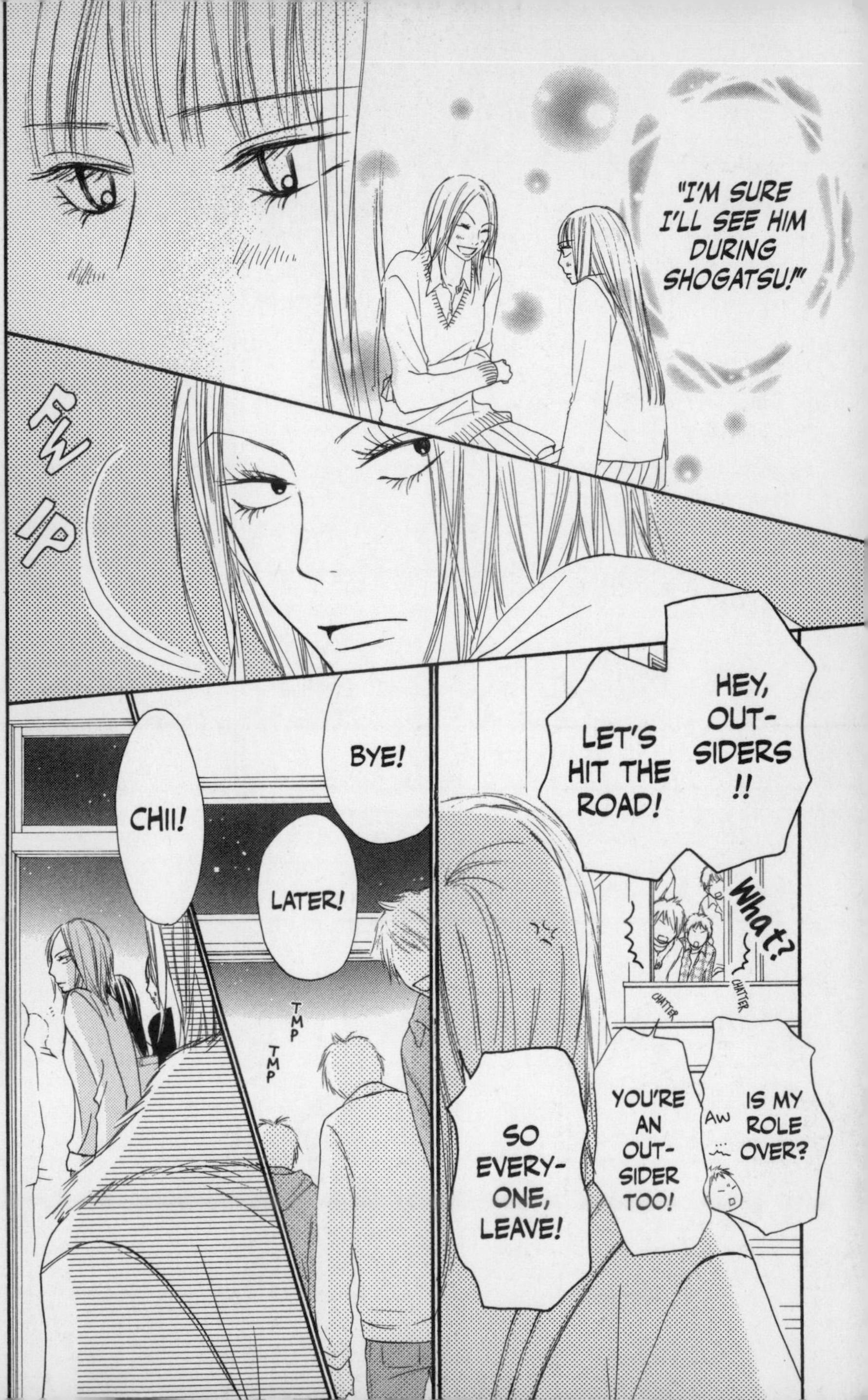
"I'M SURE I'LL SEE HIM DURING SHOGATSU!"
FWIP
HEY, OUT-SIDERS!!
LET'S HIT THE ROAD!
What?
CHATTER
CHATTER
IS MY ROLE OVER?
AW
YOU'RE AN OUT-SIDER TOO!
SO EVERY-ONE, LEAVE!
BYE!
CHII!
LATER!
TMP
TMP

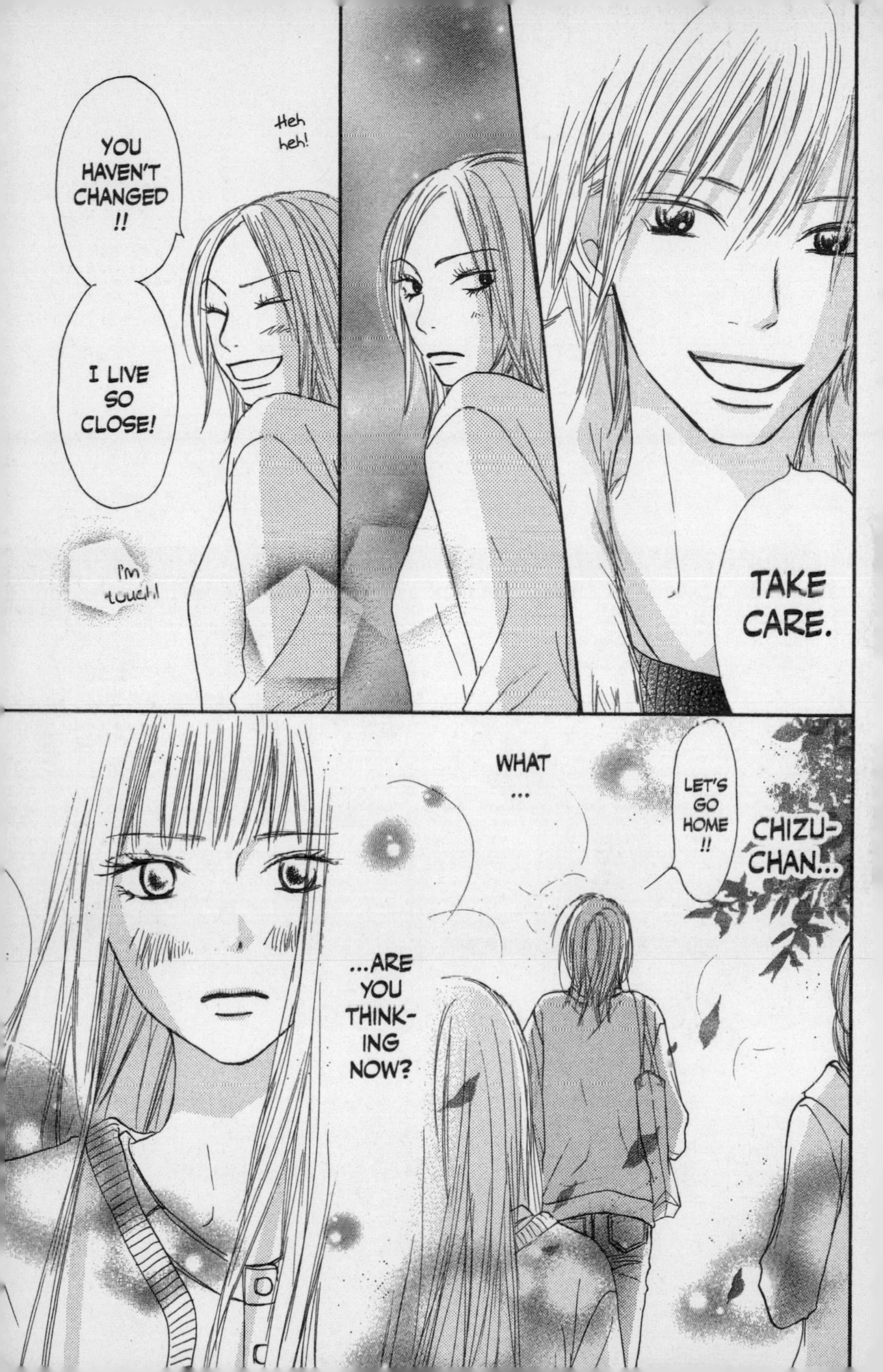
TAKE CARE.
Heh heh!
YOU HAVEN'T CHANGED !!
I LIVE SO CLOSE!
I'm touch!
CHIZU-CHAN...
LET'S GO HOME !!
WHAT ...
...ARE YOU THINKING NOW?

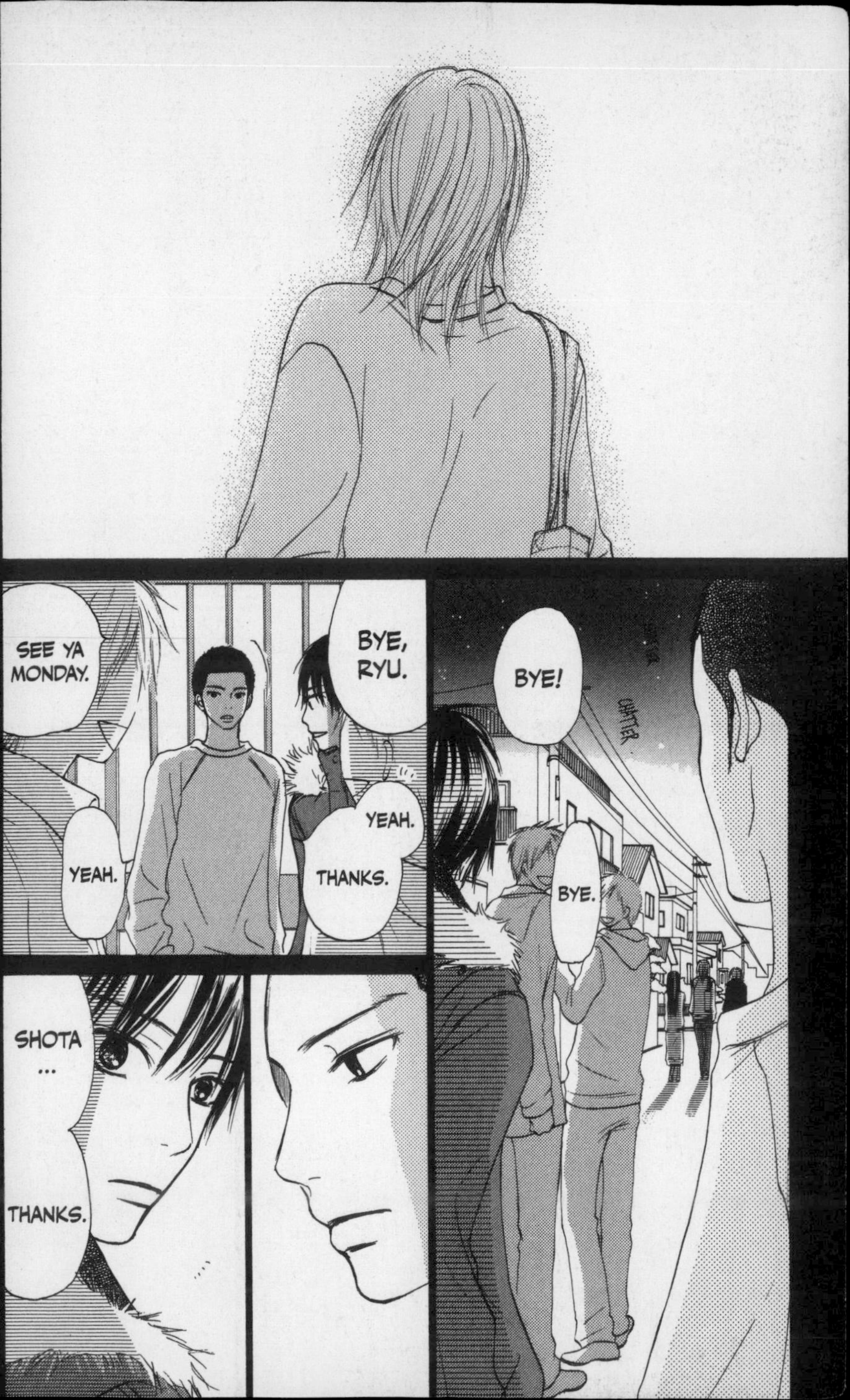
BYE!
BYE.
BYE, RYU.
YEAH.
THANKS.
SEE YA MONDAY.
YEAH.
SHOTA ...
THANKS.
...

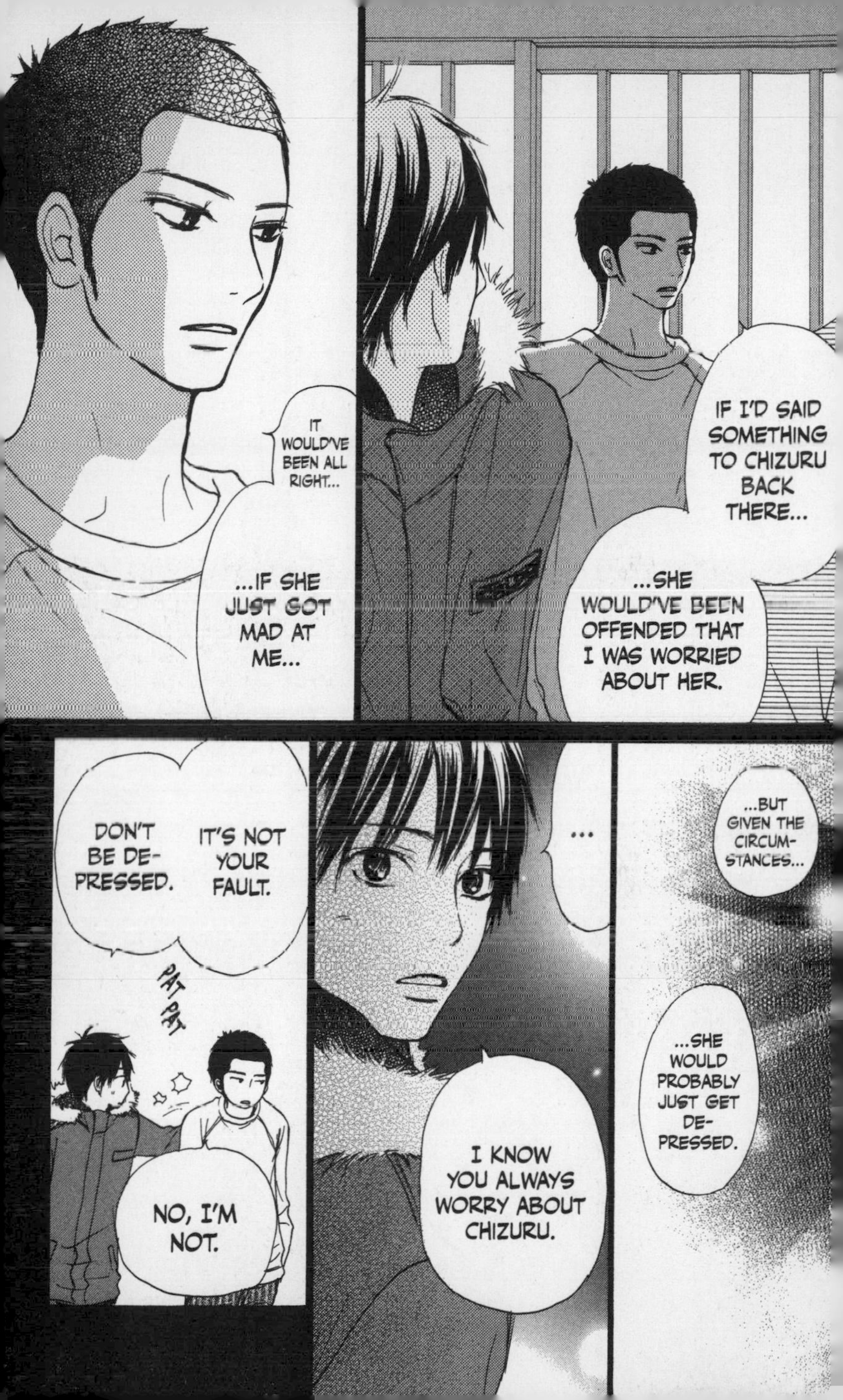
IF I'D SAID SOMETHING TO CHIZURU BACK THERE...
...SHE WOULD'VE BEEN OFFENDED THAT I WAS WORRIED ABOUT HER.
IT WOULD'VE BEEN ALL RIGHT...
...IF SHE JUST GOT MAD AT ME...
...BUT GIVEN THE CIRCUM-STANCES...
...SHE WOULD PROBABLY JUST GET DE-PRESSED.
...
I KNOW YOU ALWAYS WORRY ABOUT CHIZURU.
IT'S NOT YOUR FAULT.
DON'T BE DE-PRESSED.
PAT PAT
NO, I'M NOT.

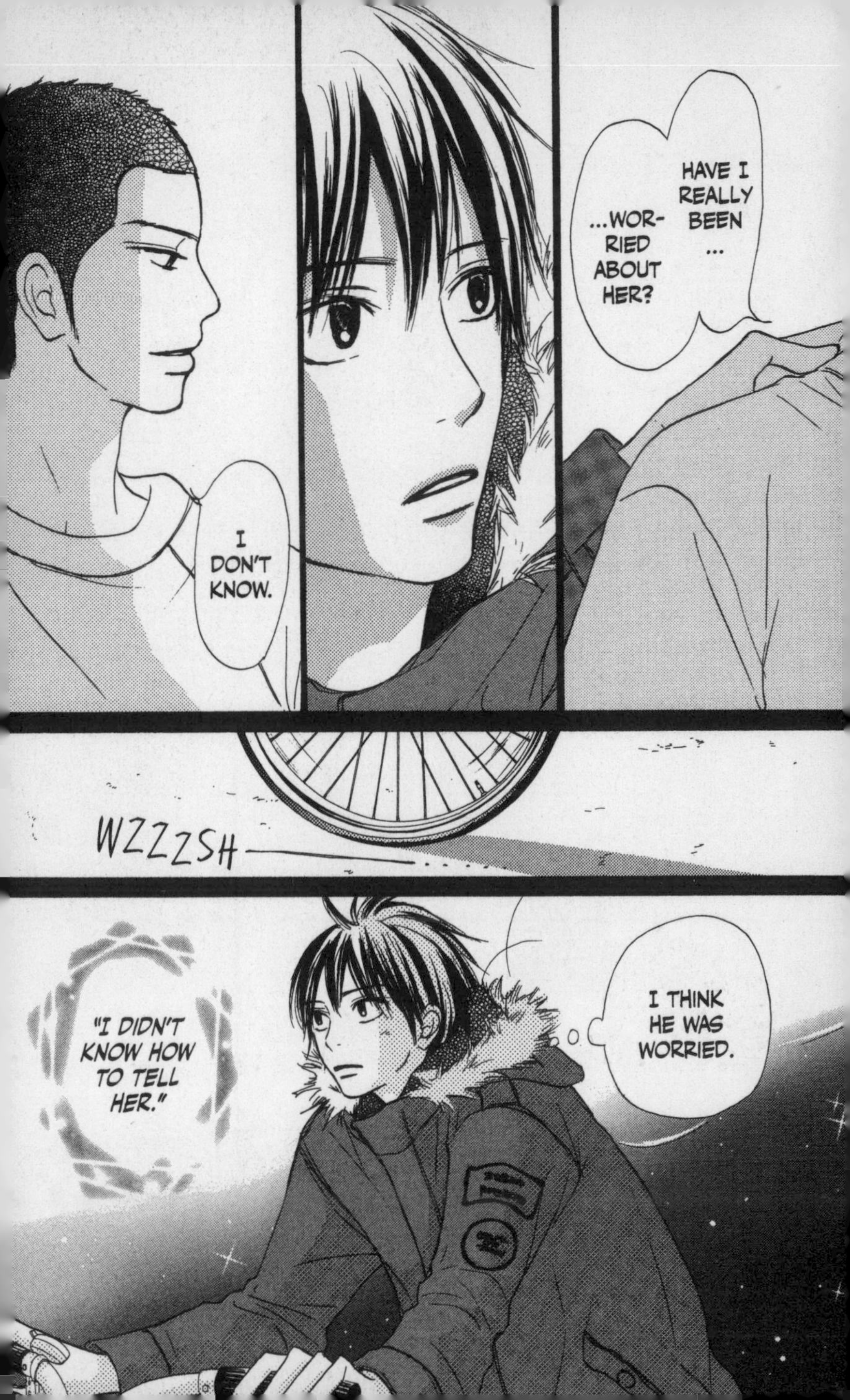
HAVE I REALLY BEEN ... ...WOR-RIED ABOUT HER?
I DON'T KNOW.
WZZZSH
I THINK HE WAS WORRIED.
"I DIDN'T KNOW HOW TO TELL HER."

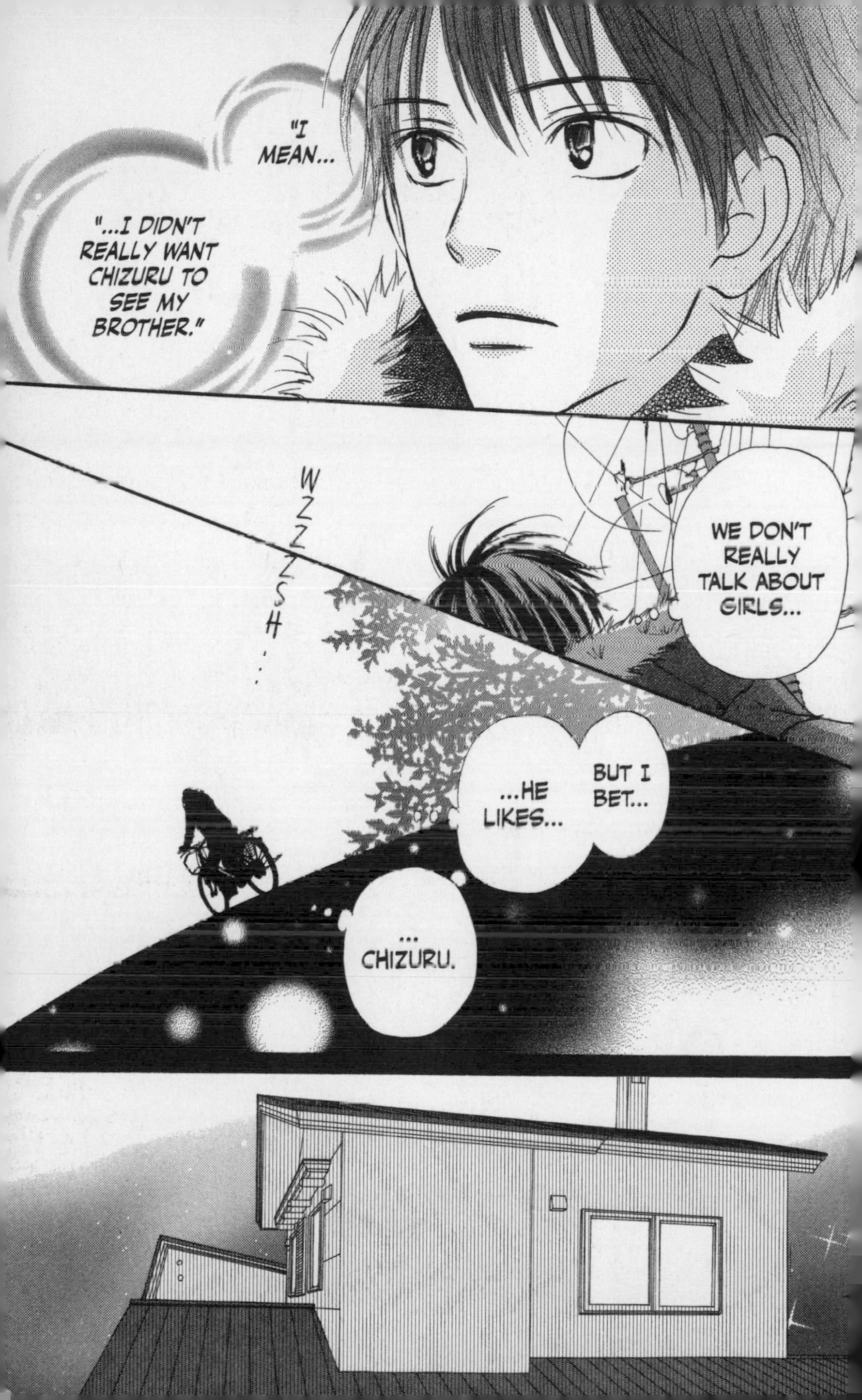

"I MEAN...
"...I DIDN'T REALLY WANT CHIZURU TO SEE MY BROTHER."
WE DON'T REALLY TALK ABOUT GIRLS...
WZZZSH...
BUT I BET...
...HE LIKES...
...CHIZURU.

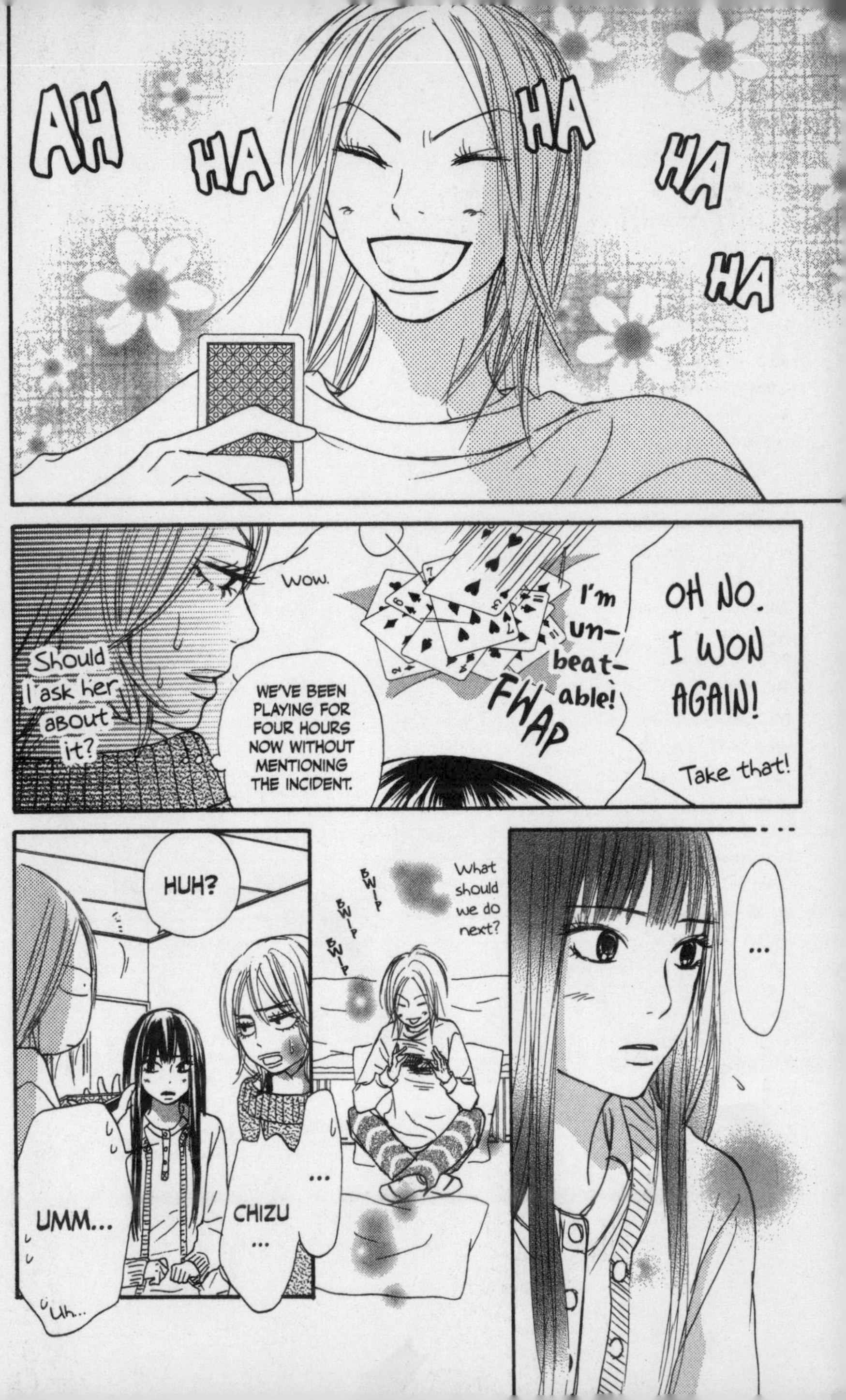
AH
HA
HA
HA
HA
OH NO. I WON AGAIN!
Take that!
I'm un-beat-able!
FWAP
Wow.
WE'VE BEEN PLAYING FOR FOUR HOURS NOW WITHOUT MENTIONING THE INCIDENT.
Should I ask her about it?
...
What should we do next?
BWIP
BWIP
BWIP
HUH?
...
CHIZU ...
UMM...
Uh...

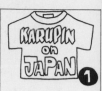

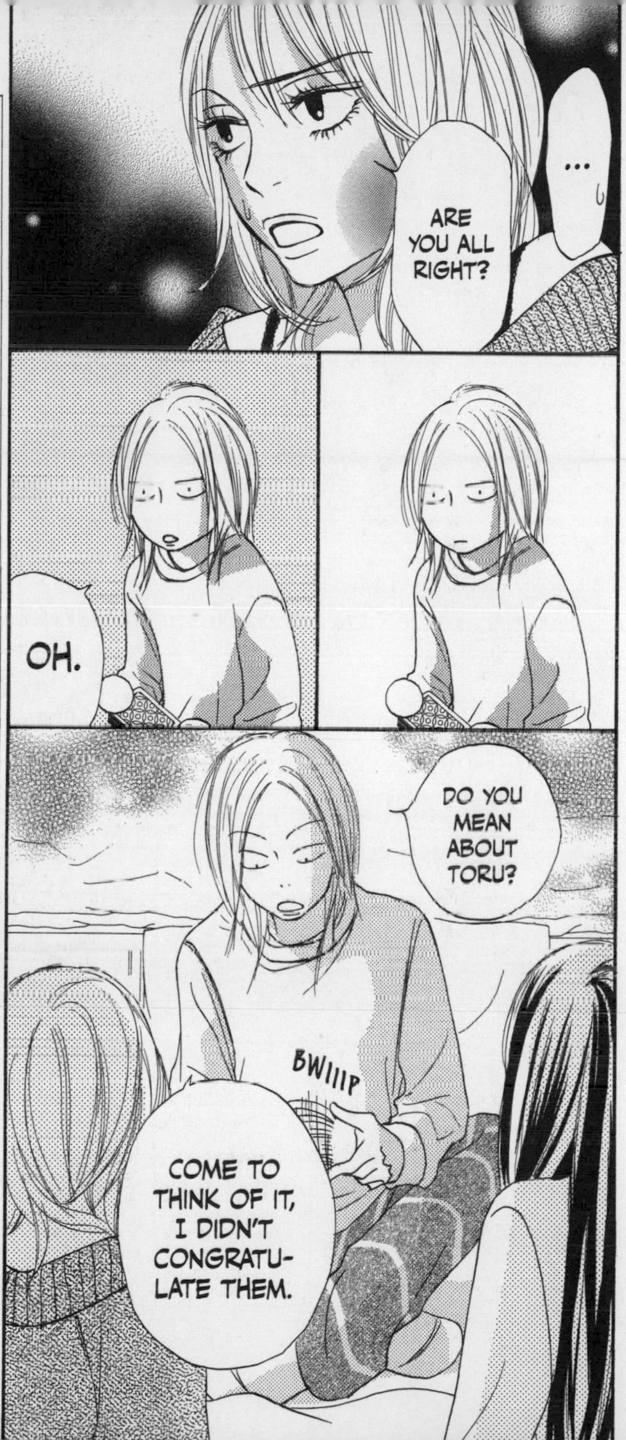
...
ARE YOU ALL RIGHT?
OH.
DO YOU MEAN ABOUT TORU?
BWIIIP
COME TO THINK OF IT, I DIDN'T CONGRATU-LATE THEM.

KARUPIN on JAPAN 1

Hi! How are you? This is Shiina. Pleased to meet you!

This is the sixth volume. There was a long interval after the fourth volume, so when I was working on the fifth volume, it felt like I hadn't worked on a graphic novel for a long time. But this time, it was a quick four months. Already volume 6? That's weird.

It's not related, but my parents got a dog recently. She was abandoned and when we rescued her, her eyes weren't even open. But she's grown up now. She's not only healthy but also rowdy.

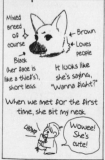

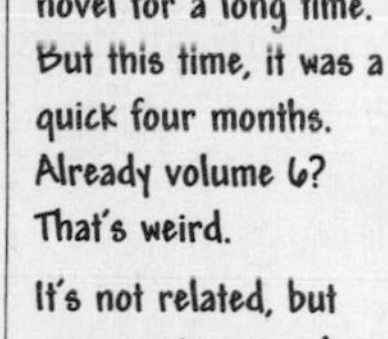
Mixed Breed of course
Brown
Loves people
Black (her face is like a thief's), short legs.
It looks like she's saying, "Wanna fight?"

When we met for the first time, she bit my neck.

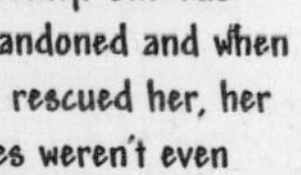
CHOMP
Wowee! She's cute!

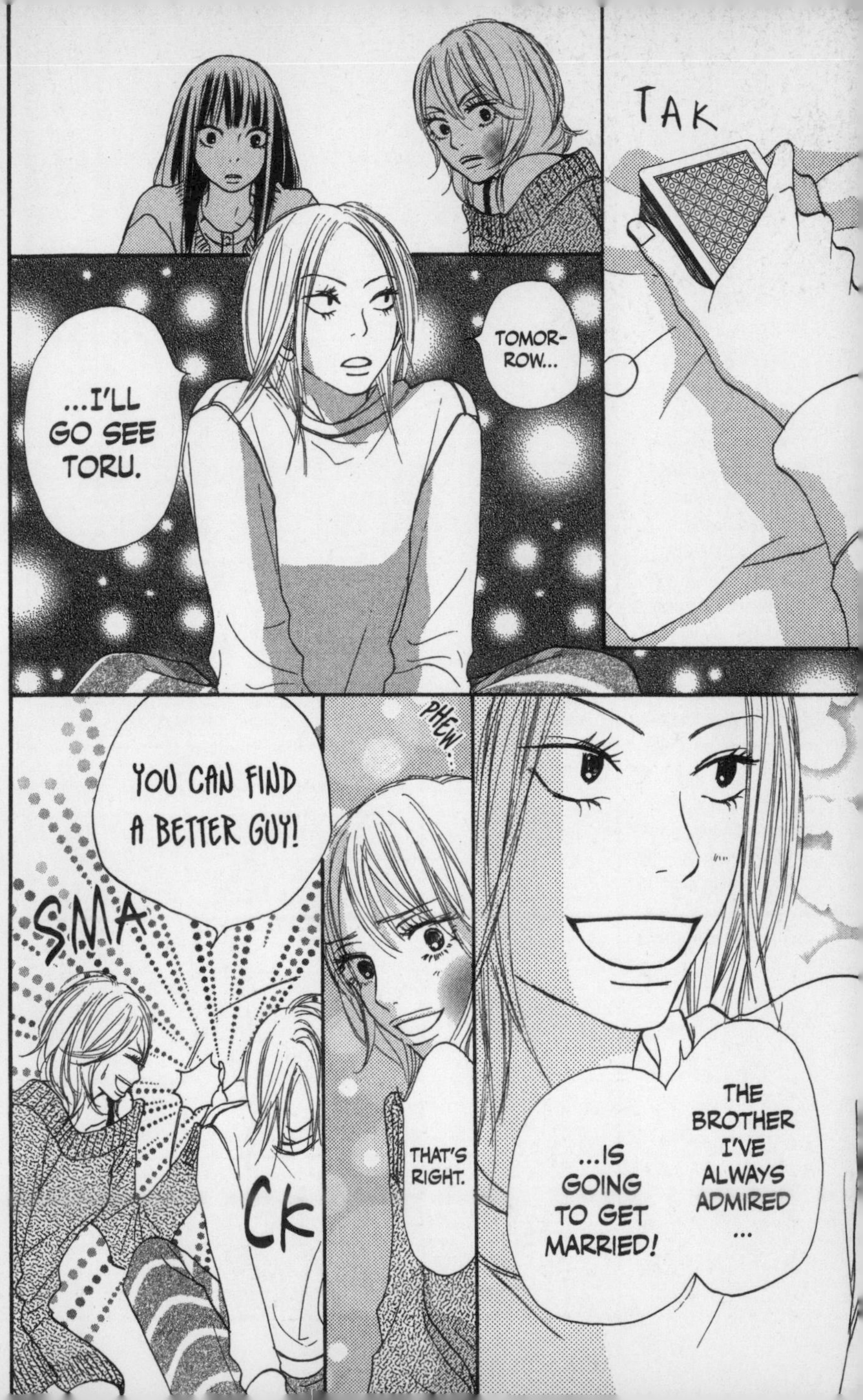
TAK
TOMORROW...
...I'LL GO SEE TORU.
THE BROTHER I'VE ALWAYS ADMIRED...
...IS GOING TO GET MARRIED!
PHEW...
THAT'S RIGHT.
YOU CAN FIND A BETTER GUY!
SMA
CK

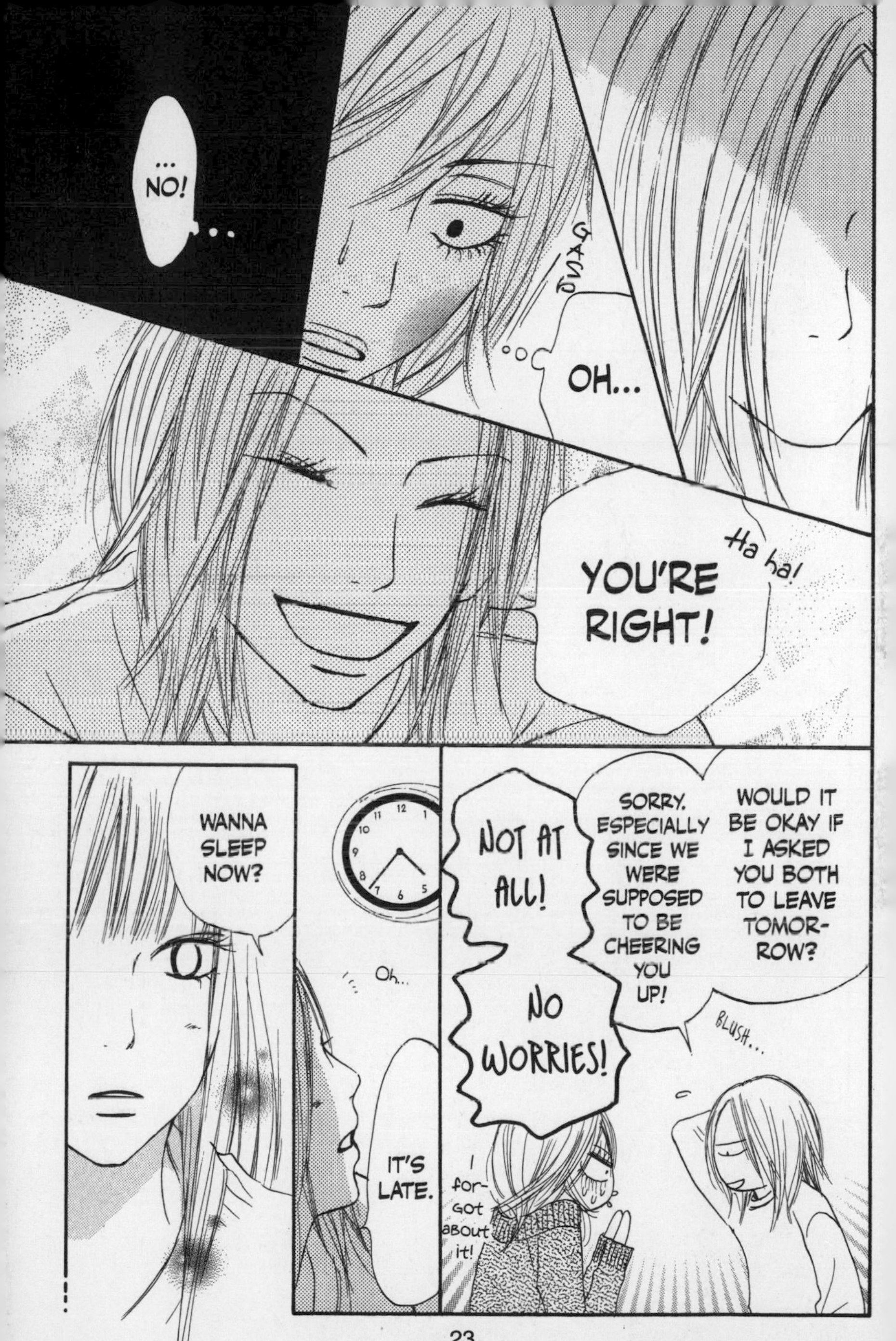
OH...
GASP
...NO!
YOU'RE RIGHT!
Ha ha!
WOULD IT BE OKAY IF I ASKED YOU BOTH TO LEAVE TOMOR-ROW?
SORRY. ESPECIALLY SINCE WE WERE SUPPOSED TO BE CHEERING YOU UP!
NOT AT ALL!
NO WORRIES!
BLUSH...
I for-got about it!
WANNA SLEEP NOW?
Oh...
IT'S LATE.

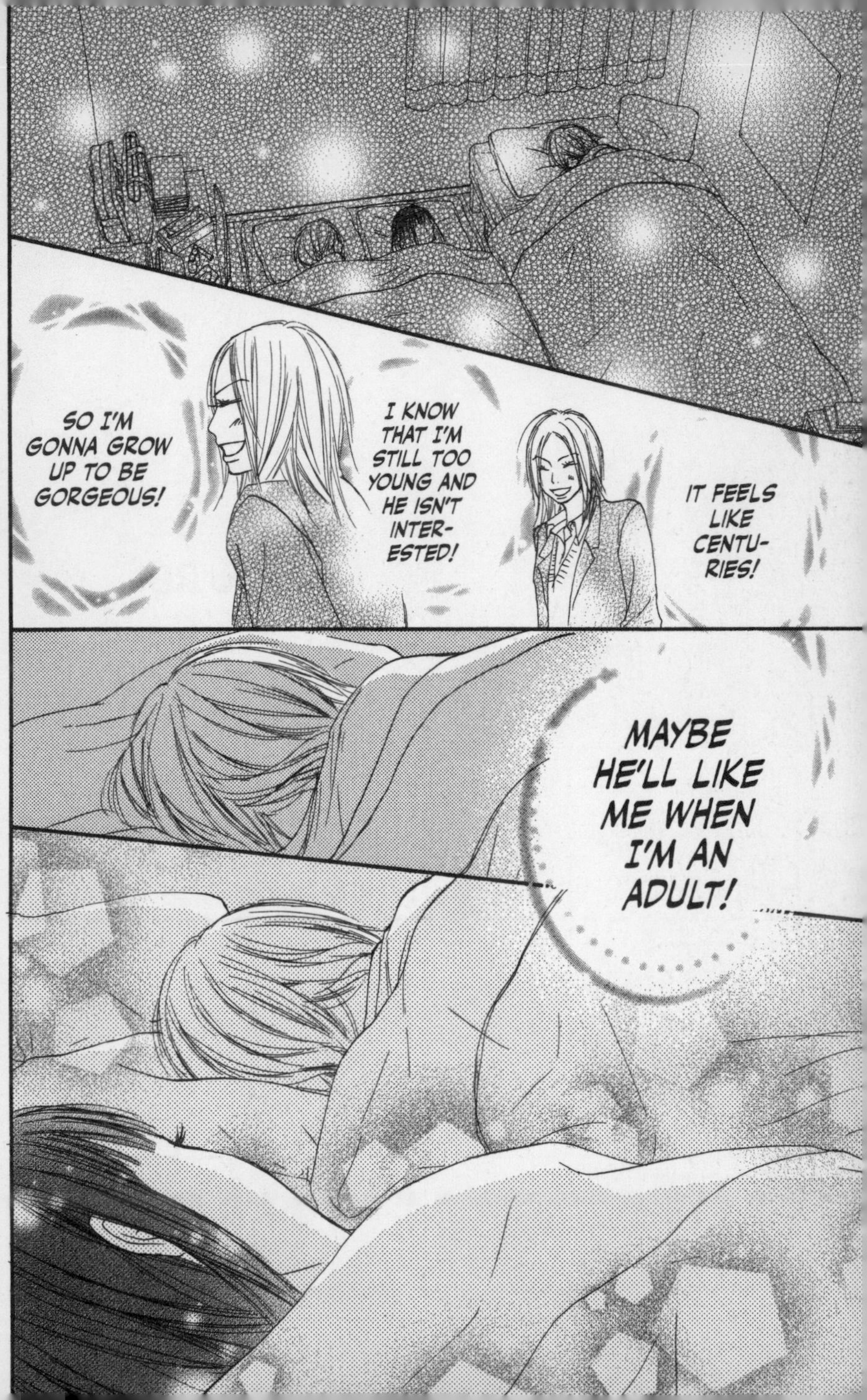
IT FEELS LIKE CENTURIES!
I KNOW THAT I'M STILL TOO YOUNG AND HE ISN'T INTERESTED!
SO I'M GONNA GROW UP TO BE GORGEOUS!
MAYBE HE'LL LIKE ME WHEN I'M AN ADULT!

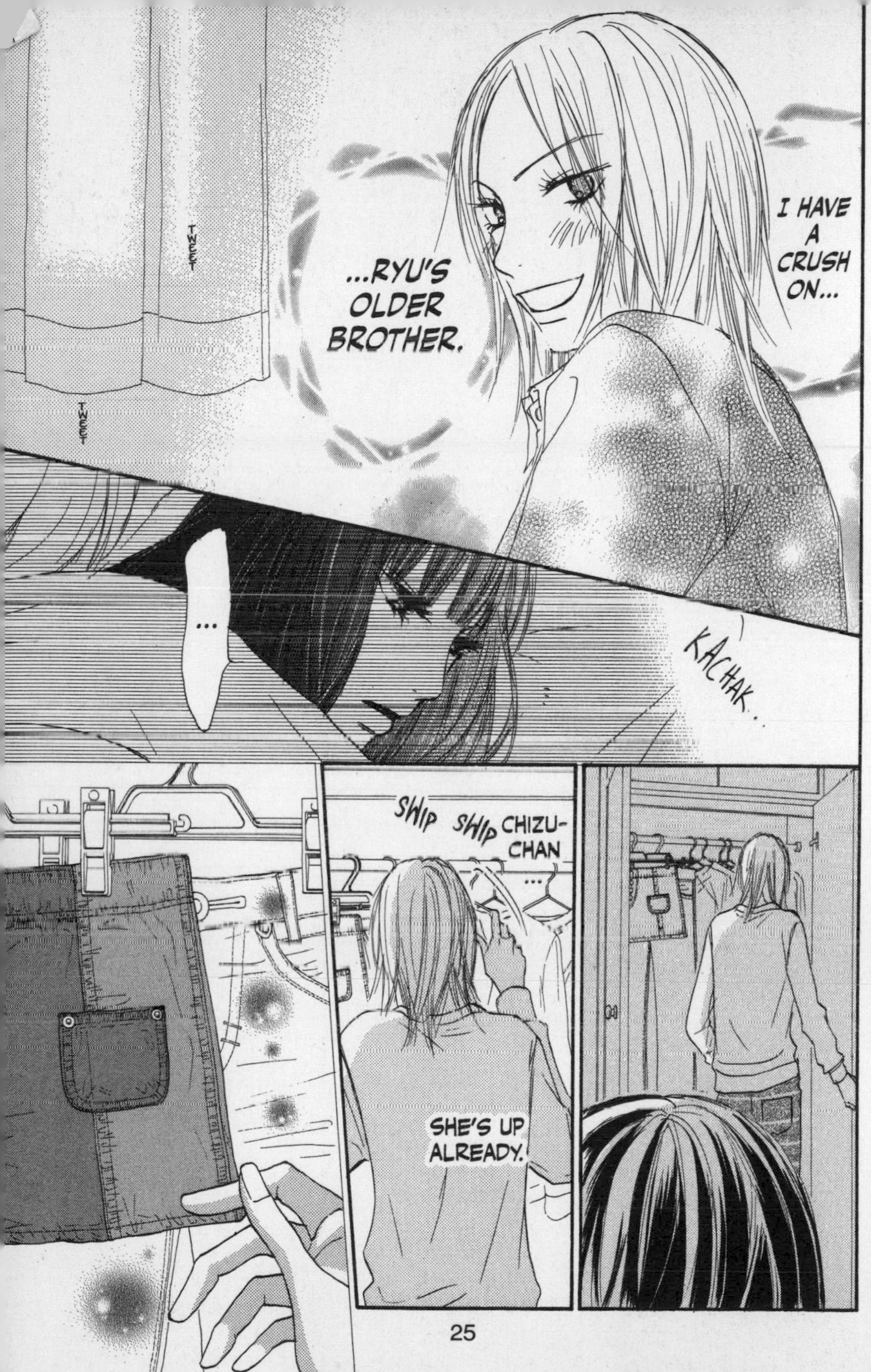
I HAVE A CRUSH ON...
...RYU'S OLDER BROTHER.
TWEET
TWEET
KACHAK...
...
CHIZU-CHAN...
SWIP
SWIP
SHE'S UP ALREADY.

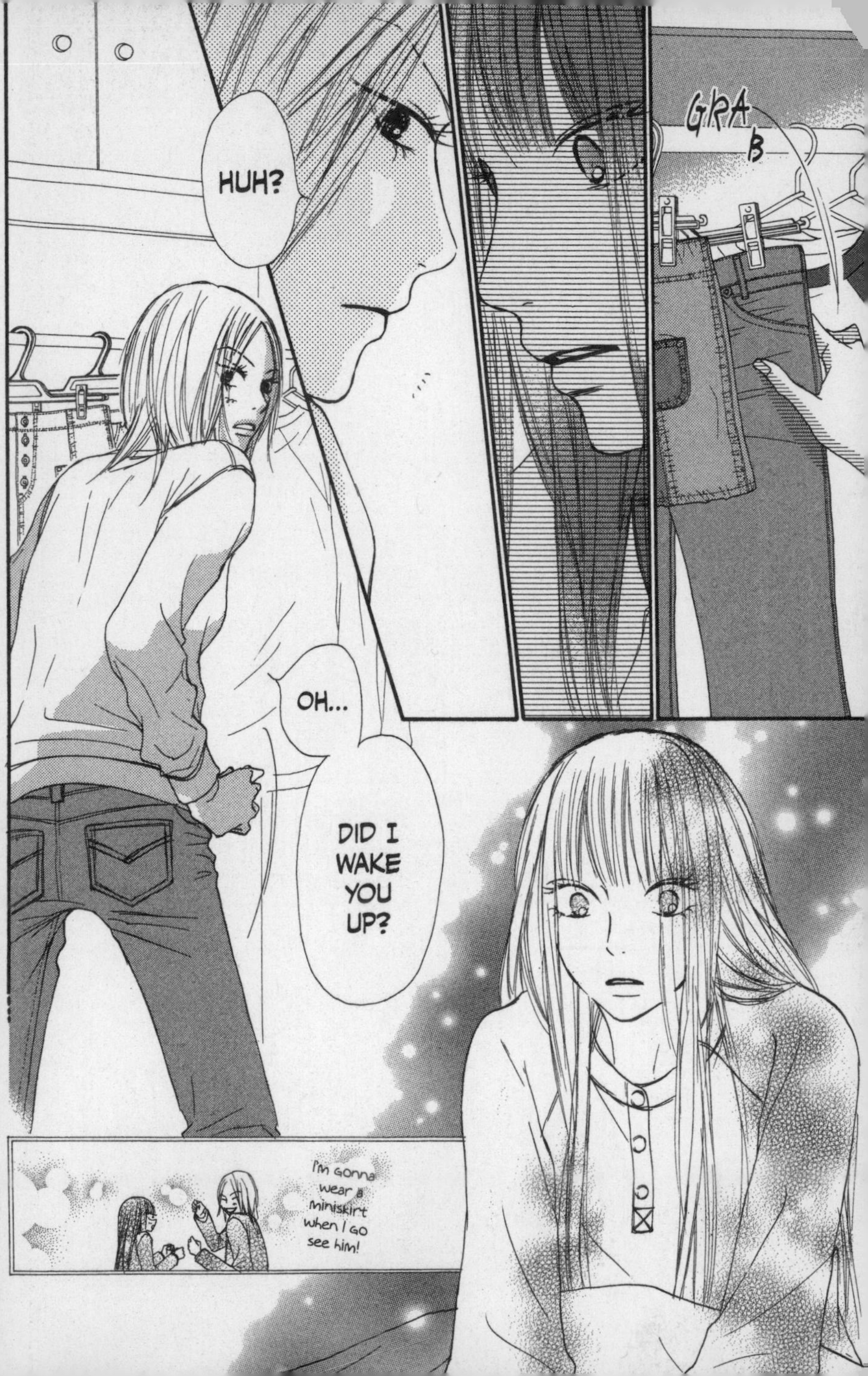
GRAB
HUH?
OH...
DID I WAKE YOU UP?
I'm gonna wear a miniskirt when I go see him!

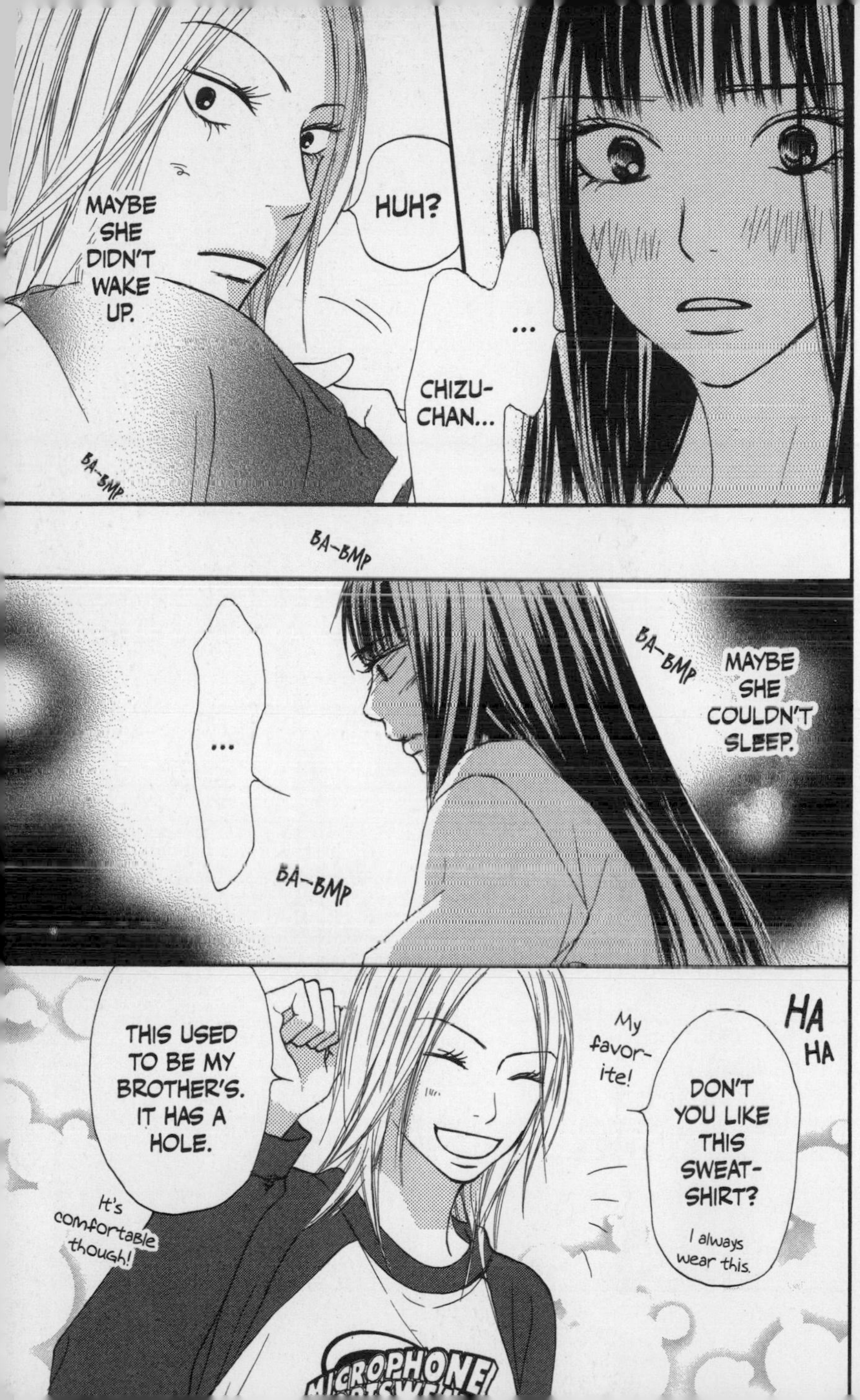
...
CHIZU-CHAN...
HUH?
MAYBE SHE DIDN'T WAKE UP.
BA-BMP
BA-BMP
BA-BMP
MAYBE SHE COULDN'T SLEEP.
...
BA-BMP
HA HA
DON'T YOU LIKE THIS SWEAT-SHIRT?
My favor-ite!
I always wear this.
THIS USED TO BE MY BROTHER'S. IT HAS A HOLE.
It's comfortable though!

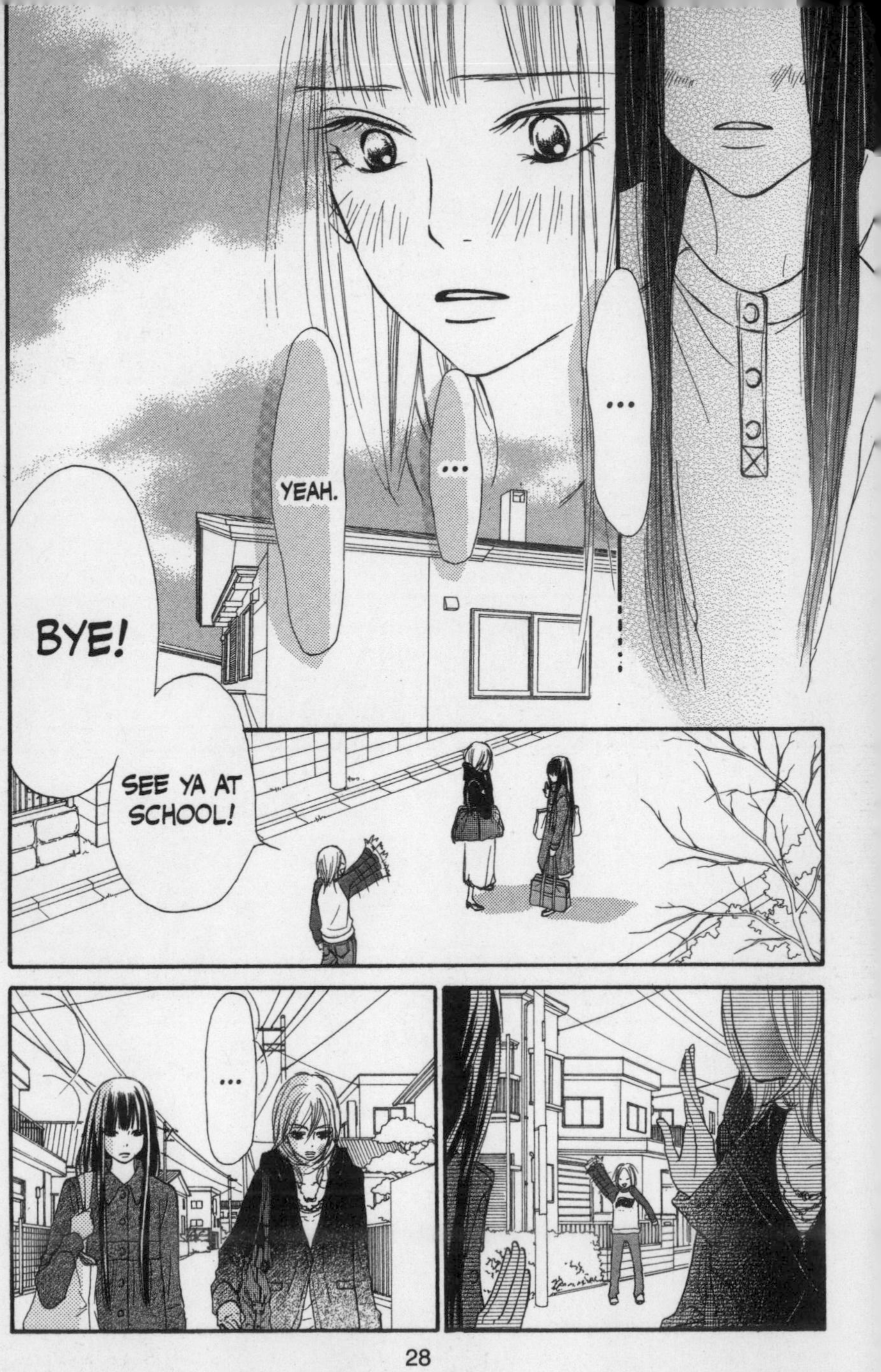
...
...
YEAH.
BYE!
SEE YA AT SCHOOL!
...

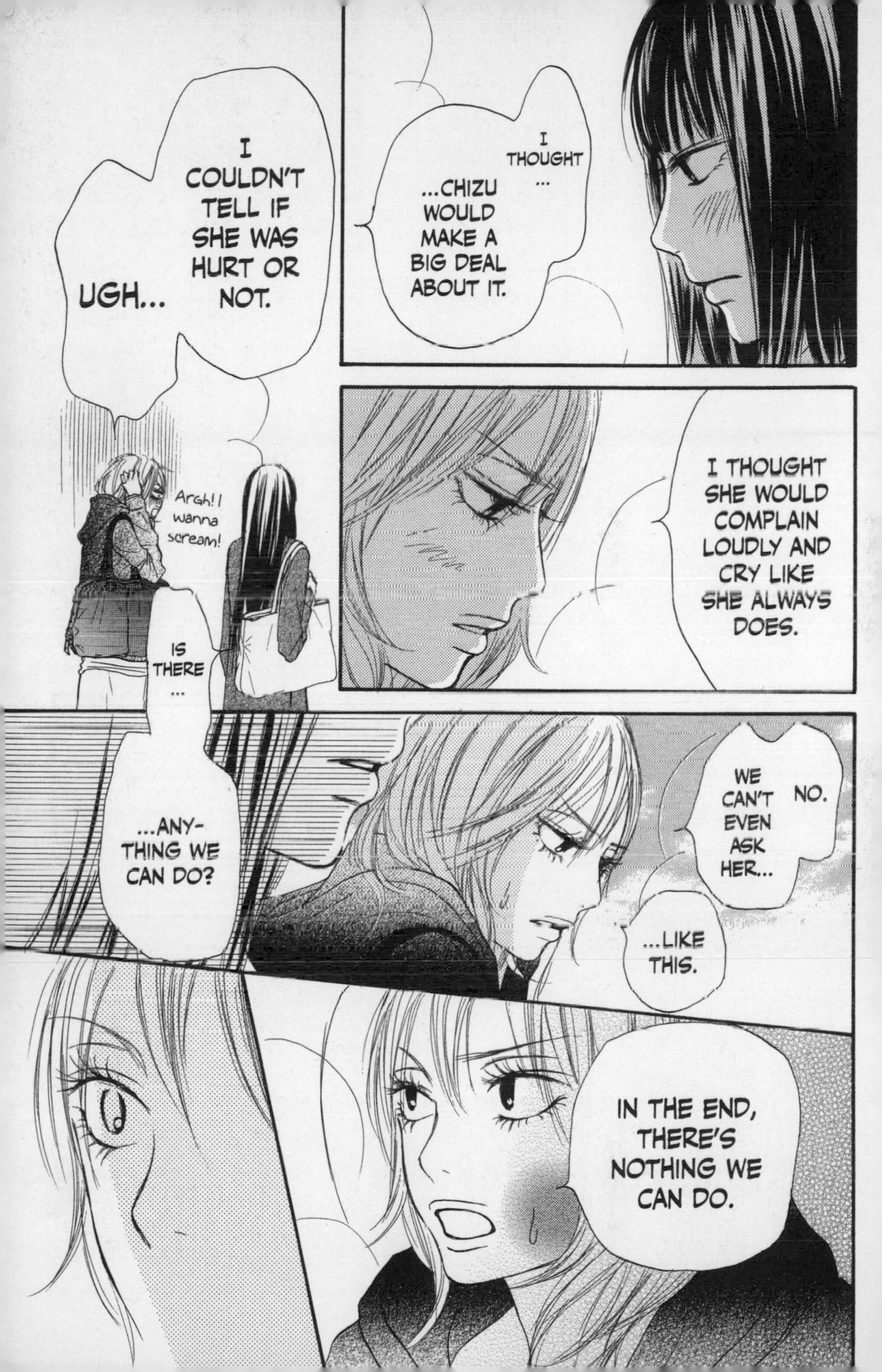
I THOUGHT...
...CHIZU WOULD MAKE A BIG DEAL ABOUT IT.
I THOUGHT SHE WOULD COMPLAIN LOUDLY AND CRY LIKE SHE ALWAYS DOES.
I COULDN'T TELL IF SHE WAS HURT OR NOT.
UGH...
Argh! I wanna scream!
IS THERE...
...ANY-THING WE CAN DO?
NO.
WE CAN'T EVEN ASK HER...
...LIKE THIS.
IN THE END, THERE'S NOTHING WE CAN DO.

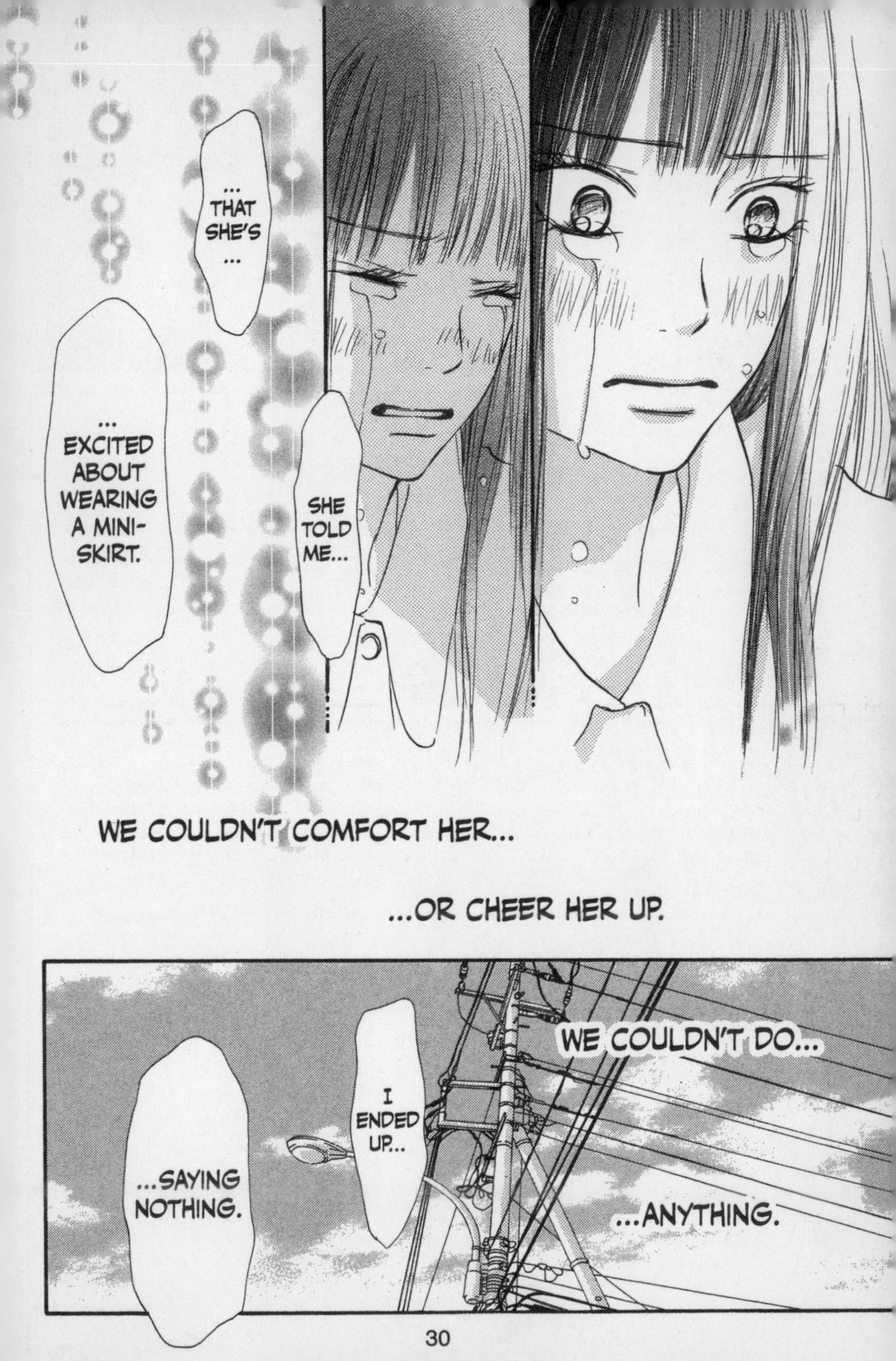
SHE TOLD ME...
...THAT SHE'S...
...EXCITED ABOUT WEARING A MINI-SKIRT.
WE COULDN'T COMFORT HER...
...OR CHEER HER UP.
WE COULDN'T DO...
...ANYTHING.
I ENDED UP...
...SAYING NOTHING.

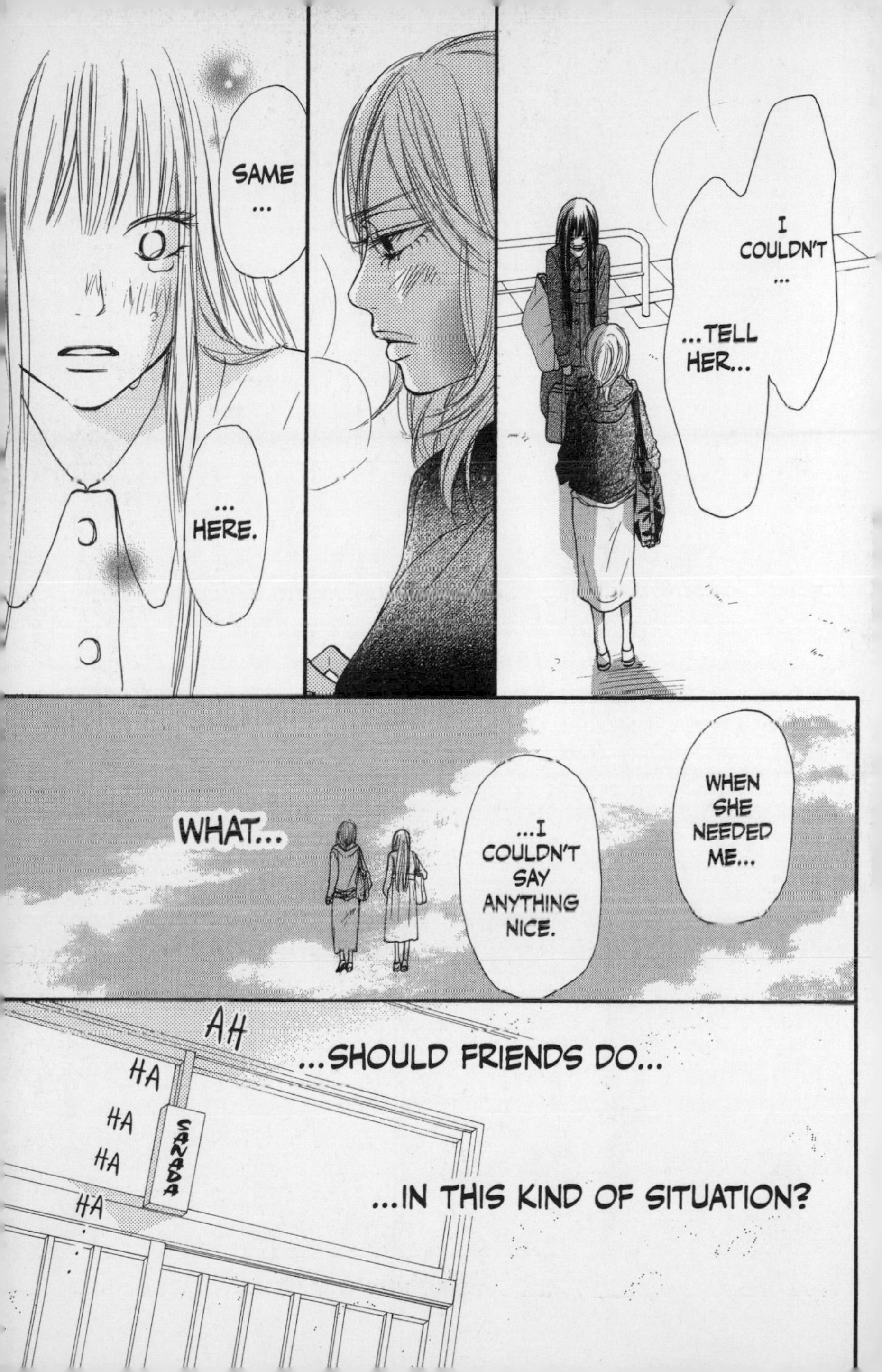
I COULDN'T ...
...TELL HER...
SAME ...
... HERE.
WHEN SHE NEEDED ME...
...I COULDN'T SAY ANYTHING NICE.
WHAT...
...SHOULD FRIENDS DO...
...IN THIS KIND OF SITUATION?
AH HA HA HA HA
SANADA

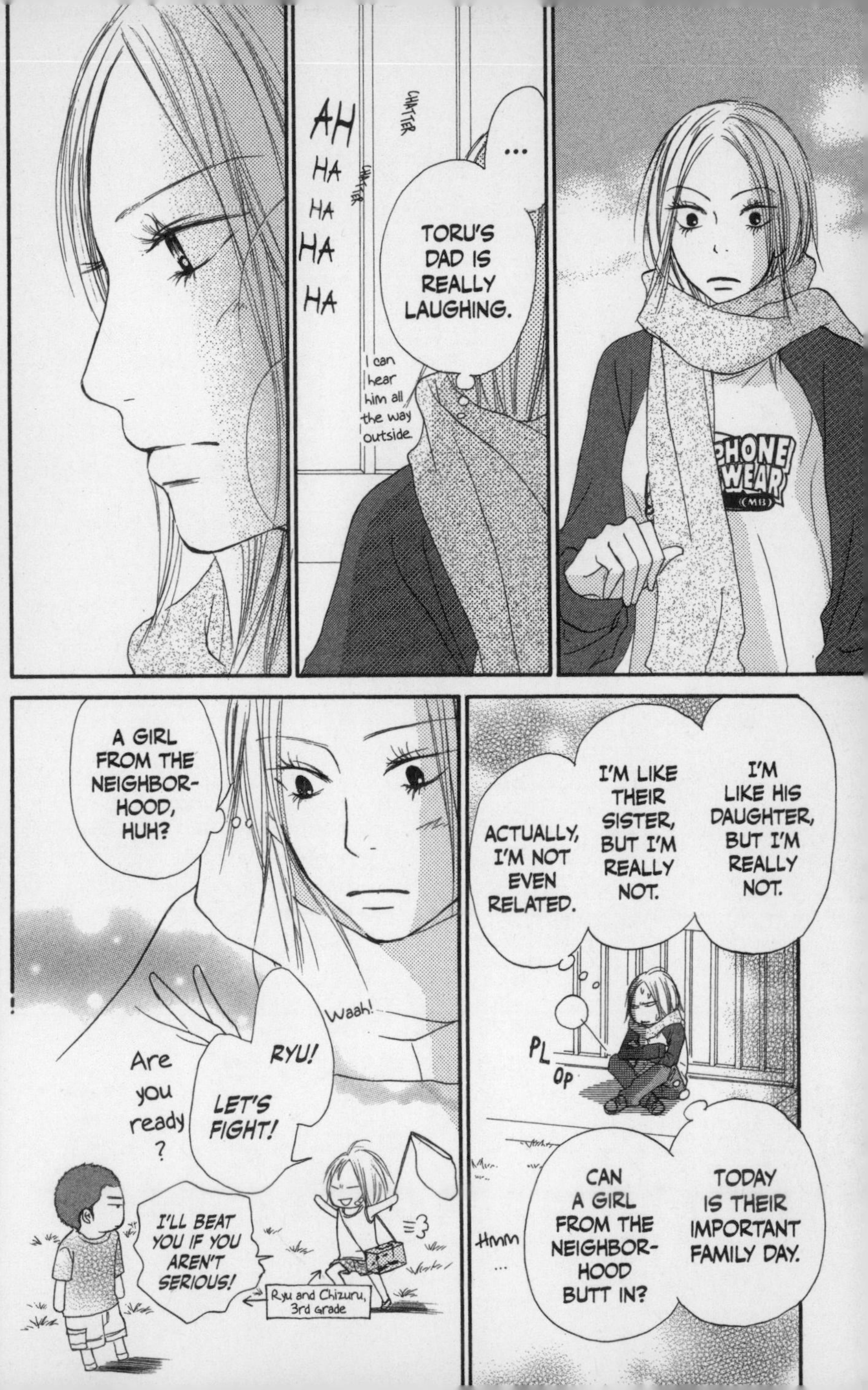
...
TORU'S DAD IS REALLY LAUGHING.
I can hear him all the way outside.
CHATTER
CHATTER
AH HA HA HA HA
I'M LIKE HIS DAUGHTER, BUT I'M REALLY NOT.
I'M LIKE THEIR SISTER, BUT I'M REALLY NOT.
ACTUALLY, I'M NOT EVEN RELATED.
PLOP
TODAY IS THEIR IMPORTANT FAMILY DAY.
CAN A GIRL FROM THE NEIGHBOR-HOOD BUTT IN?
Hmm...
A GIRL FROM THE NEIGHBOR-HOOD, HUH?
Waah!
RYU! LET'S FIGHT!
Are you ready?
I'LL BEAT YOU IF YOU AREN'T SERIOUS!
Ryu and Chizuru, 3rd Grade

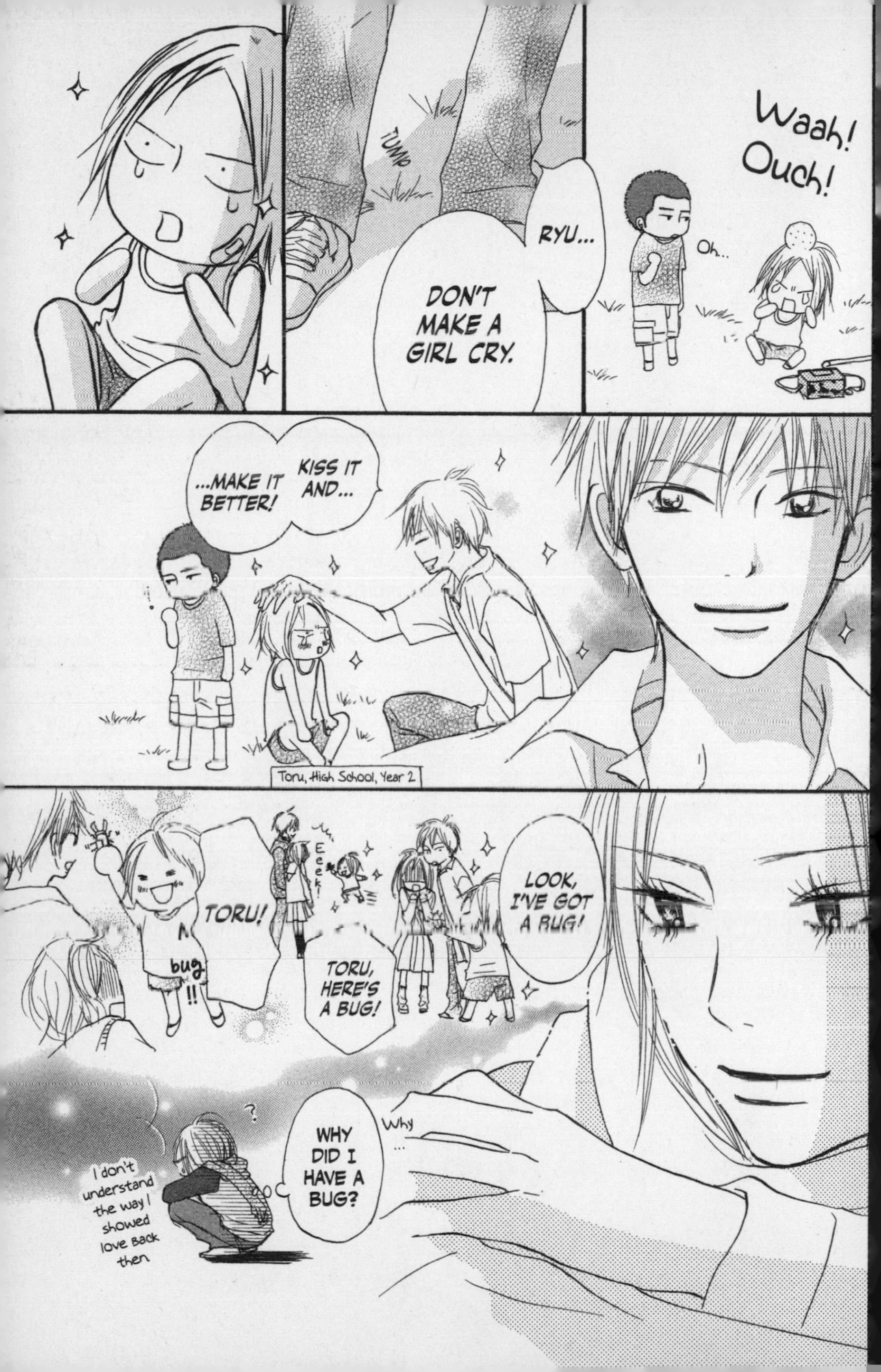
Waah! Ouch!
Oh...
RYU...
DON'T MAKE A GIRL CRY.
TUMP
KISS IT AND...
...MAKE IT BETTER!
Toru, High School, Year 2
LOOK, I'VE GOT A BUG!
TORU, HERE'S A BUG!
Eeek!
TORU!
bug!!
Why...
WHY DID I HAVE A BUG?
I don't understand the way I showed love back then

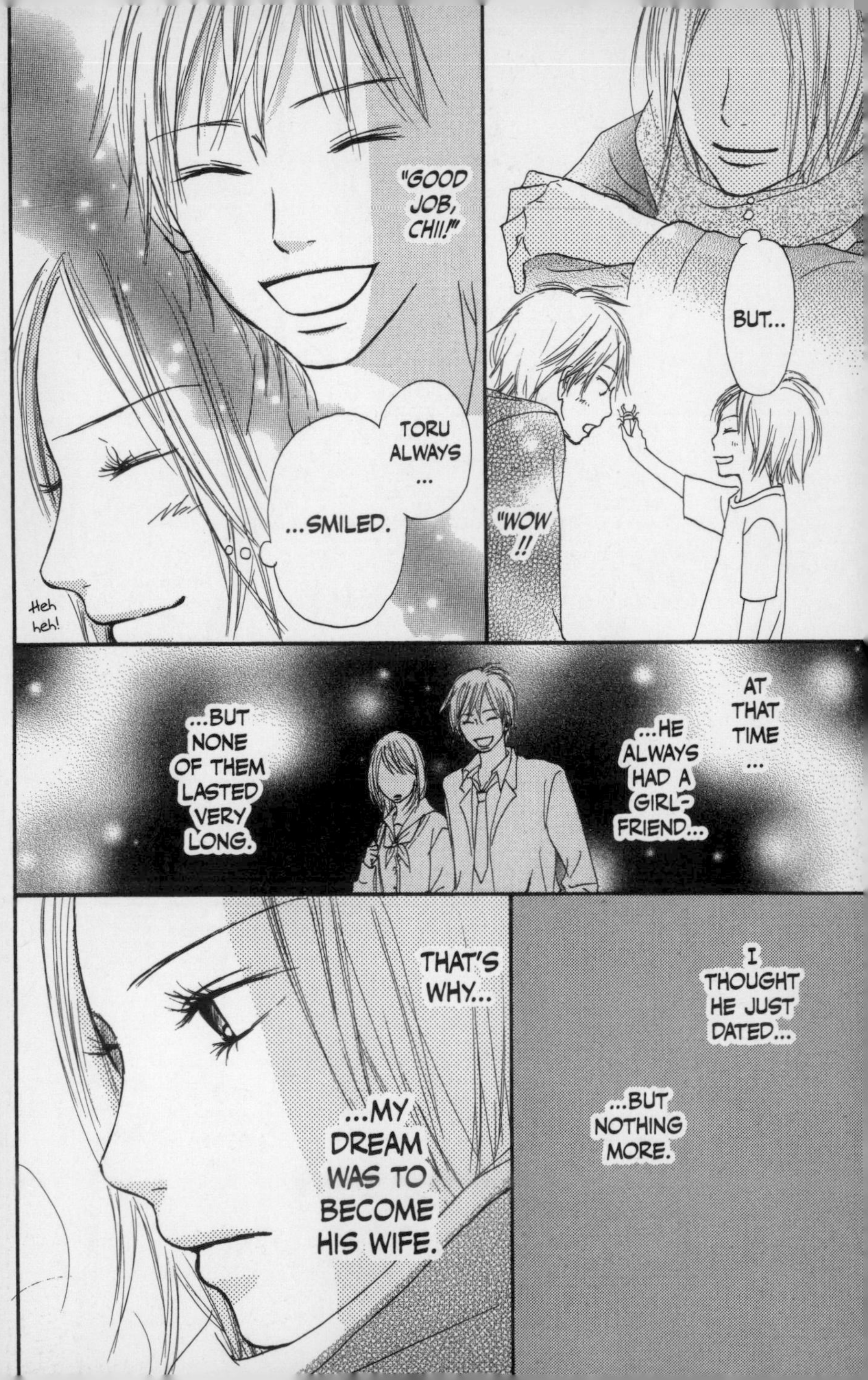
BUT...
"WOW!!"
"GOOD JOB, CHII!"
TORU ALWAYS...
...SMILED.
Heh heh!
AT THAT TIME...
...HE ALWAYS HAD A GIRL-FRIEND...
...BUT NONE OF THEM LASTED VERY LONG.
I THOUGHT HE JUST DATED...
...BUT NOTHING MORE.
THAT'S WHY...
...MY DREAM WAS TO BECOME HIS WIFE.

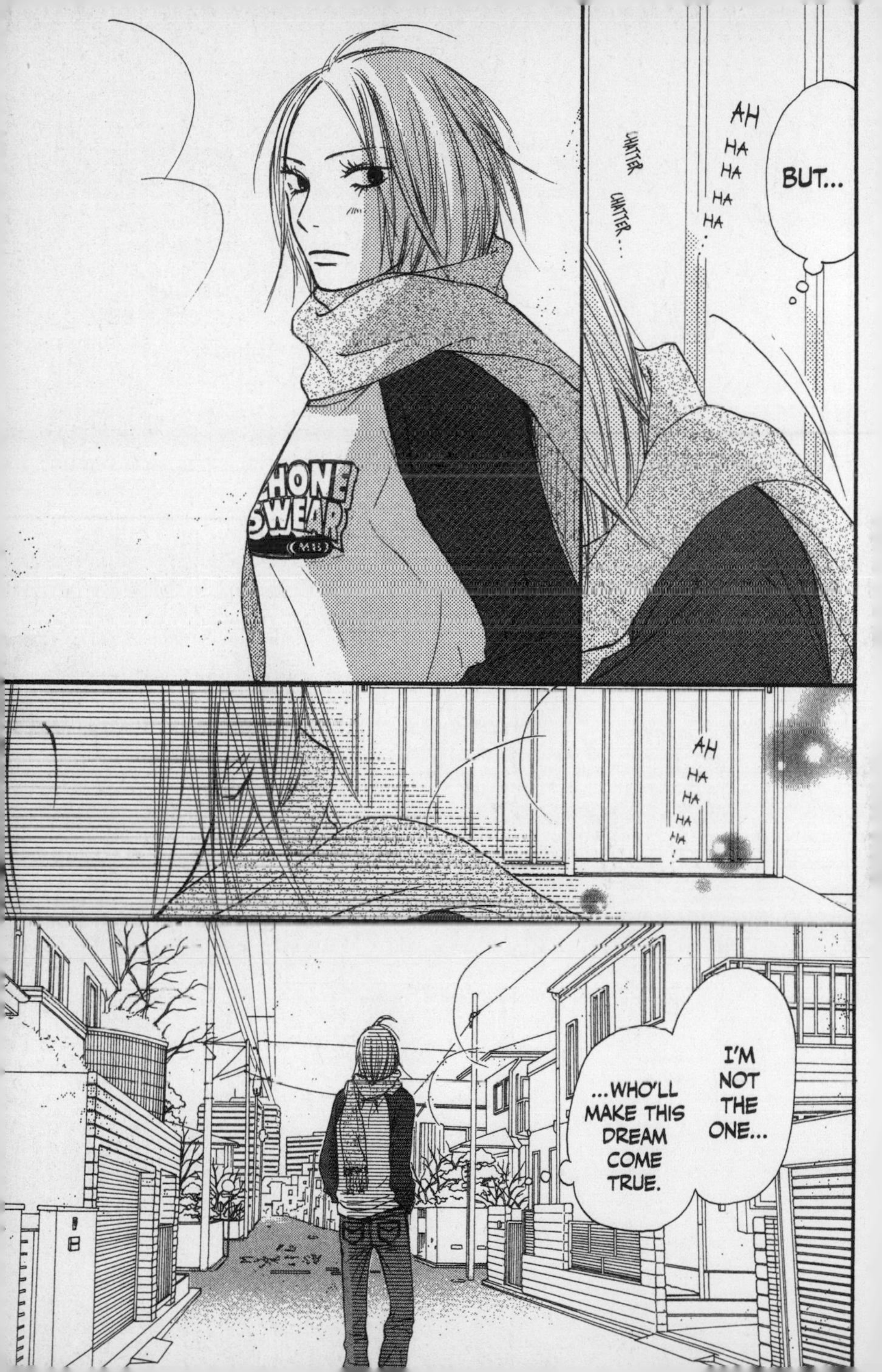
BUT...
AH HA HA HA HA
CHATTER CHATTER...
AH HA HA HA HA
I'M NOT THE ONE...
...WHO'LL MAKE THIS DREAM COME TRUE.

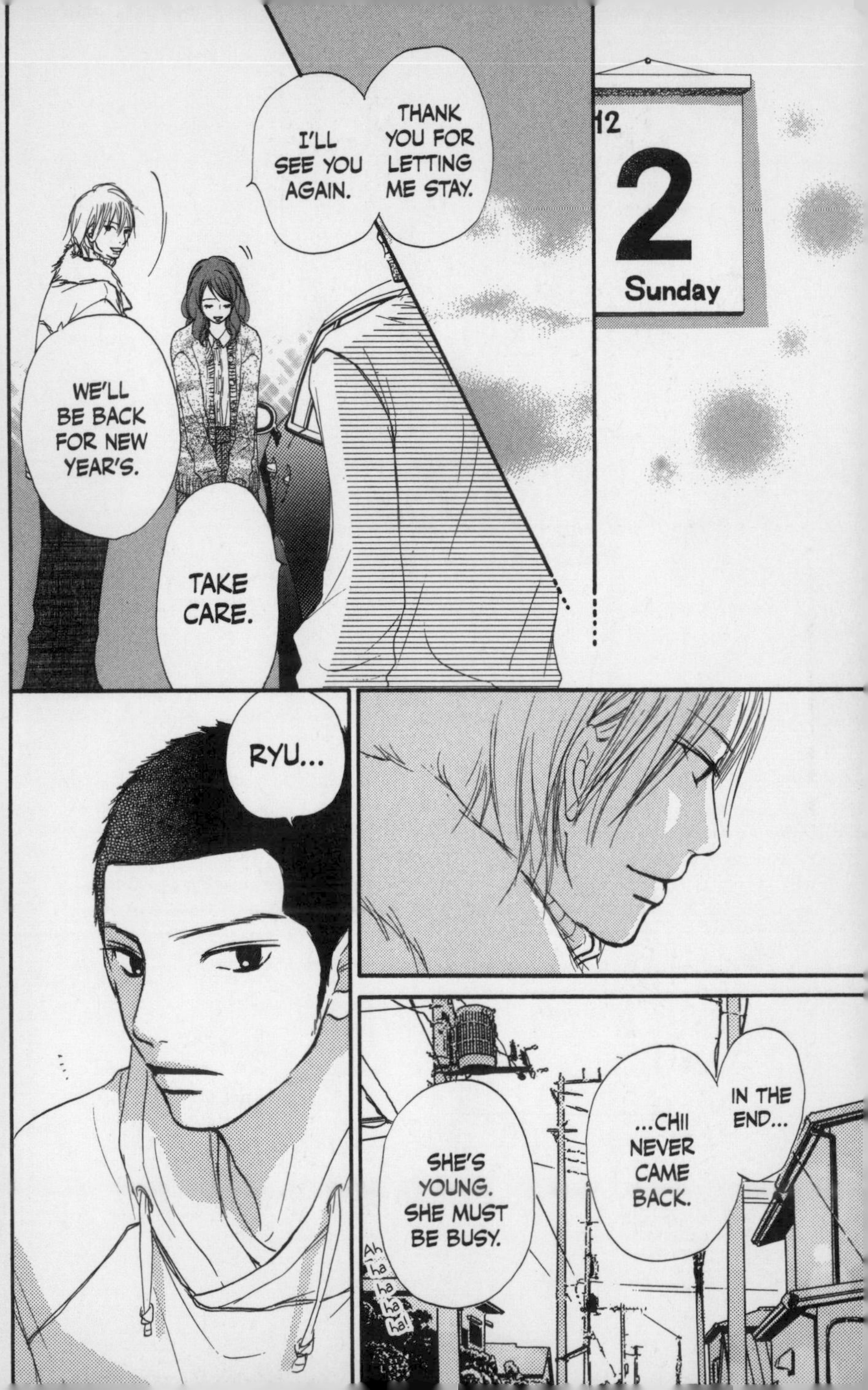
2
Sunday
THANK YOU FOR LETTING ME STAY.
I'LL SEE YOU AGAIN.
WE'LL BE BACK FOR NEW YEAR'S.
TAKE CARE.
IN THE END...
...CHII NEVER CAME BACK.
SHE'S YOUNG. SHE MUST BE BUSY.
Ah ha ha ha ha!
RYU...

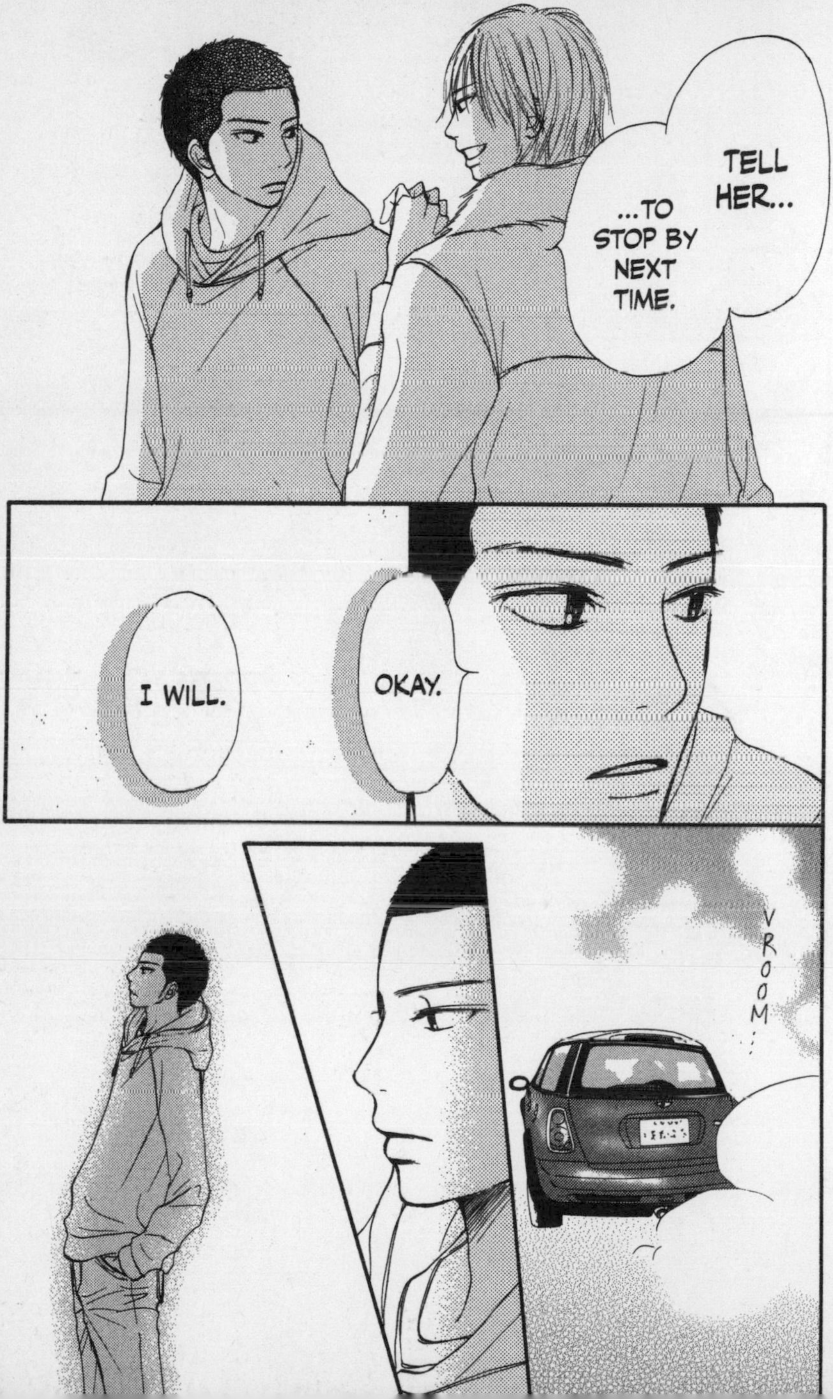
TELL HER...
...TO STOP BY NEXT TIME.
OKAY.
I WILL.
VROOM...

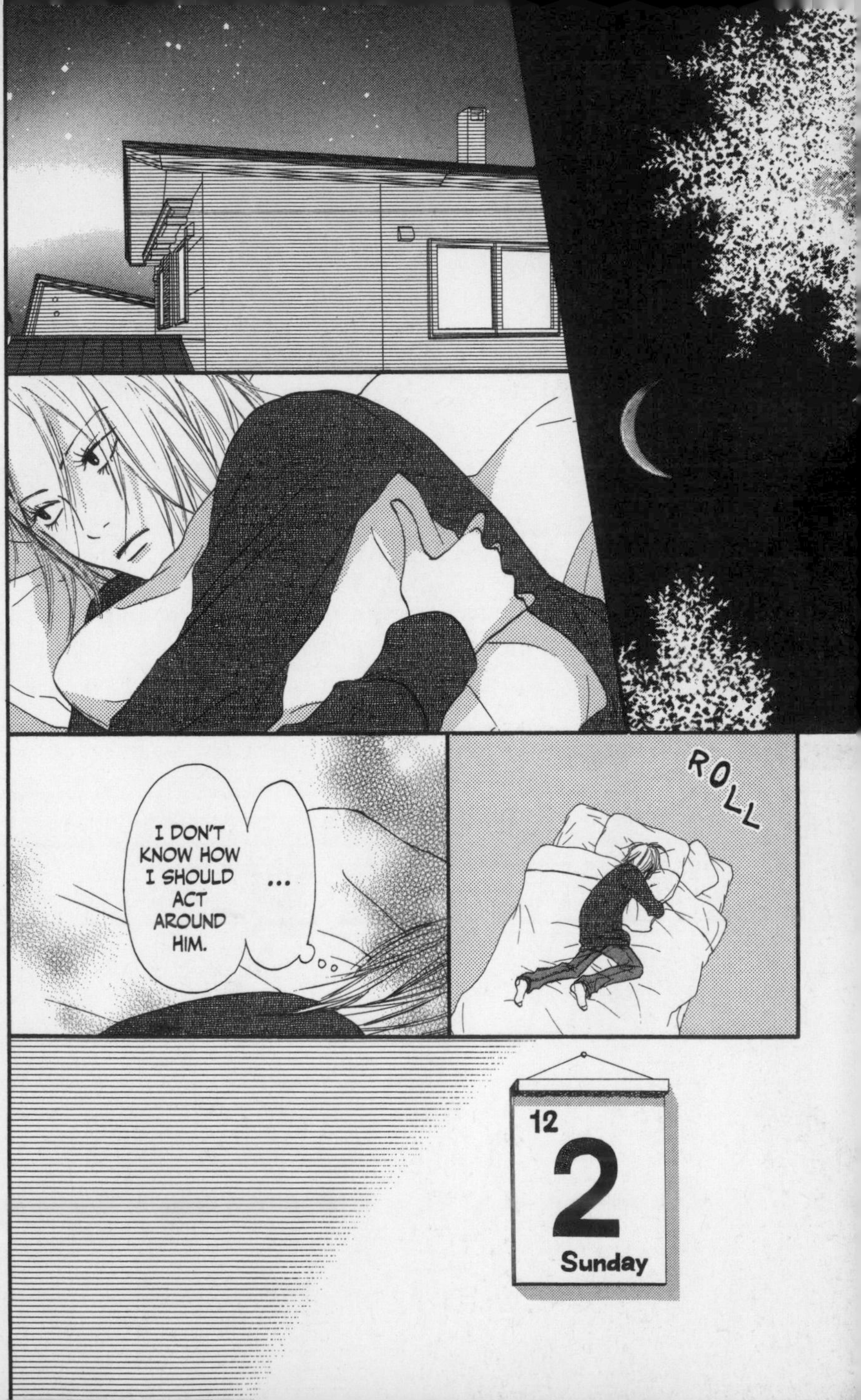
ROLL
I DON'T KNOW HOW I SHOULD ACT AROUND HIM.
...
12
2
Sunday

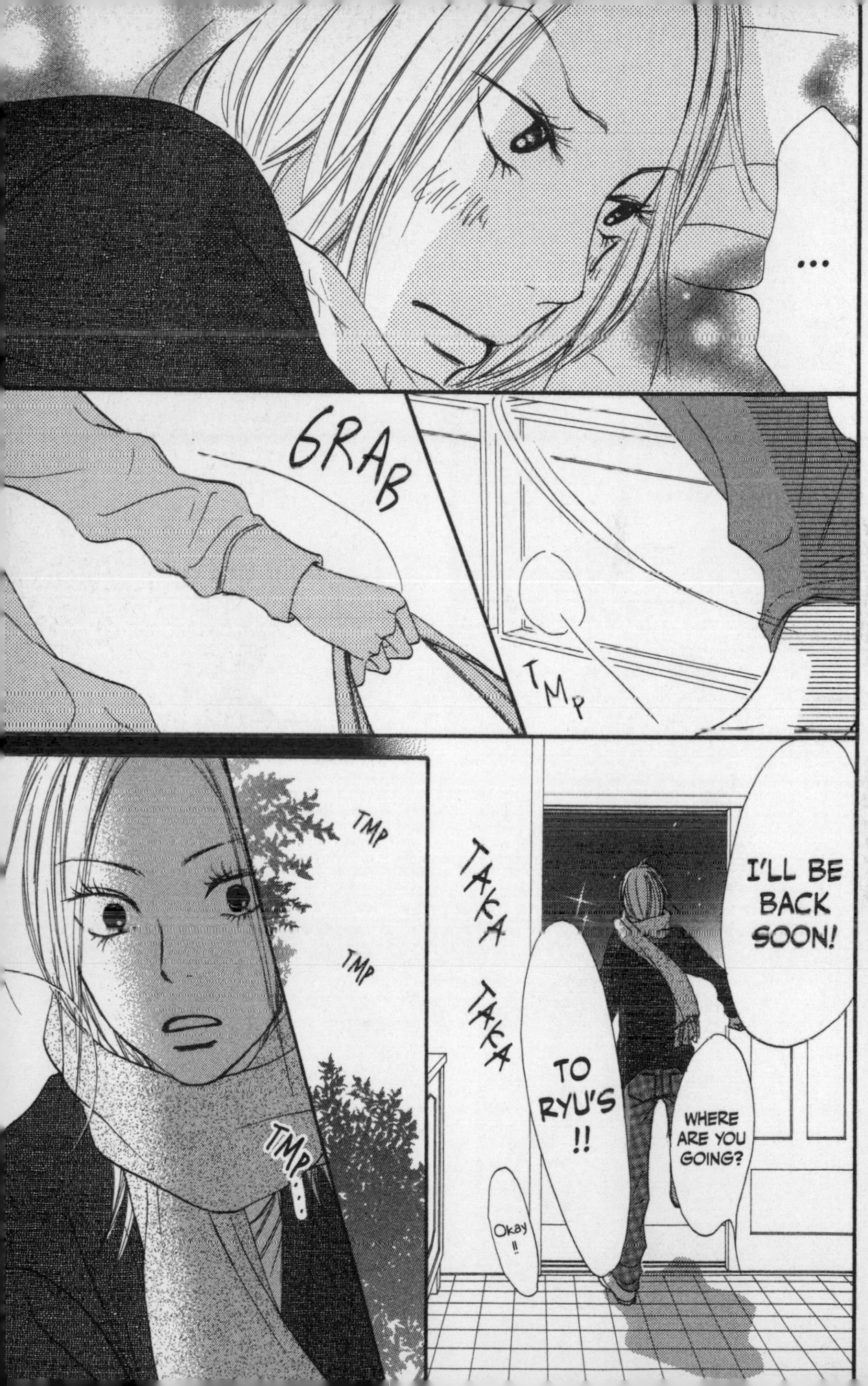
...
TMP
GRAB
I'LL BE BACK SOON!
WHERE ARE YOU GOING?
TO RYU'S!!
TAKA TAKA
Okay!!
TMP
TMP
TMP...

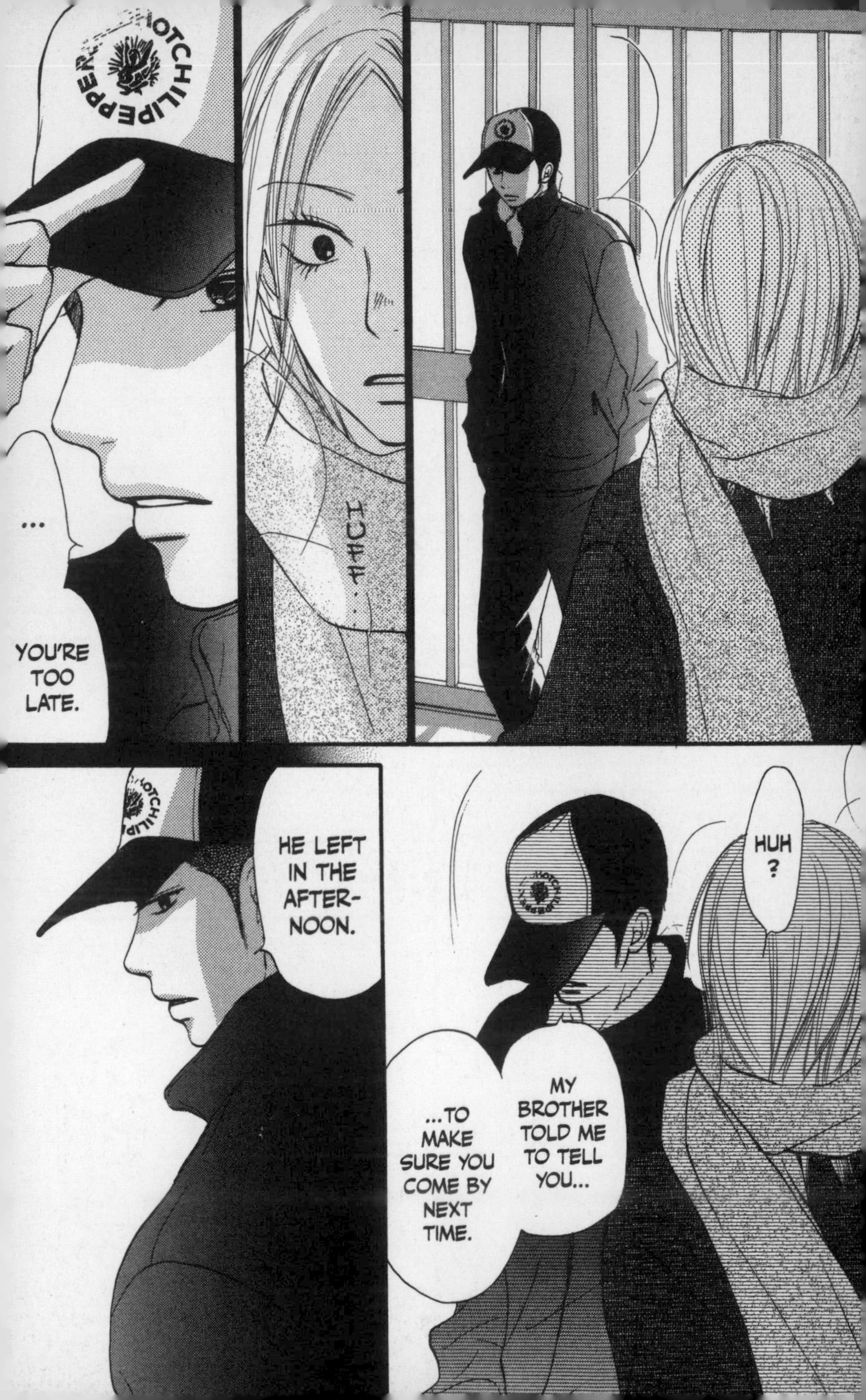
HUFF...
HOTCHILIPEPPER
...
YOU'RE TOO LATE.
HUH?
MY BROTHER TOLD ME TO TELL YOU...
...TO MAKE SURE YOU COME BY NEXT TIME.
HE LEFT IN THE AFTER-NOON.

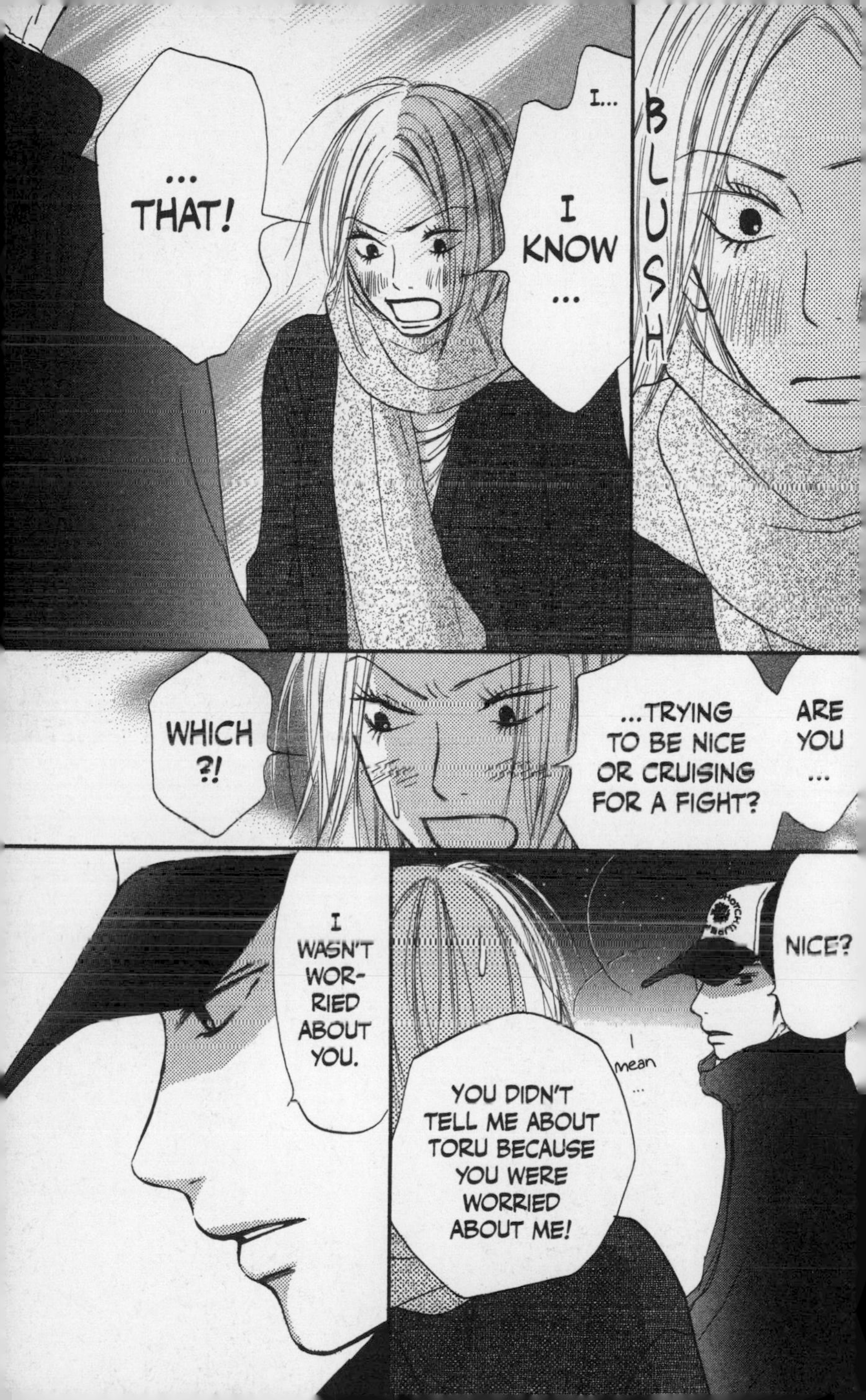
BLUSH
I... I KNOW ...
... THAT!
ARE YOU ...
...TRYING TO BE NICE OR CRUISING FOR A FIGHT?
WHICH ?!
NICE?
I mean ...
YOU DIDN'T TELL ME ABOUT TORU BECAUSE YOU WERE WORRIED ABOUT ME!
I WASN'T WOR-RIED ABOUT YOU.

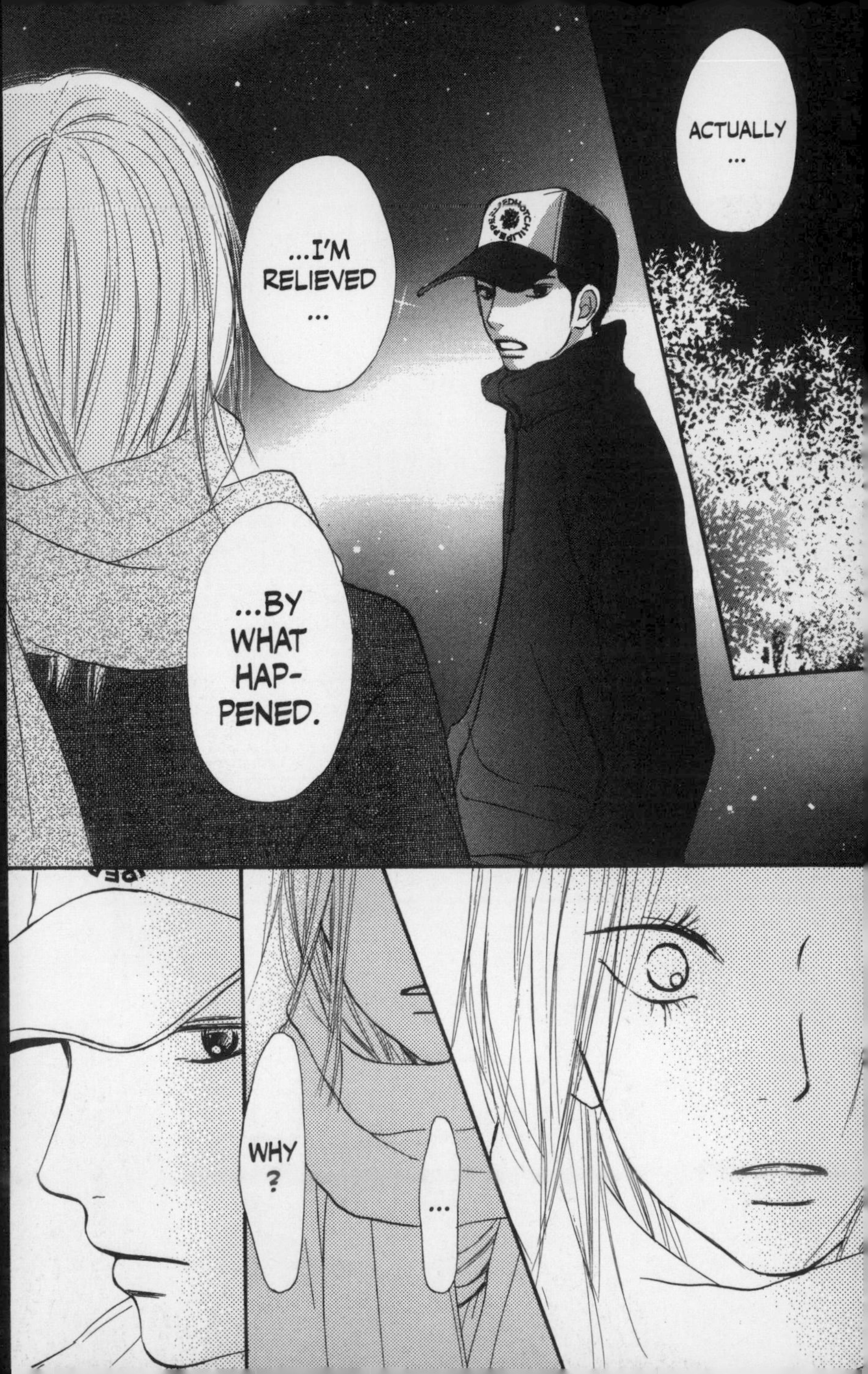
ACTUALLY ...
...I'M RELIEVED ...
...BY WHAT HAP-PENED.
...
WHY ?

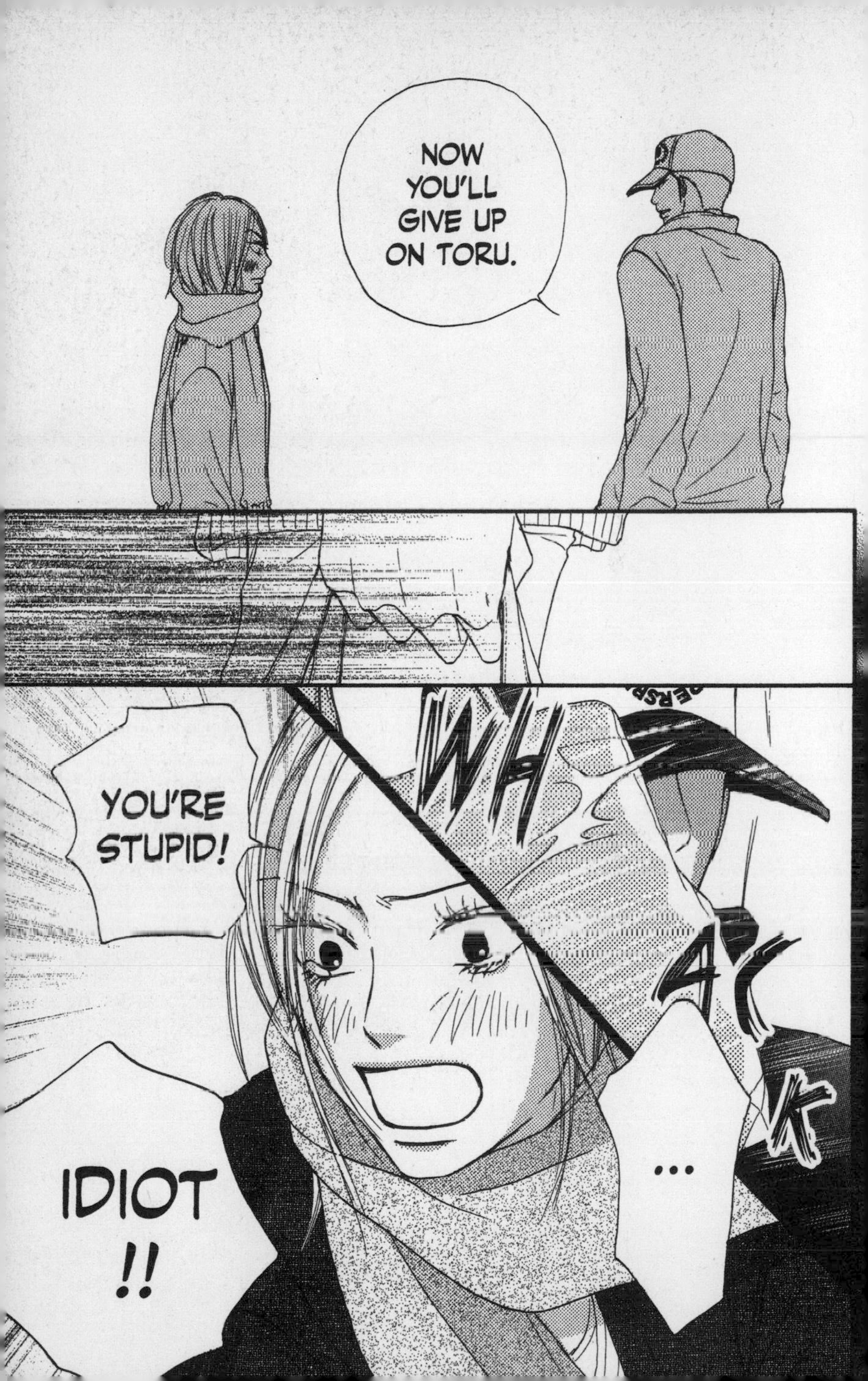
NOW YOU'LL GIVE UP ON TORU.
WH
ACK
YOU'RE STUPID!
...
IDIOT !!

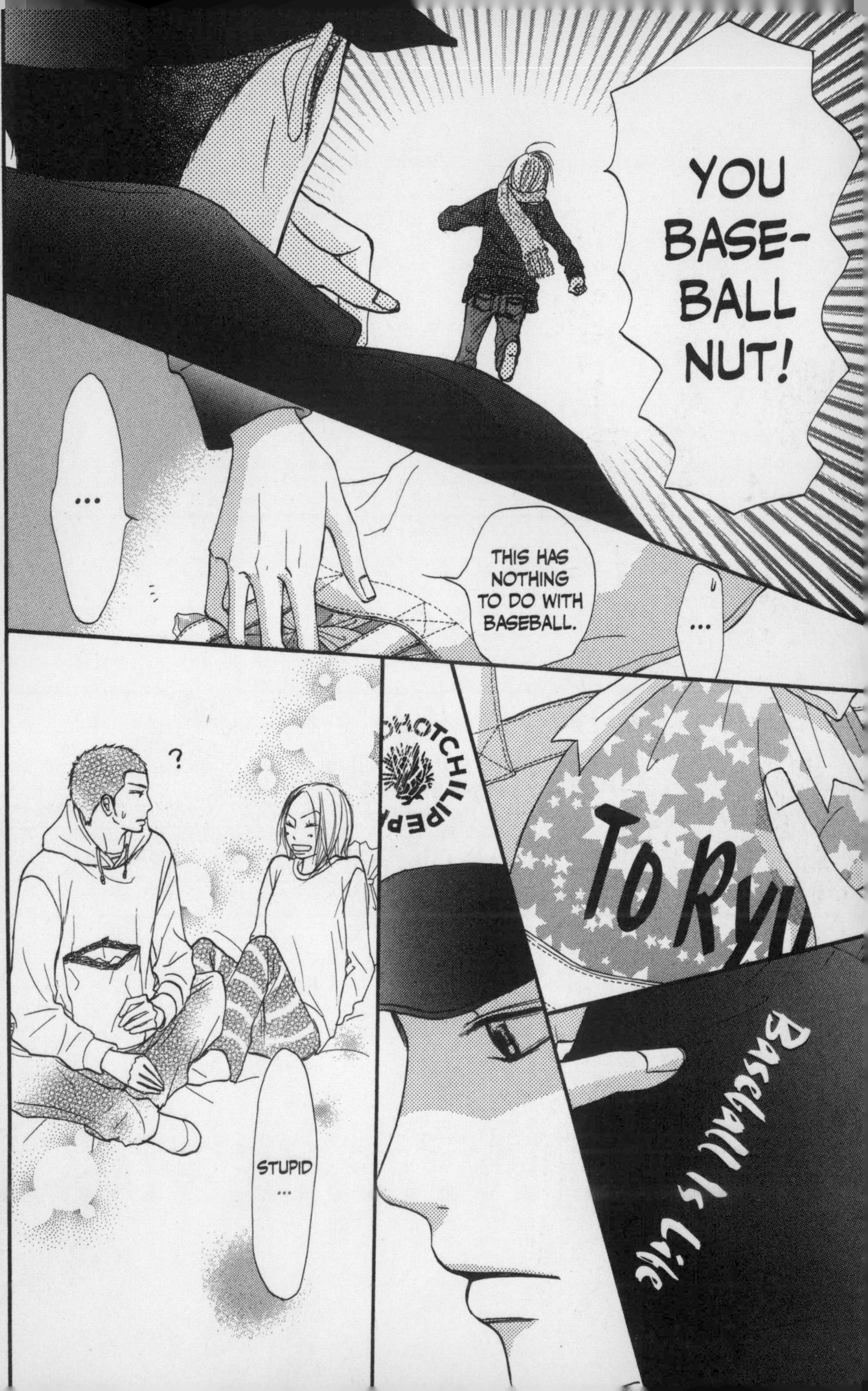
YOU BASE-BALL NUT!
...
THIS HAS NOTHING TO DO WITH BASEBALL.
...
TO RYU
Baseball Is Life
?
STUPID ...

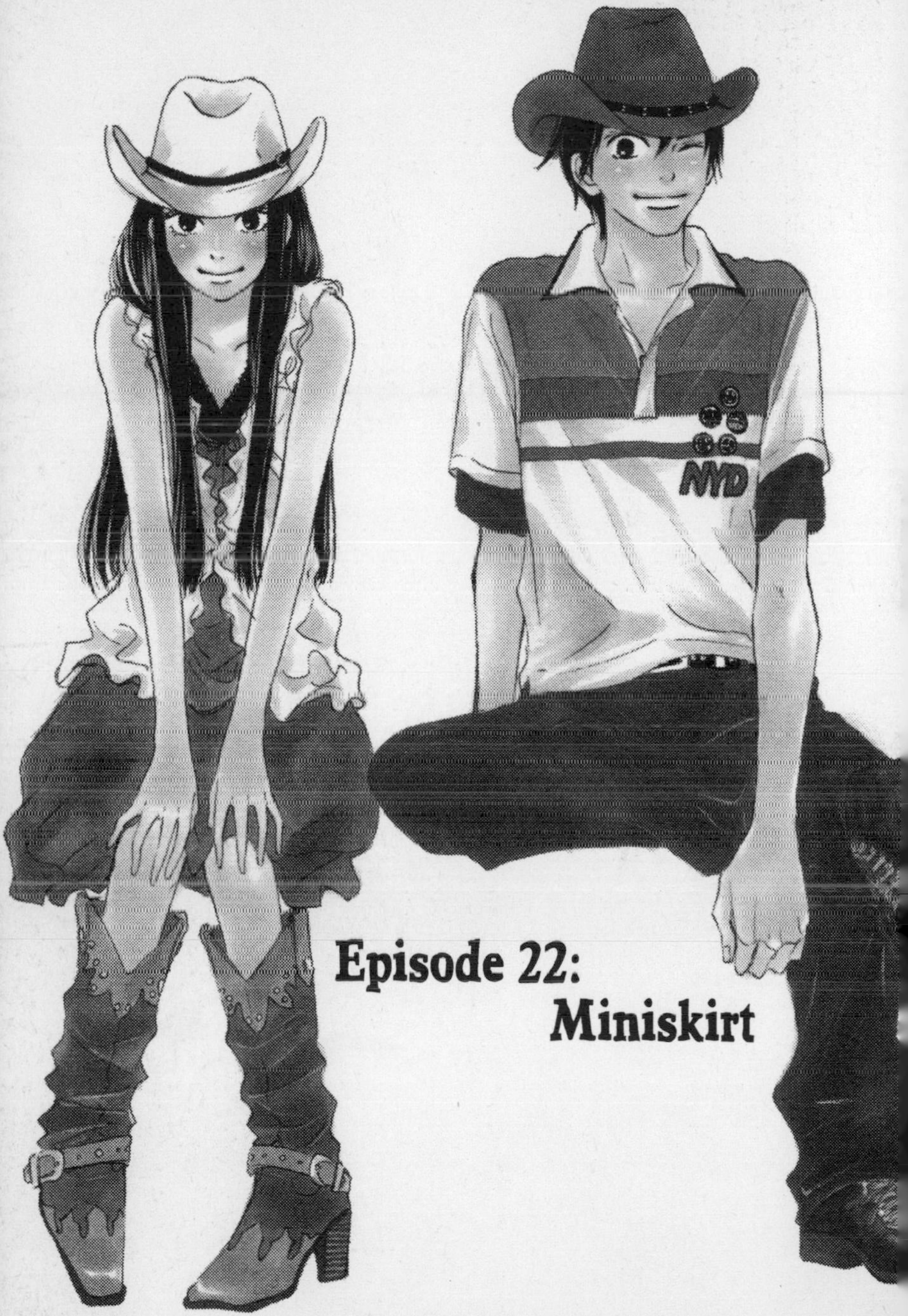
NYD

Episode 22: Miniskirt

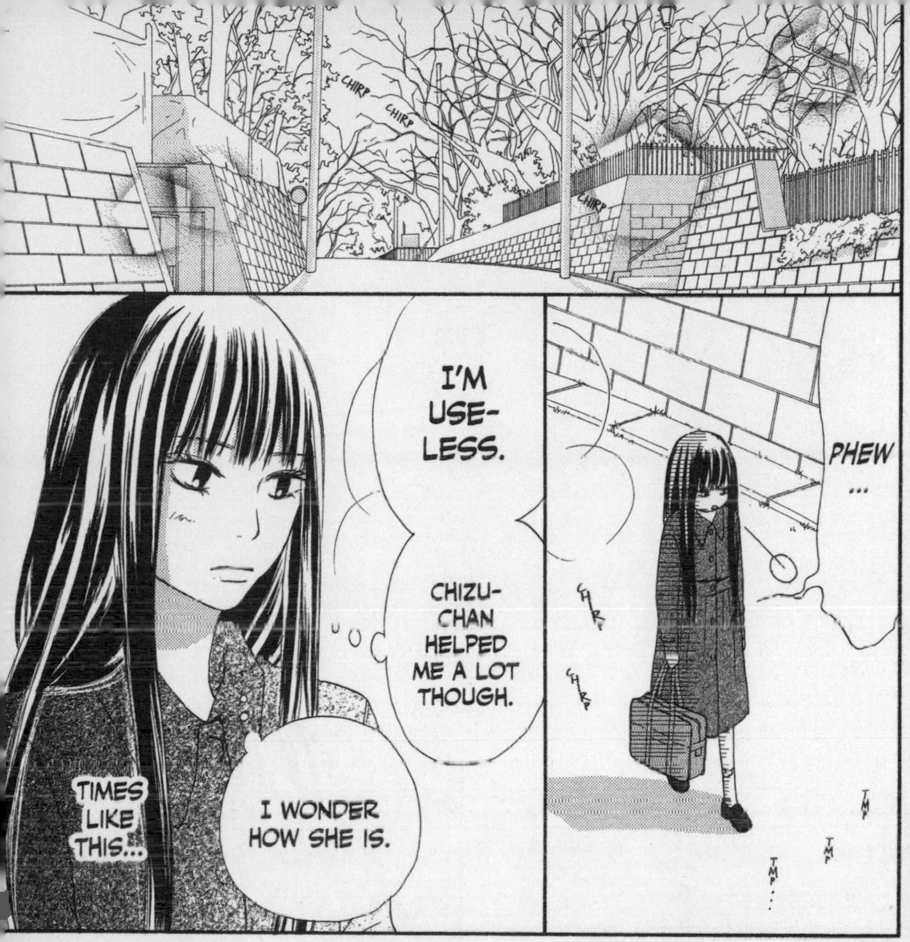
CHIRP
CHIRP
CHIRP
PHEW...
CHIRP
CHIRP
TMP
TMP
TMP...
I'M USELESS.
CHIZU-CHAN HELPED ME A LOT THOUGH.
I WONDER HOW SHE IS.
TIMES LIKE THIS...

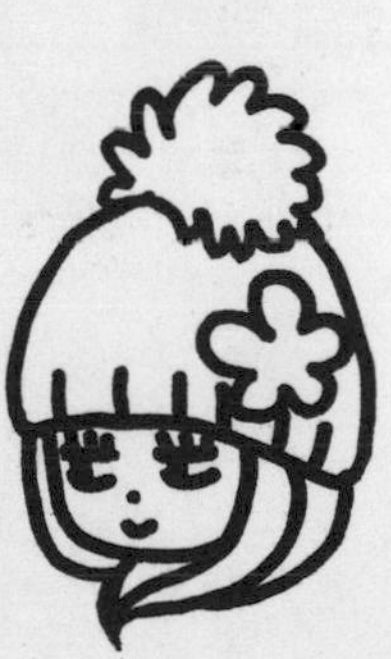

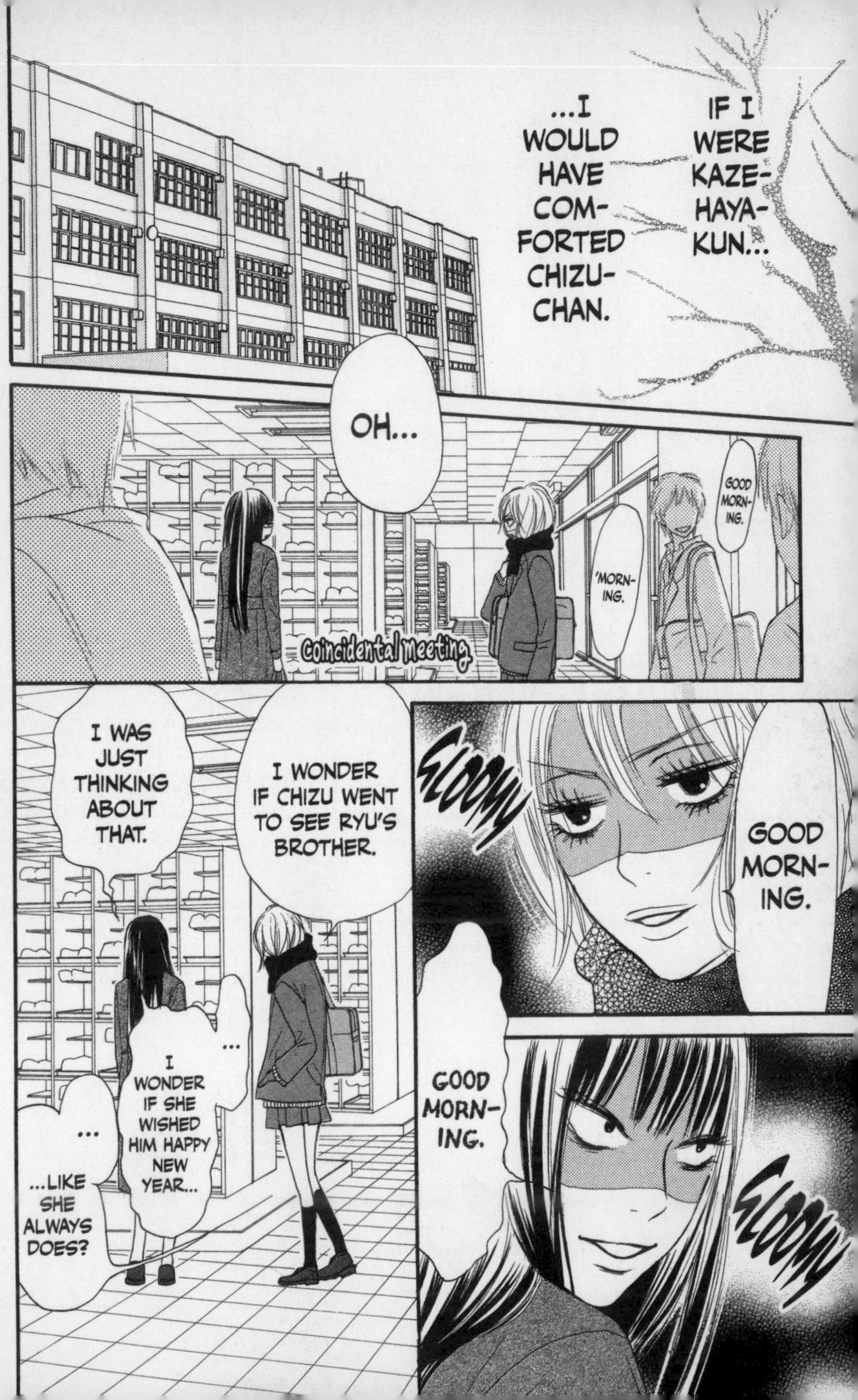
IF I WERE KAZE-HAYA-KUN...
...I WOULD HAVE COM-FORTED CHIZU-CHAN.
GOOD MORN-ING.
'MORN-ING.
OH...
Coincidental meeting
GLOOMY
GOOD MORN-ING.
GOOD MORN-ING.
GLOOMY
I WONDER IF CHIZU WENT TO SEE RYU'S BROTHER.
I WAS JUST THINKING ABOUT THAT.
...
I WONDER IF SHE WISHED HIM HAPPY NEW YEAR...
...
...LIKE SHE ALWAYS DOES?

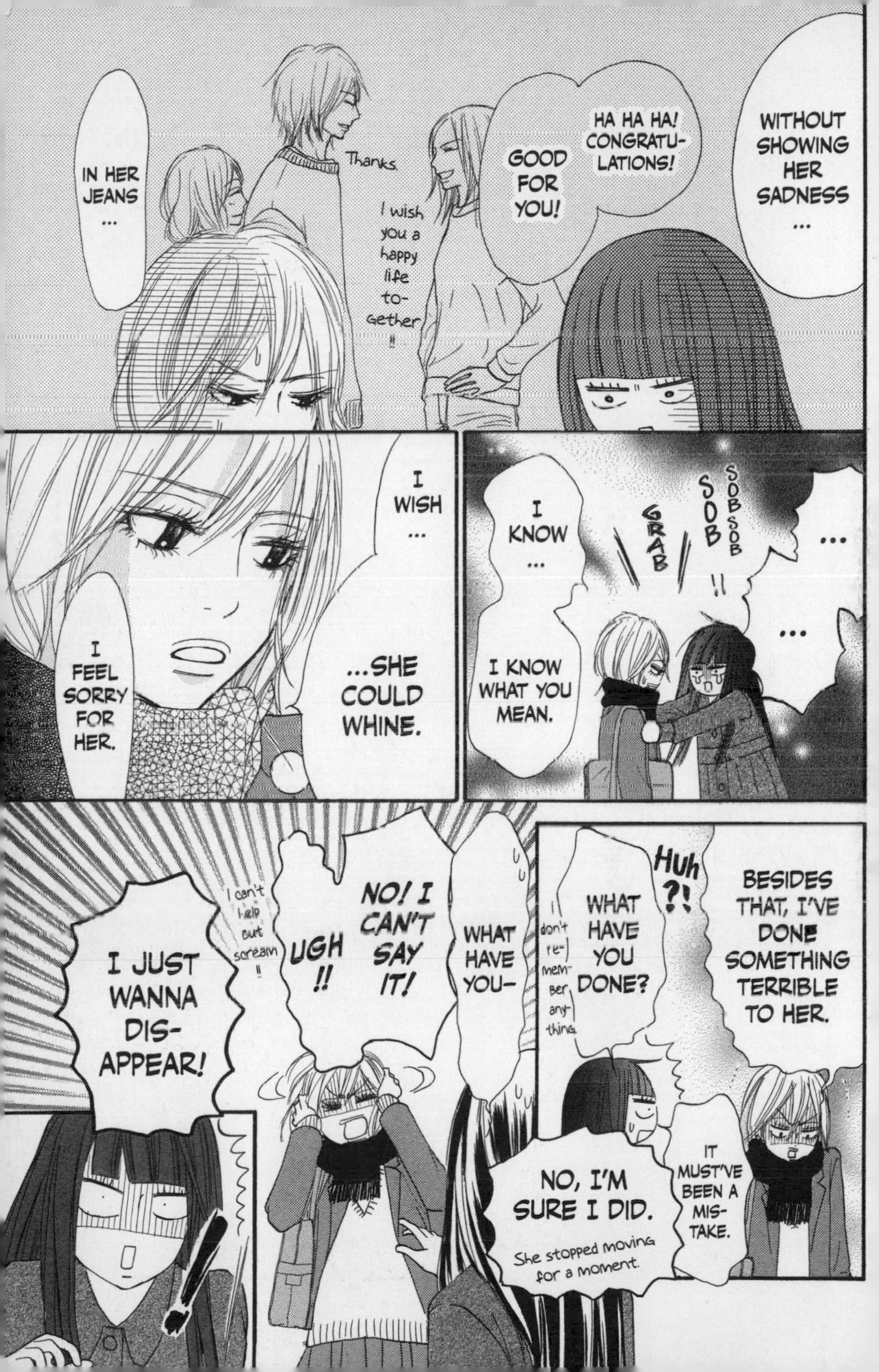
WITHOUT SHOWING HER SADNESS ...
HA HA HA! CONGRATU-LATIONS!
GOOD FOR YOU!
I wish you a happy life to-gether!!
Thanks.
IN HER JEANS ...
...
...
SOB SOB SOB
!!
GRAB
I KNOW ...
I KNOW WHAT YOU MEAN.
I WISH ...
...SHE COULD WHINE.
I FEEL SORRY FOR HER.
BESIDES THAT, I'VE DONE SOMETHING TERRIBLE TO HER.
Huh?!
WHAT HAVE YOU DONE?
I don't re-mem-ber any-thing.
IT MUST'VE BEEN A MIS-TAKE.
NO, I'M SURE I DID.
She stopped moving for a moment.
WHAT HAVE YOU-
NO! I CAN'T SAY IT!
UGH!!
I can't help but scream!!
I JUST WANNA DIS-APPEAR!

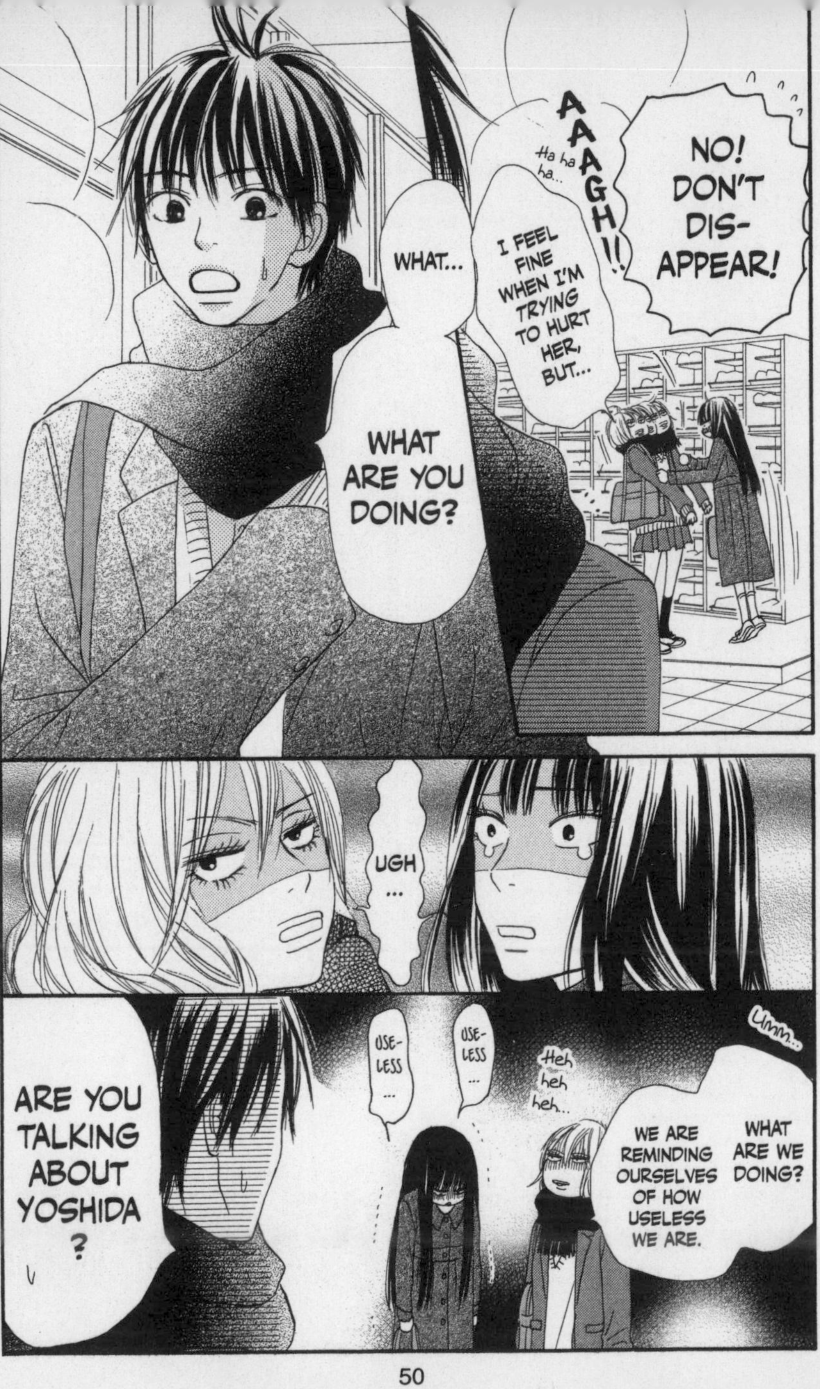
NO! DON'T DIS-APPEAR!
AAAAGH!!
Ha ha ha...
I FEEL FINE WHEN I'M TRYING TO HURT HER, BUT...
WHAT...
WHAT ARE YOU DOING?
UGH ...
Umm...
WHAT ARE WE DOING?
WE ARE REMINDING OURSELVES OF HOW USELESS WE ARE.
Heh heh heh...
USE-LESS ...
USE-LESS ...
ARE YOU TALKING ABOUT YOSHIDA ?

KARUPIN on JAPAN 2

Anyway, that puppy is completely looking down on me, but when I spend time with her at my parent's house...

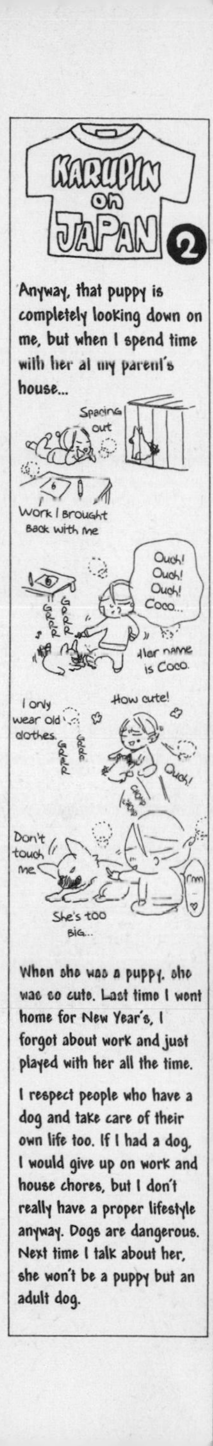
Spacing out
Work I brought back with me
Ouch! Ouch! Ouch! Coco...
Her name is Coco.
How cute!
I only wear old clothes.
Ouch!
Don't touch me.
She's too big...

When she was a puppy, she was so cute. Last time I went home for New Year's, I forgot about work and just played with her all the time.

I respect people who have a dog and take care of their own life too. If I had a dog, I would give up on work and house chores, but I don't really have a proper lifestyle anyway. Dogs are dangerous. Next time I talk about her, she won't be a puppy but an adult dog.

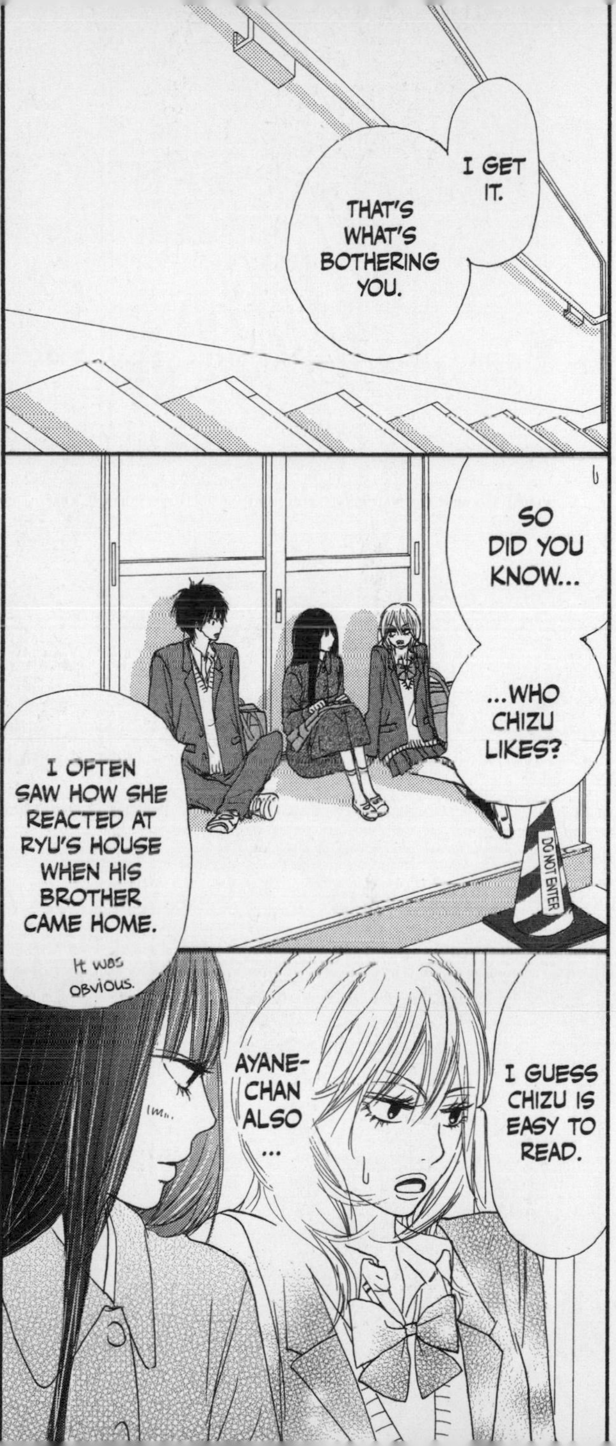
I GET IT.
THAT'S WHAT'S BOTHERING YOU.
SO DID YOU KNOW...
...WHO CHIZU LIKES?
I OFTEN SAW HOW SHE REACTED AT RYU'S HOUSE WHEN HIS BROTHER CAME HOME.
It was obvious.
DO NOT ENTER
I GUESS CHIZU IS EASY TO READ.
AYANE-CHAN ALSO ...

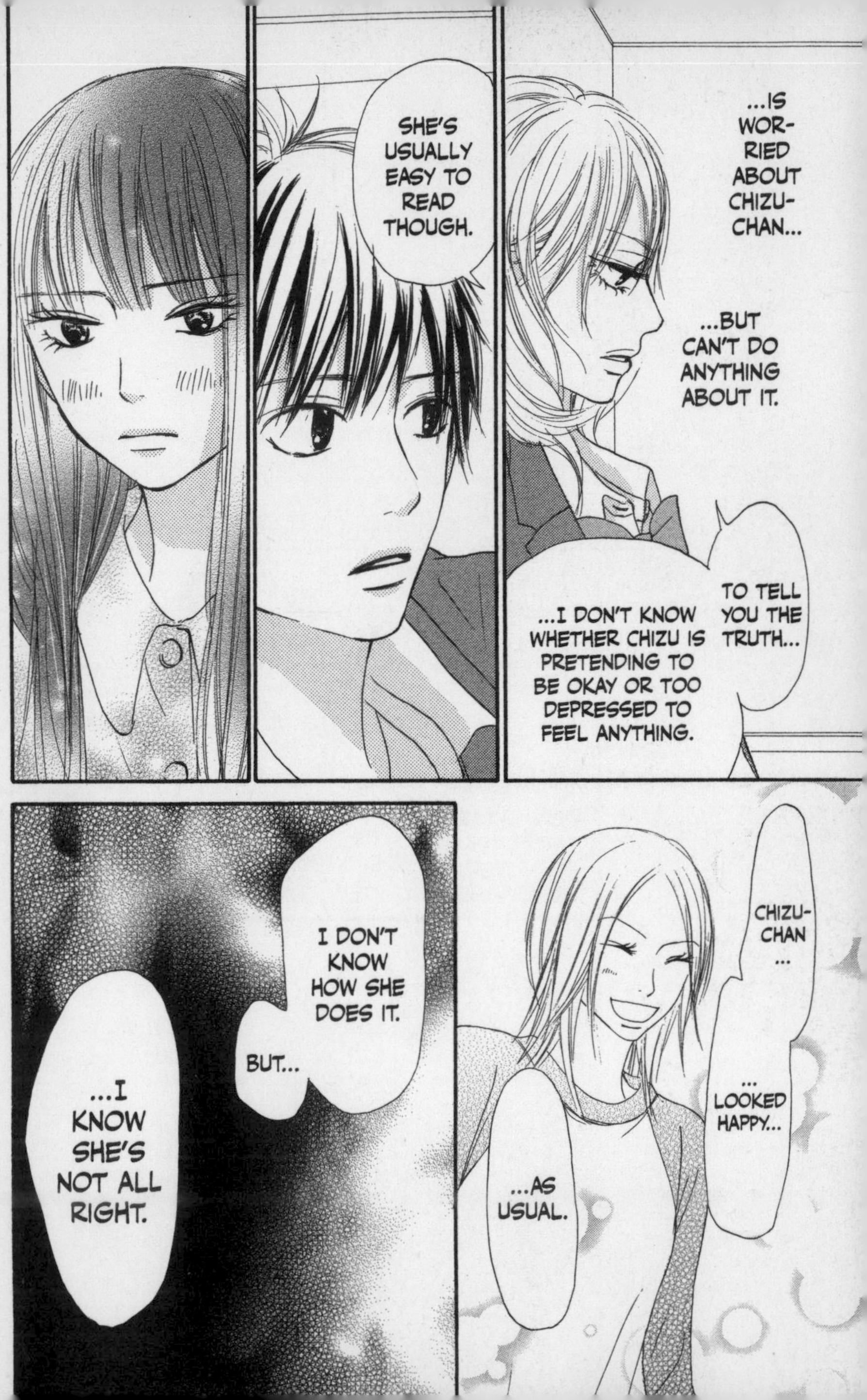
...IS WORRIED ABOUT CHIZU-CHAN...
...BUT CAN'T DO ANYTHING ABOUT IT.
TO TELL YOU THE TRUTH...
...I DON'T KNOW WHETHER CHIZU IS PRETENDING TO BE OKAY OR TOO DEPRESSED TO FEEL ANYTHING.
SHE'S USUALLY EASY TO READ THOUGH.
CHIZU-CHAN...
...LOOKED HAPPY...
...AS USUAL.
I DON'T KNOW HOW SHE DOES IT.
BUT...
...I KNOW SHE'S NOT ALL RIGHT.

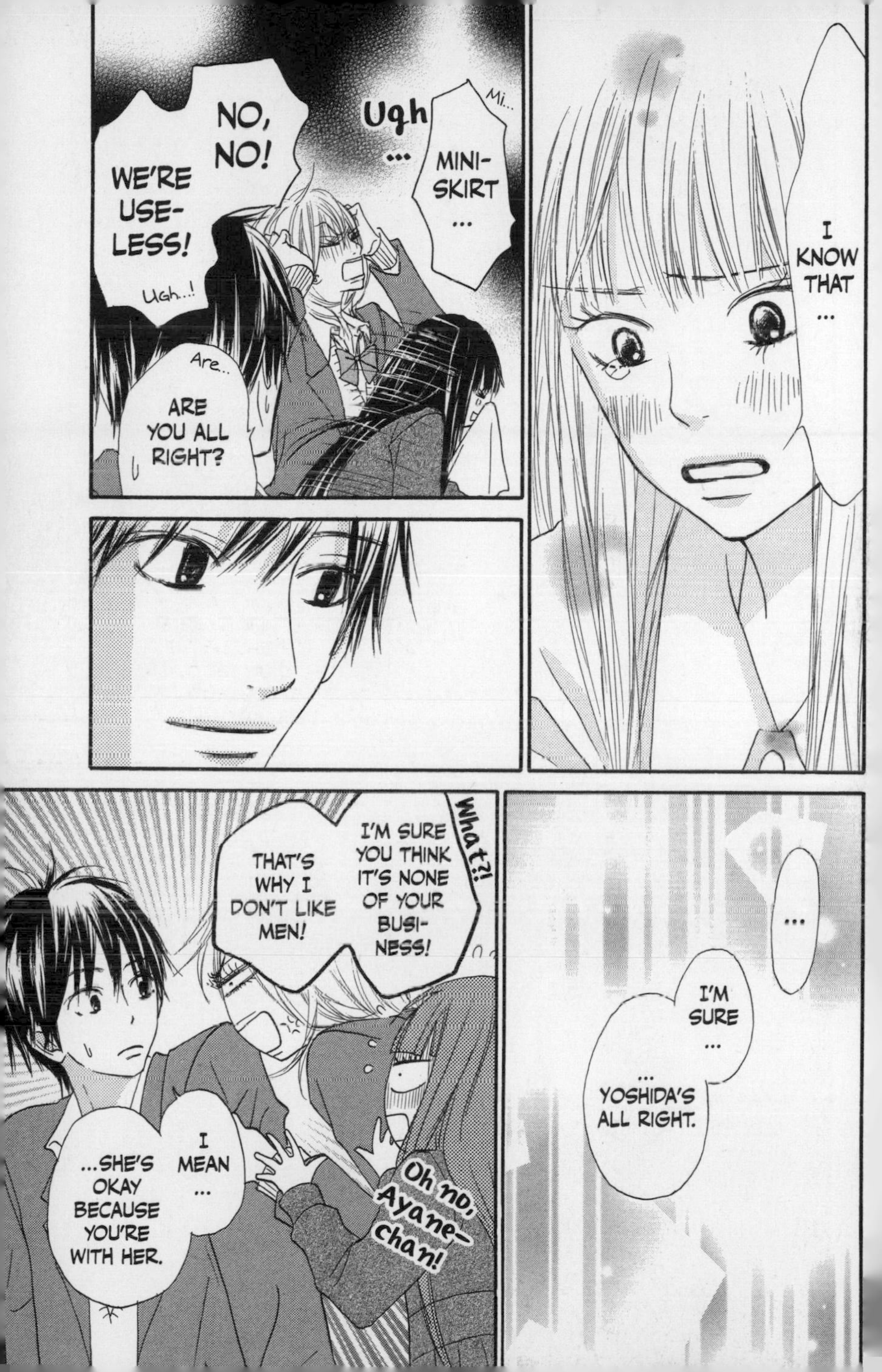
I KNOW THAT ...
Mi...
MINI-SKIRT ...
Ugh ...
NO, NO!
WE'RE USE-LESS!
Ugh...!
Are...
ARE YOU ALL RIGHT?
...
I'M SURE ...
... YOSHIDA'S ALL RIGHT.
What?!
I'M SURE YOU THINK IT'S NONE OF YOUR BUSI-NESS!
THAT'S WHY I DON'T LIKE MEN!
Oh no, Ayane-chan!
I MEAN ...
...SHE'S OKAY BECAUSE YOU'RE WITH HER.

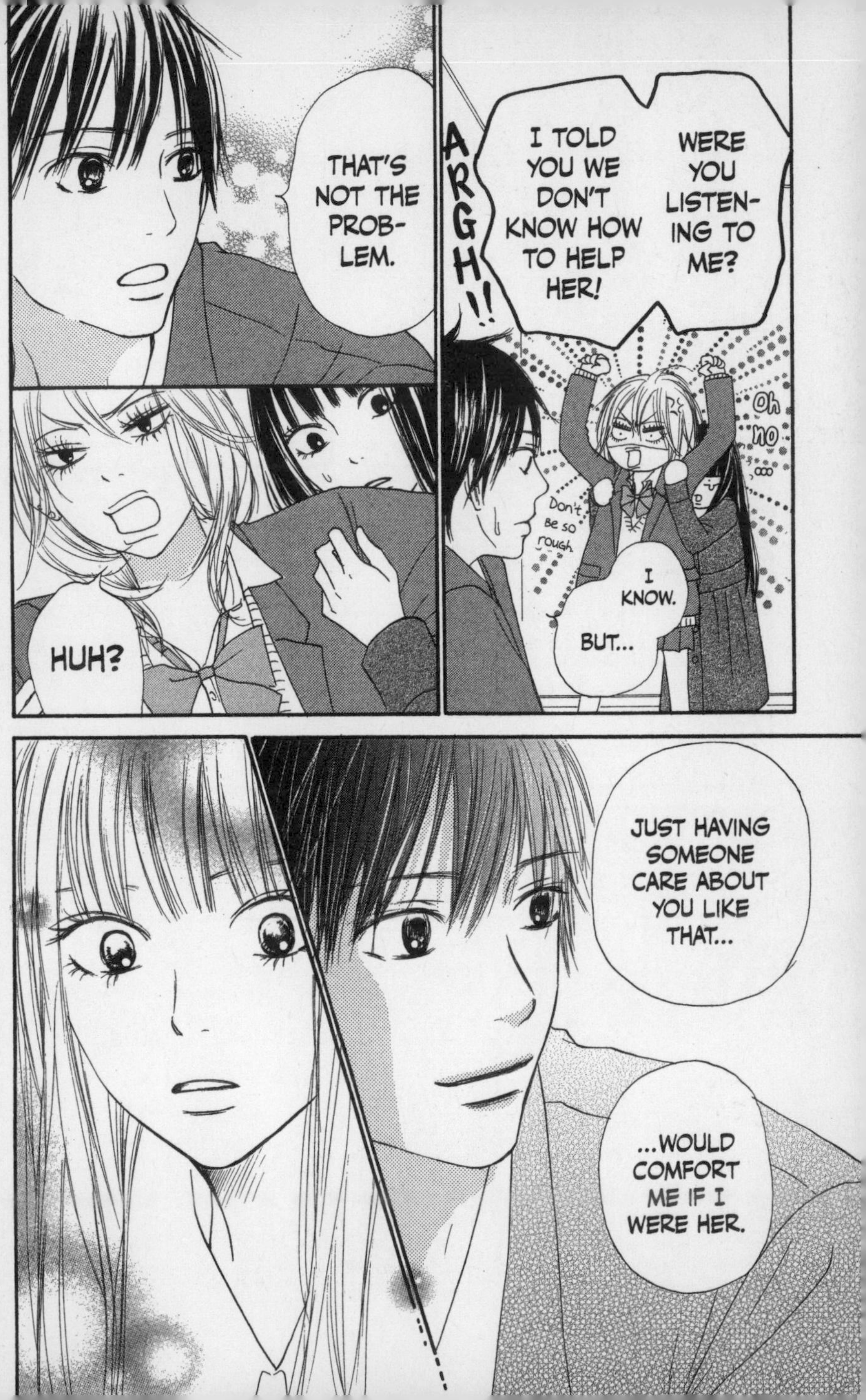
WERE YOU LISTENING TO ME? I TOLD YOU WE DON'T KNOW HOW TO HELP HER!
ARGH!!
Oh no...
Don't be so rough
I KNOW. BUT...
THAT'S NOT THE PROBLEM.
HUH?
JUST HAVING SOMEONE CARE ABOUT YOU LIKE THAT...
...WOULD COMFORT ME IF I WERE HER.

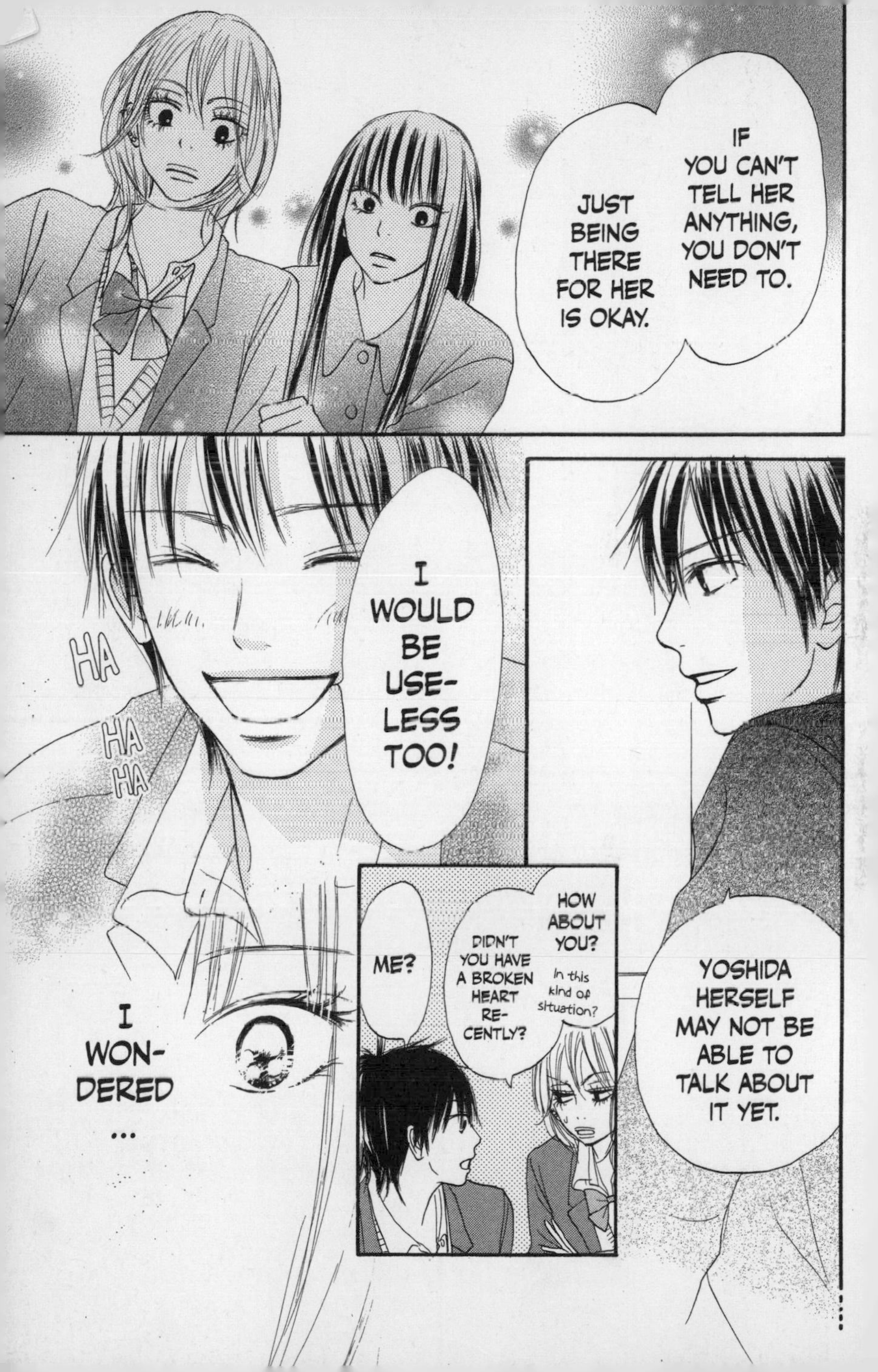
IF YOU CAN'T TELL HER ANYTHING, YOU DON'T NEED TO.
JUST BEING THERE FOR HER IS OKAY.
YOSHIDA HERSELF MAY NOT BE ABLE TO TALK ABOUT IT YET.
I WOULD BE USE-LESS TOO!
HA
HA
HA
HOW ABOUT YOU?
In this kind of situation?
DIDN'T YOU HAVE A BROKEN HEART RE-CENTLY?
ME?
I WON-DERED ...

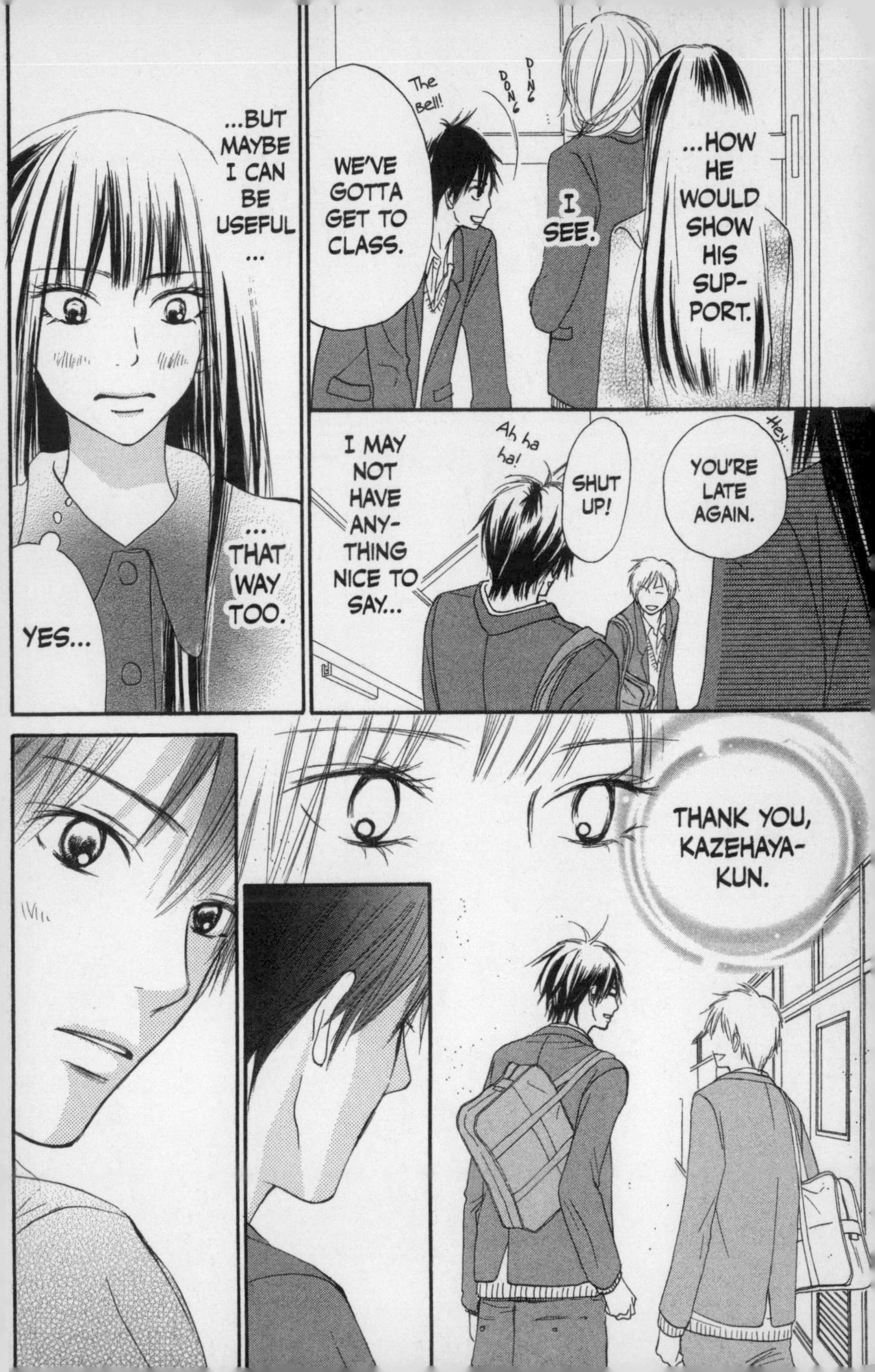
...HOW HE WOULD SHOW HIS SUP-PORT.
I SEE.
DING DONG
The bell!
WE'VE GOTTA GET TO CLASS.
Hey...
YOU'RE LATE AGAIN.
SHUT UP!
Ah ha ha!
I MAY NOT HAVE ANY-THING NICE TO SAY...
...BUT MAYBE I CAN BE USEFUL...
...THAT WAY TOO.
YES...
THANK YOU, KAZEHAYA-KUN.

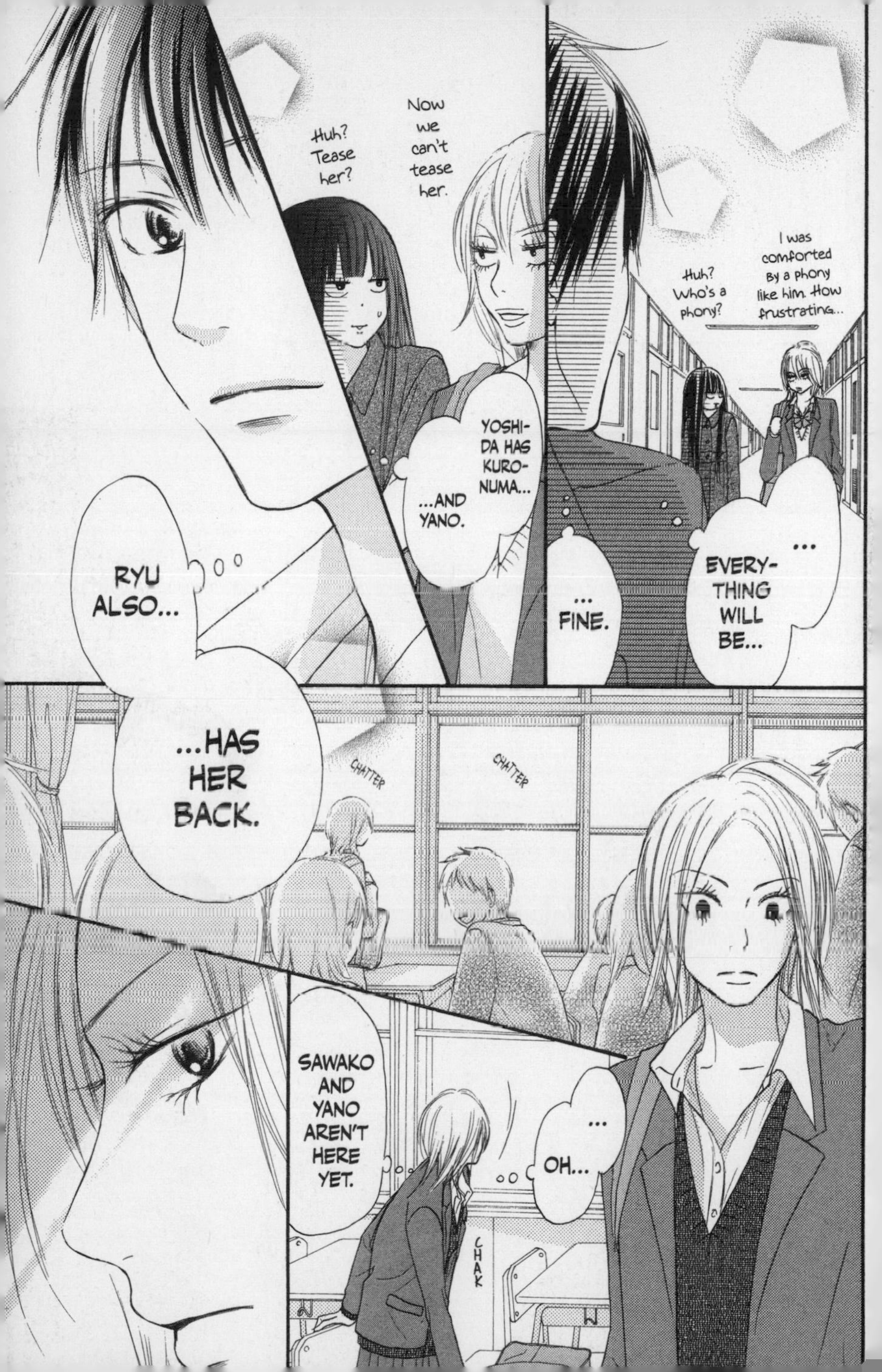
I was comforted by a phony like him. How frustrating...
Huh? Who's a phony?
... EVERYTHING WILL BE...
... FINE.
Now we can't tease her.
Huh? Tease her?
YOSHIDA HAS KURONUMA...
...AND YANO.
RYU ALSO...
...HAS HER BACK.
CHATTER
CHATTER
... OH...
SAWAKO AND YANO AREN'T HERE YET.
CHAK

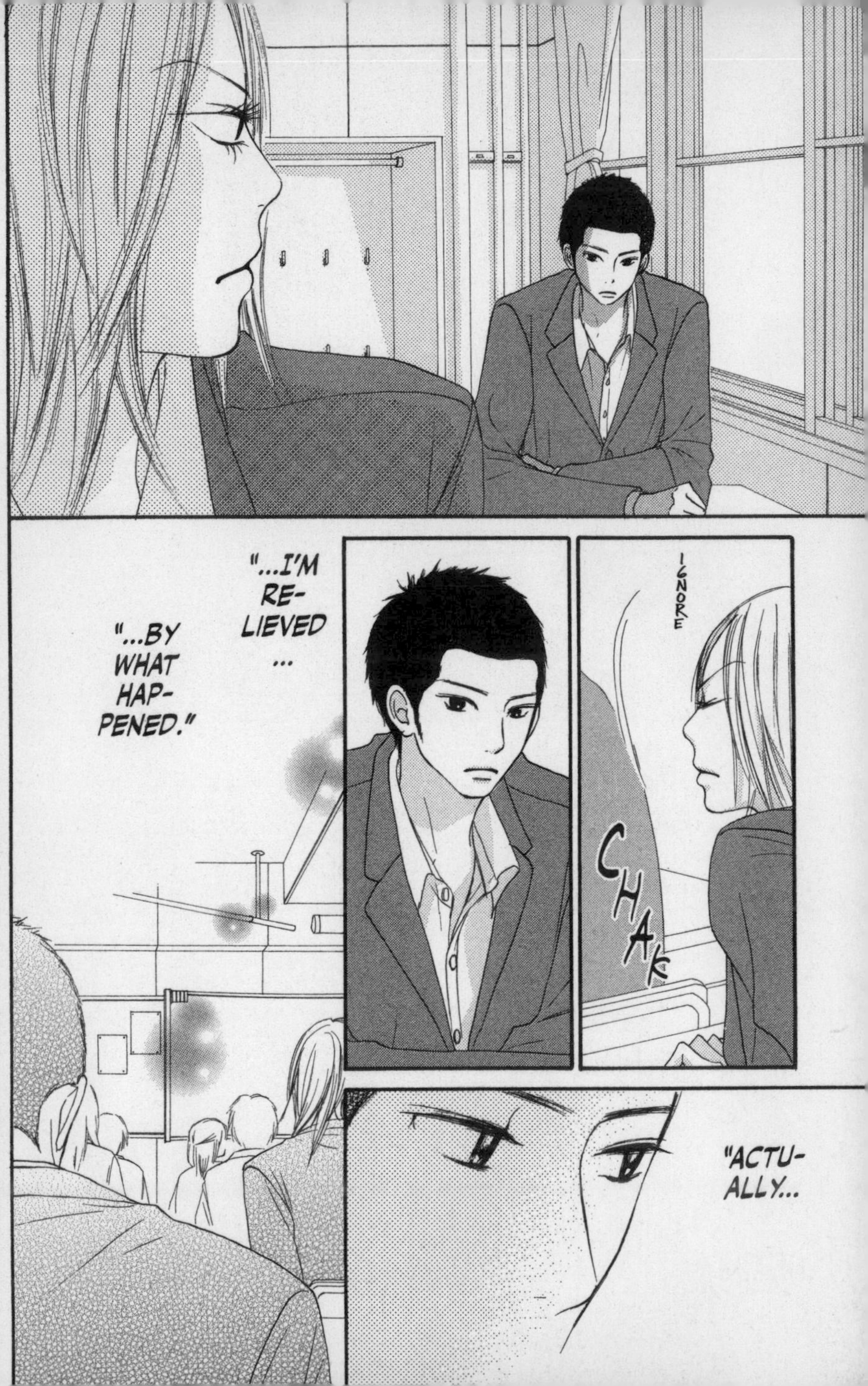
IGNORE
CHAK
"ACTU-ALLY...
"...I'M RE-LIEVED...
"...BY WHAT HAP-PENED."

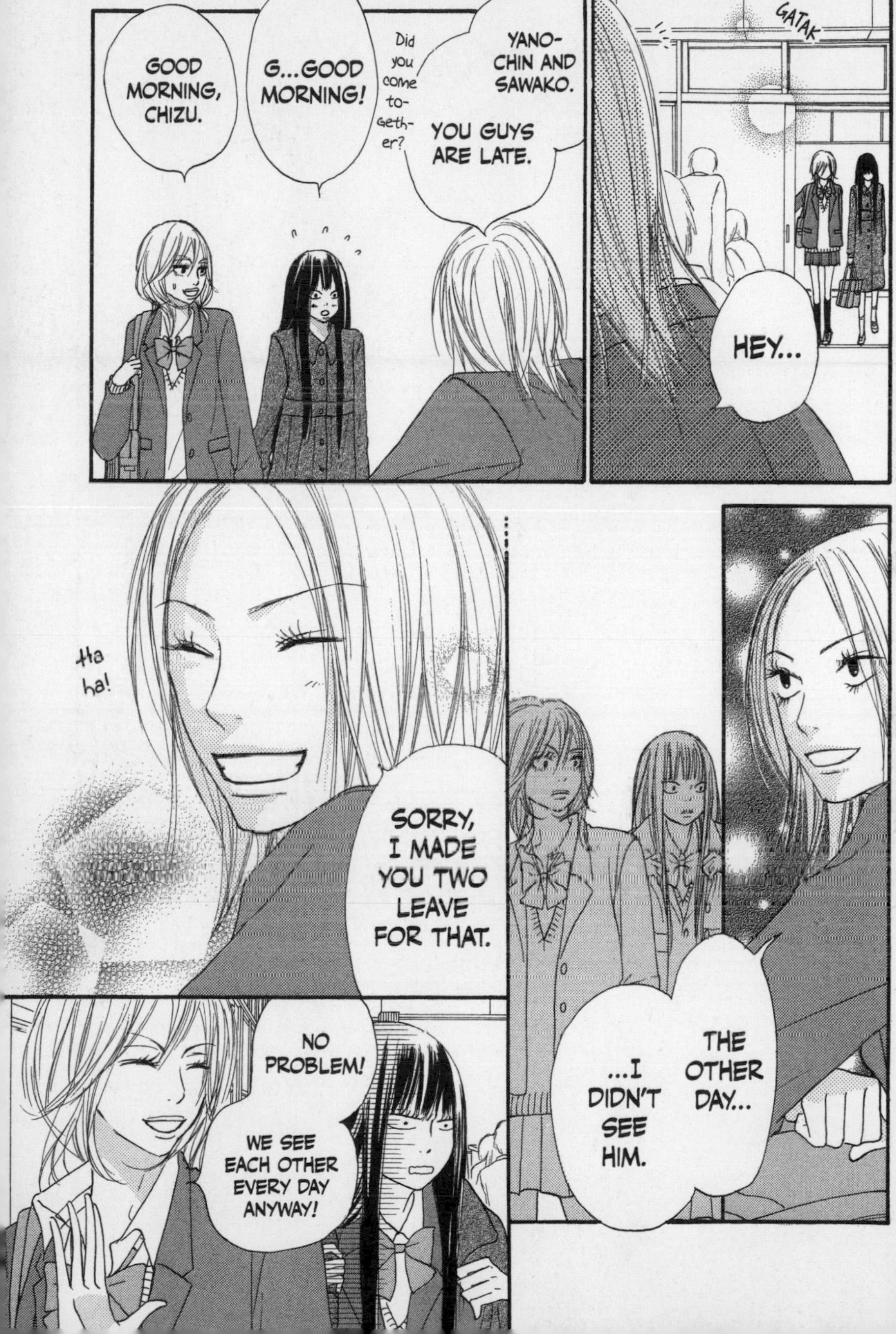
GATAK
HEY...
YANO-CHIN AND SAWAKO.
YOU GUYS ARE LATE.
Did you come to-geth-er?
G...GOOD MORNING!
GOOD MORNING, CHIZU.
THE OTHER DAY...
...I DIDN'T SEE HIM.
SORRY, I MADE YOU TWO LEAVE FOR THAT.
Ha ha!
NO PROBLEM!
WE SEE EACH OTHER EVERY DAY ANYWAY!

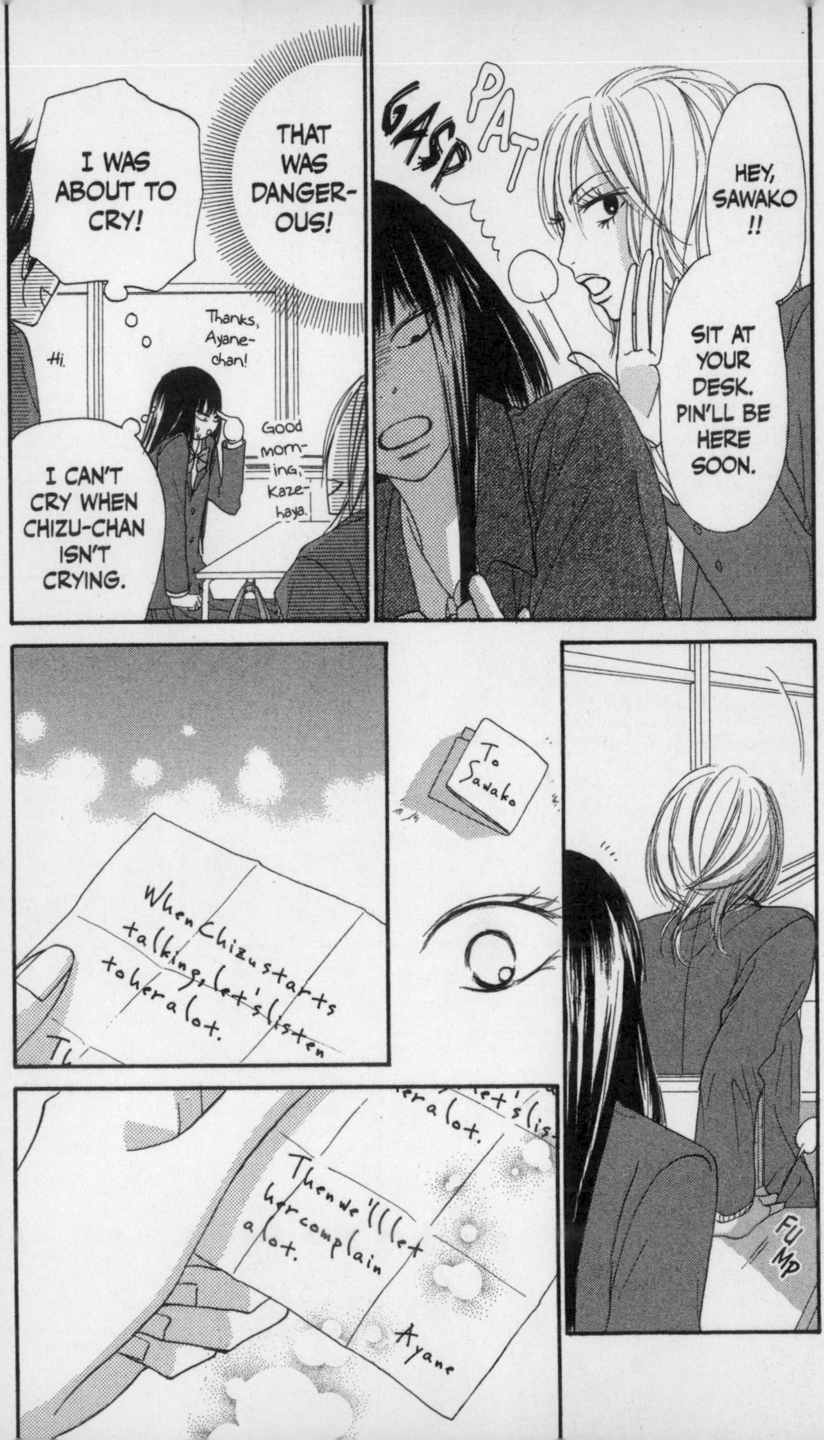
HEY, SAWAKO !!
SIT AT YOUR DESK. PIN'LL BE HERE SOON.
PAT
GASP
THAT WAS DANGER-OUS!
I WAS ABOUT TO CRY!
Thanks, Ayane-chan!
Good morn-ing, Kaze-haya.
Hi.
I CAN'T CRY WHEN CHIZU-CHAN ISN'T CRYING.
To Sawako
FUMP
When Chizu starts
talking, let's listen
to her a lot.
her a lot.
Then we'll let
her complain
a lot.
Ayane

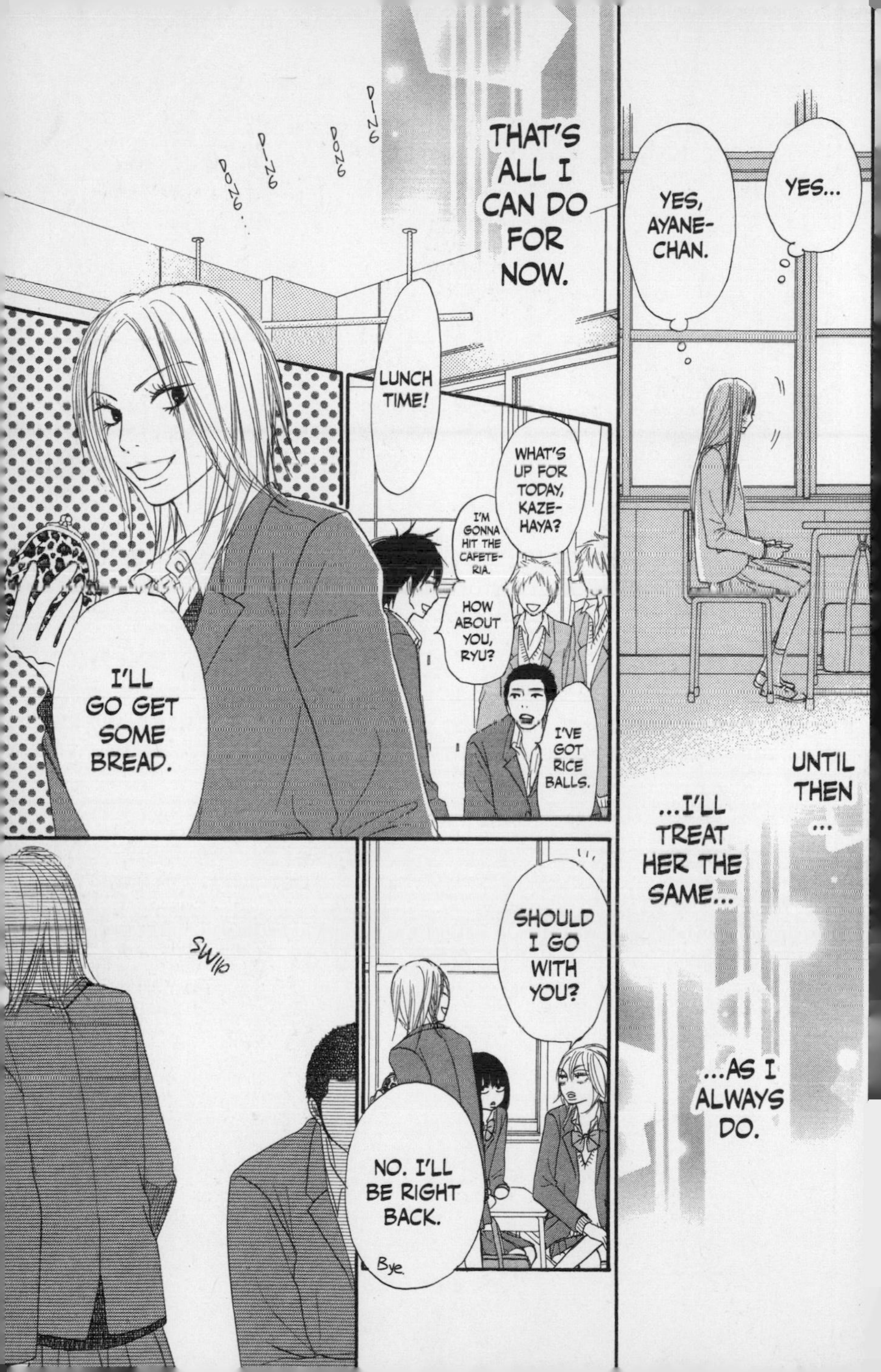
YES...
YES, AYANE-CHAN.
UNTIL THEN...
...I'LL TREAT HER THE SAME...
...AS I ALWAYS DO.
THAT'S ALL I CAN DO FOR NOW.
DING DONG
DING DONG...
LUNCH TIME!
WHAT'S UP FOR TODAY, KAZE-HAYA?
I'M GONNA HIT THE CAFETERIA.
HOW ABOUT YOU, RYU?
I'VE GOT RICE BALLS.
I'LL GO GET SOME BREAD.
SHOULD I GO WITH YOU?
NO. I'LL BE RIGHT BACK.
Bye.
SWIP

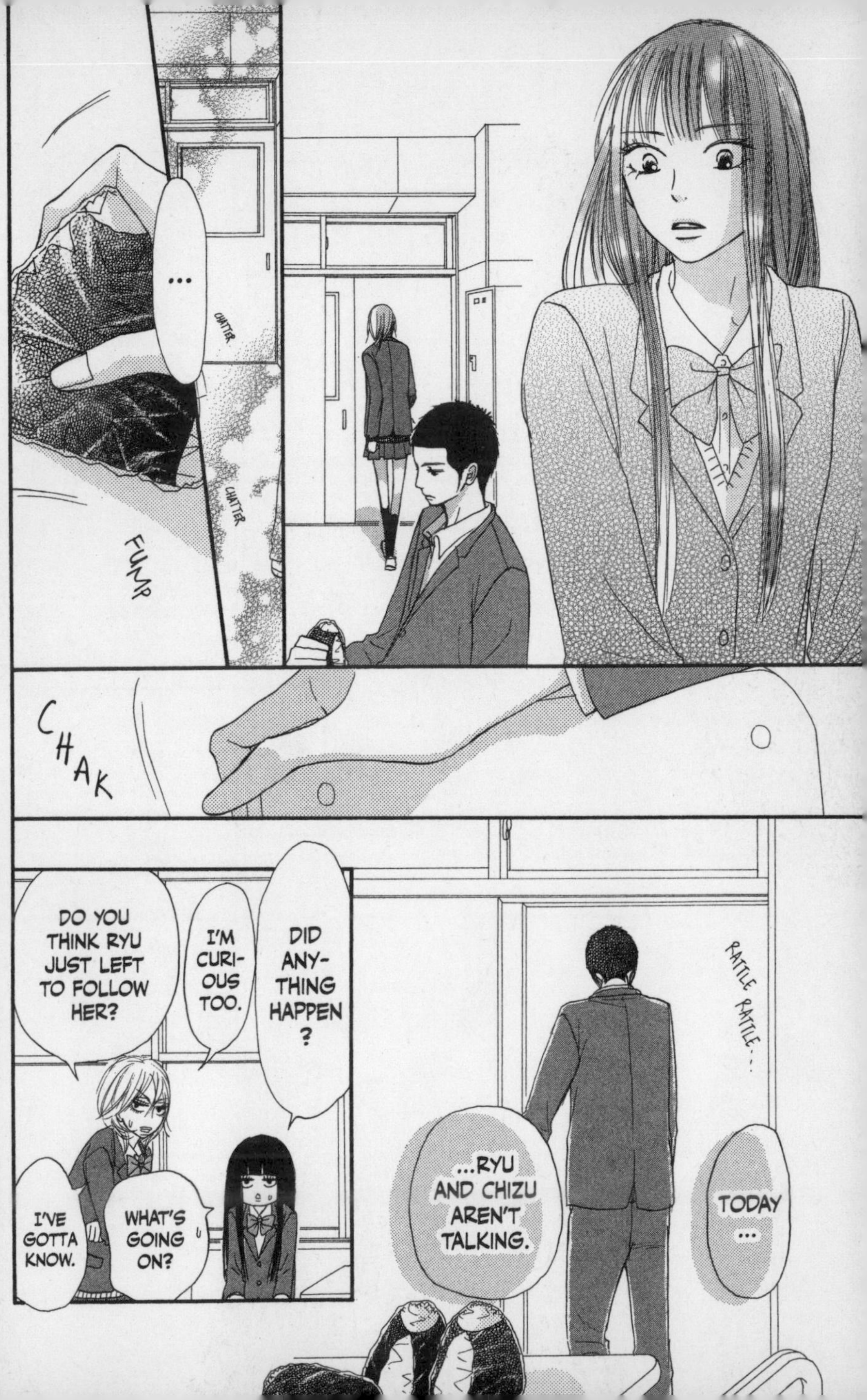
...
CHATTER
CHATTER
FUMP
CHAK
RATTLE RATTLE...
TODAY...
...RYU AND CHIZU AREN'T TALKING.
DID ANYTHING HAPPEN?
I'M CURIOUS TOO.
DO YOU THINK RYU JUST LEFT TO FOLLOW HER?
WHAT'S GOING ON?
I'VE GOTTA KNOW.

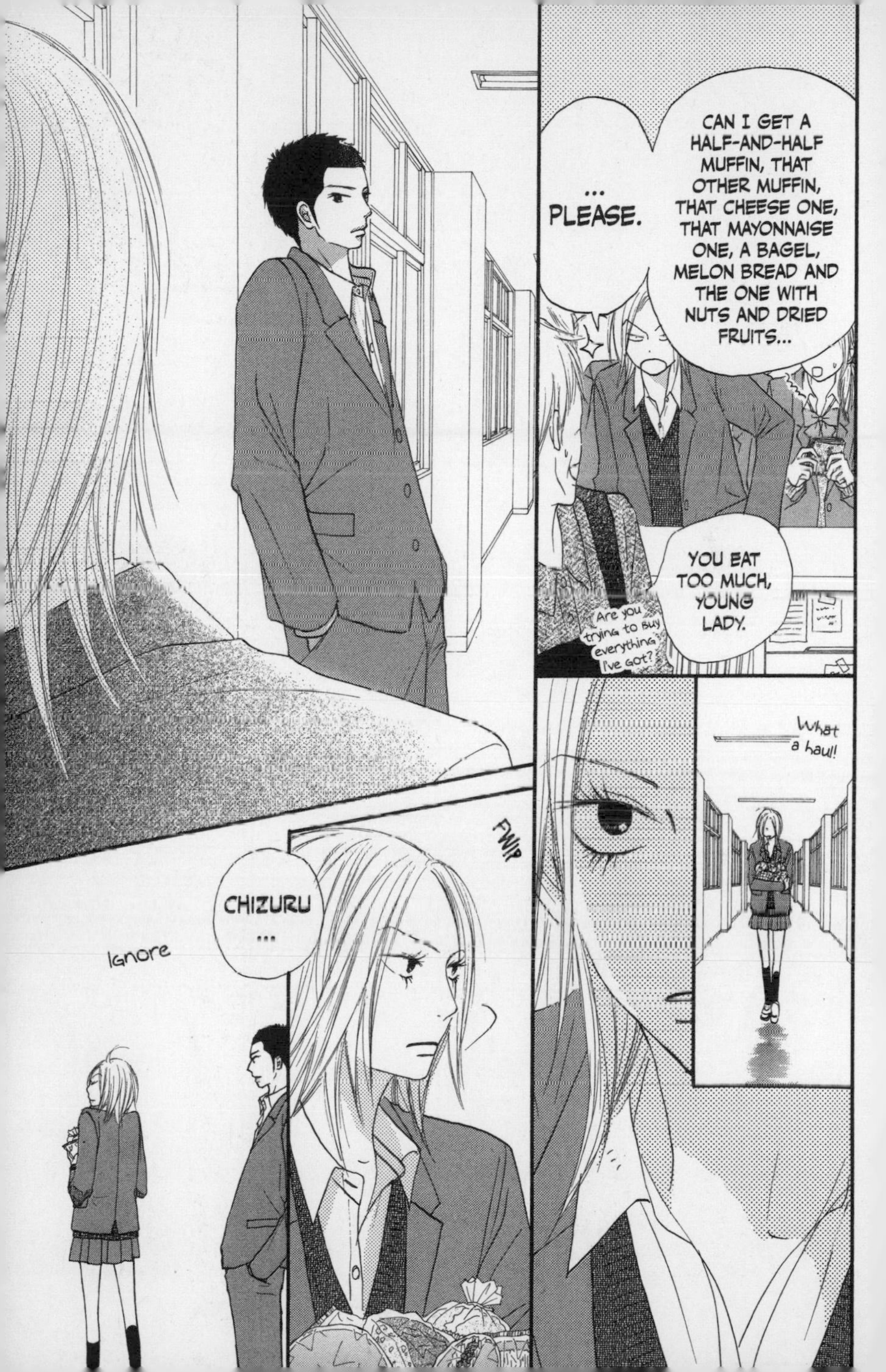
CAN I GET A HALF-AND-HALF MUFFIN, THAT OTHER MUFFIN, THAT CHEESE ONE, THAT MAYONNAISE ONE, A BAGEL, MELON BREAD AND THE ONE WITH NUTS AND DRIED FRUITS...
... PLEASE.
YOU EAT TOO MUCH, YOUNG LADY.
Are you trying to buy everything I've got?
What a haul!
FWIP
CHIZURU ...
Ignore

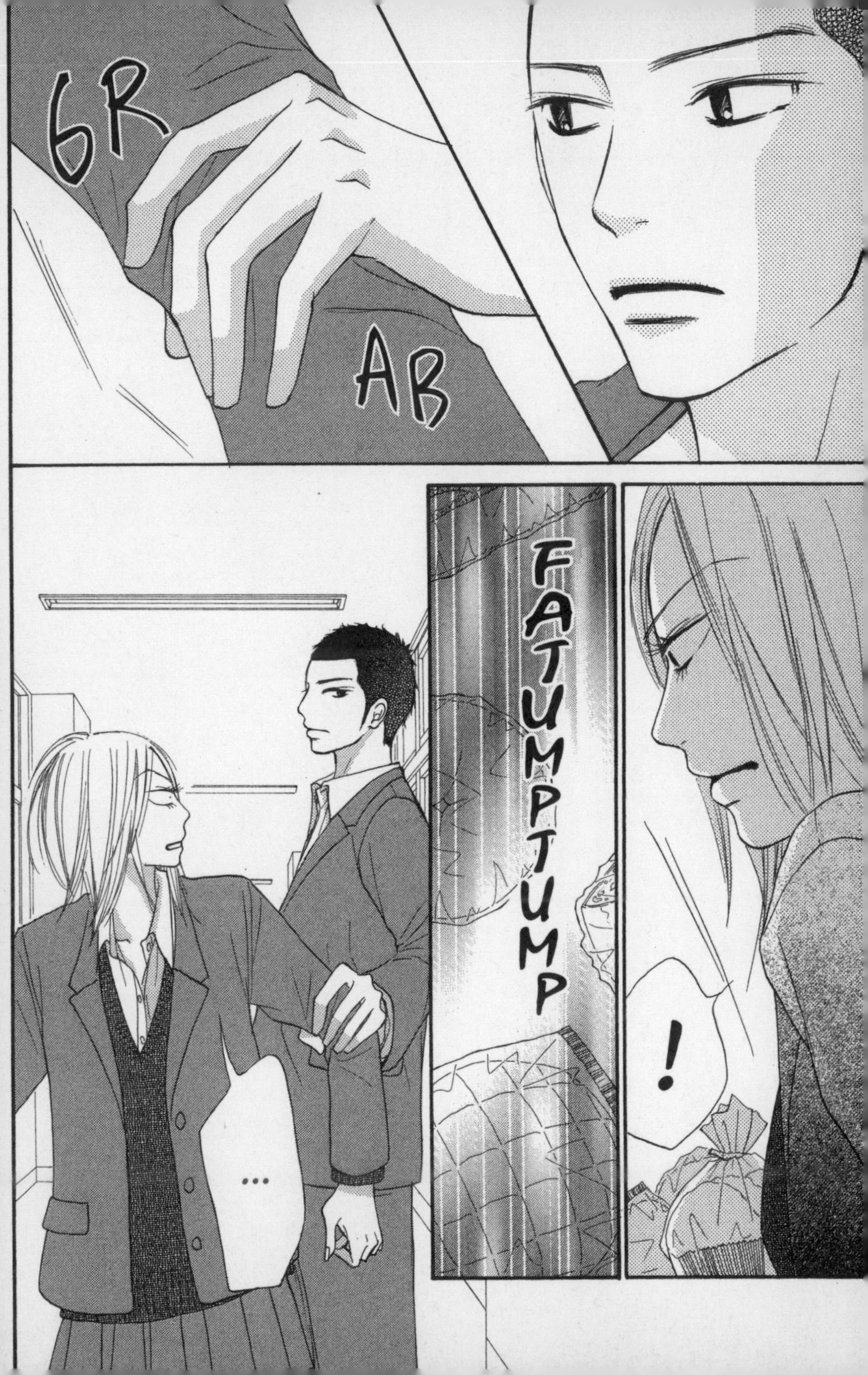
GR
AB
!
FATUMPTUMP
...

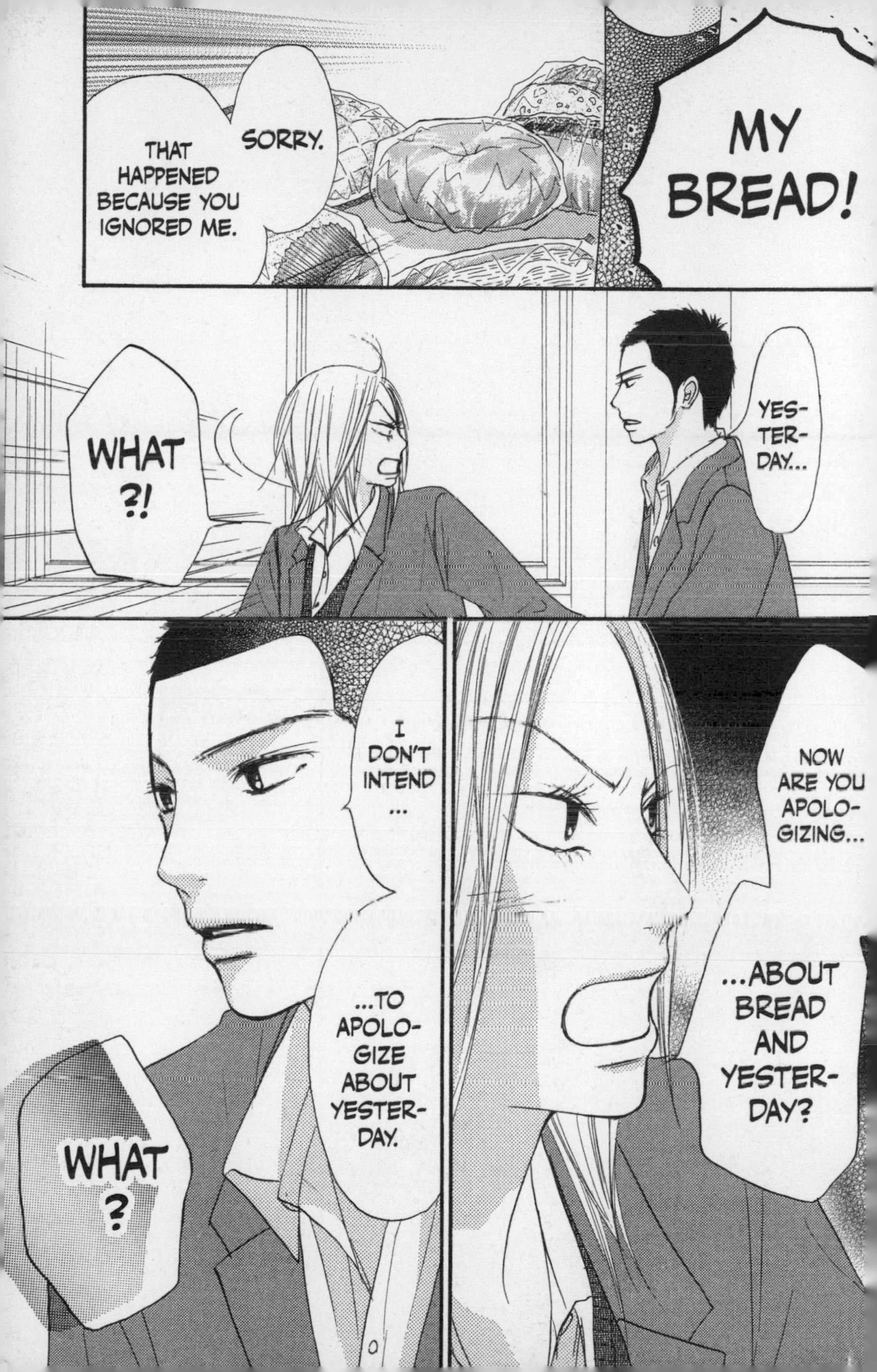
MY BREAD!
SORRY.
THAT HAPPENED BECAUSE YOU IGNORED ME.
YES-TER-DAY...
WHAT ?!
NOW ARE YOU APOLO-GIZING...
...ABOUT BREAD AND YESTER-DAY?
I DON'T INTEND ...
...TO APOLO-GIZE ABOUT YESTER-DAY.
WHAT ?

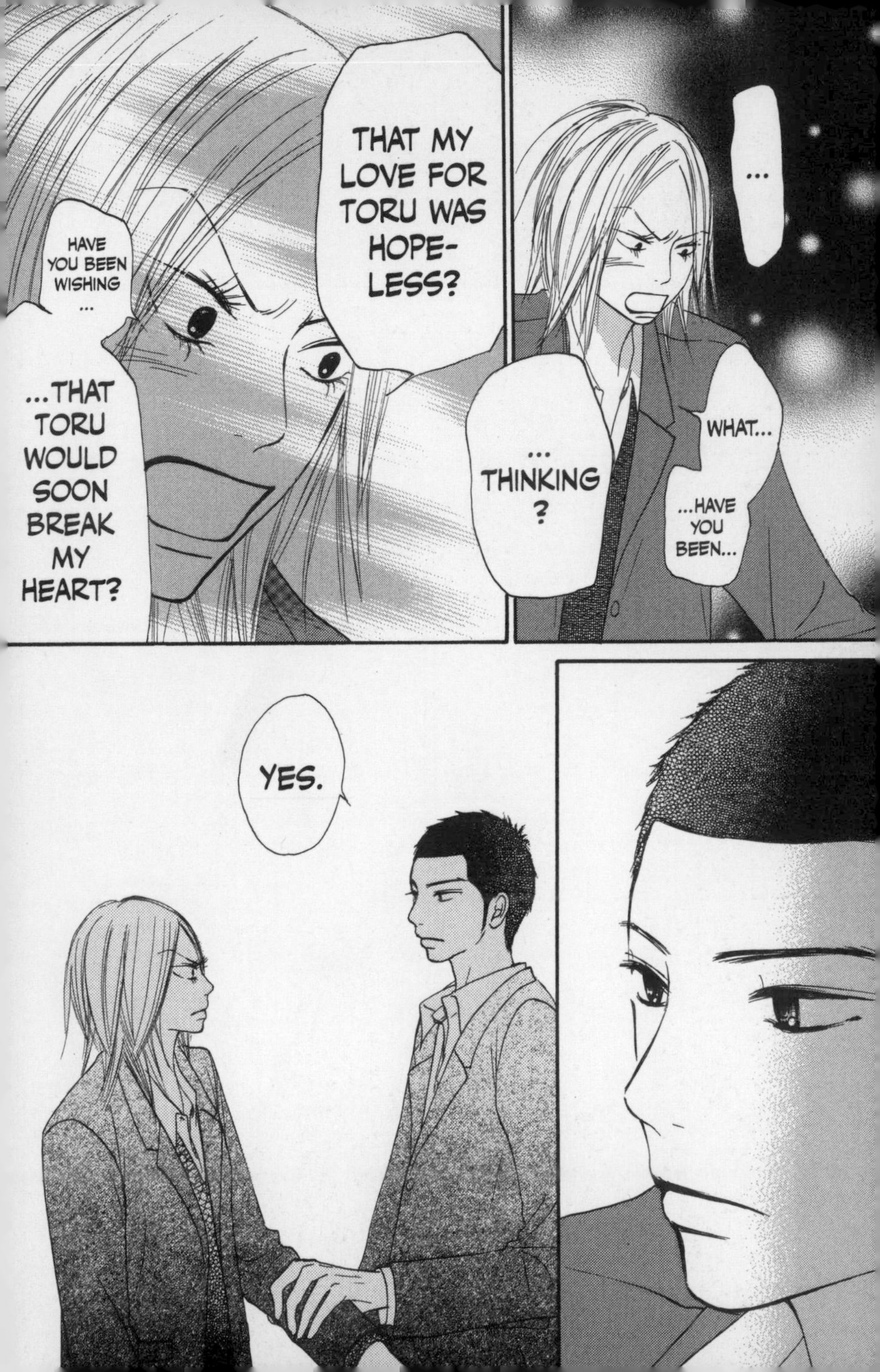
...
WHAT...
...HAVE YOU BEEN...
... THINKING?
THAT MY LOVE FOR TORU WAS HOPE-LESS?
HAVE YOU BEEN WISHING ...
...THAT TORU WOULD SOON BREAK MY HEART?
YES.

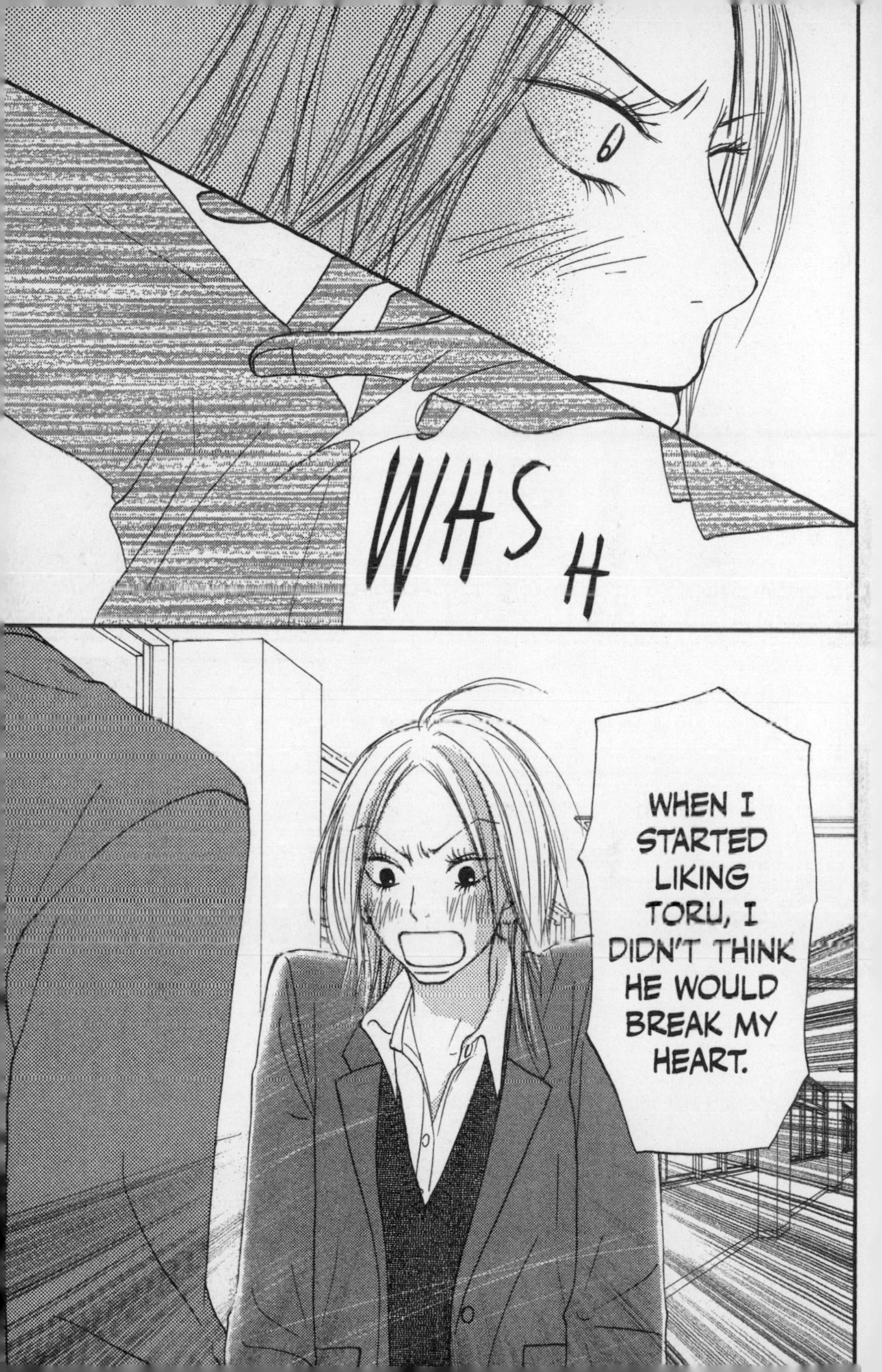
WHSH
WHEN I STARTED LIKING TORU, I DIDN'T THINK HE WOULD BREAK MY HEART.

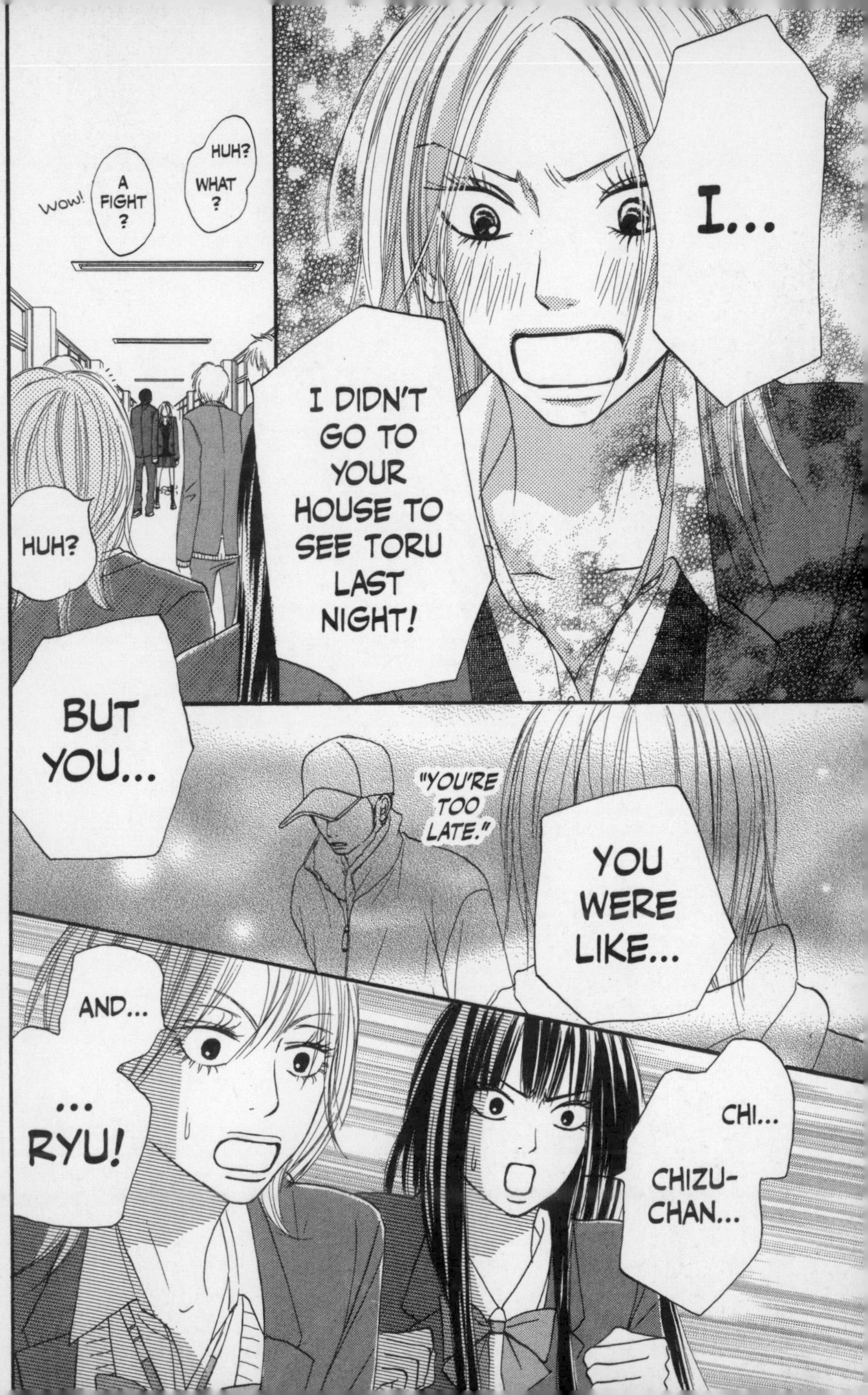
I...
I DIDN'T GO TO YOUR HOUSE TO SEE TORU LAST NIGHT!
HUH? WHAT?
A FIGHT?
WOW!
HUH?
BUT YOU...
YOU WERE LIKE...
"YOU'RE TOO LATE."
CHI... CHIZU-CHAN...
AND... ...RYU!

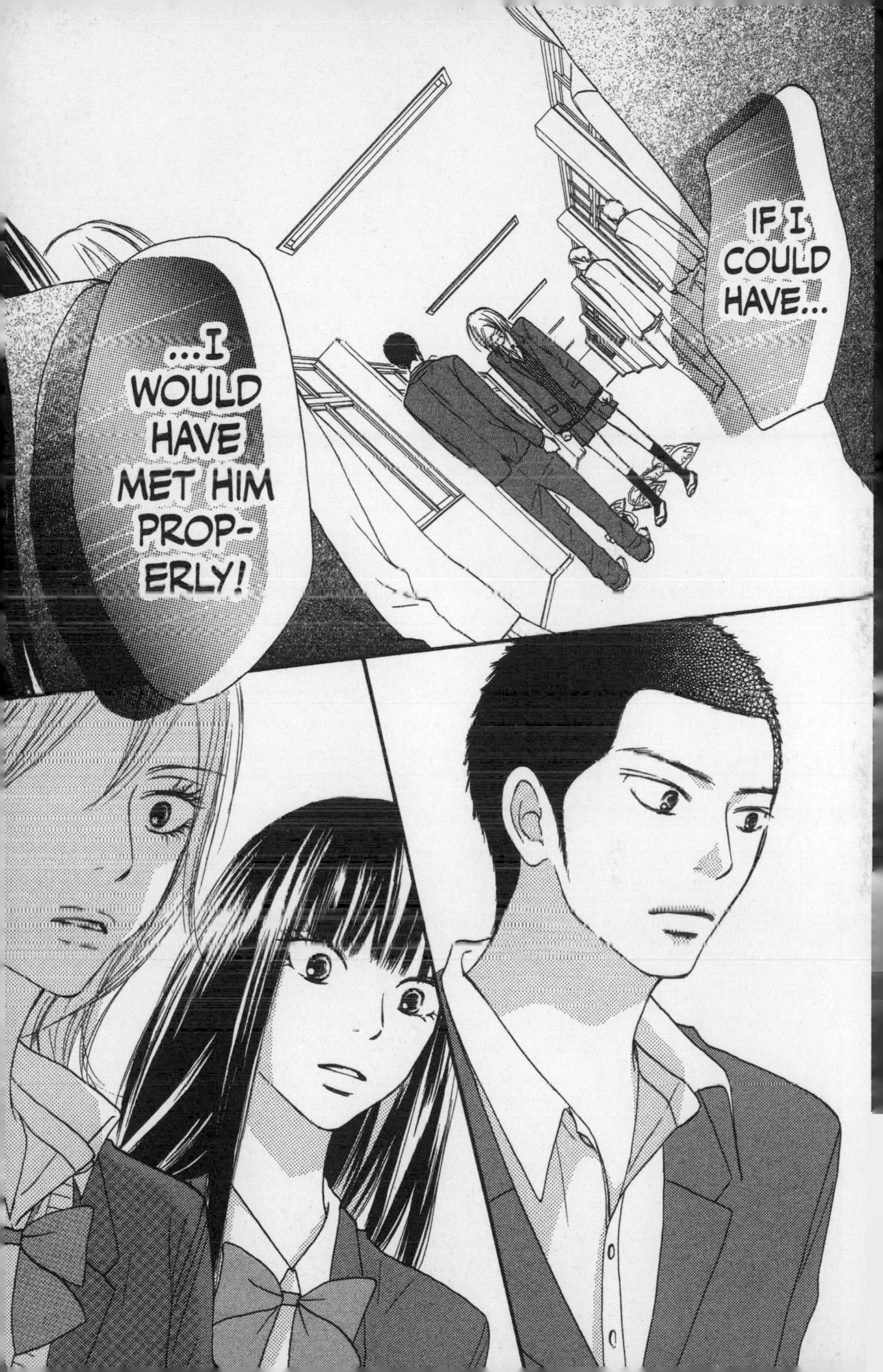
IF I COULD HAVE...
...I WOULD HAVE MET HIM PROP-ERLY!

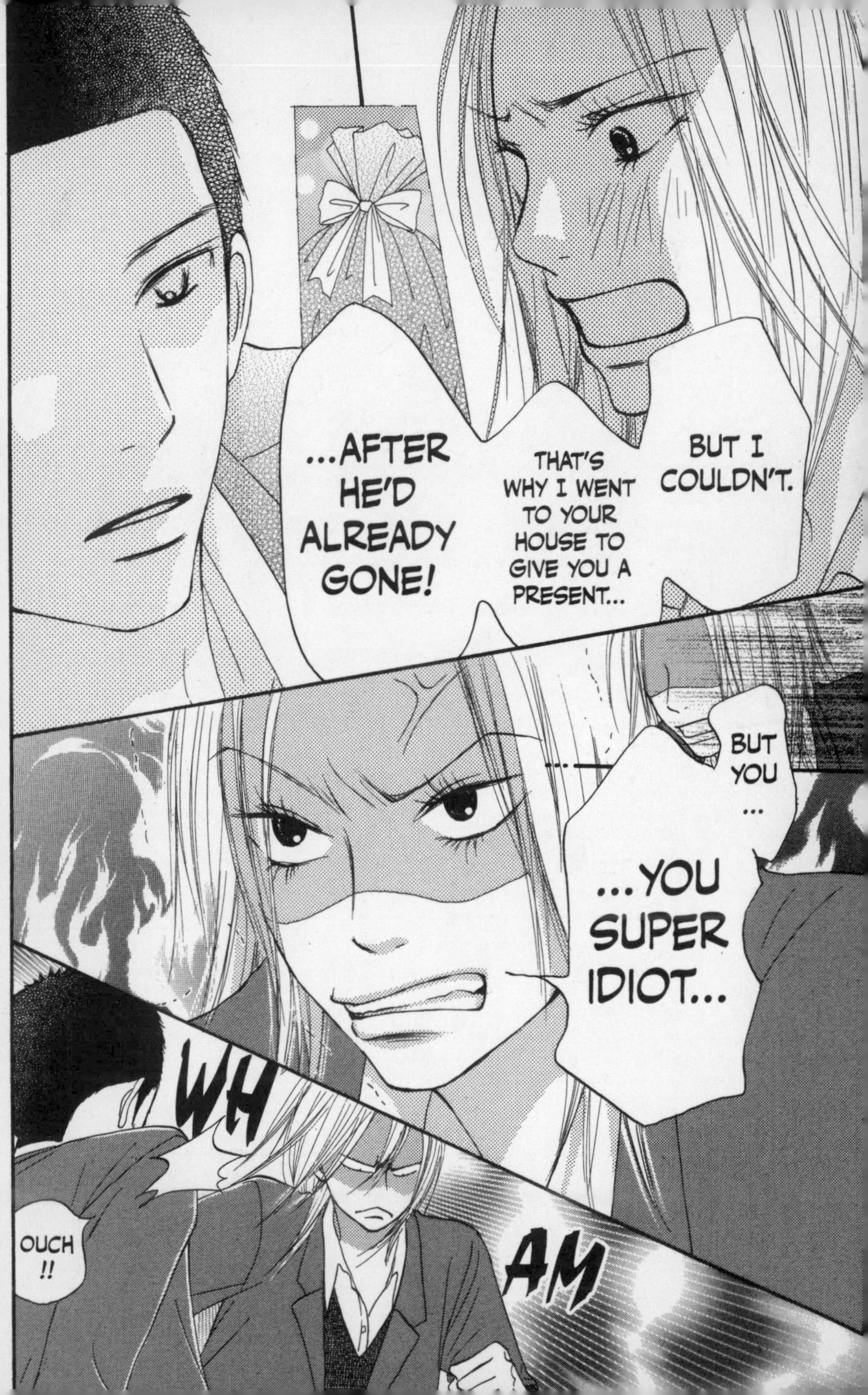
BUT I COULDN'T.
THAT'S WHY I WENT TO YOUR HOUSE TO GIVE YOU A PRESENT...
...AFTER HE'D ALREADY GONE!
BUT YOU ...
...YOU SUPER IDIOT...
WH
AM
OUCH !!

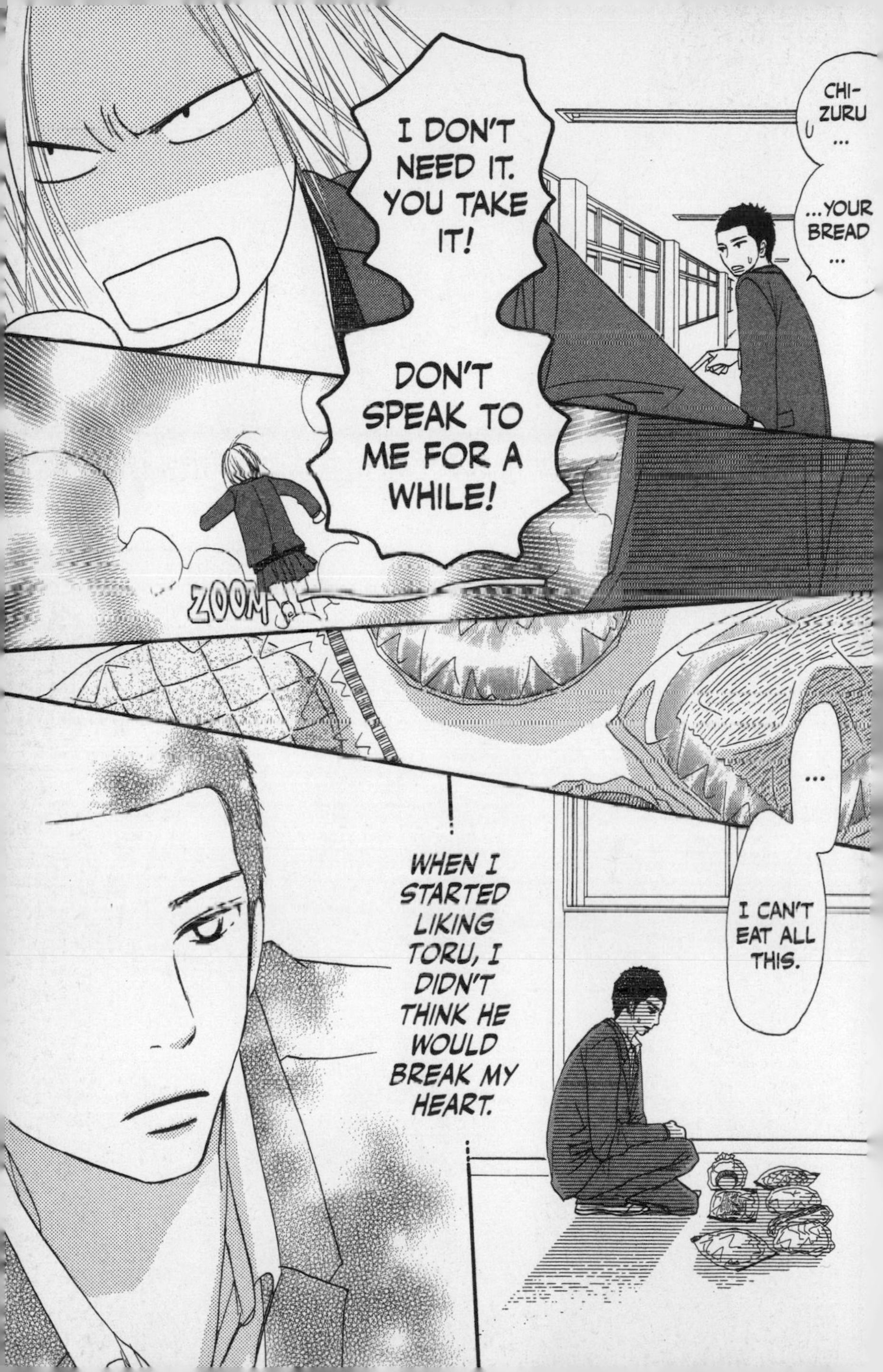
CHI-ZURU...
...YOUR BREAD...
I DON'T NEED IT. YOU TAKE IT!
DON'T SPEAK TO ME FOR A WHILE!
ZOOM
...
I CAN'T EAT ALL THIS.
WHEN I STARTED LIKING TORU, I DIDN'T THINK HE WOULD BREAK MY HEART.

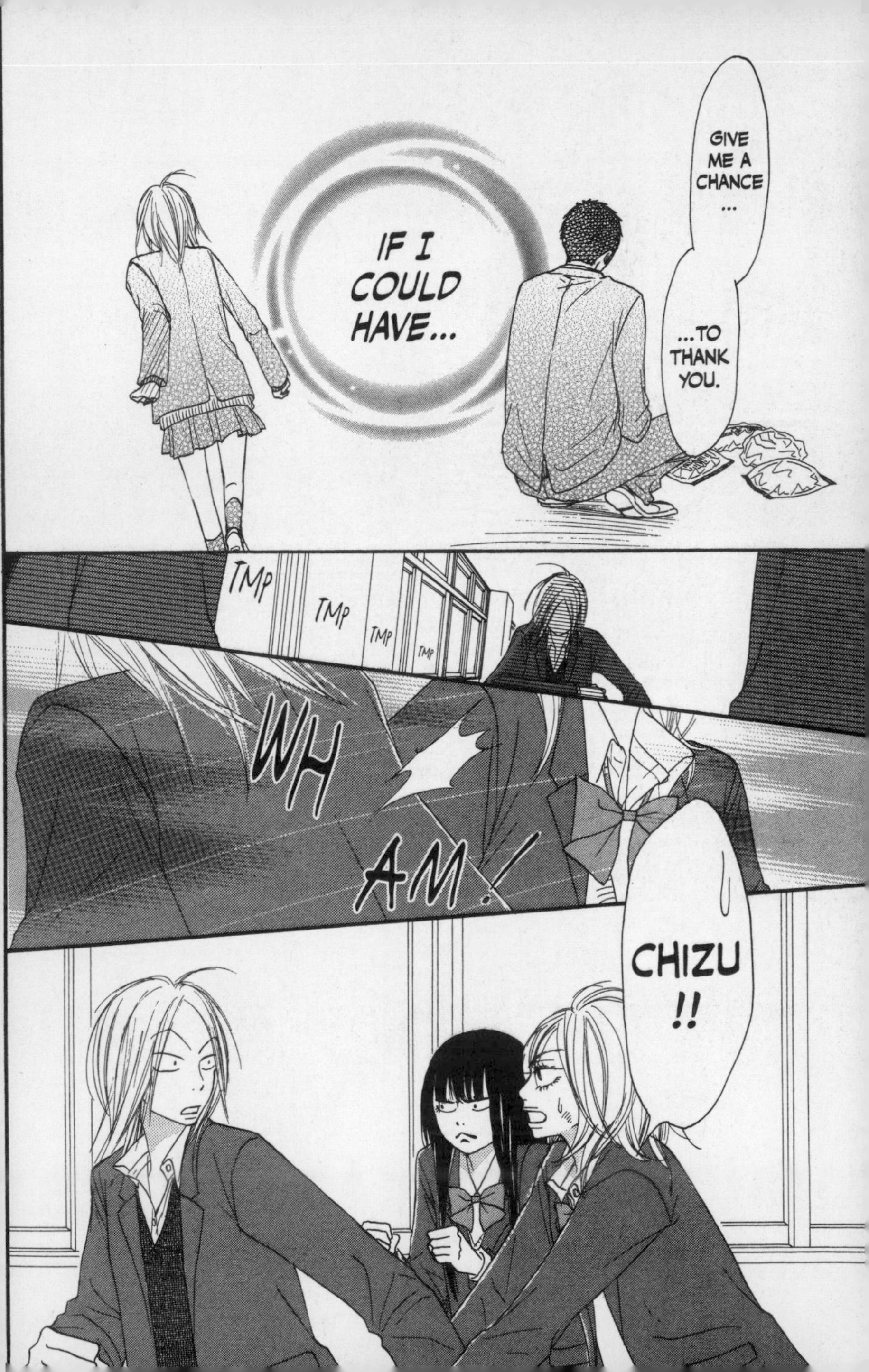
GIVE ME A CHANCE ...
...TO THANK YOU.
IF I COULD HAVE...
TMP
TMP
TMP
TMP
WHAM!
CHIZU !!

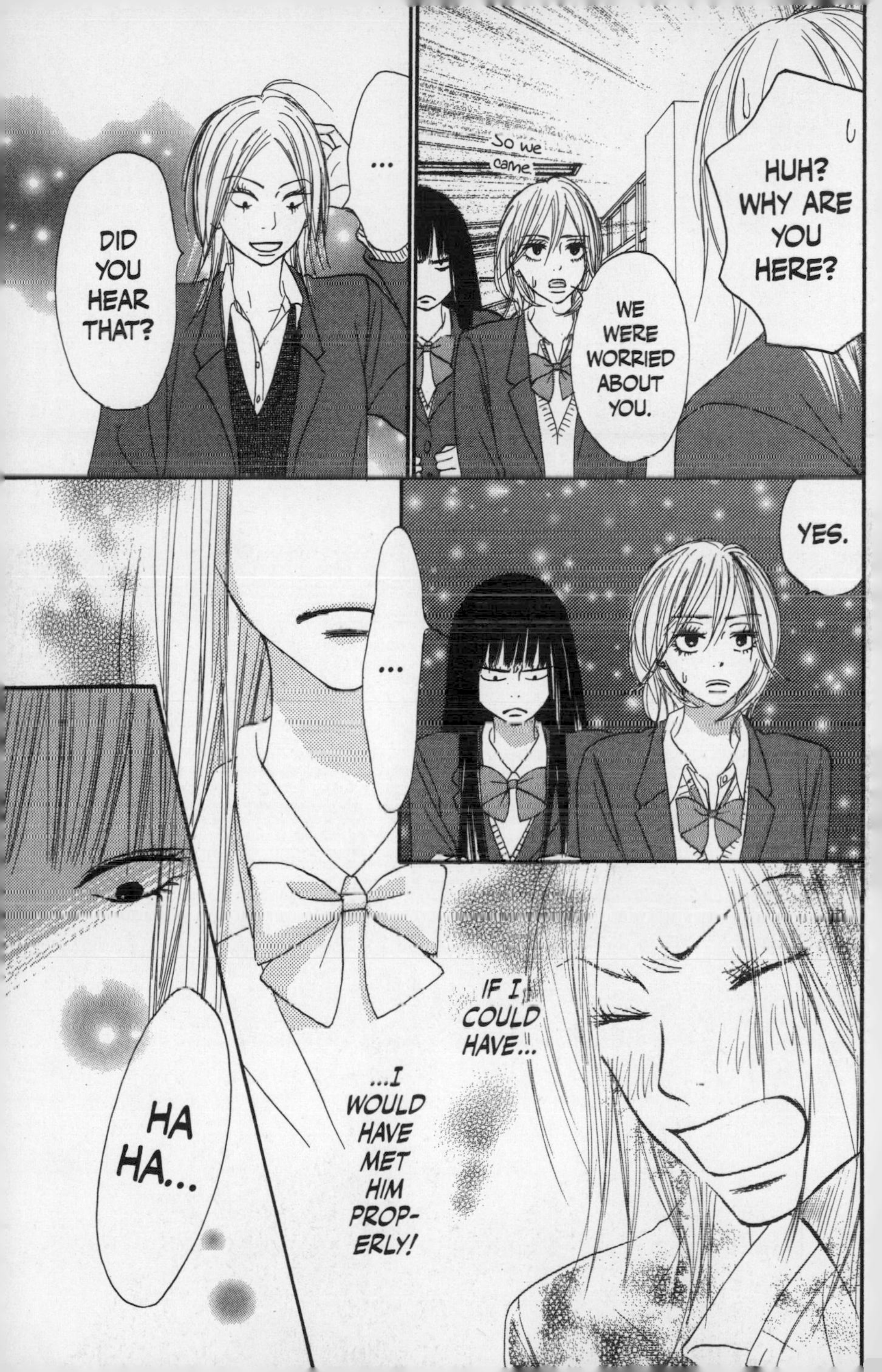
HUH? WHY ARE YOU HERE?
WE WERE WORRIED ABOUT YOU.
So we came.
...
DID YOU HEAR THAT?
YES.
...
IF I COULD HAVE...!!
...I WOULD HAVE MET HIM PROPERLY!
HA HA...

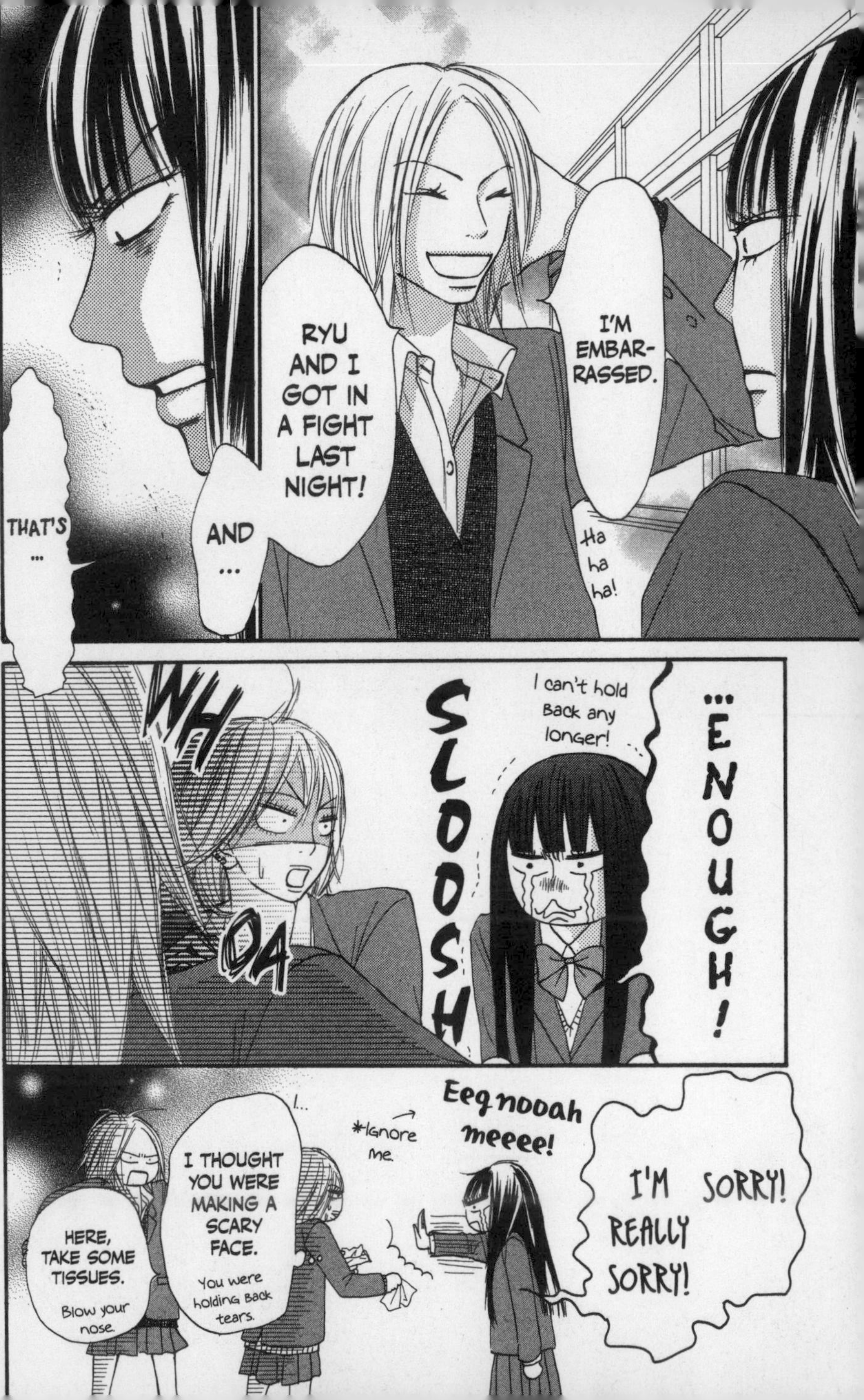
I'M EMBARRASSED.
Ha ha ha!
RYU AND I GOT IN A FIGHT LAST NIGHT!
AND ...
THAT'S ...
...ENOUGH!
I can't hold Back any longer!
SLOOSH
WHOA
I'M SORRY! REALLY SORRY!
Eeqnooah meeee!
*Ignore me.
I...
I THOUGHT YOU WERE MAKING A SCARY FACE.
You were holding Back tears.
HERE, TAKE SOME TISSUES.
Blow your nose.

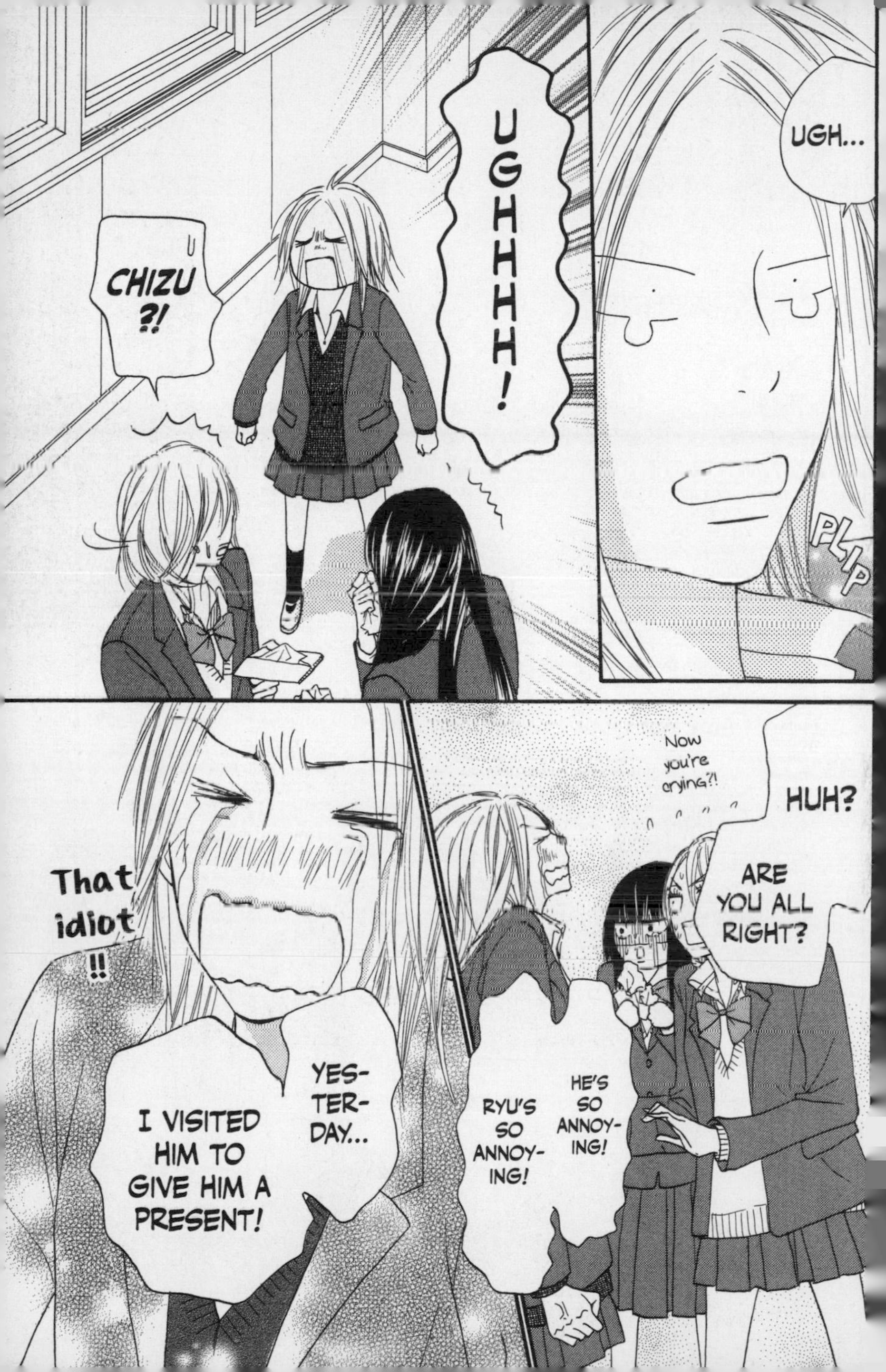
UGH...
PLIP
UGHHHHH!
CHIZU?!
Now you're crying?!
HUH?
ARE YOU ALL RIGHT?
HE'S SO ANNOYING!
RYU'S SO ANNOYING!
That idiot!!
YESTERDAY...
I VISITED HIM TO GIVE HIM A PRESENT!

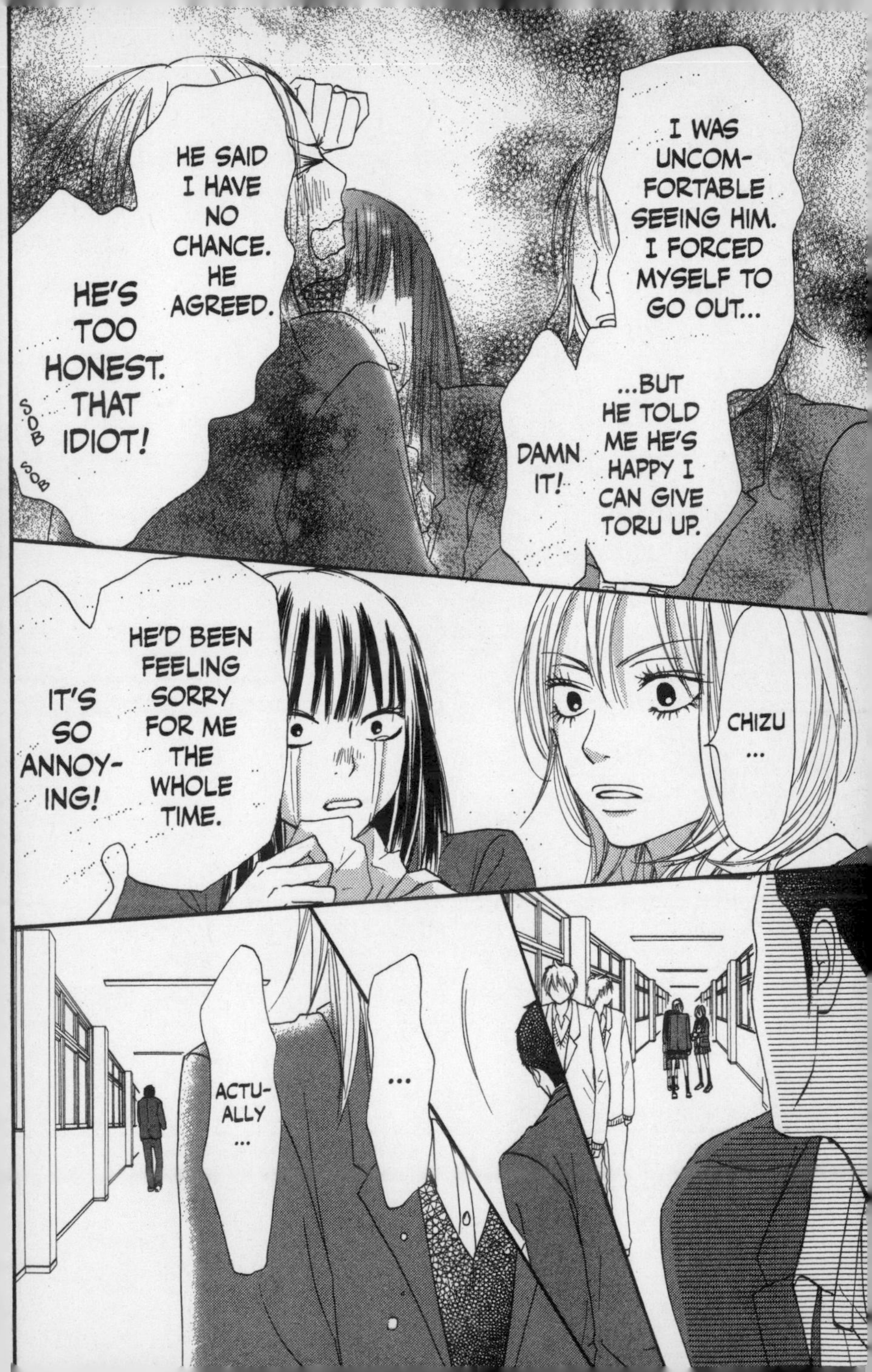
I WAS UNCOMFORTABLE SEEING HIM. I FORCED MYSELF TO GO OUT...
...BUT HE TOLD ME HE'S HAPPY I CAN GIVE TORU UP.
DAMN IT!
HE SAID I HAVE NO CHANCE. HE AGREED.
HE'S TOO HONEST. THAT IDIOT!
SOB
SOB
CHIZU ...
HE'D BEEN FEELING SORRY FOR ME THE WHOLE TIME.
IT'S SO ANNOYING!
...
ACTUALLY ...

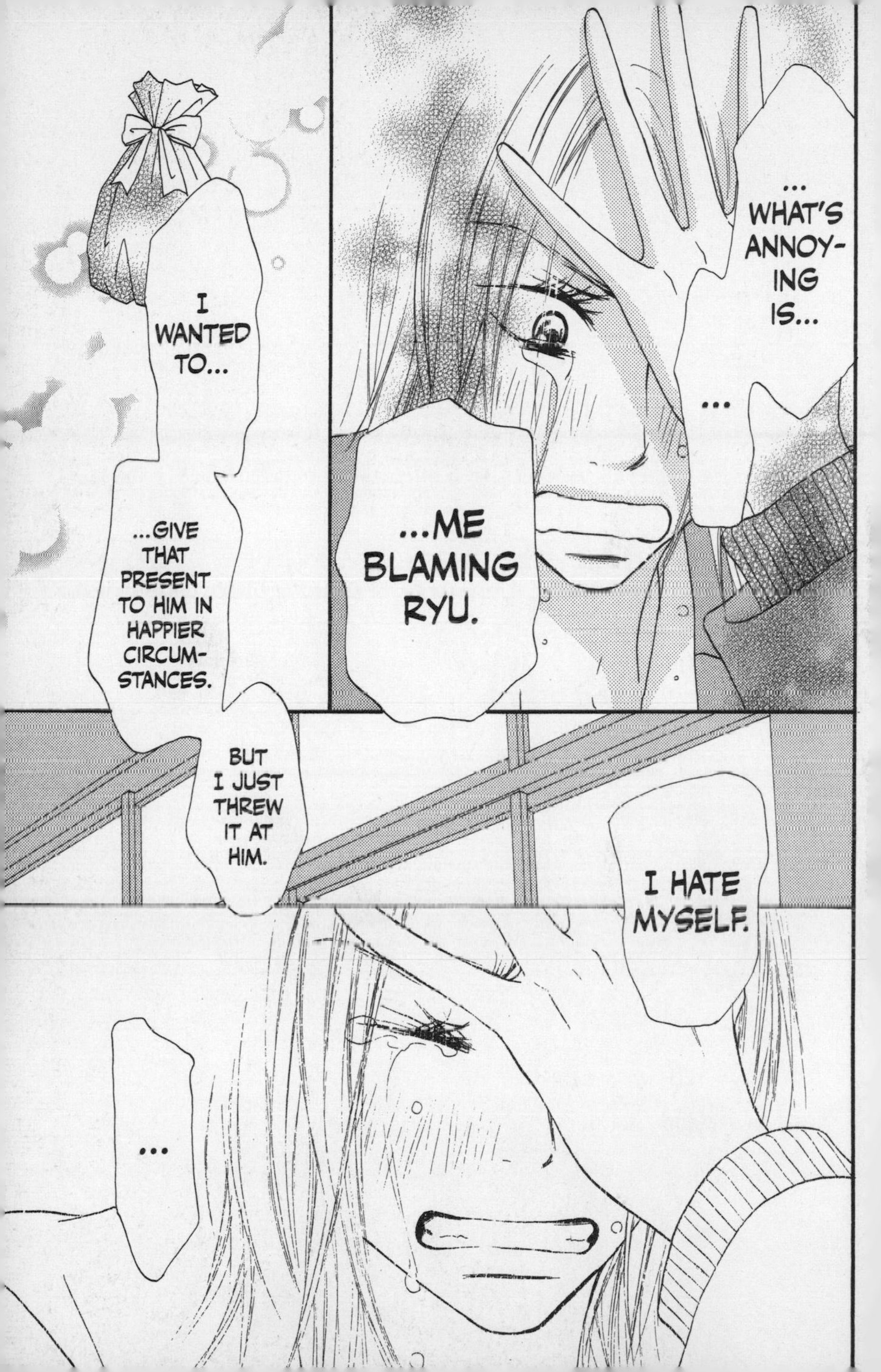
... WHAT'S ANNOY-ING IS...
...
...ME BLAMING RYU.
I WANTED TO...
...GIVE THAT PRESENT TO HIM IN HAPPIER CIRCUM-STANCES.
BUT I JUST THREW IT AT HIM.
I HATE MYSELF.
...

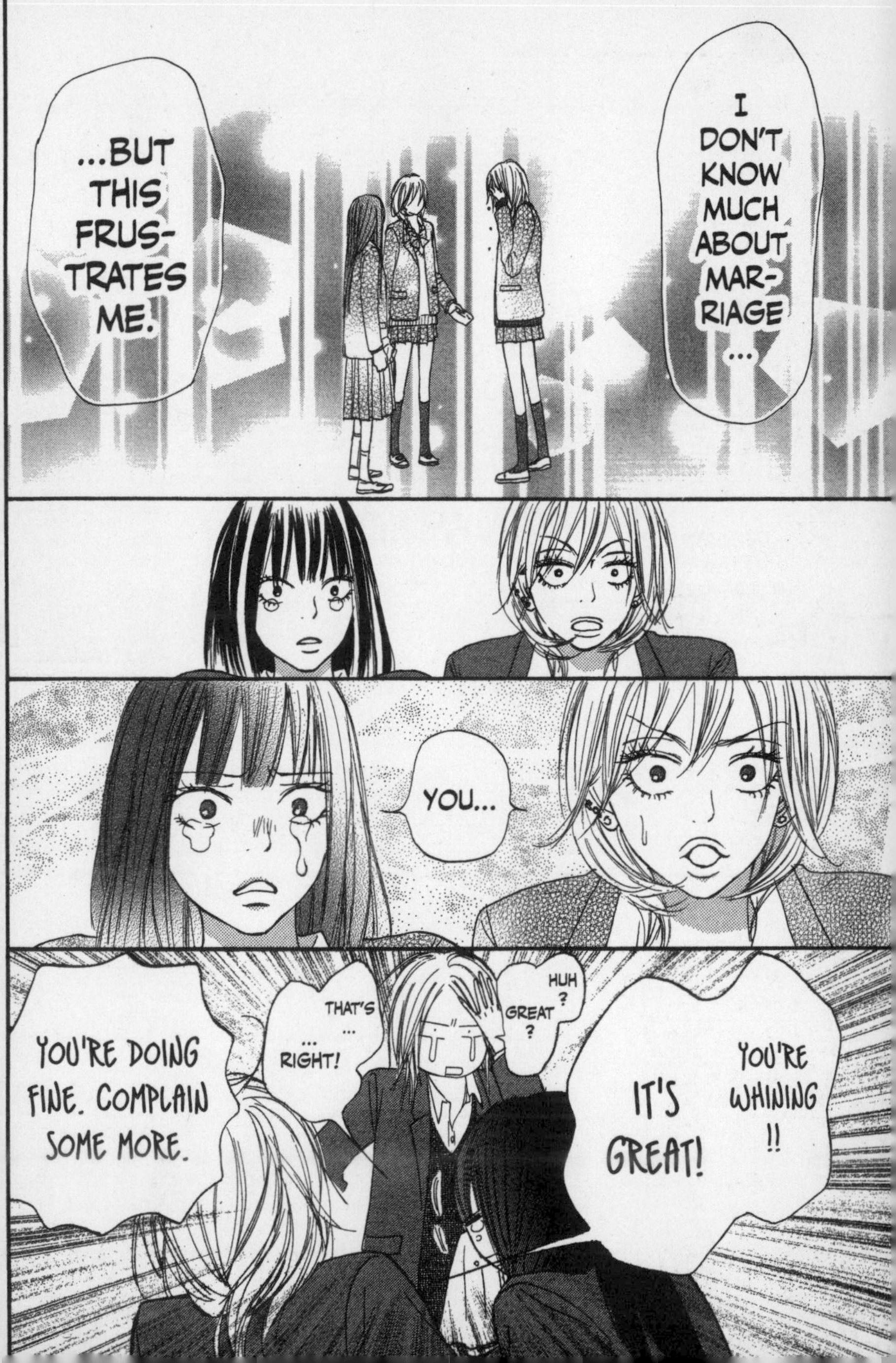
I DON'T KNOW MUCH ABOUT MARRIAGE...
...BUT THIS FRUSTRATES ME.
YOU...
YOU'RE WHINING!!
IT'S GREAT!
HUH? GREAT?
THAT'S... ...RIGHT!
YOU'RE DOING FINE. COMPLAIN SOME MORE.

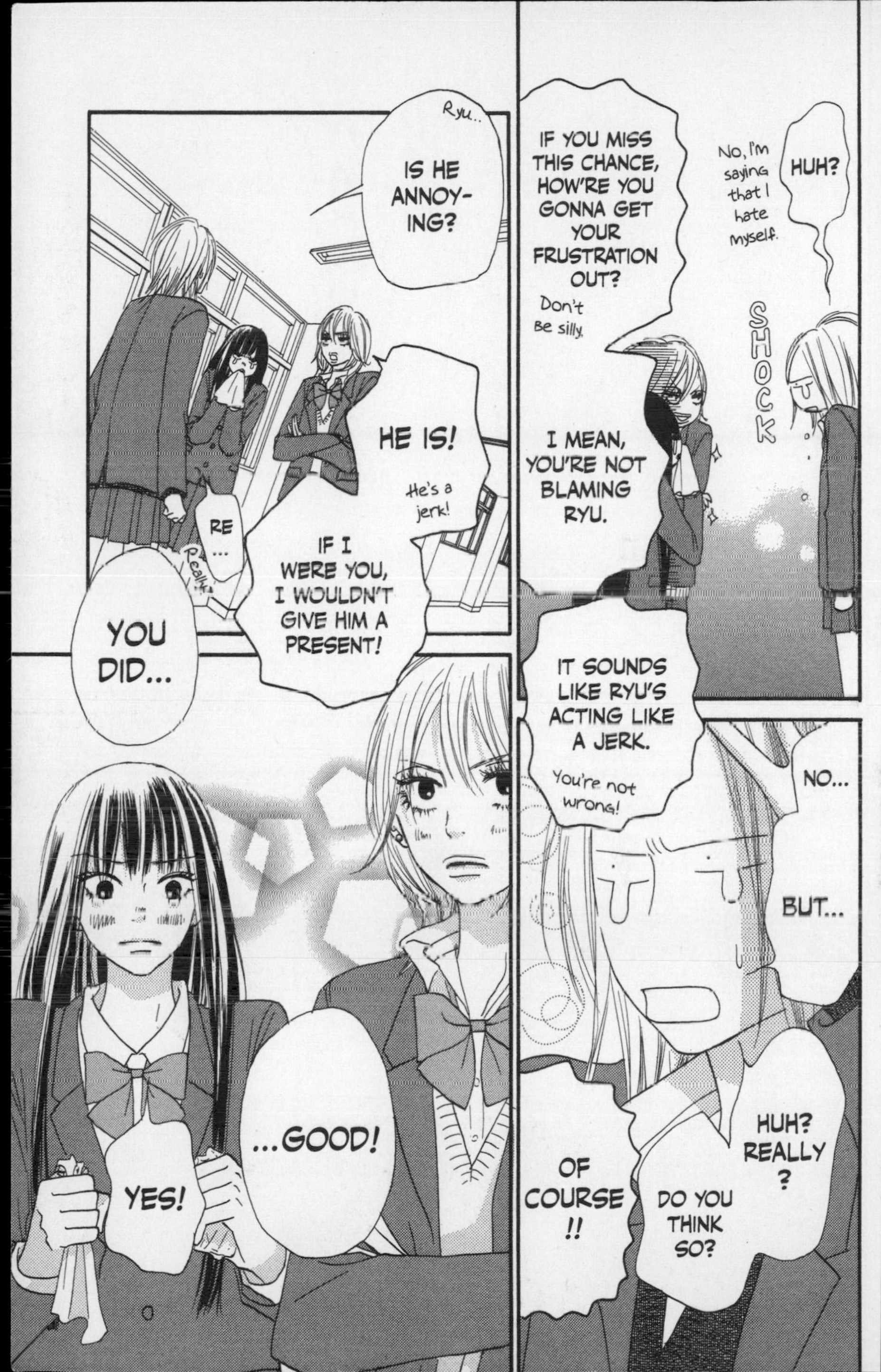
HUH?
No, I'm saying that I hate myself.
IF YOU MISS THIS CHANCE, HOW'RE YOU GONNA GET YOUR FRUSTRATION OUT?
Don't Be silly.
SHOCK
I MEAN, YOU'RE NOT BLAMING RYU.
IT SOUNDS LIKE RYU'S ACTING LIKE A JERK.
You're not wrong!
NO...
BUT...
HUH? REALLY?
DO YOU THINK SO?
OF COURSE!!
Ryu..
IS HE ANNOYING?
HE IS!
He's a jerk!
RE...
Really
IF I WERE YOU, I WOULDN'T GIVE HIM A PRESENT!
YOU DID...
...GOOD!
YES!

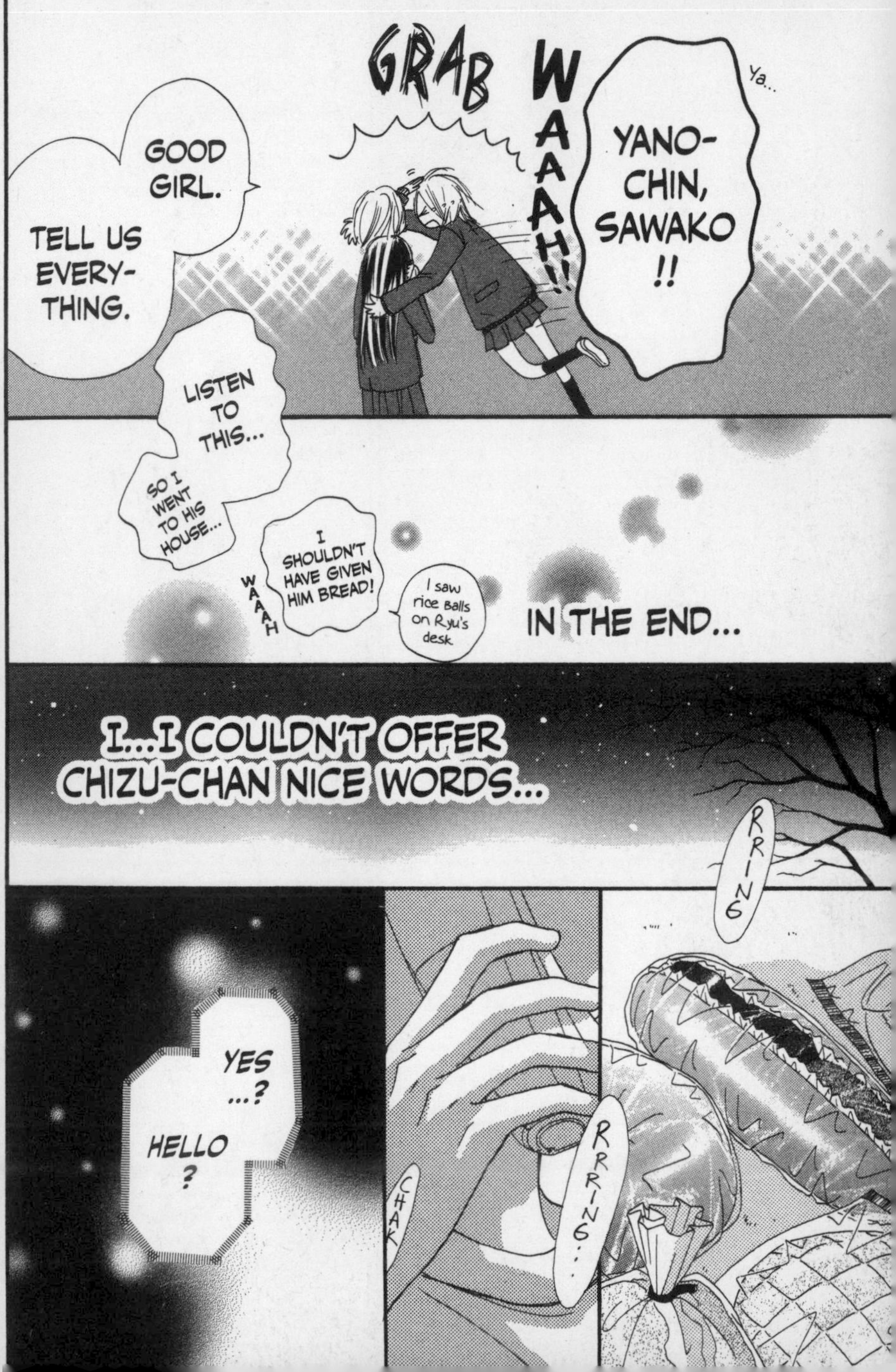
Ya...
YANO-CHIN, SAWAKO !!
WAAAAH!!
GRAB
GOOD GIRL.
TELL US EVERY-THING.
IN THE END...
I saw rice balls on Ryu's desk
I SHOULDN'T HAVE GIVEN HIM BREAD!
WAAAH
LISTEN TO THIS...
SO I WENT TO HIS HOUSE...
I...I COULDN'T OFFER CHIZU-CHAN NICE WORDS...
RRING
RRRING...
CHAK
YES ...?
HELLO ?

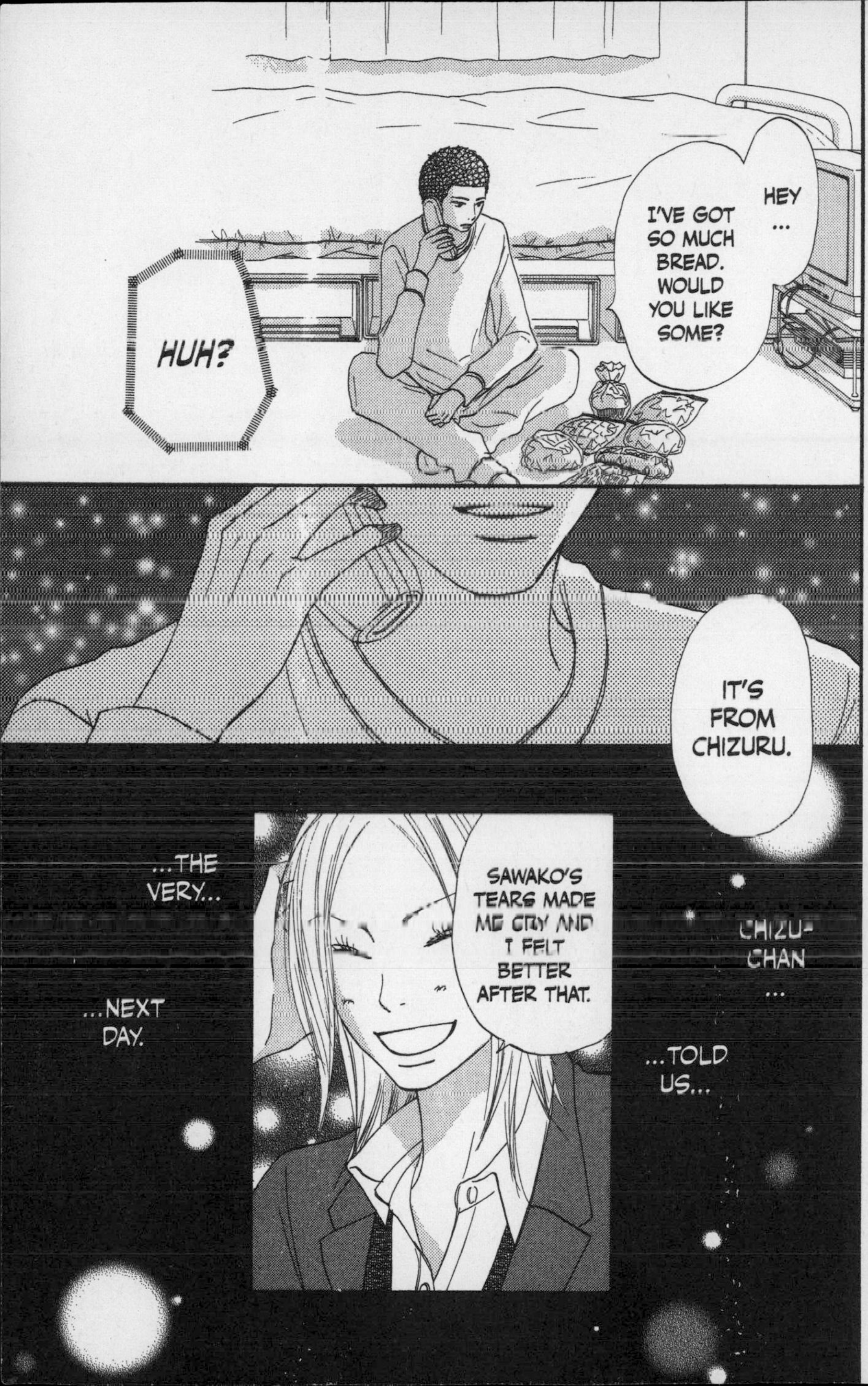
HEY ... I'VE GOT SO MUCH BREAD. WOULD YOU LIKE SOME?
HUH?
IT'S FROM CHIZURU.
CHIZU-CHAN ...
...TOLD US...
SAWAKO'S TEARS MADE ME CRY AND I FELT BETTER AFTER THAT.
...THE VERY...
...NEXT DAY.

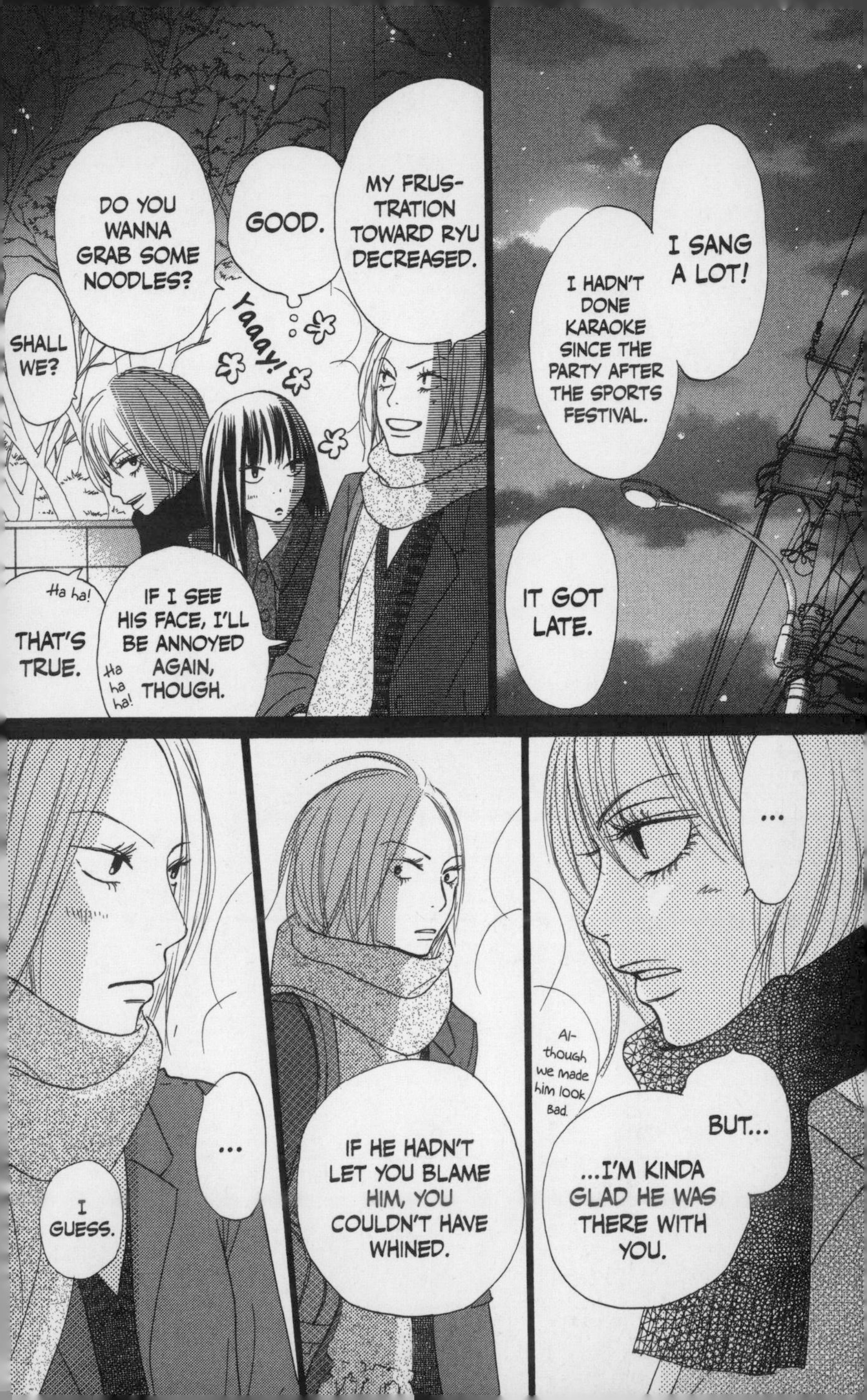
I SANG A LOT!
I HADN'T DONE KARAOKE SINCE THE PARTY AFTER THE SPORTS FESTIVAL.
IT GOT LATE.
MY FRUSTRATION TOWARD RYU DECREASED.
GOOD.
Yaaay!
DO YOU WANNA GRAB SOME NOODLES?
SHALL WE?
IF I SEE HIS FACE, I'LL BE ANNOYED AGAIN, THOUGH.
Ha ha ha!
Ha ha!
THAT'S TRUE.
...
Although we made him look bad.
BUT...
...I'M KINDA GLAD HE WAS THERE WITH YOU.
IF HE HADN'T LET YOU BLAME HIM, YOU COULDN'T HAVE WHINED.
...
I GUESS.

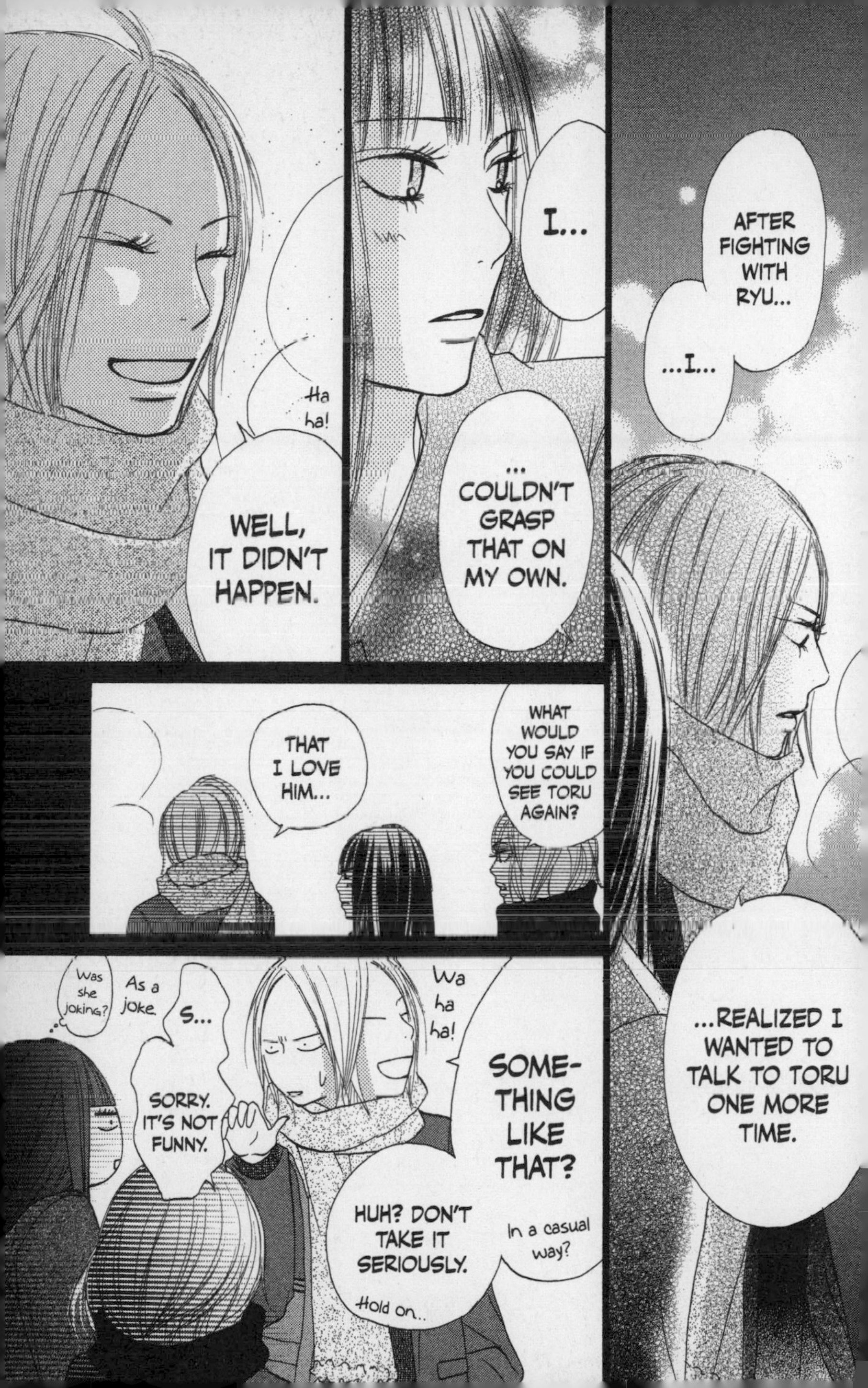

AFTER FIGHTING WITH RYU...
...I...
...REALIZED I WANTED TO TALK TO TORU ONE MORE TIME.
I...
... COULDN'T GRASP THAT ON MY OWN.
Ha ha!
WELL, IT DIDN'T HAPPEN.
WHAT WOULD YOU SAY IF YOU COULD SEE TORU AGAIN?
THAT I LOVE HIM...
Wa ha ha!
SOME-THING LIKE THAT?
In a casual way?
HUH? DON'T TAKE IT SERIOUSLY.
Hold on..
S...
SORRY. IT'S NOT FUNNY.
As a joke
Was she joking?

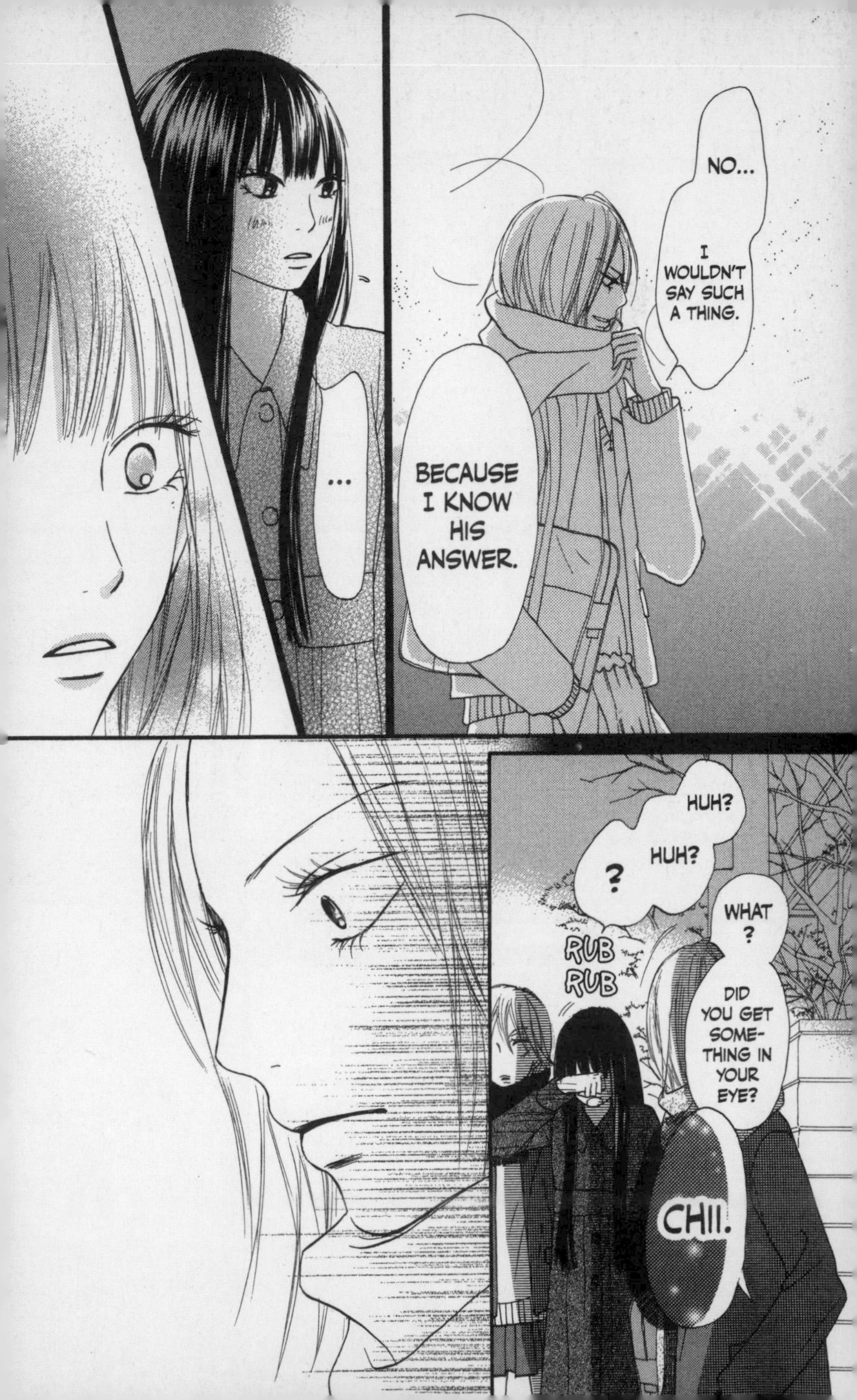
NO...
I WOULDN'T SAY SUCH A THING.
BECAUSE I KNOW HIS ANSWER.
...
HUH?
WHAT?
HUH?
?
DID YOU GET SOME-THING IN YOUR EYE?
RUB RUB
CHII.

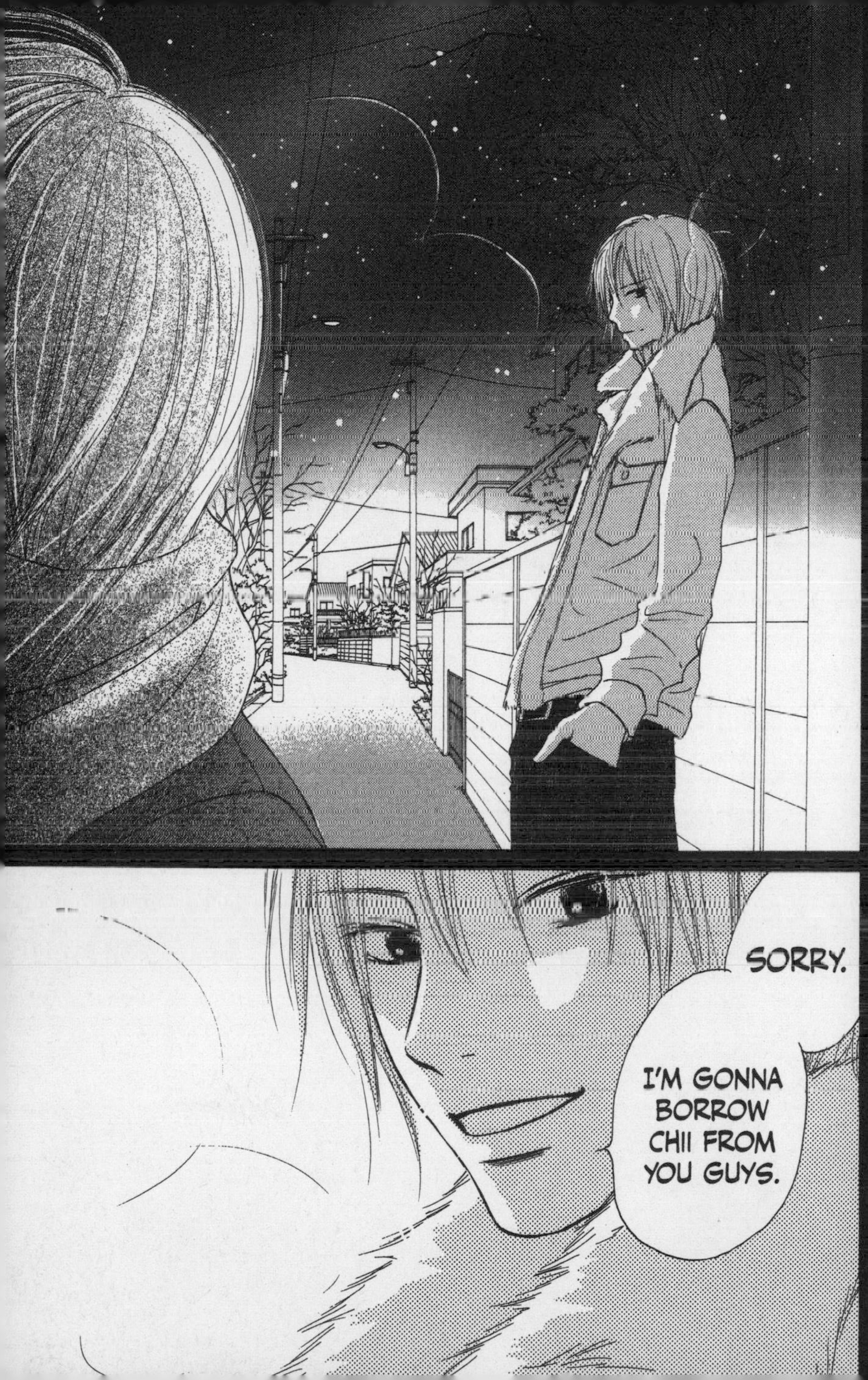
SORRY.
I'M GONNA BORROW CHII FROM YOU GUYS.

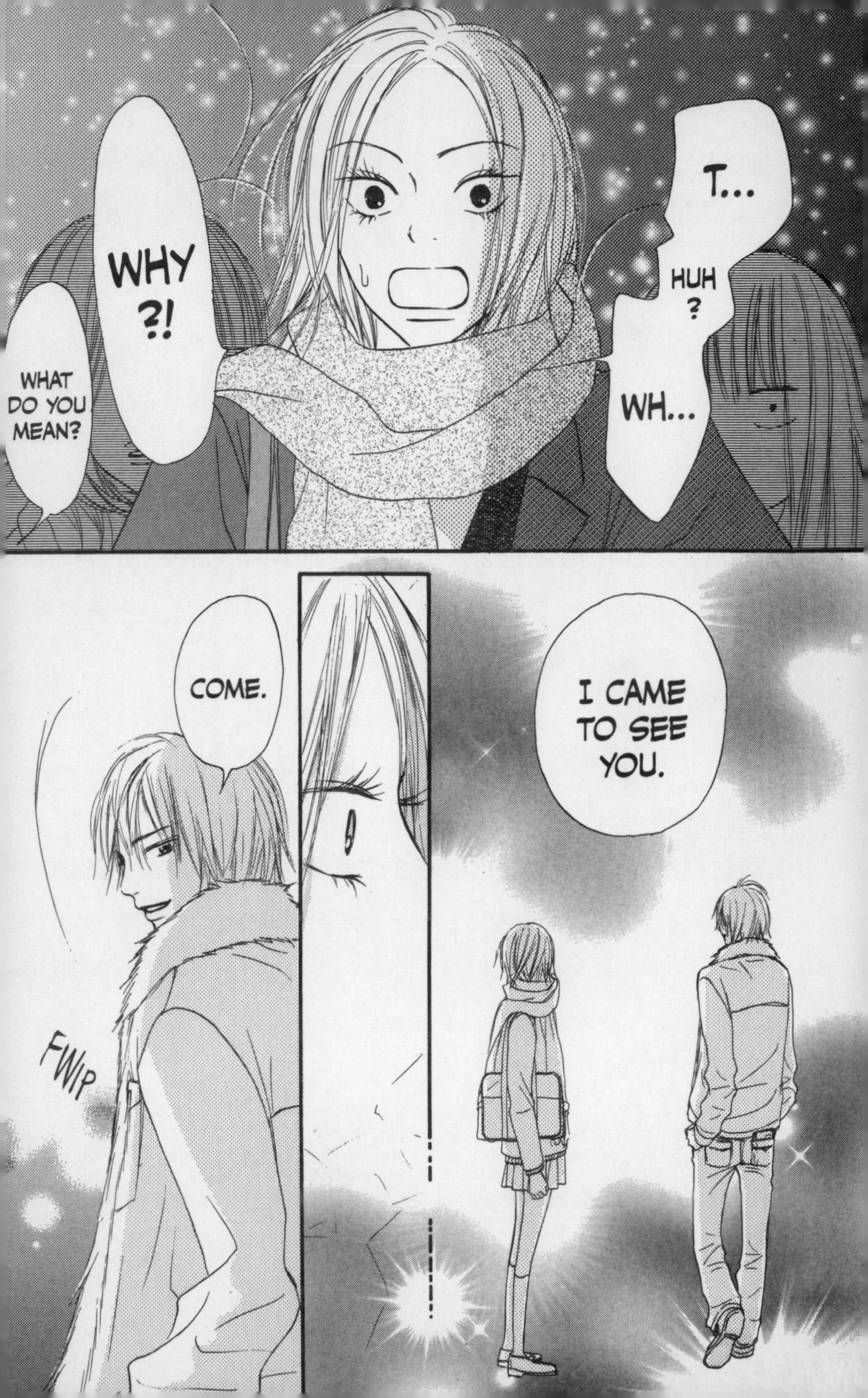
T...
HUH?
WH...
WHY?!
WHAT DO YOU MEAN?
I CAME TO SEE YOU.
COME.
FWIP

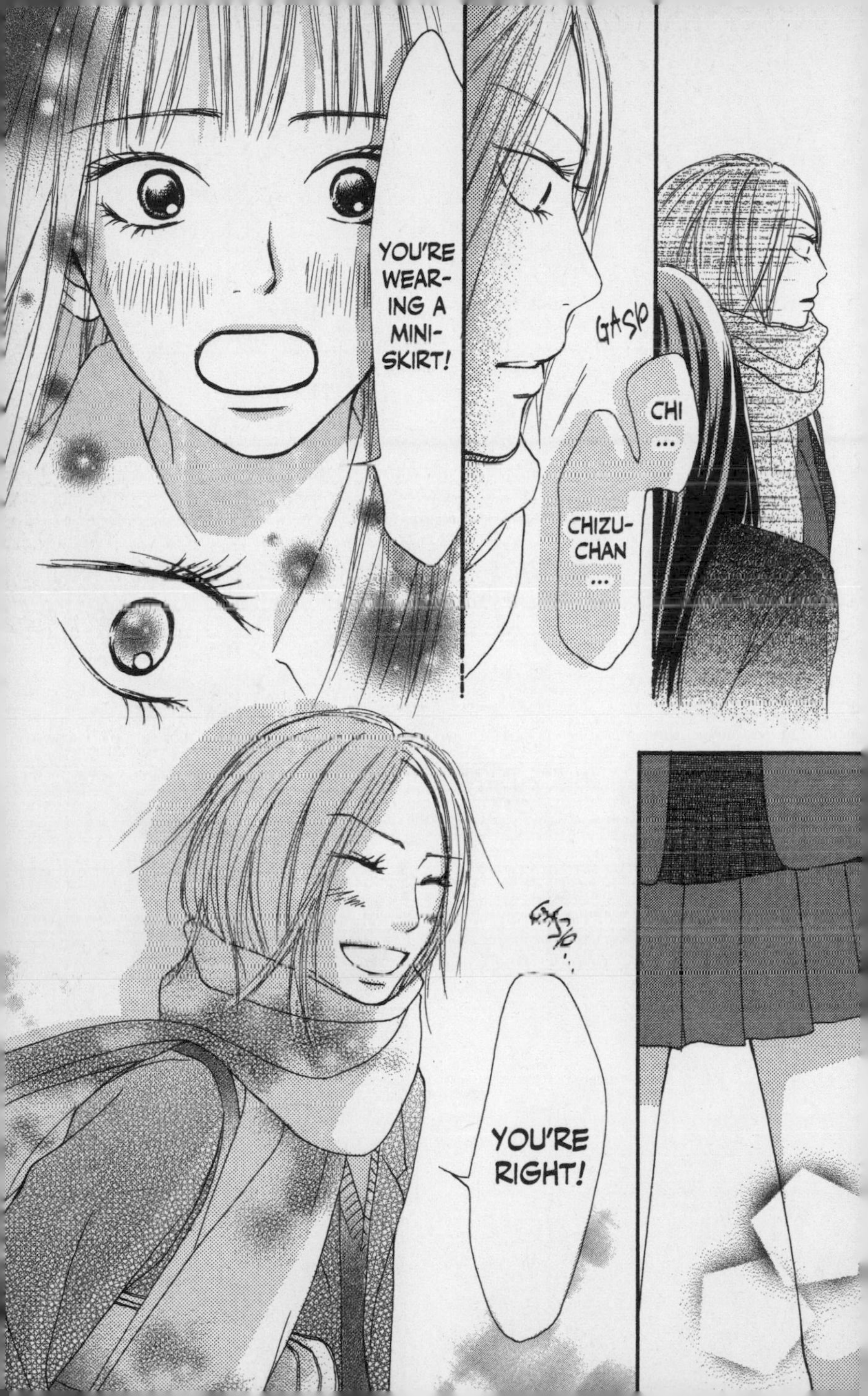
GASP
CHI ...
CHIZU-CHAN ...
YOU'RE WEARING A MINISKIRT!
GASP...
YOU'RE RIGHT!

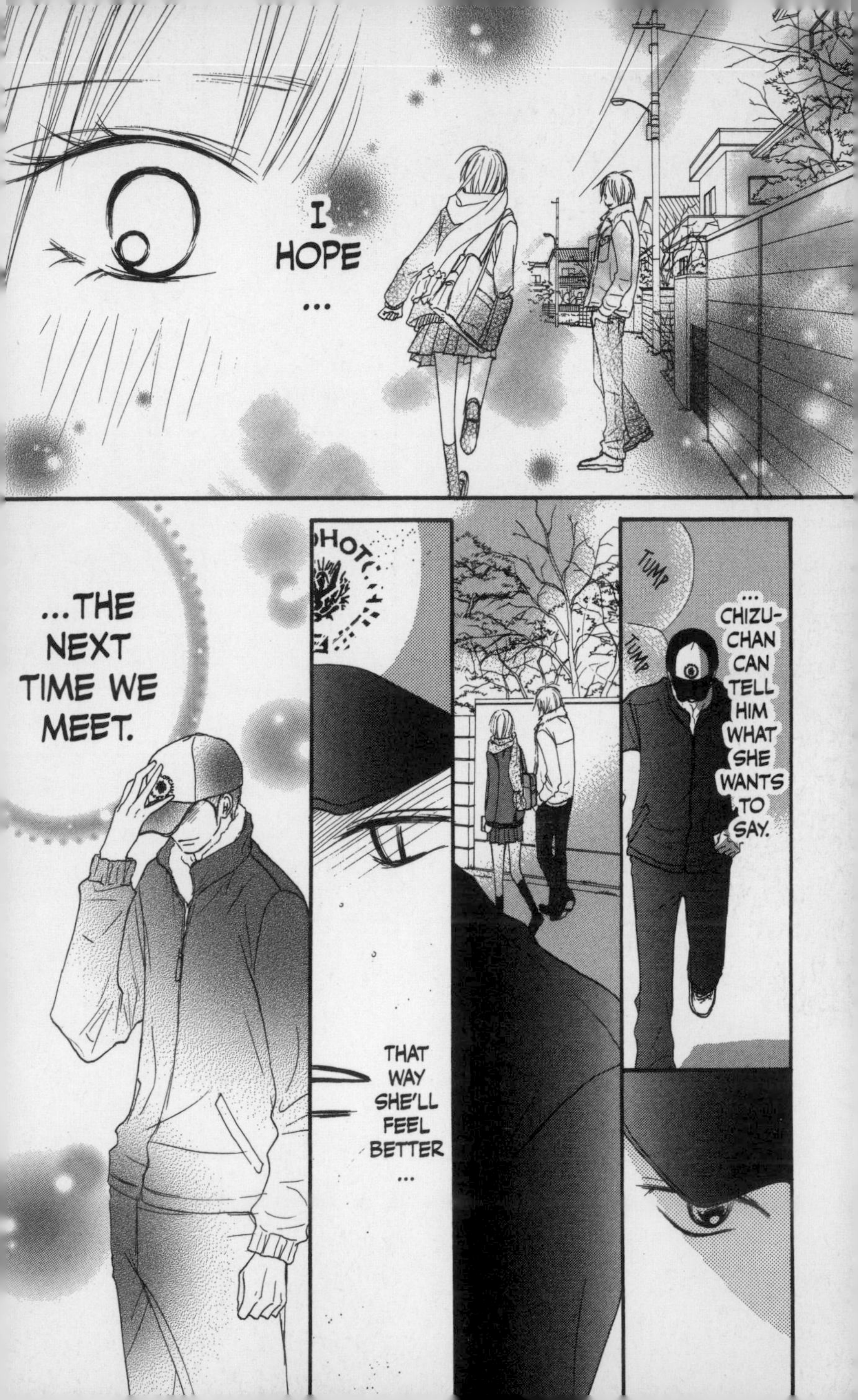
I HOPE ...
TUMP
TUMP
...CHIZU-CHAN CAN TELL HIM WHAT SHE WANTS TO SAY.
THAT WAY SHE'LL FEEL BETTER ...
...THE NEXT TIME WE MEET.

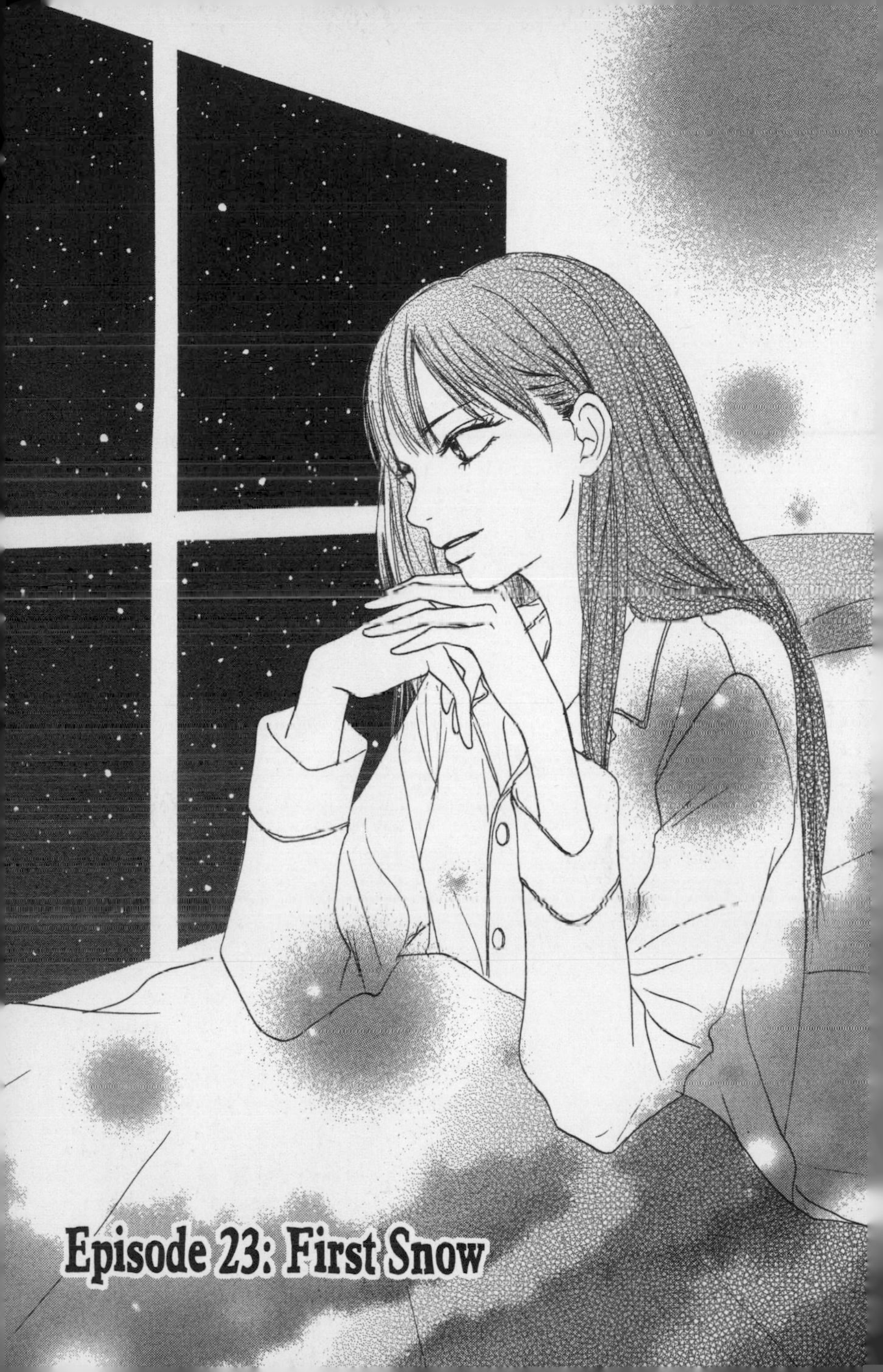
Episode 23: First Snow

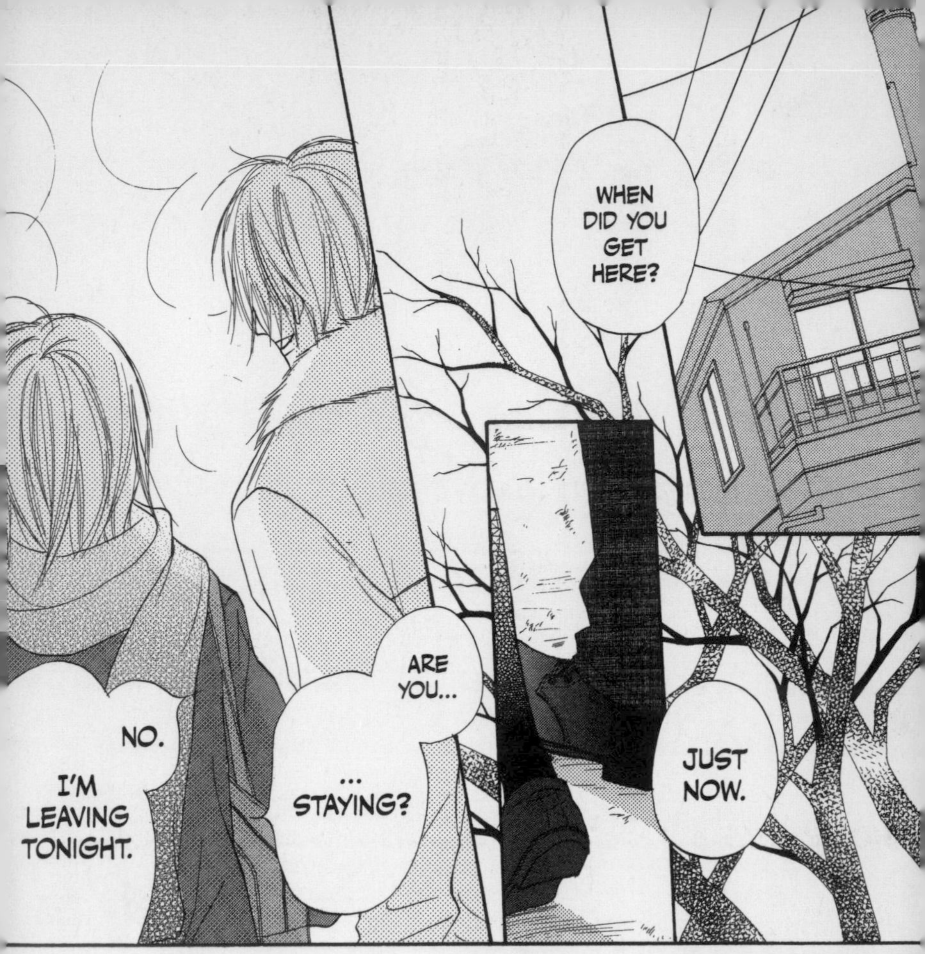
WHEN DID YOU GET HERE?
JUST NOW.
ARE YOU...
... STAYING?
NO.
I'M LEAVING TONIGHT.

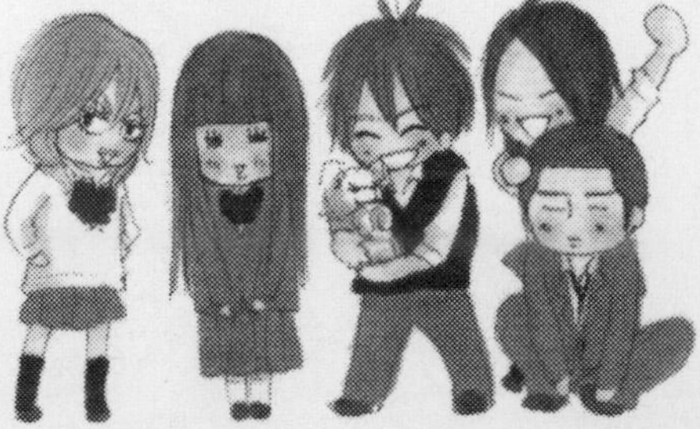

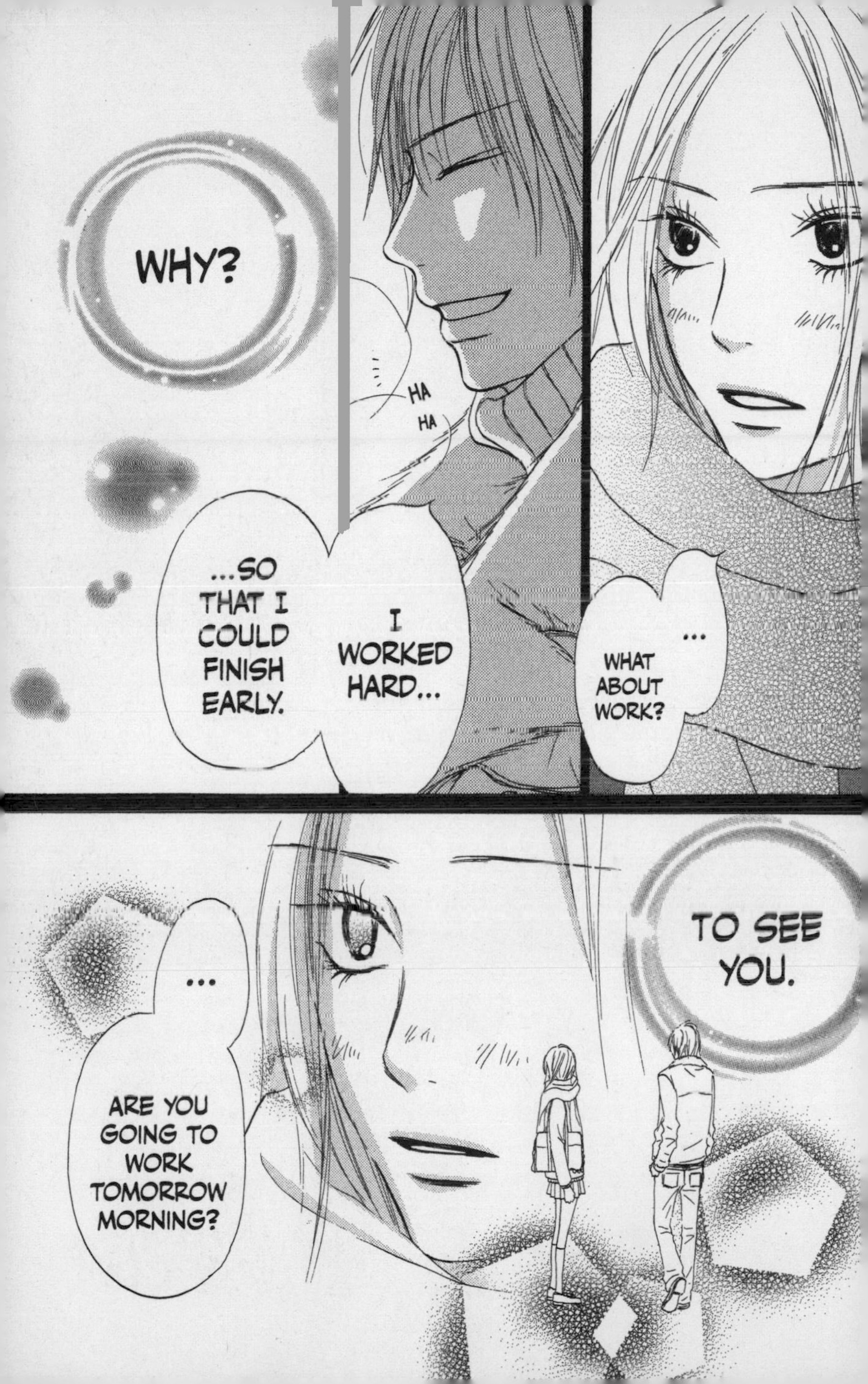
...
WHAT ABOUT WORK?
HA HA
I WORKED HARD...
...SO THAT I COULD FINISH EARLY.
WHY?
TO SEE YOU.
...
ARE YOU GOING TO WORK TOMORROW MORNING?

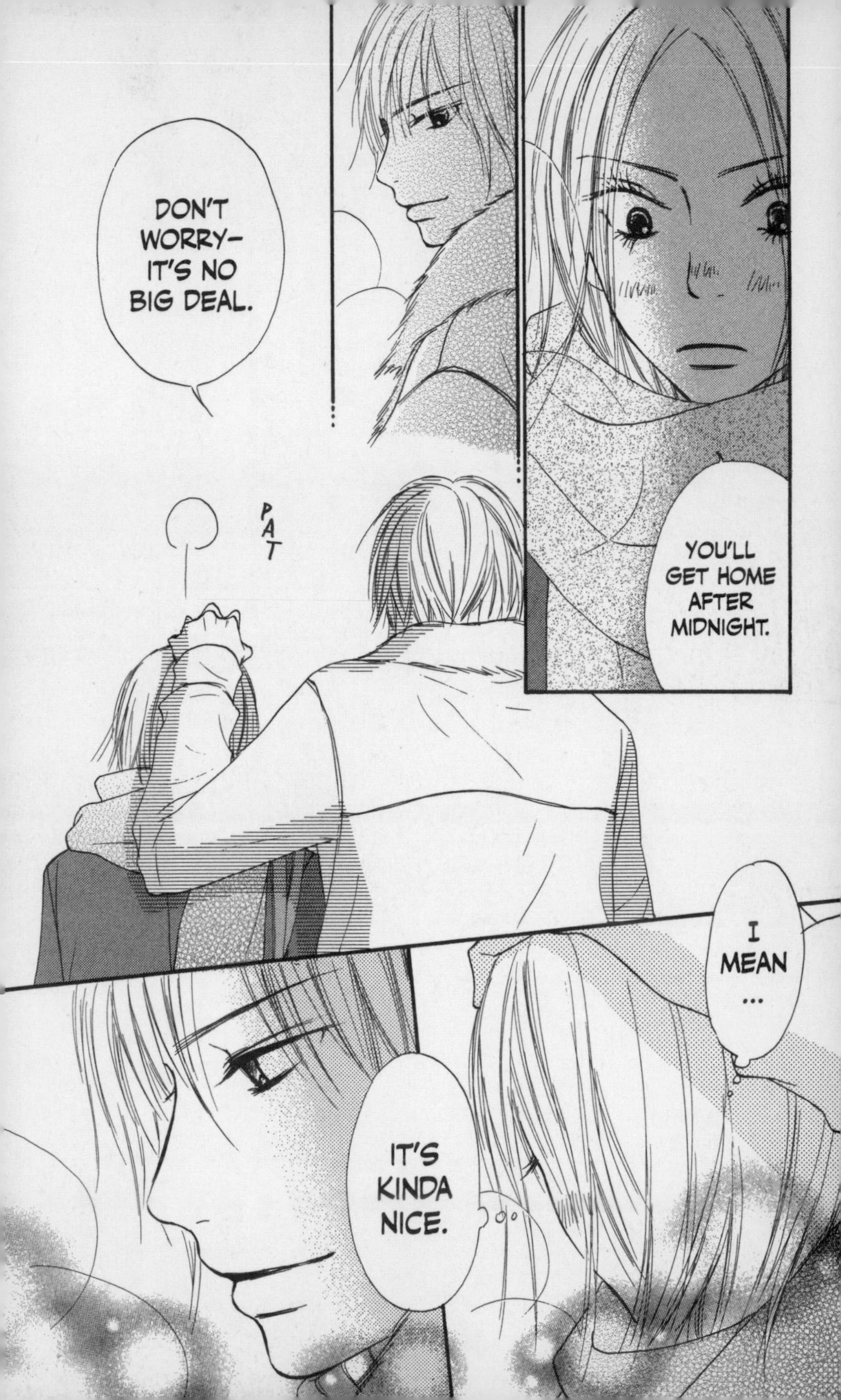
YOU'LL GET HOME AFTER MIDNIGHT.
DON'T WORRY- IT'S NO BIG DEAL.
PAT
I MEAN ...
IT'S KINDA NICE.

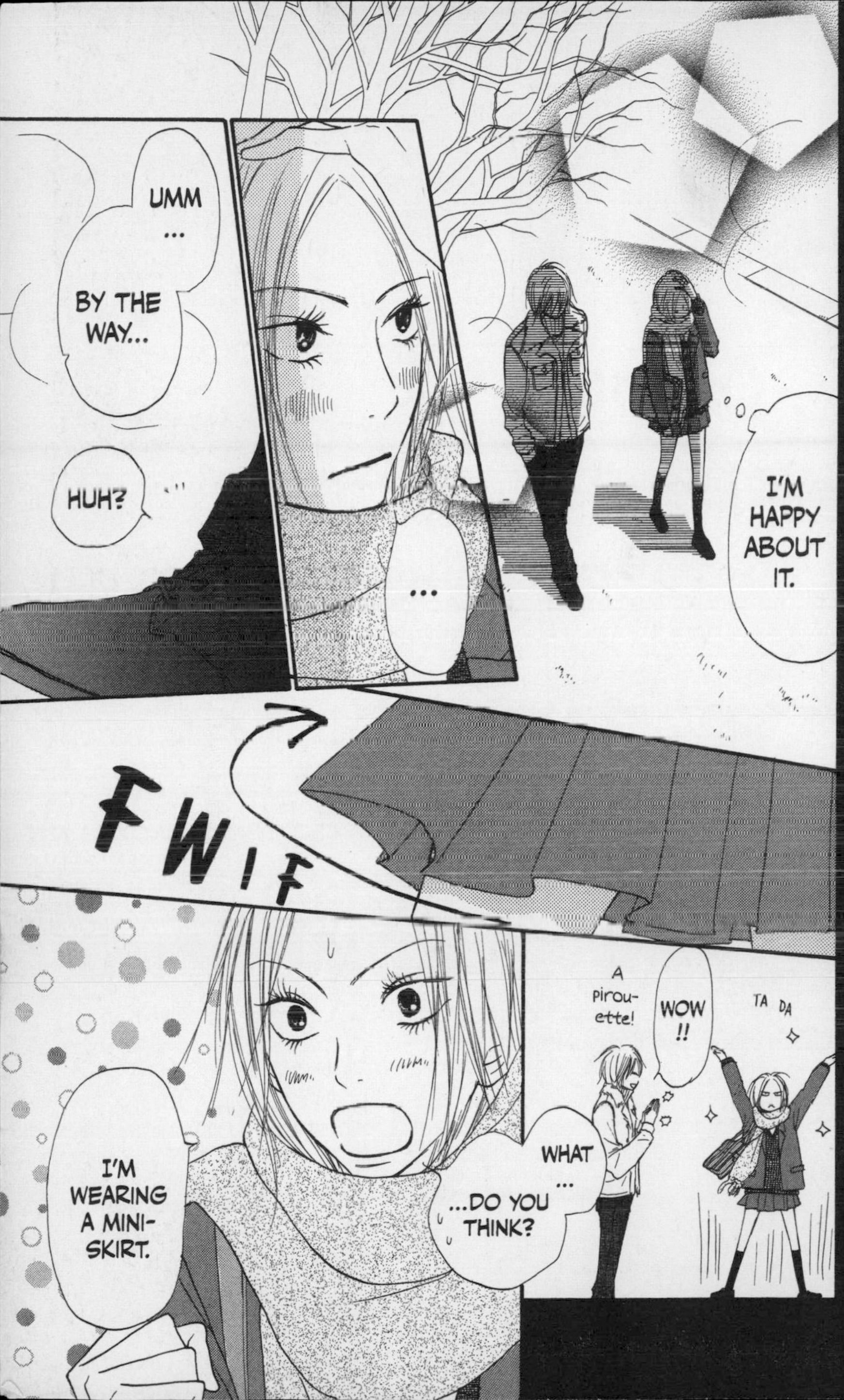
I'M HAPPY ABOUT IT.
...
UMM ... BY THE WAY...
HUH?
FWIF
TA DA
WOW !!
A pirou-ette!
WHAT ... ...DO YOU THINK?
I'M WEARING A MINI-SKIRT.

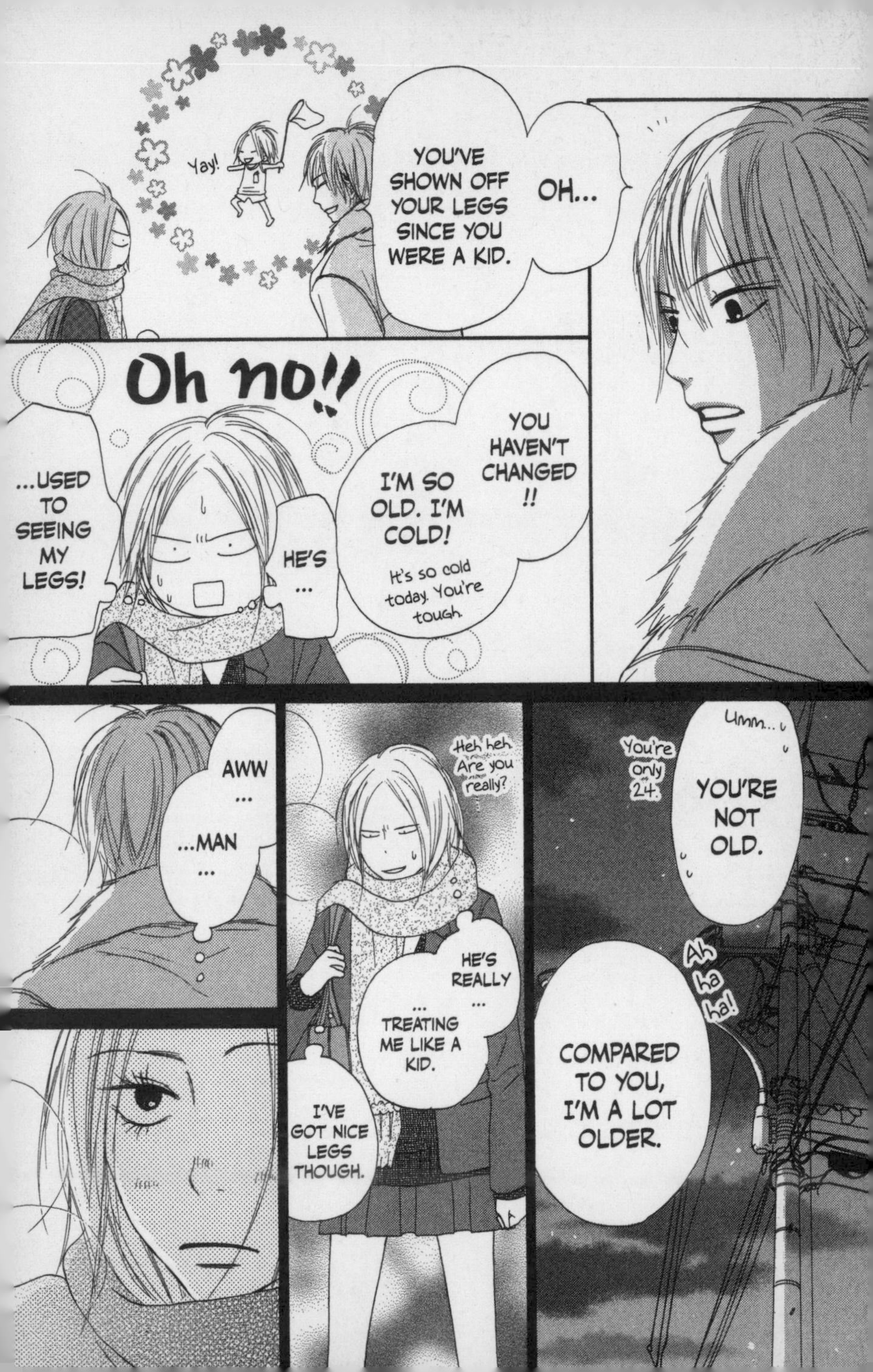
OH...
YOU'VE SHOWN OFF YOUR LEGS SINCE YOU WERE A KID.
Yay!
YOU HAVEN'T CHANGED!!
I'M SO OLD. I'M COLD!
It's so cold today. You're tough.
Oh no!!
HE'S ...
...USED TO SEEING MY LEGS!
Umm...
YOU'RE NOT OLD.
You're only 24.
Ah ha ha!
COMPARED TO YOU, I'M A LOT OLDER.
Heh heh. Are you really? ...
HE'S REALLY ...
... TREATING ME LIKE A KID.
I'VE GOT NICE LEGS THOUGH.
AWW ...
...MAN ...

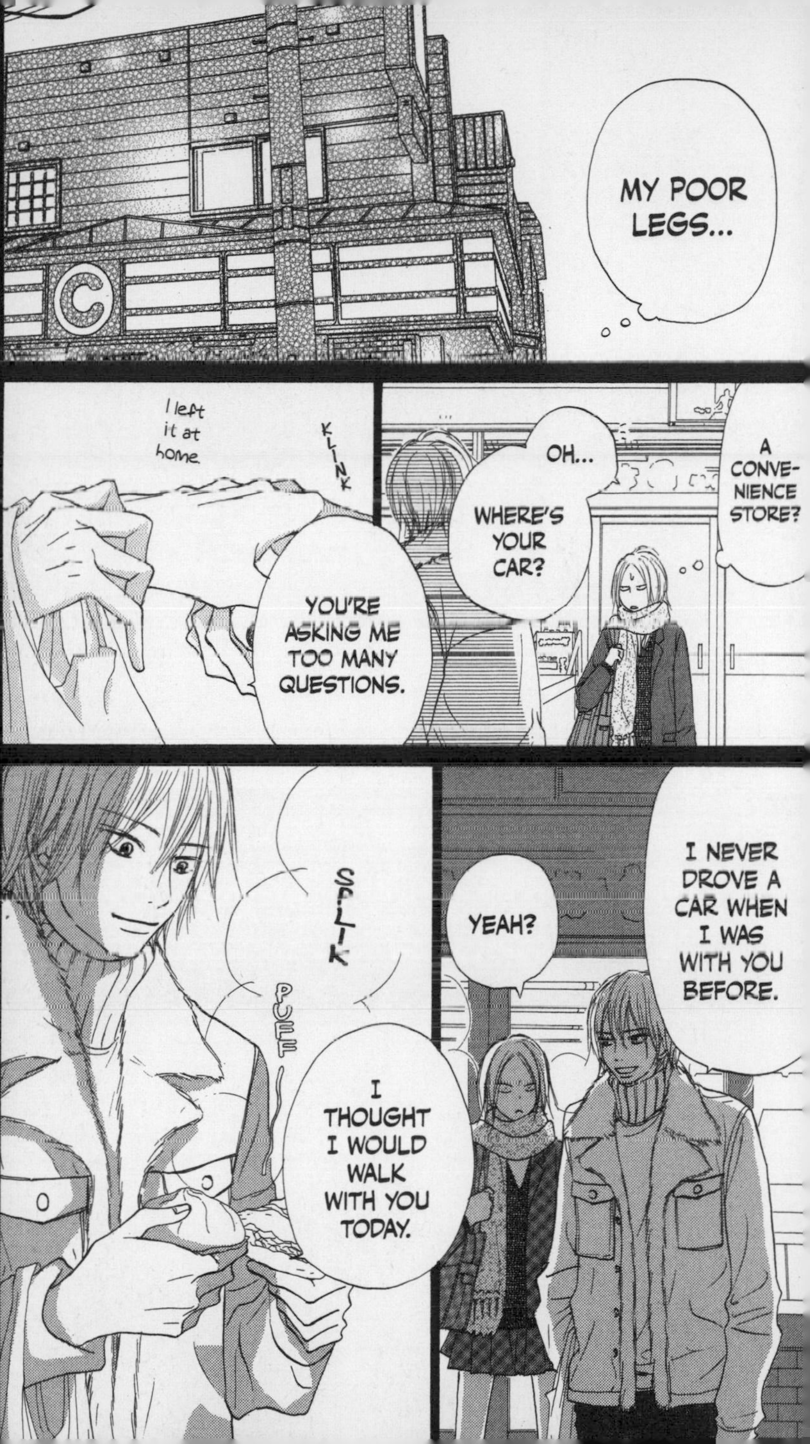
MY POOR LEGS...
A CONVE-NIENCE STORE?
...
OH...
WHERE'S YOUR CAR?
KLINK
YOU'RE ASKING ME TOO MANY QUESTIONS.
I left it at home.
I NEVER DROVE A CAR WHEN I WAS WITH YOU BEFORE.
YEAH?
SPLIK
PUFF
I THOUGHT I WOULD WALK WITH YOU TODAY.

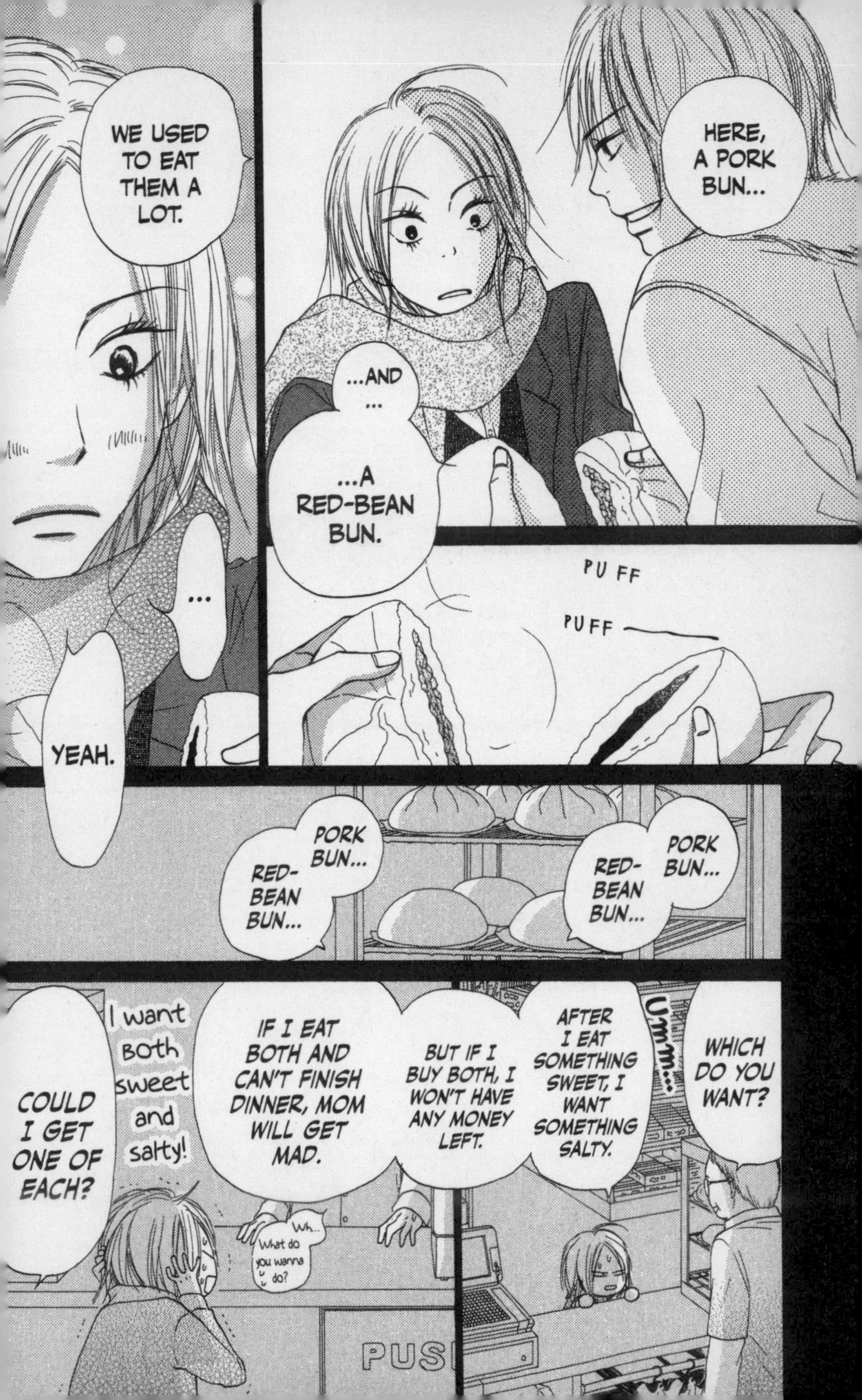
HERE, A PORK BUN...
...AND ...
...A RED-BEAN BUN.
PU FF
PUFF
WE USED TO EAT THEM A LOT.
...
YEAH.
PORK BUN...
RED-BEAN BUN...
PORK BUN...
RED-BEAN BUN...
WHICH DO YOU WANT?
Umm...
AFTER I EAT SOMETHING SWEET, I WANT SOMETHING SALTY.
BUT IF I BUY BOTH, I WON'T HAVE ANY MONEY LEFT.
IF I EAT BOTH AND CAN'T FINISH DINNER, MOM WILL GET MAD.
I want both sweet and salty!
COULD I GET ONE OF EACH?
Wh... What do you wanna do?
PUS

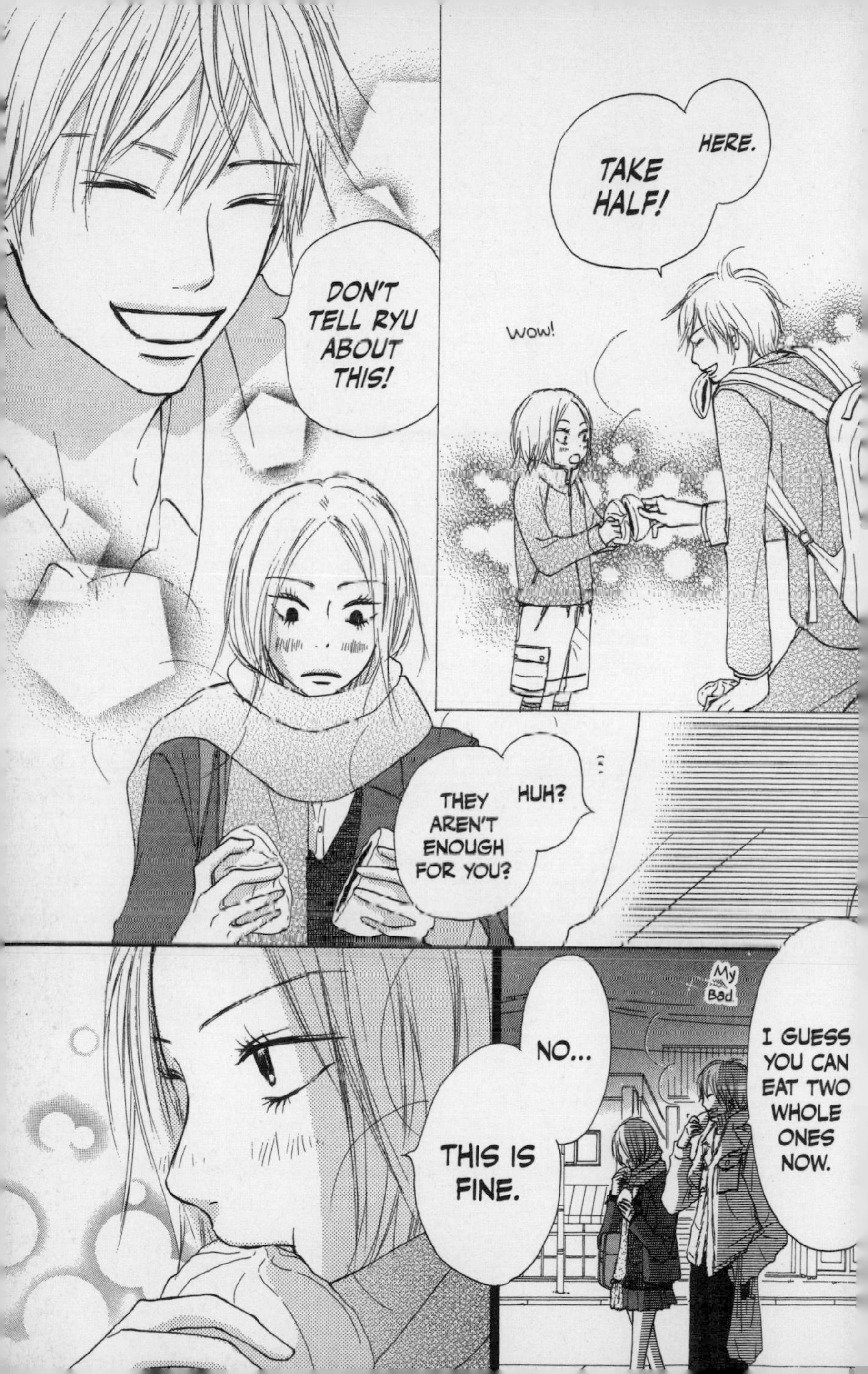
HERE.
TAKE HALF!
Wow!
DON'T TELL RYU ABOUT THIS!
...
HUH?
THEY AREN'T ENOUGH FOR YOU?
My Bad
I GUESS YOU CAN EAT TWO WHOLE ONES NOW.
NO...
THIS IS FINE.

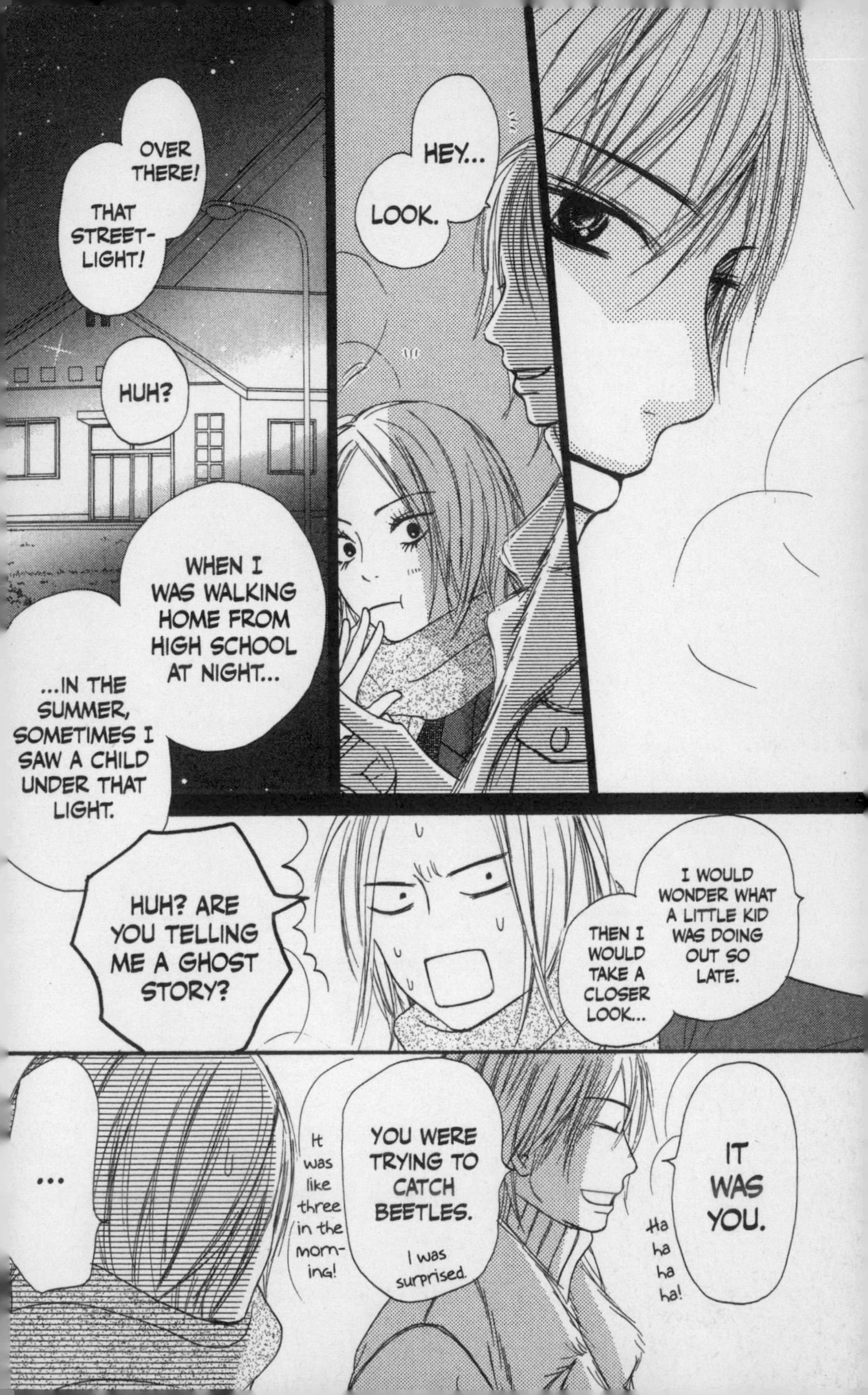
HEY... LOOK.
OVER THERE!
THAT STREET-LIGHT!
HUH?
WHEN I WAS WALKING HOME FROM HIGH SCHOOL AT NIGHT...
...IN THE SUMMER, SOMETIMES I SAW A CHILD UNDER THAT LIGHT.
I WOULD WONDER WHAT A LITTLE KID WAS DOING OUT SO LATE.
THEN I WOULD TAKE A CLOSER LOOK...
HUH? ARE YOU TELLING ME A GHOST STORY?
IT WAS YOU.
Ha ha ha ha!
YOU WERE TRYING TO CATCH BEETLES.
I was surprised.
It was like three in the morn-ing!
...

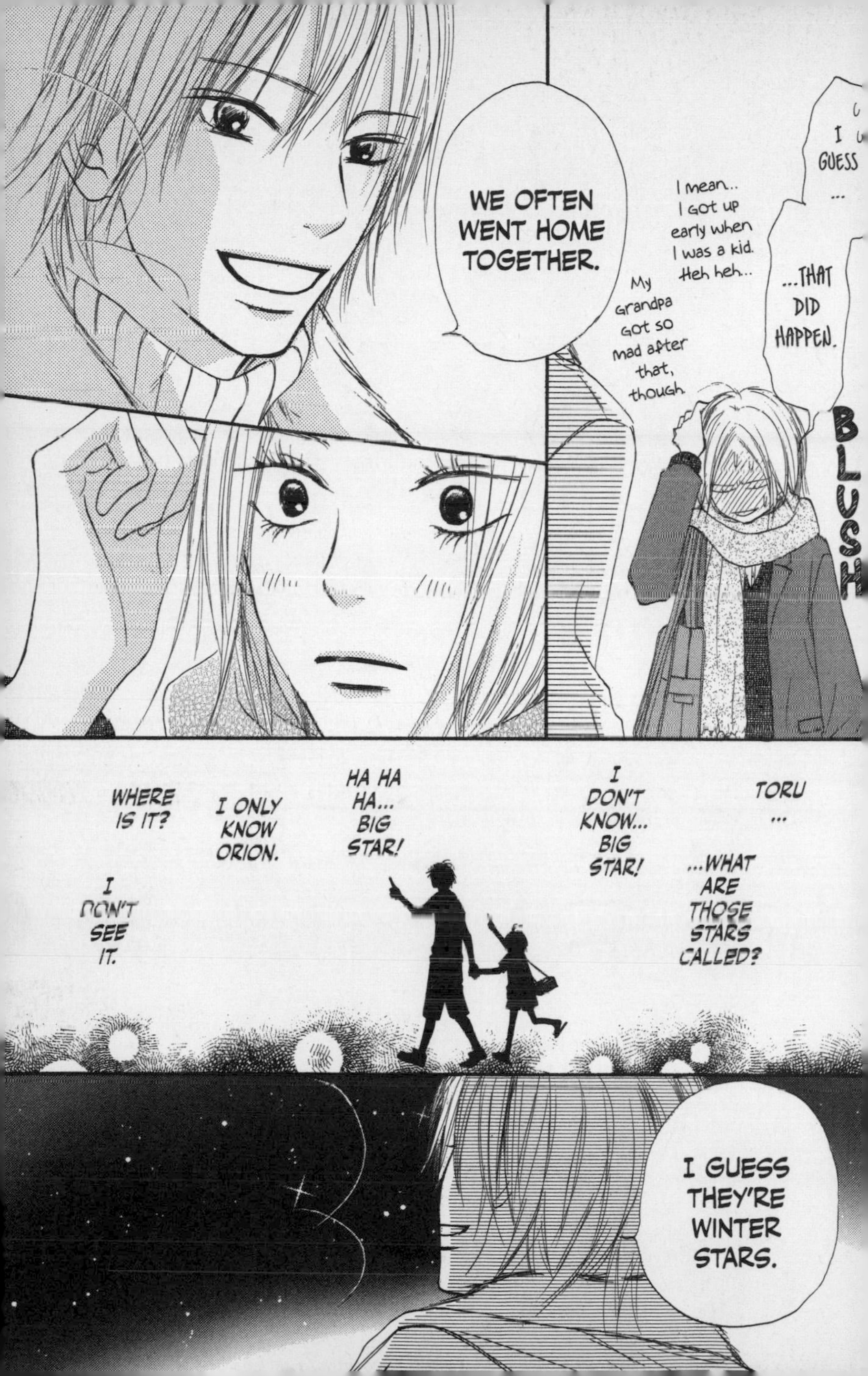
I GUESS ...
...THAT DID HAPPEN.
I mean.. I got up early when I was a kid. Heh heh...
My Grandpa got so mad after that, though.
BLUSH
WE OFTEN WENT HOME TOGETHER.
TORU ...
...WHAT ARE THOSE STARS CALLED?
I DON'T KNOW... BIG STAR!
HA HA HA... BIG STAR!
I ONLY KNOW ORION.
WHERE IS IT?
I DON'T SEE IT.
I GUESS THEY'RE WINTER STARS.

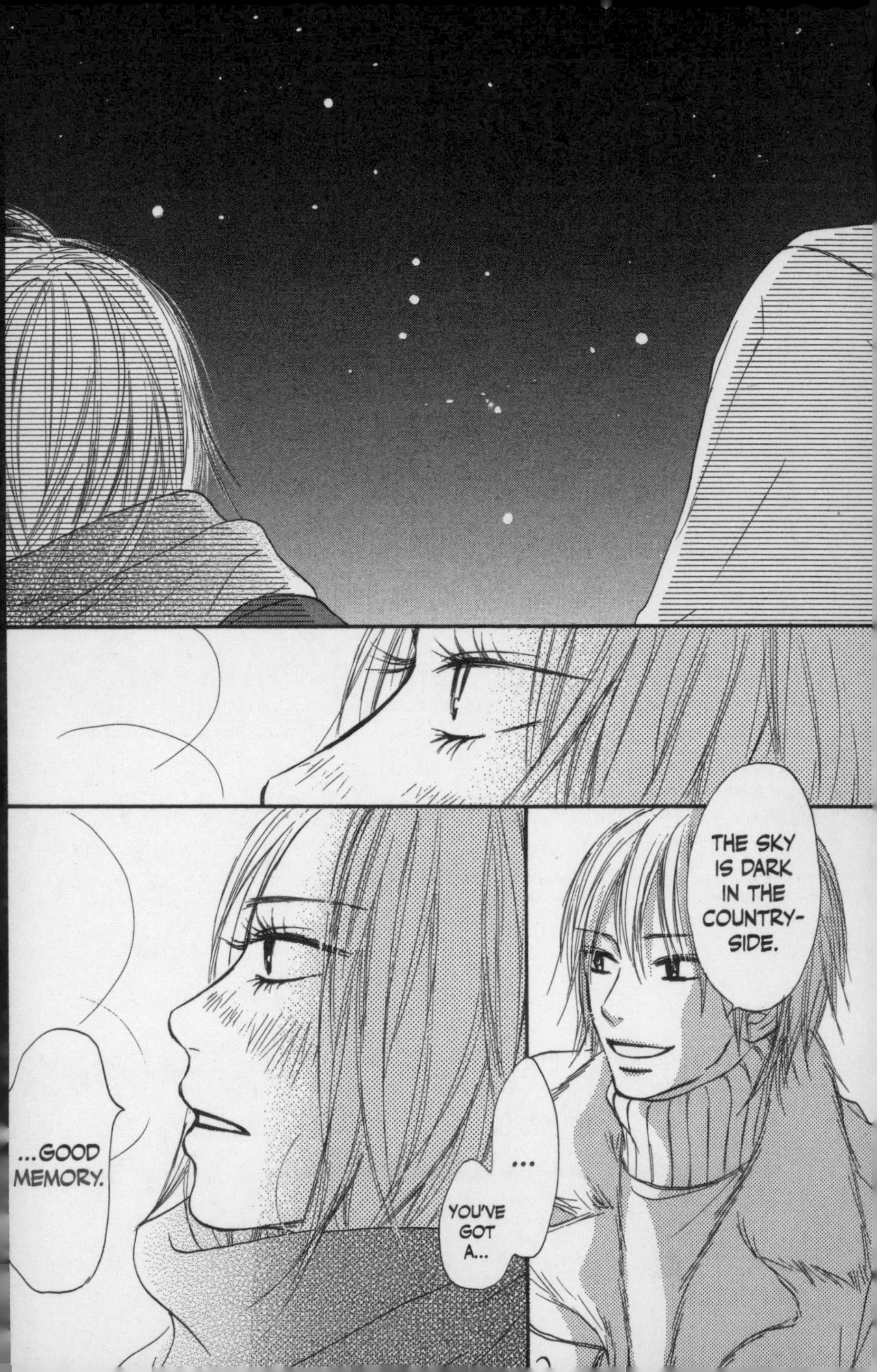
THE SKY IS DARK IN THE COUNTRY-SIDE.
...
YOU'VE GOT A...
...GOOD MEMORY.

KARUPIN on JAPAN 3

My eyesight is pretty bad. I wear glasses at home, and when I work.

I can't tell distance with contacts and it's difficult to work.

Something's wrong. Huh? Huh?

The glasses I wear as my first choice are really old. I bought them a long time ago. They're all beat up and look old, but I can't find any good glasses to replace them.

↓

Glasses I bought to replace the old ones. ①

frame

When looking down

TAK

What?!

It hurts my nose to wear them a long time.

They don't fit. I tried to adjust them though.

↓

They just became my second choice.

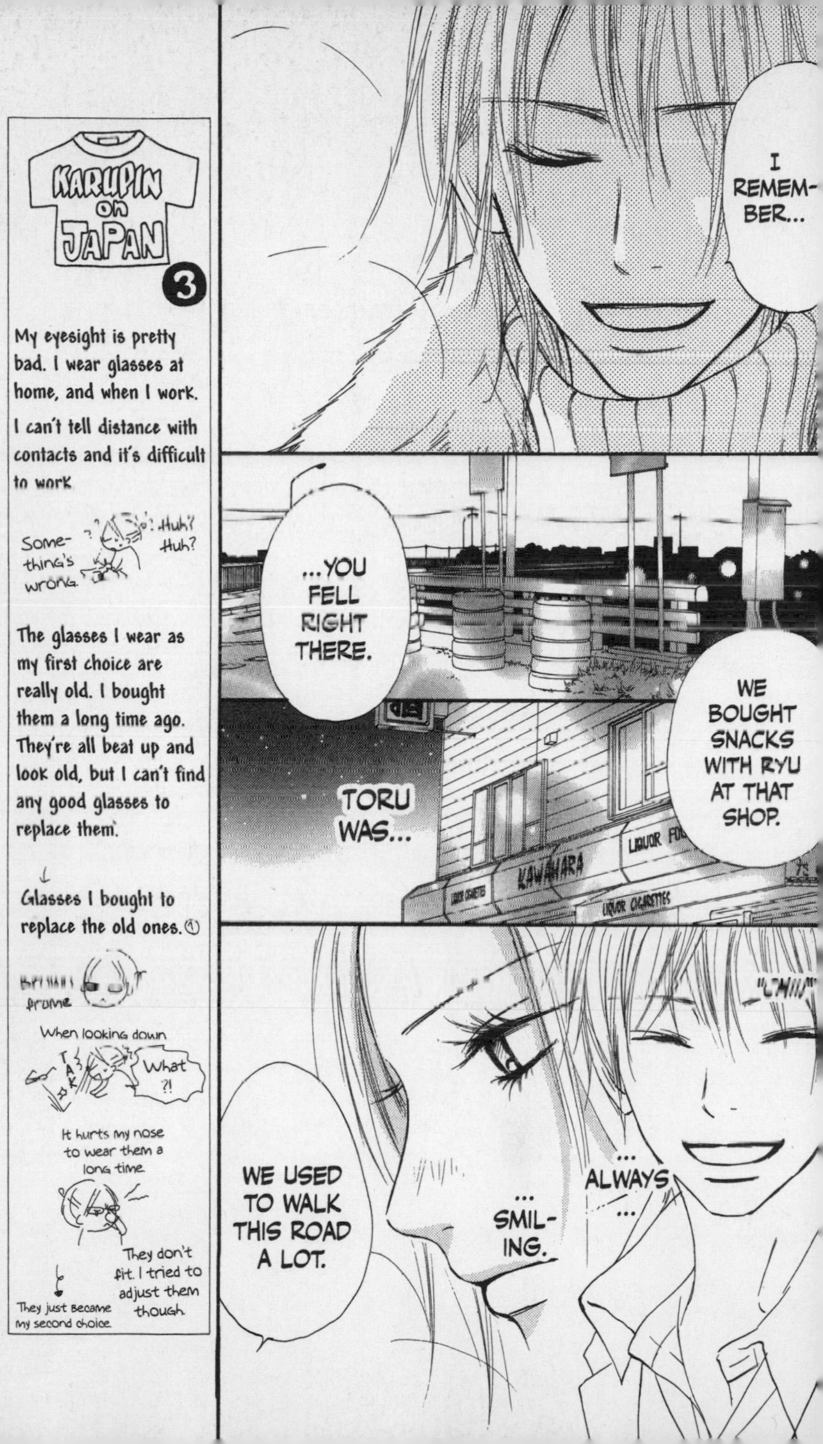
I REMEMBER...
...YOU FELL RIGHT THERE.
WE BOUGHT SNACKS WITH RYU AT THAT SHOP.
TORU WAS...
LIQUOR FO
KAWAHARA
LIQUOR CIGARETTES
LIQUOR CIGARETTES
...ALWAYS...
...SMILING.
WE USED TO WALK THIS ROAD A LOT.

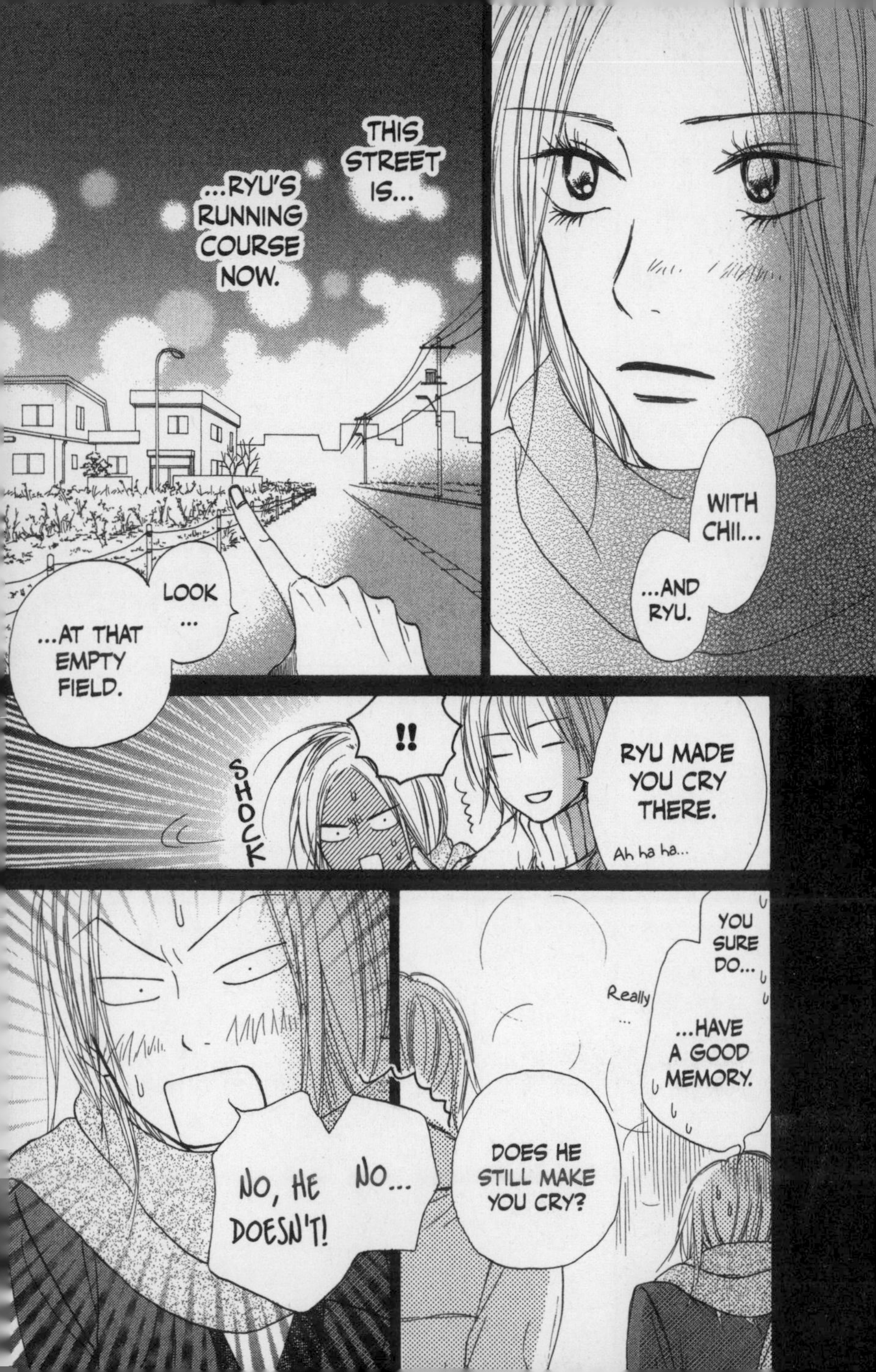
WITH CHII...
...AND RYU.
THIS STREET IS...
...RYU'S RUNNING COURSE NOW.
LOOK...
...AT THAT EMPTY FIELD.
RYU MADE YOU CRY THERE.
Ah ha ha...
!!
SHOCK
YOU SURE DO...
Really...
...HAVE A GOOD MEMORY.
DOES HE STILL MAKE YOU CRY?
NO...
NO, HE DOESN'T!

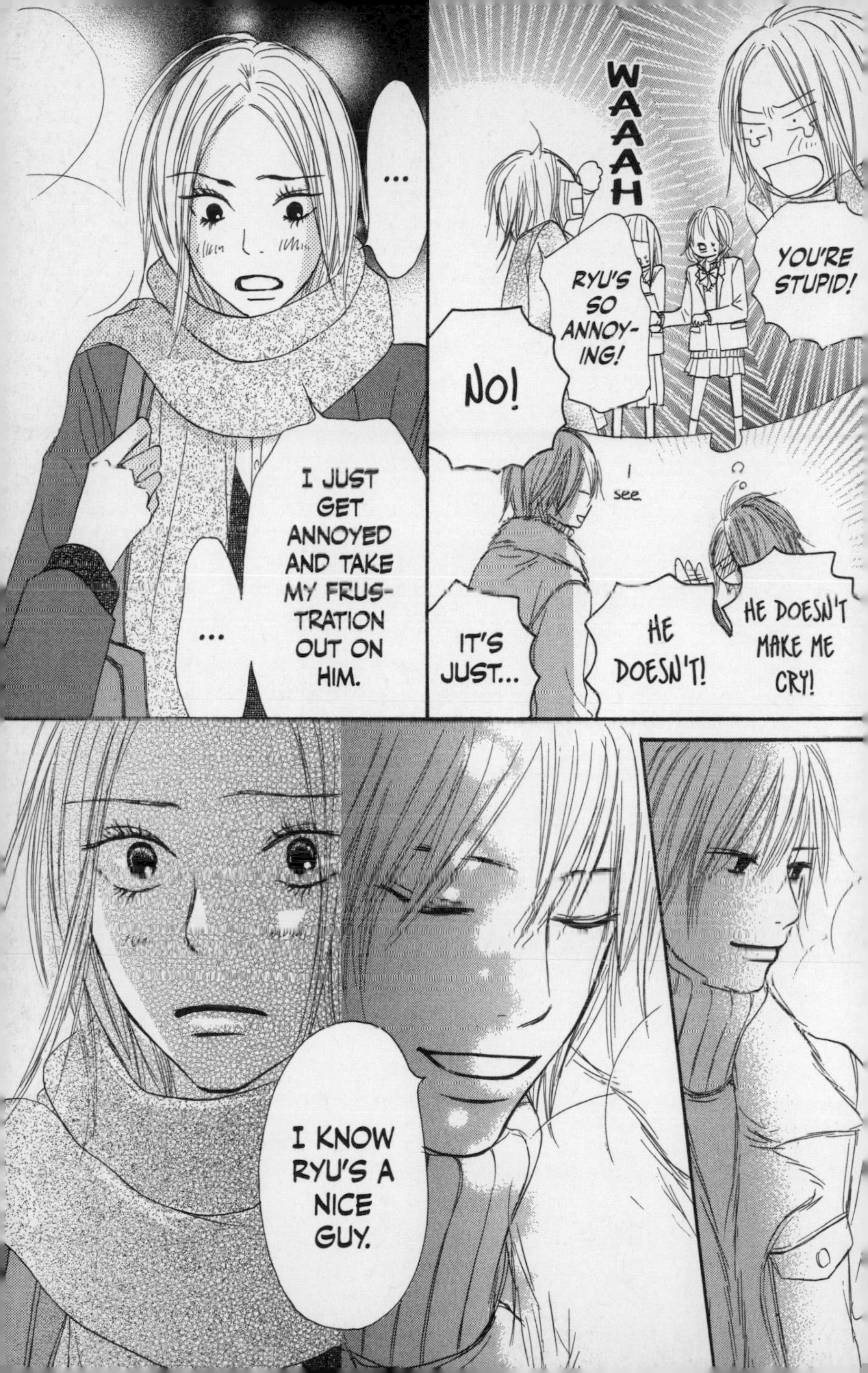
WAAAH
YOU'RE STUPID!
RYU'S SO ANNOYING!
NO!
I see.
HE DOESN'T MAKE ME CRY!
HE DOESN'T!
IT'S JUST...
...
I JUST GET ANNOYED AND TAKE MY FRUSTRATION OUT ON HIM.
...
I KNOW RYU'S A NICE GUY.

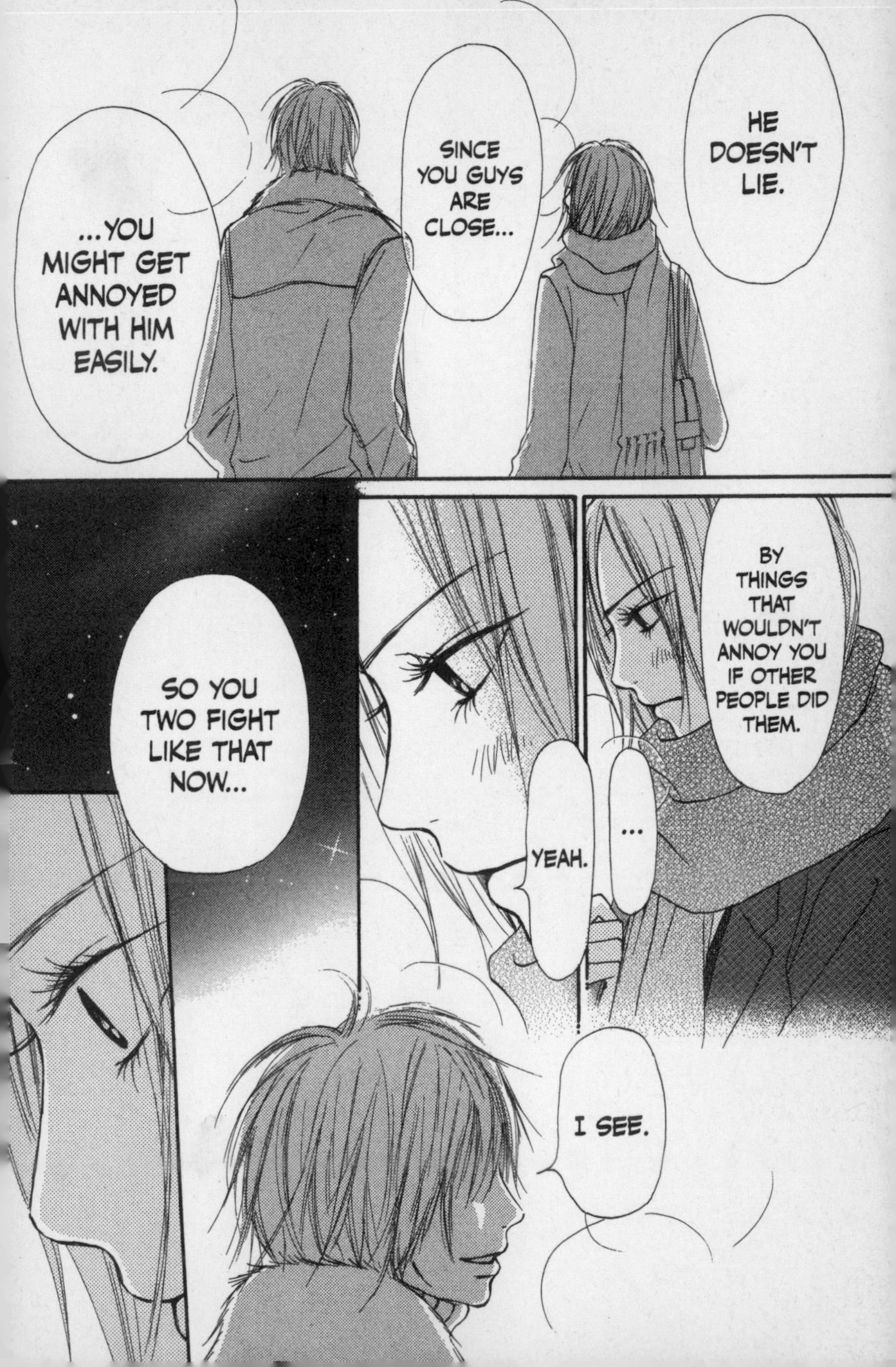
HE DOESN'T LIE.
SINCE YOU GUYS ARE CLOSE...
...YOU MIGHT GET ANNOYED WITH HIM EASILY.
BY THINGS THAT WOULDN'T ANNOY YOU IF OTHER PEOPLE DID THEM.
...
YEAH.
SO YOU TWO FIGHT LIKE THAT NOW...
I SEE.

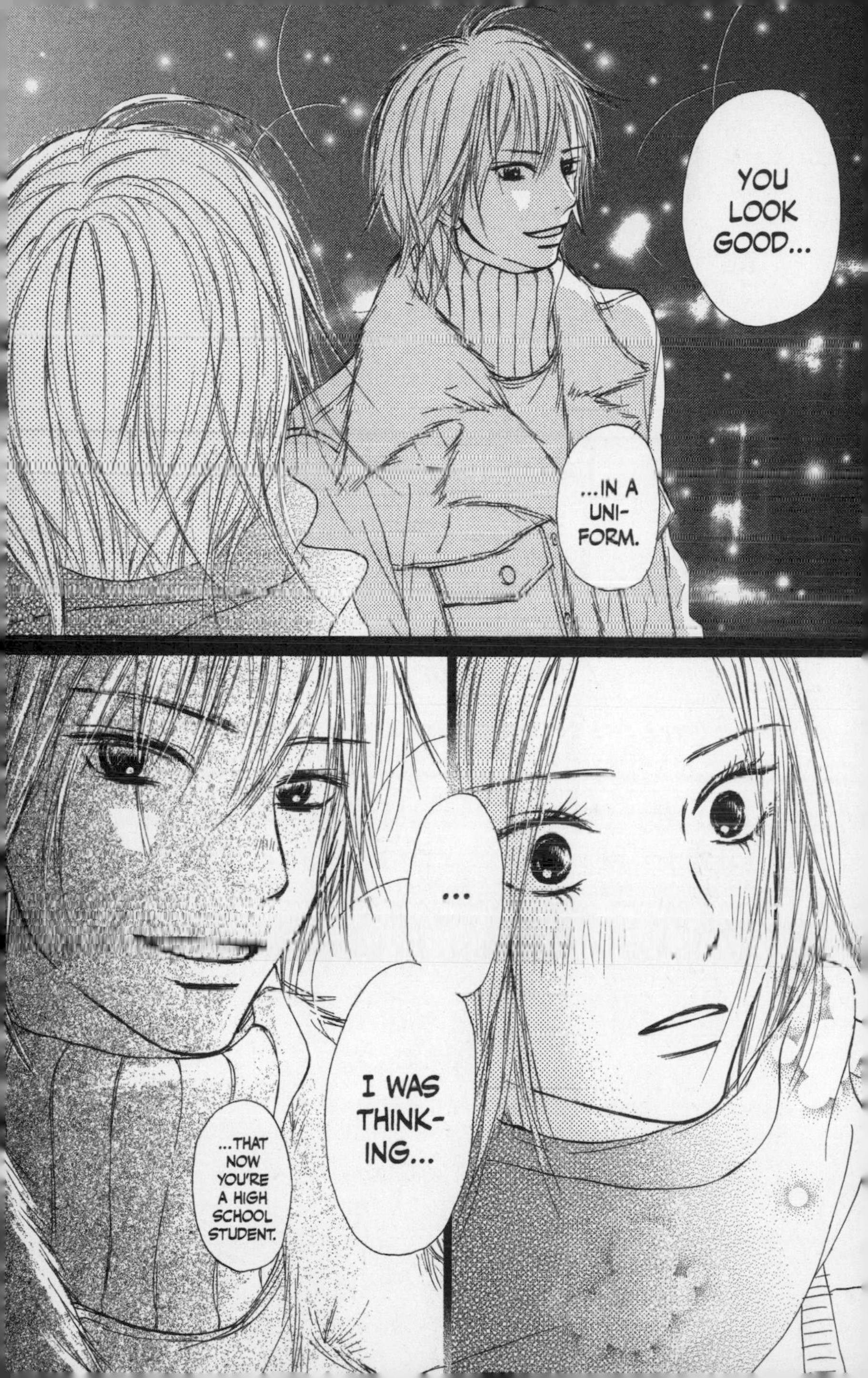
YOU LOOK GOOD...
...IN A UNI-FORM.
...
I WAS THINK-ING...
...THAT NOW YOU'RE A HIGH SCHOOL STUDENT.

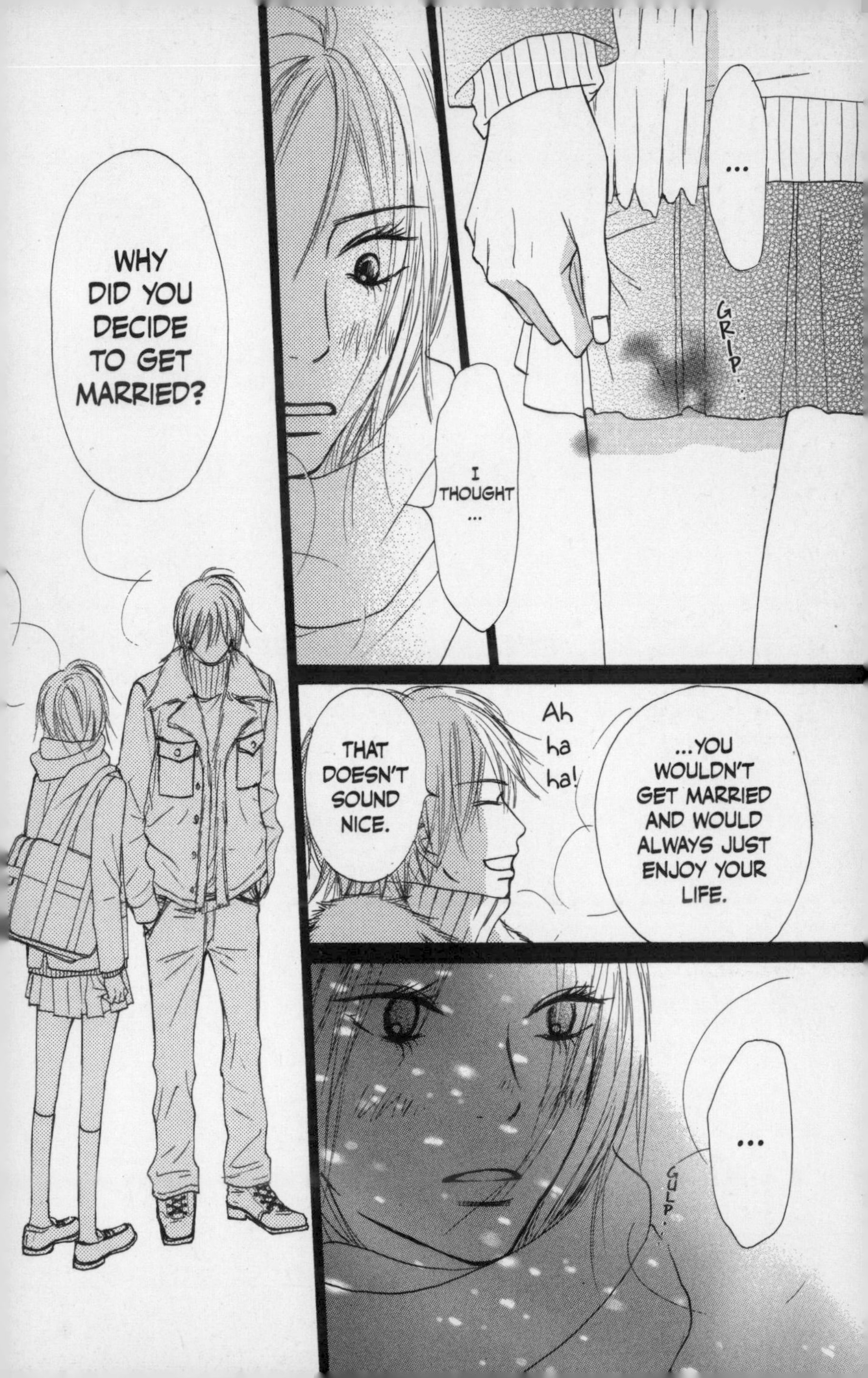
...
GRIP...
I THOUGHT ...
...YOU WOULDN'T GET MARRIED AND WOULD ALWAYS JUST ENJOY YOUR LIFE.
Ah ha ha!
THAT DOESN'T SOUND NICE.
...
GULP.
WHY DID YOU DECIDE TO GET MARRIED?

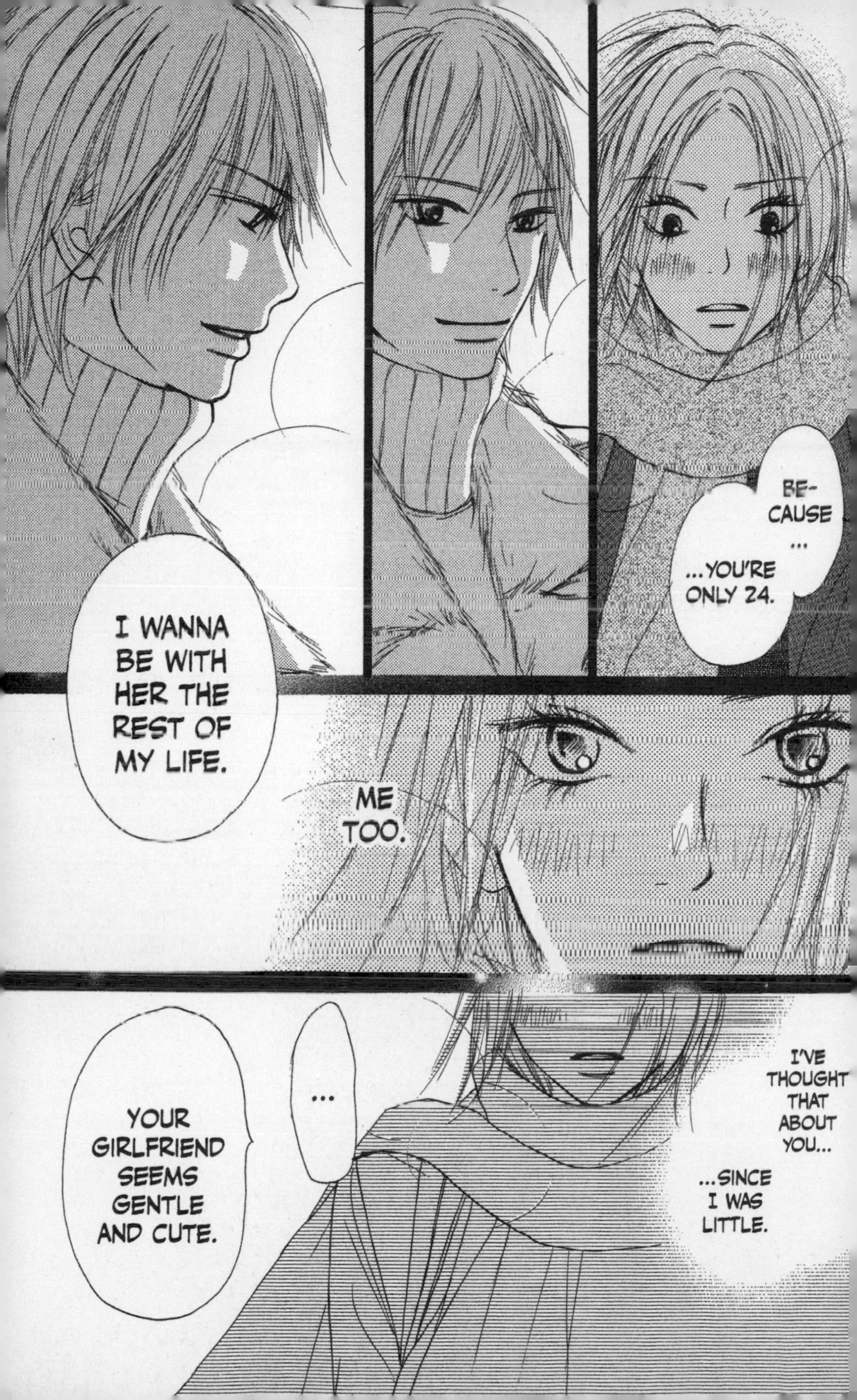
BE-CAUSE ...
...YOU'RE ONLY 24.
I WANNA BE WITH HER THE REST OF MY LIFE.
ME TOO.
I'VE THOUGHT THAT ABOUT YOU...
...SINCE I WAS LITTLE.
...
YOUR GIRLFRIEND SEEMS GENTLE AND CUTE.

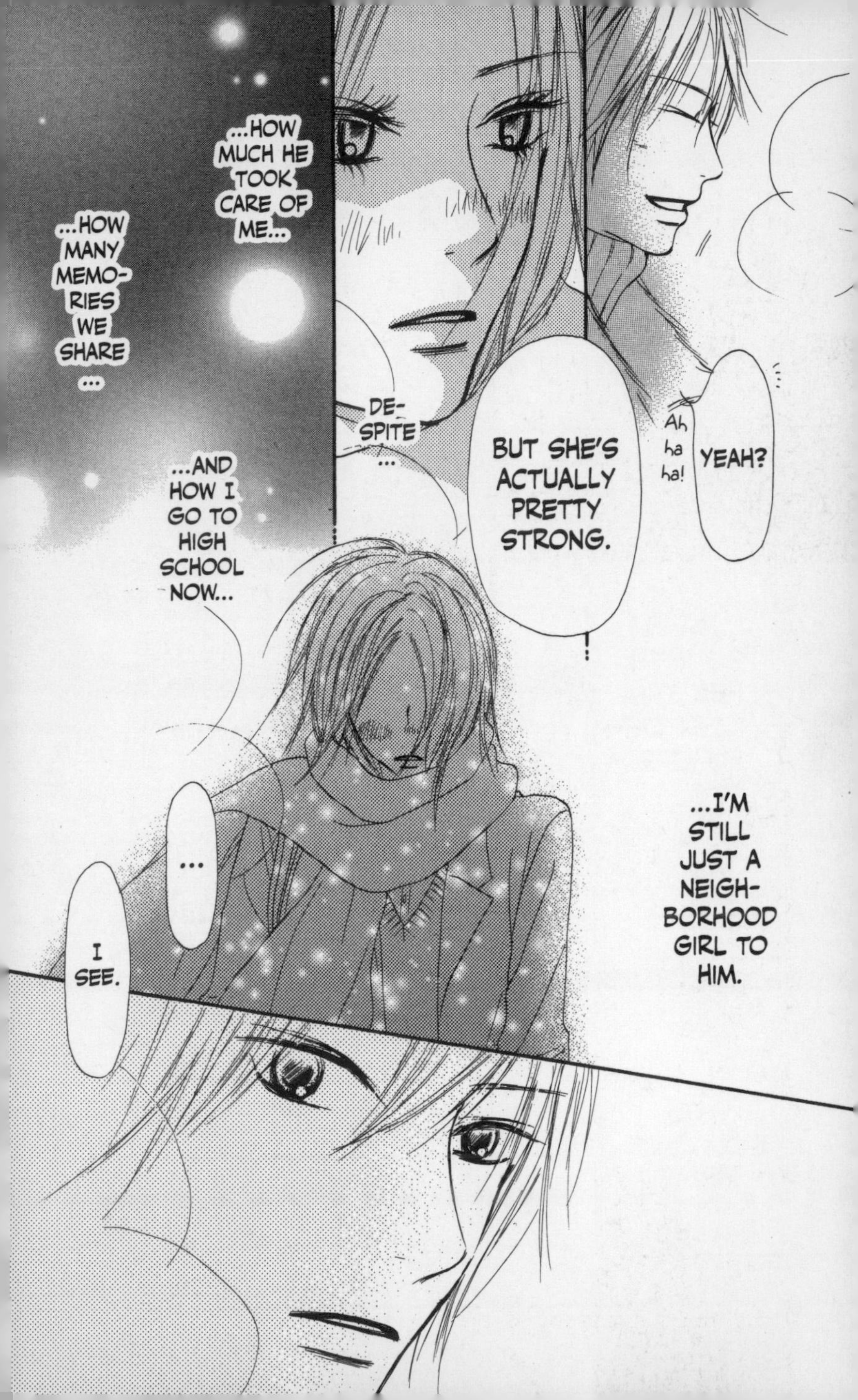
YEAH?
Ah ha ha!
BUT SHE'S ACTUALLY PRETTY STRONG.
DE-SPITE...
...HOW MUCH HE TOOK CARE OF ME...
...HOW MANY MEMO-RIES WE SHARE...
...AND HOW I GO TO HIGH SCHOOL NOW...
...I'M STILL JUST A NEIGH-BORHOOD GIRL TO HIM.
...
I SEE.

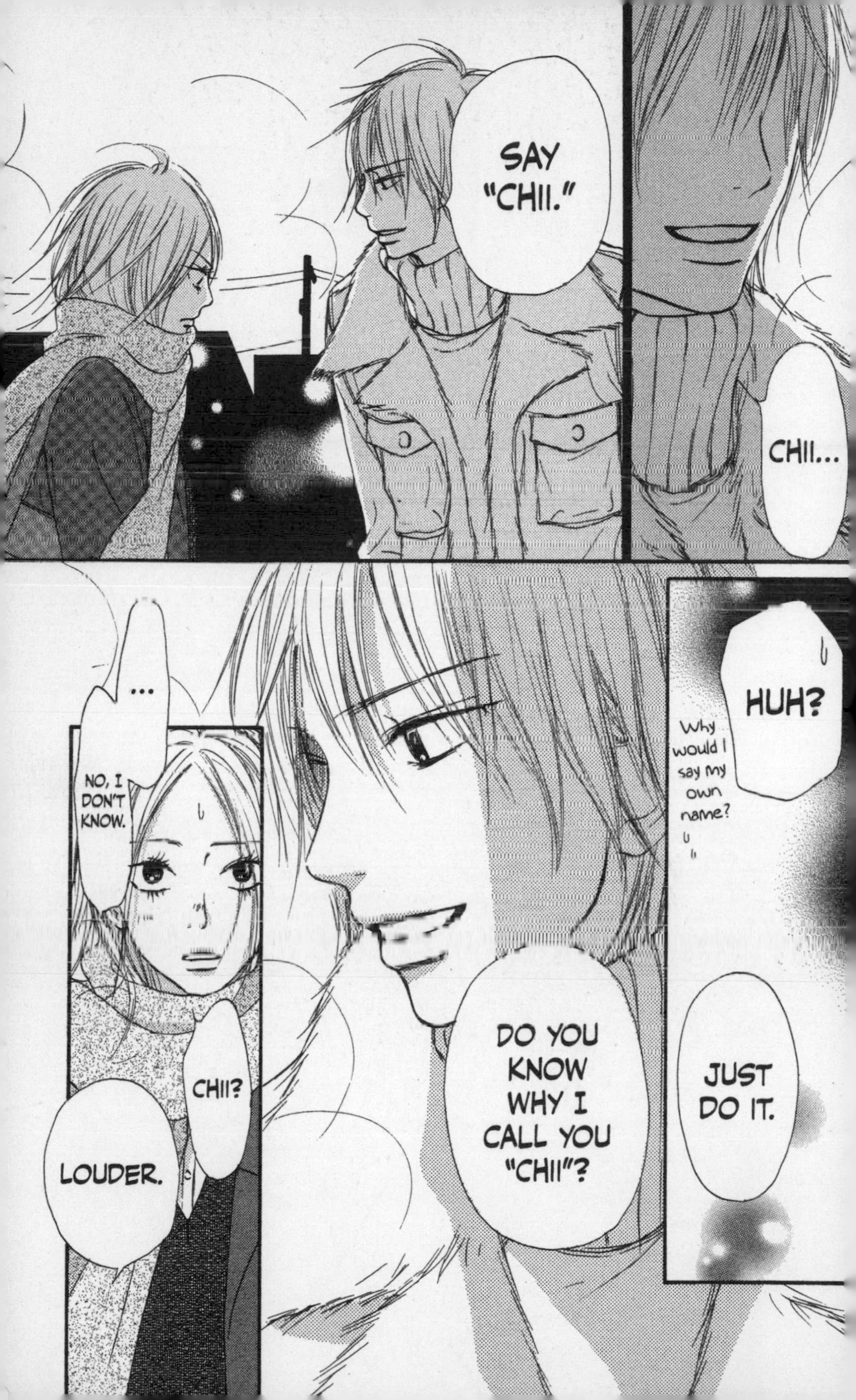
CHII...
SAY "CHII."
HUH?
Why would I say my own name?
JUST DO IT.
CHII?
LOUDER.
DO YOU KNOW WHY I CALL YOU "CHII"?
...
NO, I DON'T KNOW.

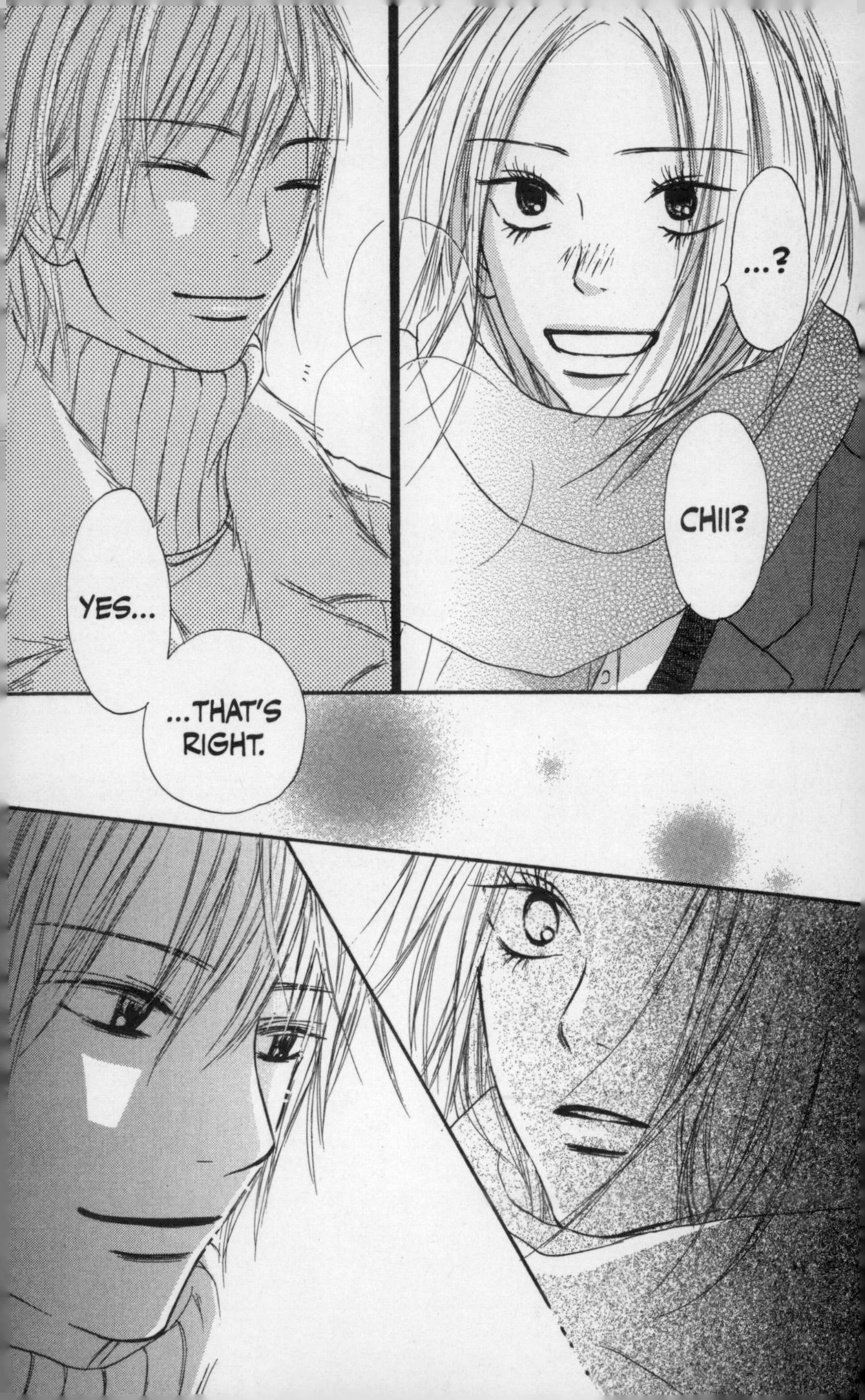
...?
CHII?
YES...
...THAT'S RIGHT.

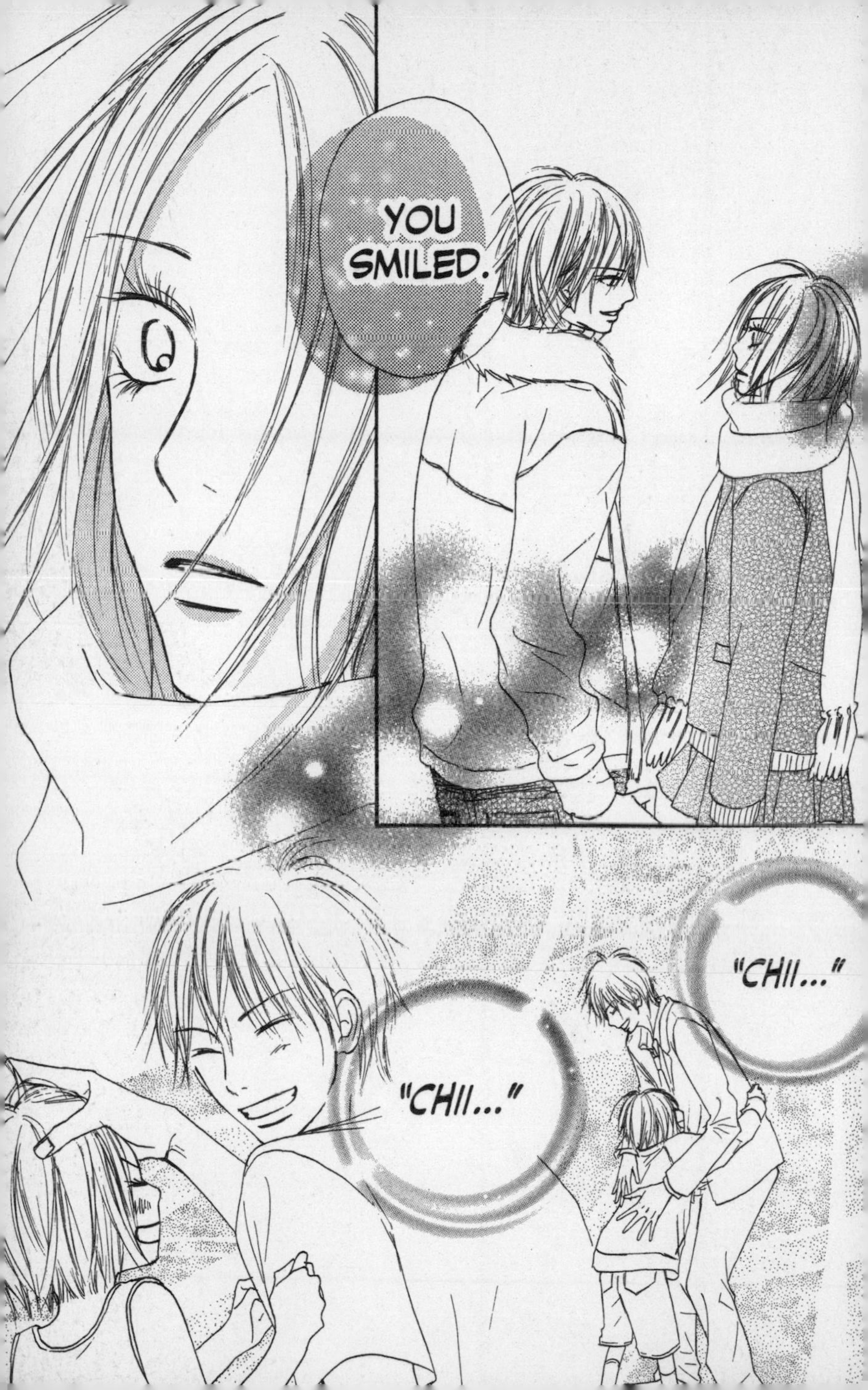
YOU SMILED.
"CHII..."
"CHII..."

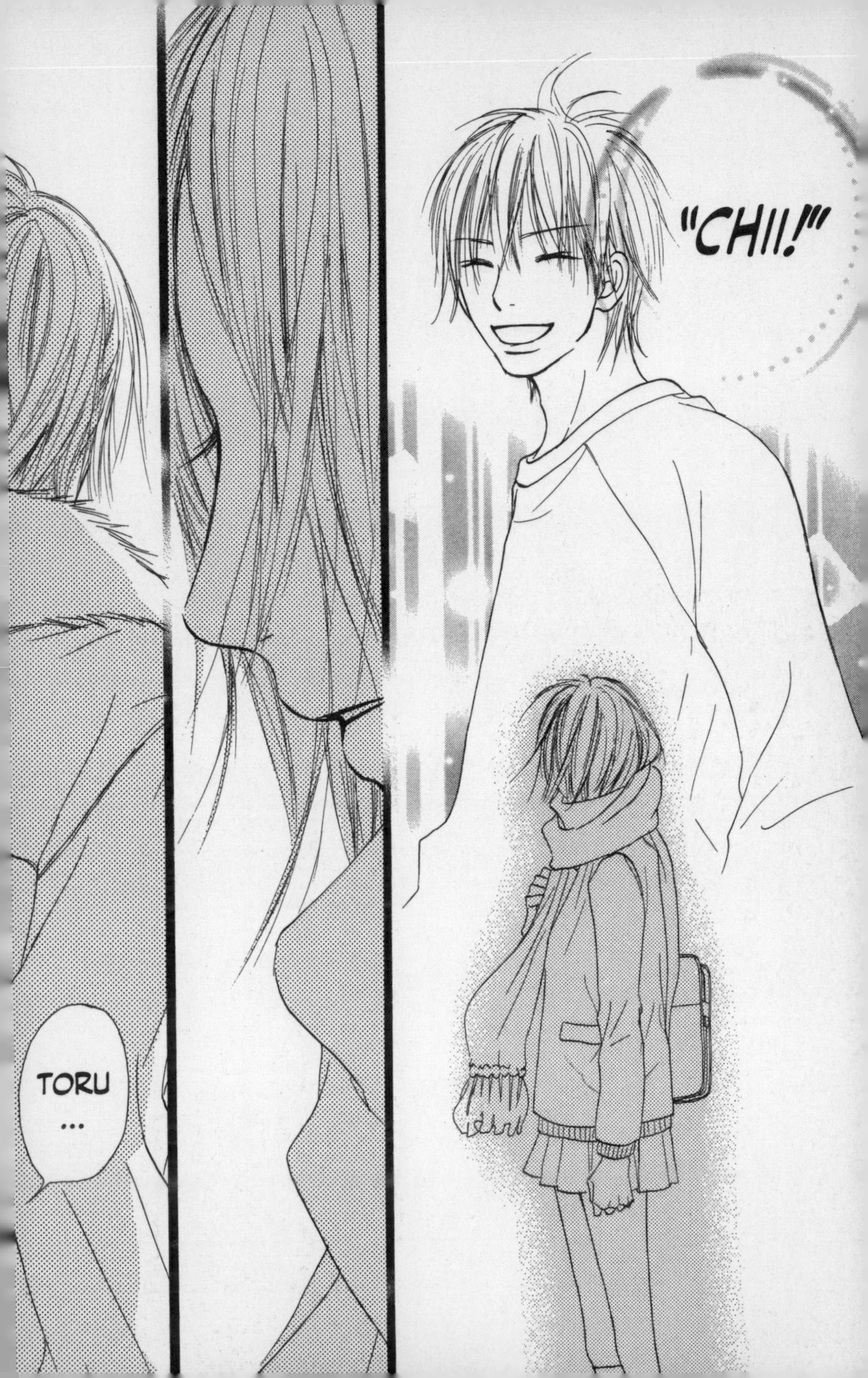
"CHII!"
TORU ...

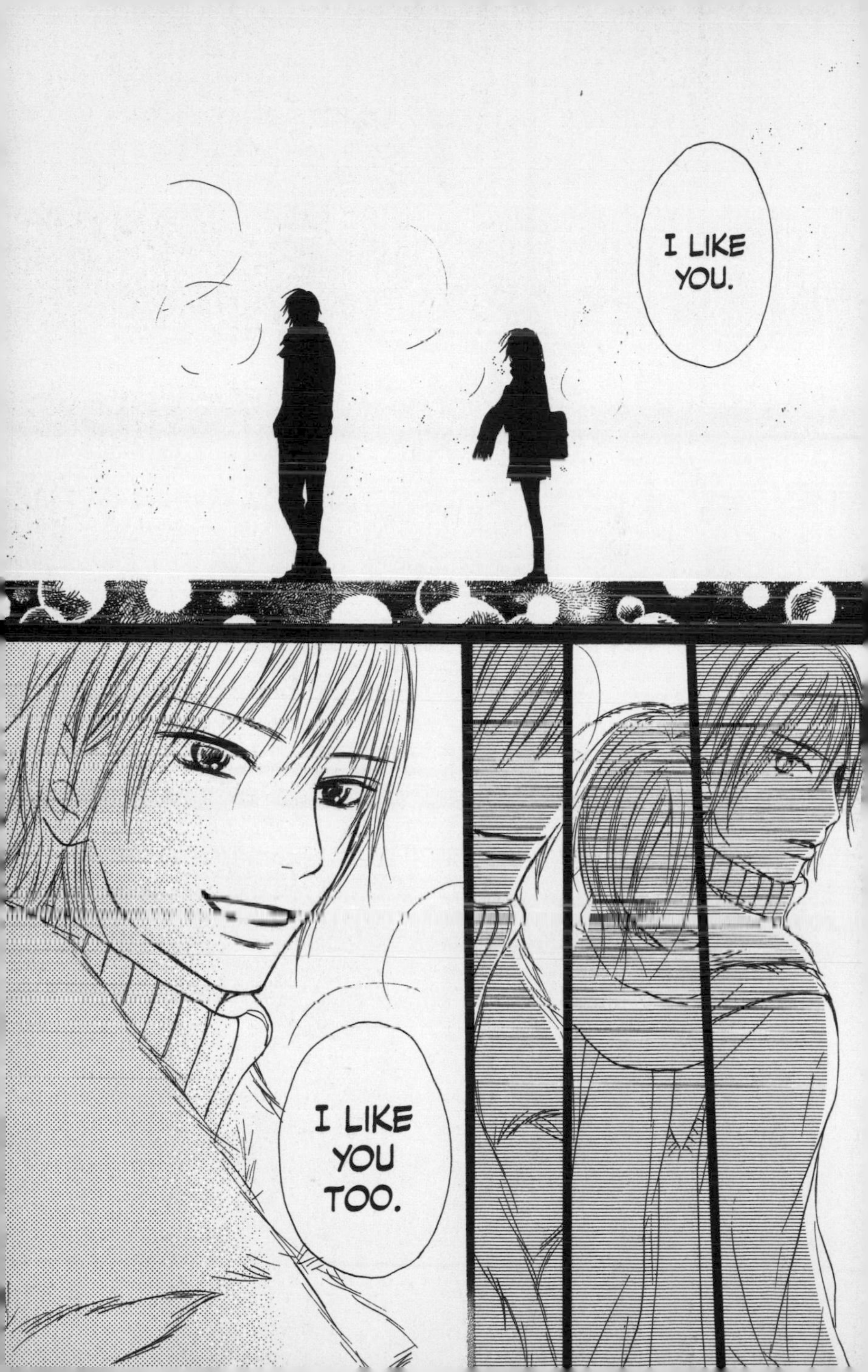
I LIKE YOU.
I LIKE YOU TOO.

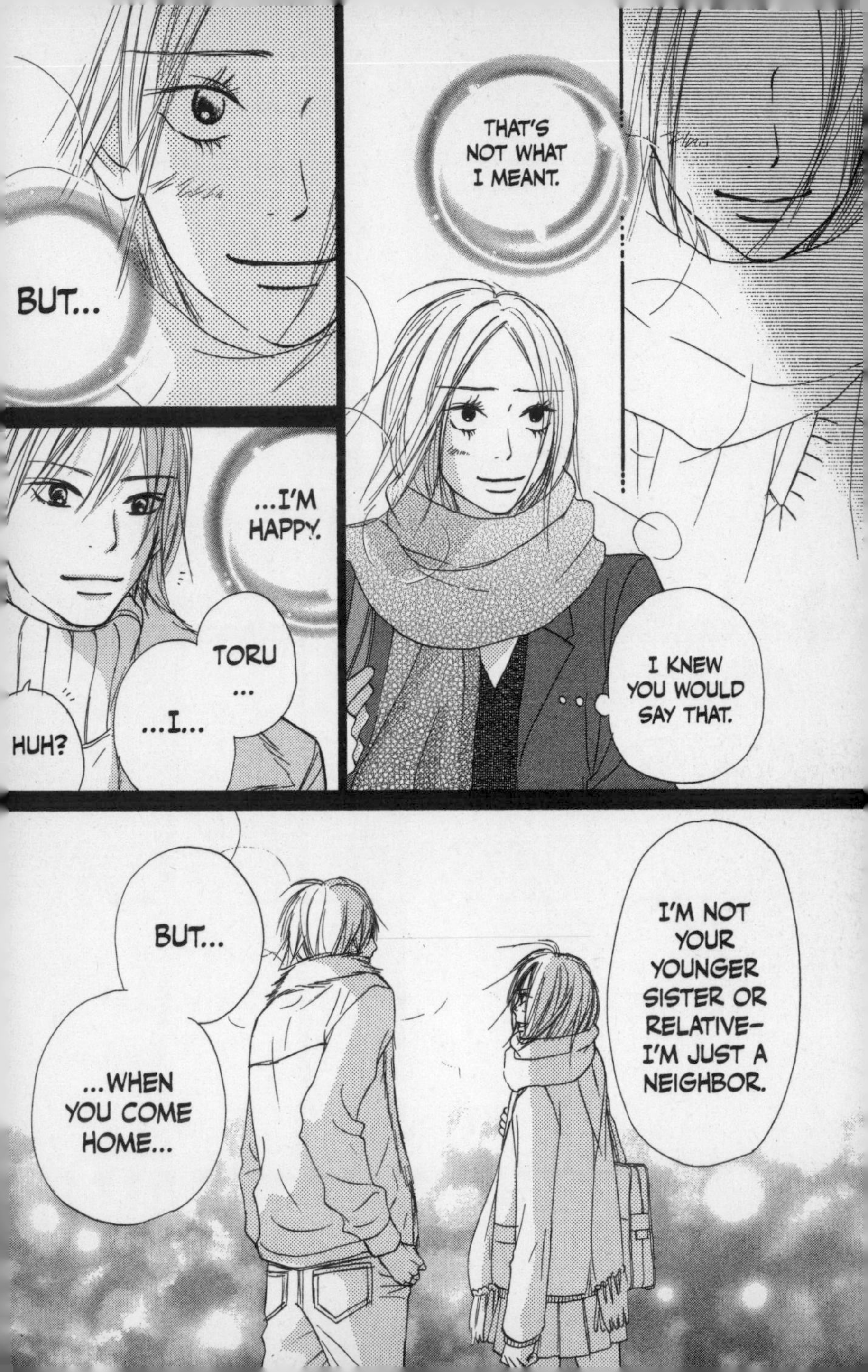
THAT'S NOT WHAT I MEANT.
I KNEW YOU WOULD SAY THAT.
BUT...
...I'M HAPPY.
TORU ...
...I...
HUH?
I'M NOT YOUR YOUNGER SISTER OR RELATIVE— I'M JUST A NEIGHBOR.
BUT...
...WHEN YOU COME HOME...

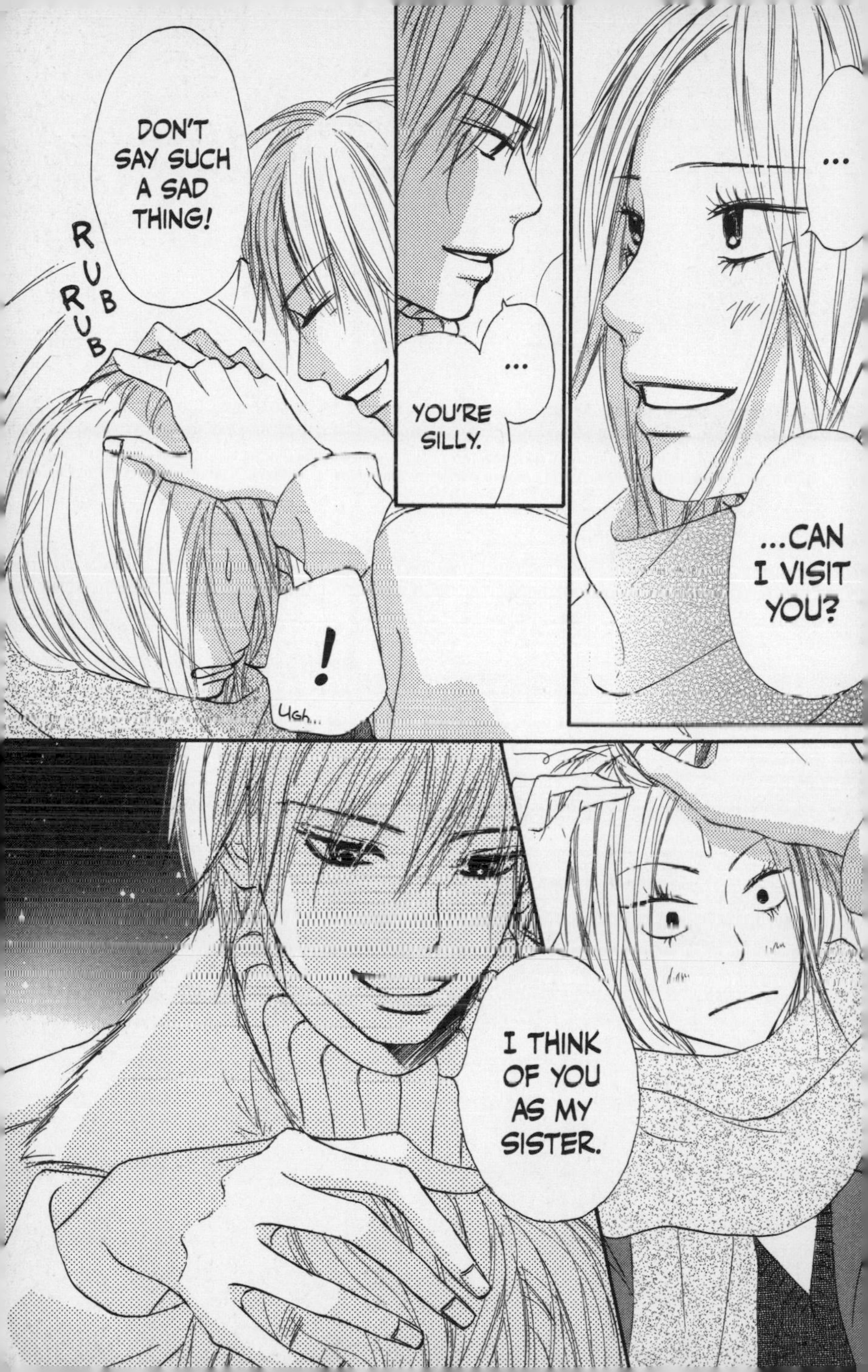
...
...CAN I VISIT YOU?
...
YOU'RE SILLY.
DON'T SAY SUCH A SAD THING!
RUB RUB
!
Ugh...
I THINK OF YOU AS MY SISTER.

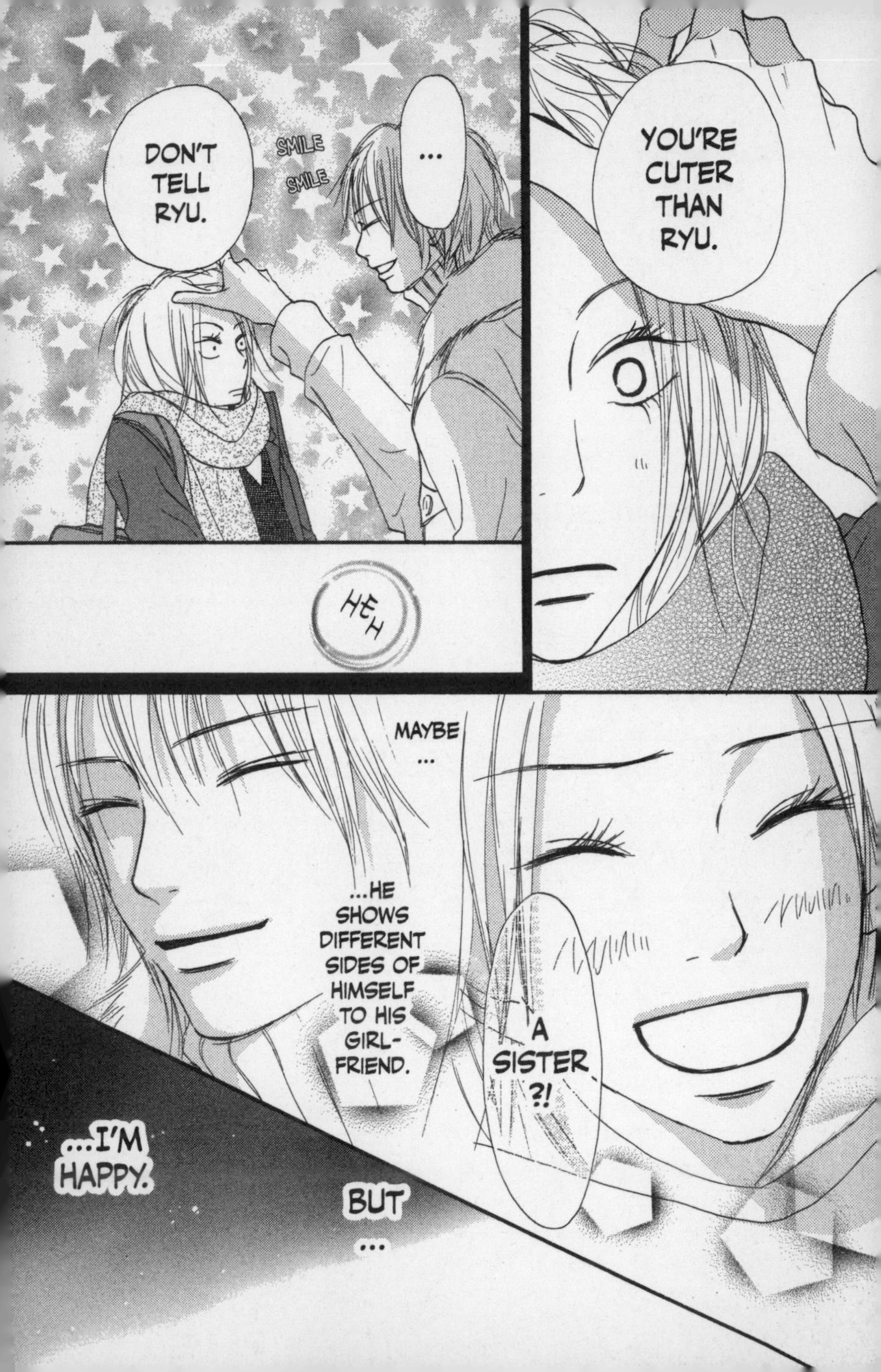
YOU'RE CUTER THAN RYU.
...
SMILE
SMILE
DON'T TELL RYU.
HEH
MAYBE ...
...HE SHOWS DIFFERENT SIDES OF HIMSELF TO HIS GIRL-FRIEND.
A SISTER?!
...I'M HAPPY.
BUT ...

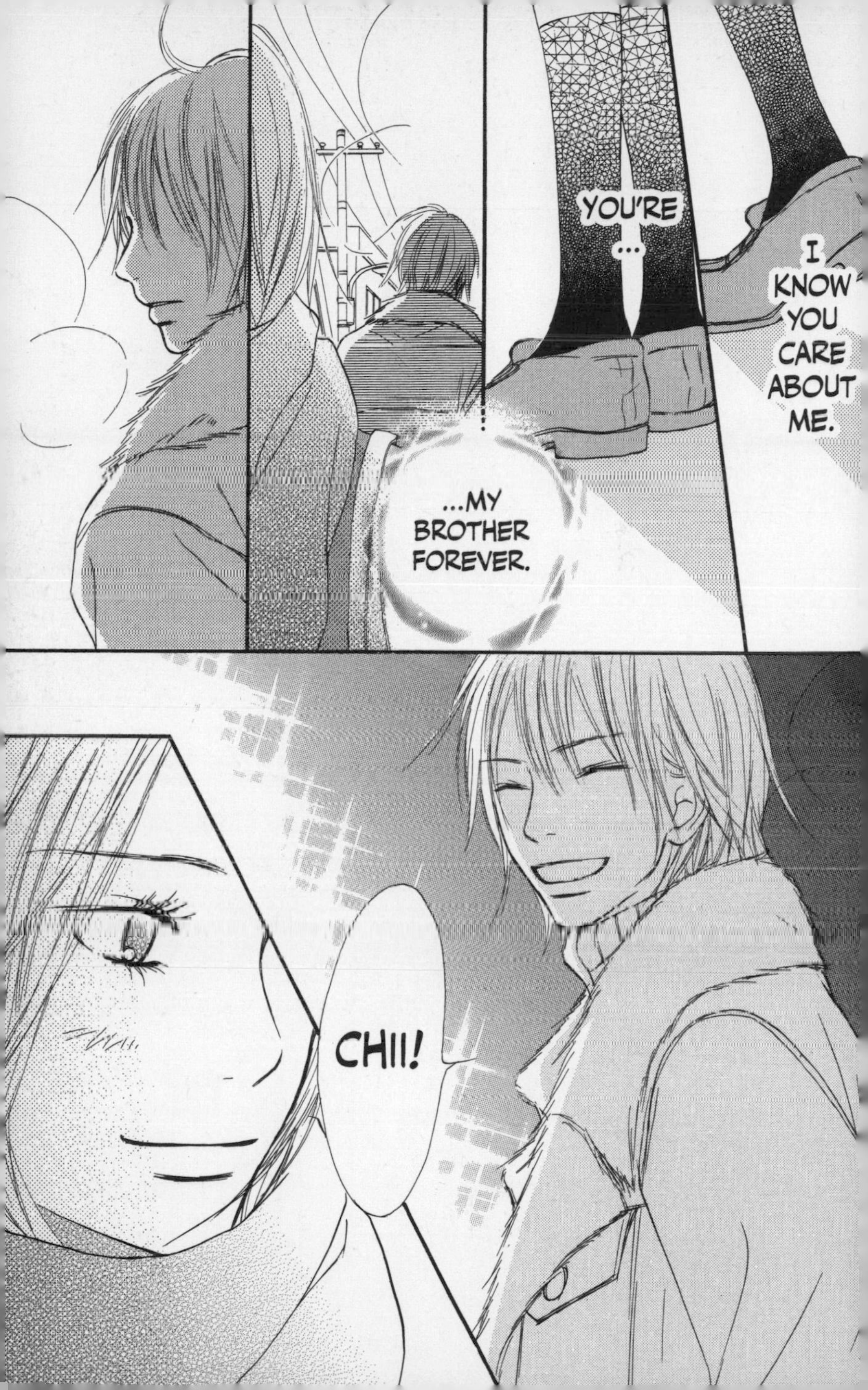
I KNOW YOU CARE ABOUT ME.
YOU'RE ...
...MY BROTHER FOREVER.
CHII!

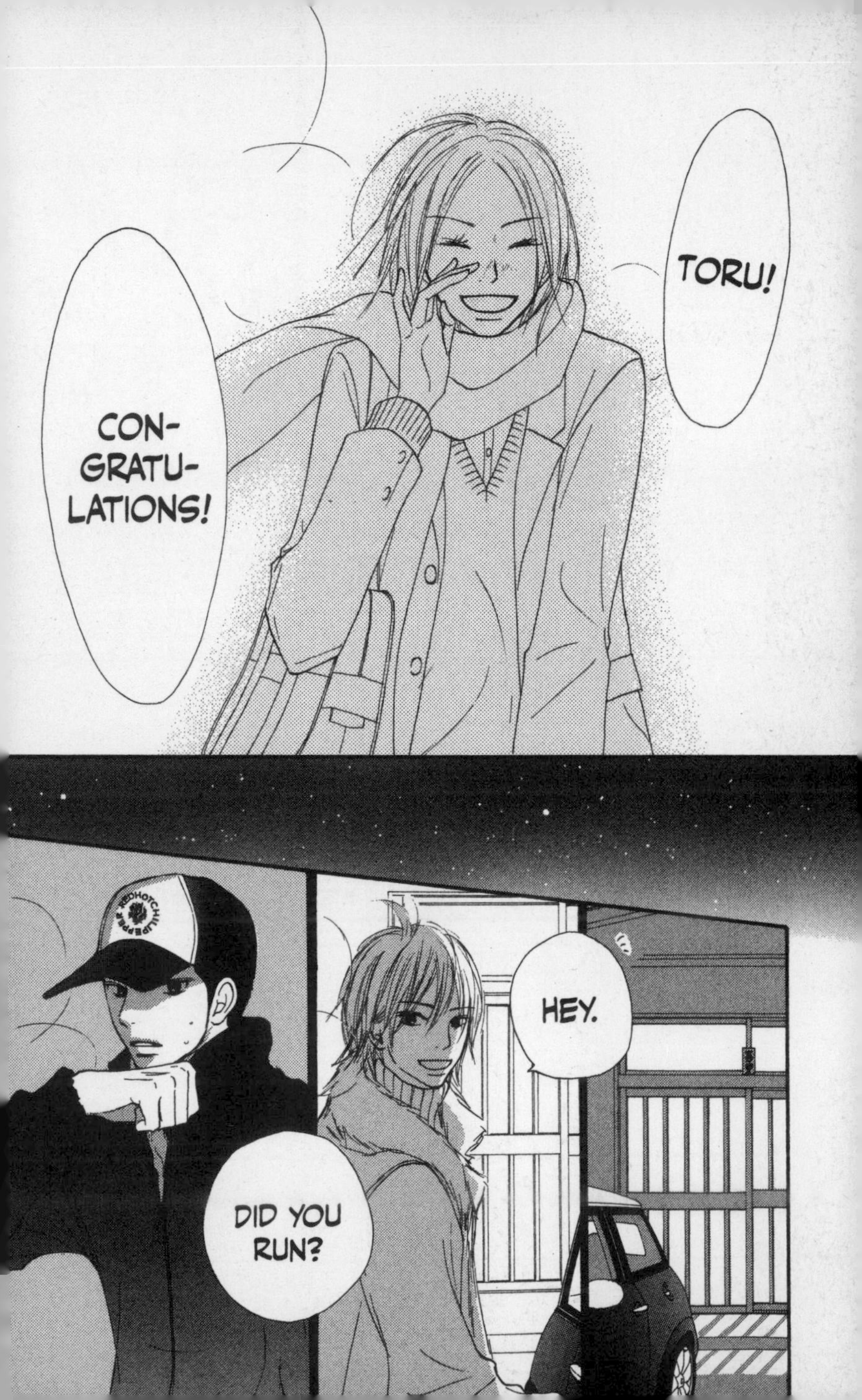
TORU!
CON-GRATU-LATIONS!
HEY.
DID YOU RUN?

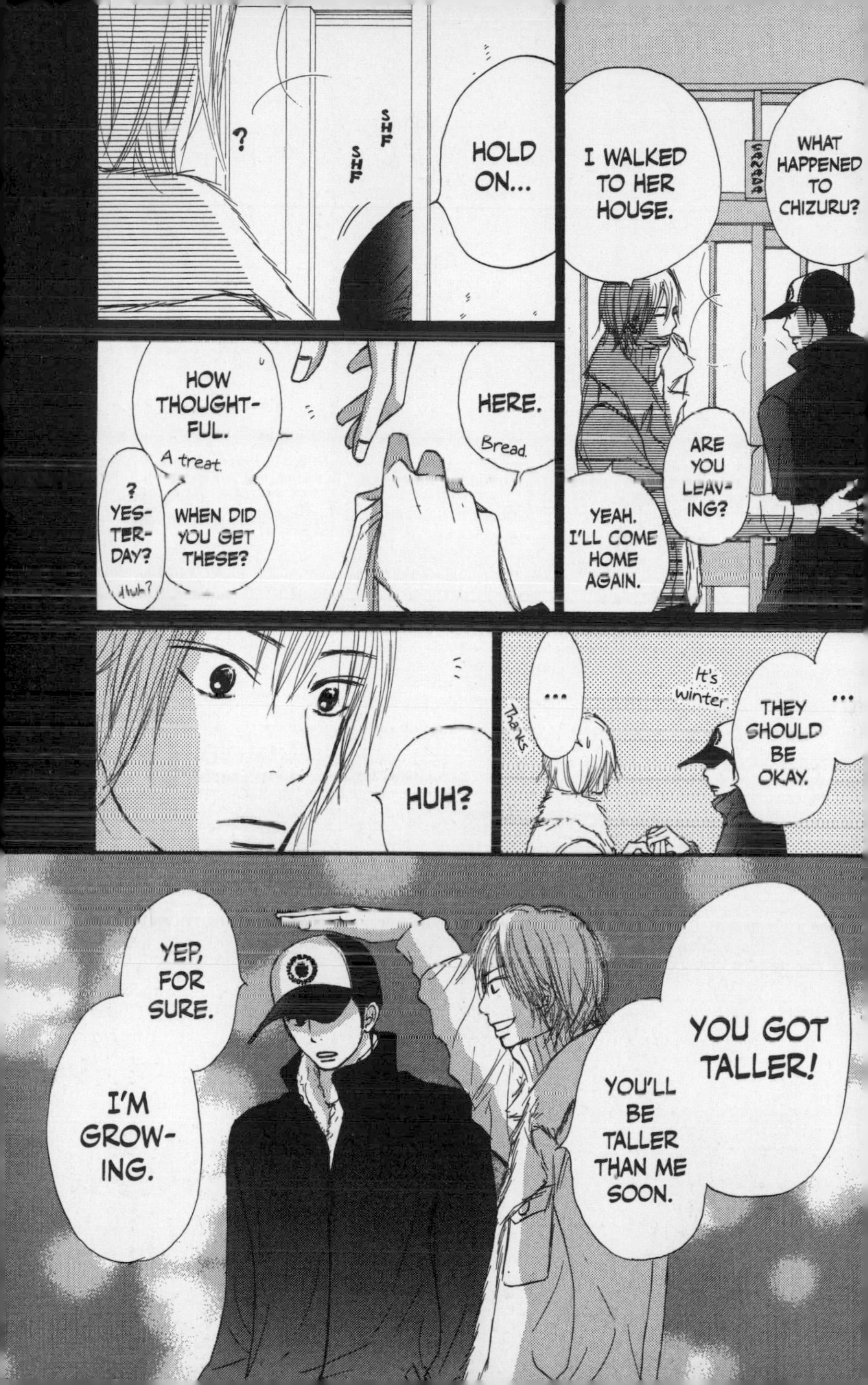
WHAT HAPPENED TO CHIZURU?
I WALKED TO HER HOUSE.
ARE YOU LEAVING?
YEAH. I'LL COME HOME AGAIN.
HOLD ON...
SHF SHF
?
HERE.
Bread.
HOW THOUGHTFUL.
A treat.
WHEN DID YOU GET THESE?
? YESTERDAY?
Huh?
...
THEY SHOULD BE OKAY.
It's winter.
...
Thanks
HUH?
YOU GOT TALLER!
YOU'LL BE TALLER THAN ME SOON.
YEP, FOR SURE.
I'M GROWING.

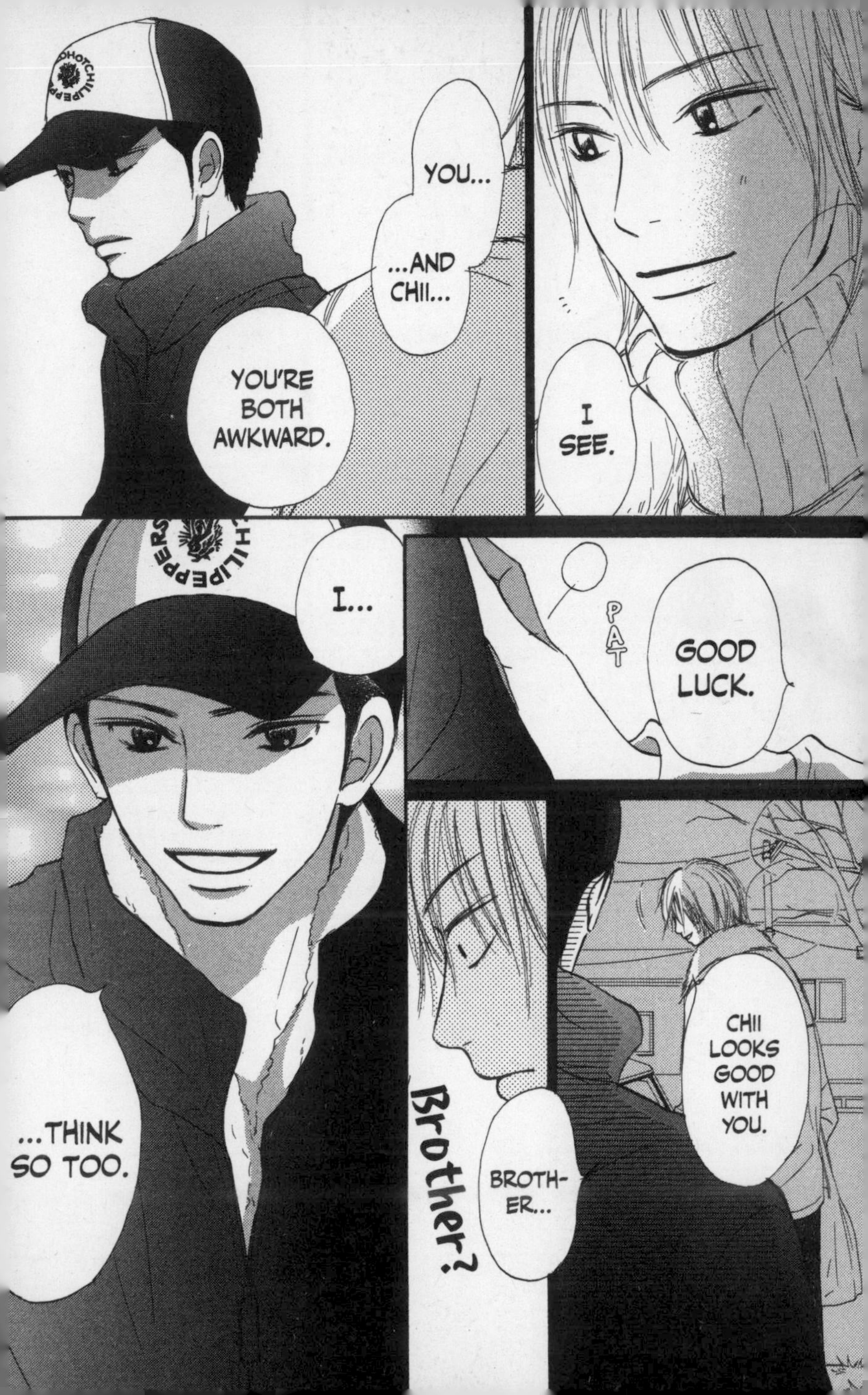
I SEE.
YOU...
...AND CHII...
YOU'RE BOTH AWKWARD.
PAT
GOOD LUCK.
CHII LOOKS GOOD WITH YOU.
BROTH-ER...
Brother?
I...
...THINK SO TOO.

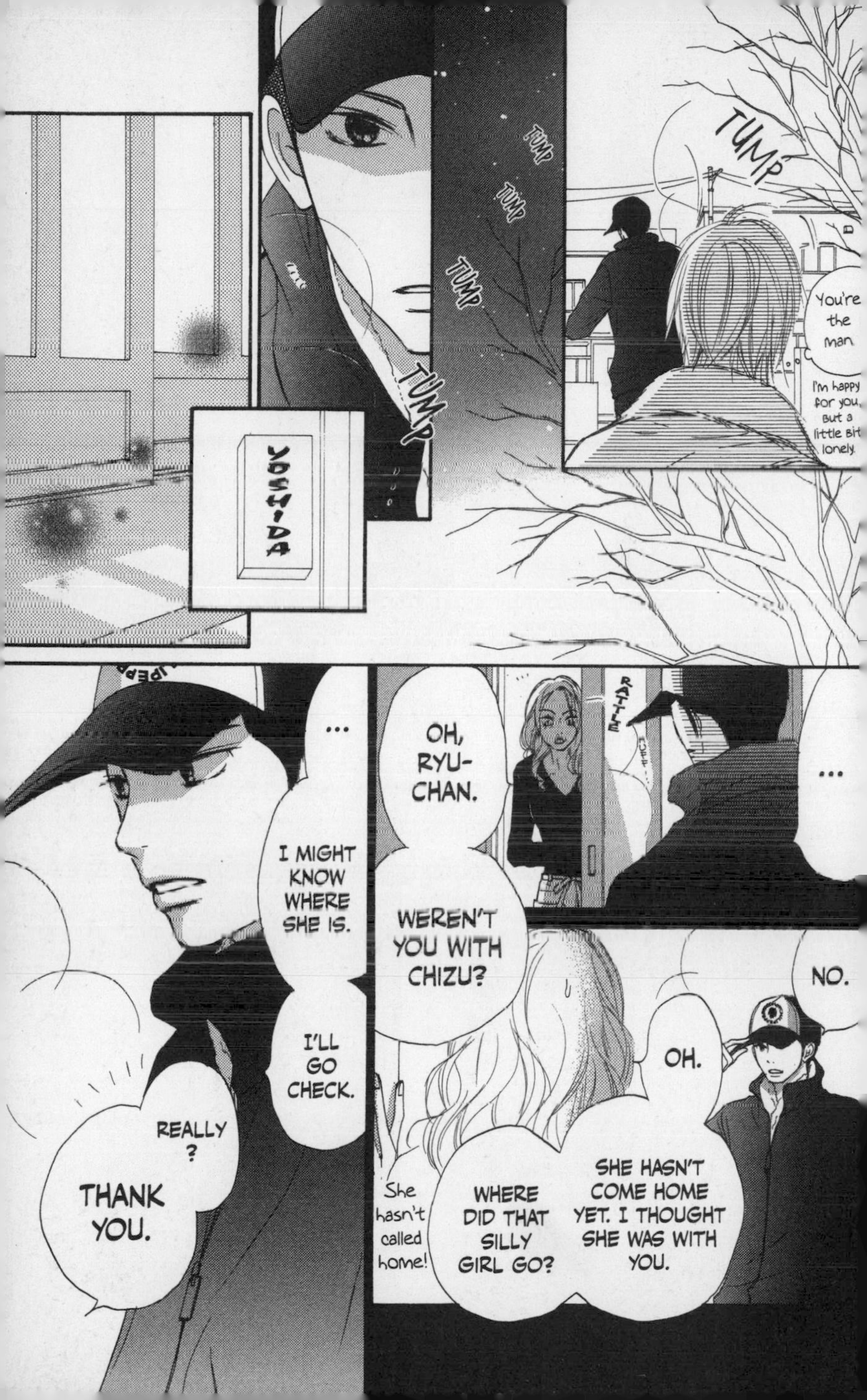

TUMP
You're the man.
I'm happy for you. But a little bit lonely.
TUMP
TUMP
TUMP
TUMP
YOSHIDA
RATTLE
HUFF...
...
OH, RYU-CHAN.
WEREN'T YOU WITH CHIZU?
NO.
OH.
SHE HASN'T COME HOME YET. I THOUGHT SHE WAS WITH YOU.
WHERE DID THAT SILLY GIRL GO?
She hasn't called home!
...
I MIGHT KNOW WHERE SHE IS.
I'LL GO CHECK.
REALLY?
THANK YOU.

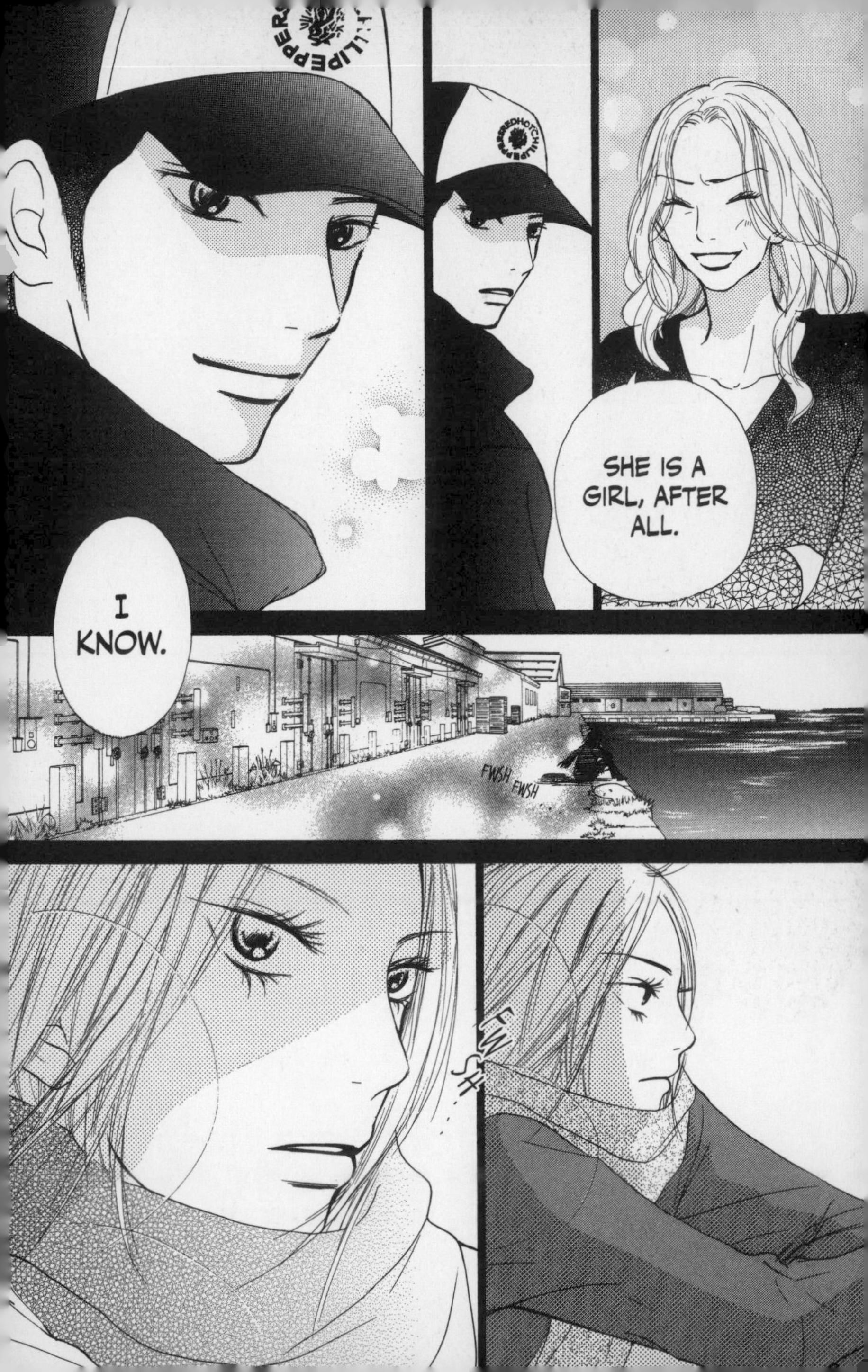
SHE IS A GIRL, AFTER ALL.
I KNOW.
FWSH FWSH
FWSH...

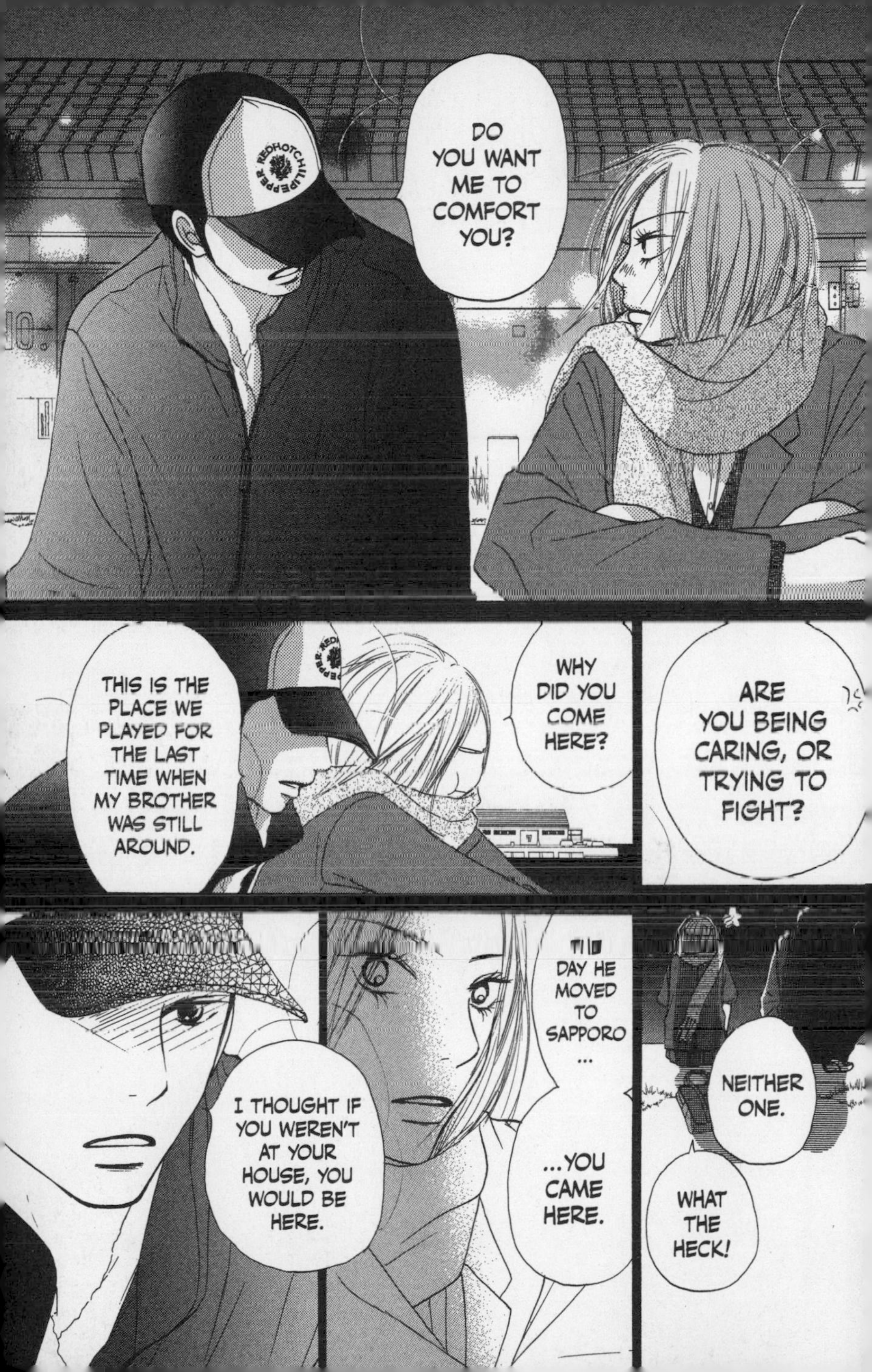
DO YOU WANT ME TO COMFORT YOU?
ARE YOU BEING CARING, OR TRYING TO FIGHT?
WHY DID YOU COME HERE?
THIS IS THE PLACE WE PLAYED FOR THE LAST TIME WHEN MY BROTHER WAS STILL AROUND.
NEITHER ONE.
WHAT THE HECK!
DAY HE MOVED TO SAPPORO ...
...YOU CAME HERE.
I THOUGHT IF YOU WEREN'T AT YOUR HOUSE, YOU WOULD BE HERE.

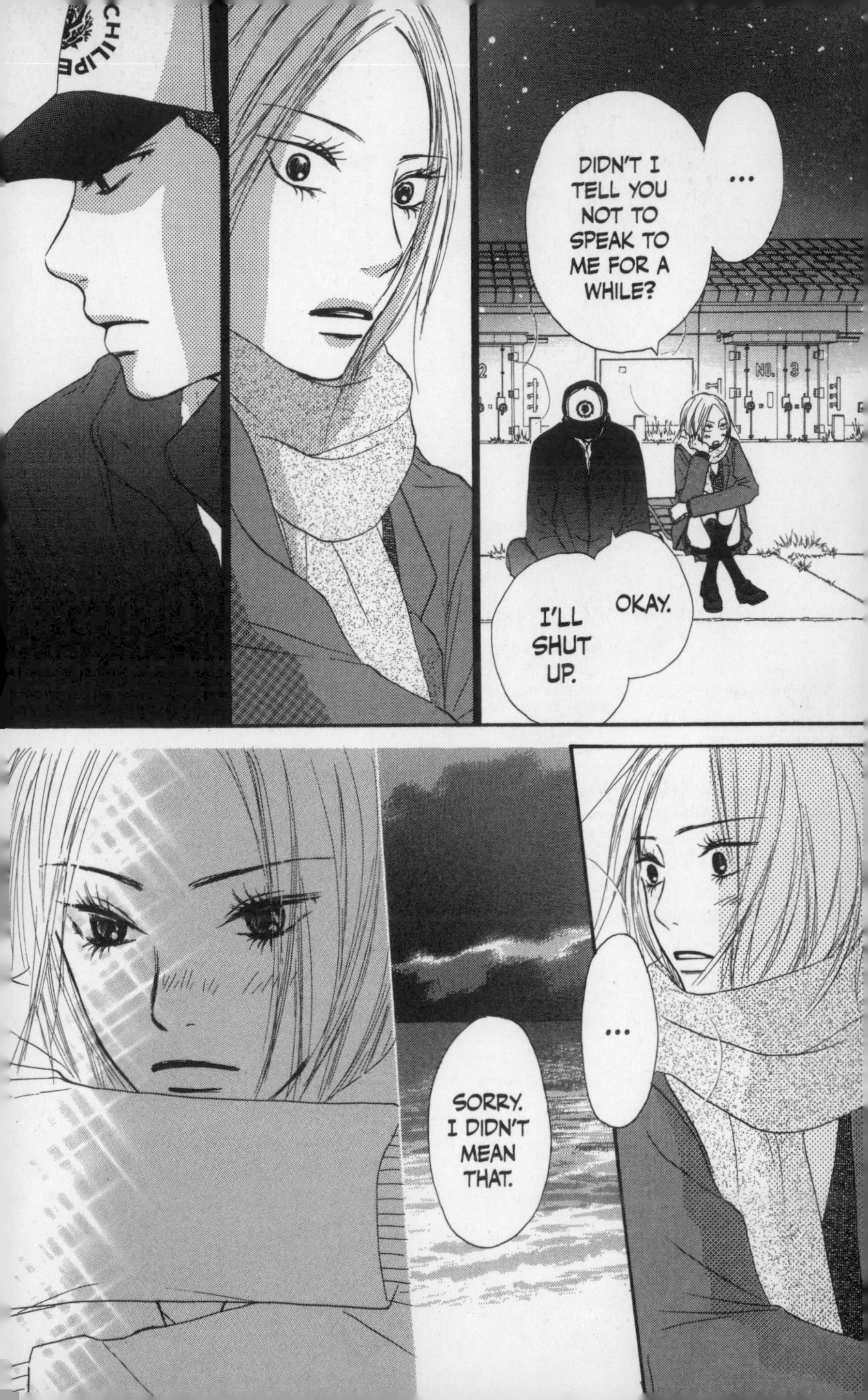
...
DIDN'T I TELL YOU NOT TO SPEAK TO ME FOR A WHILE?
OKAY.
I'LL SHUT UP.
CHILIPE
...
SORRY. I DIDN'T MEAN THAT.

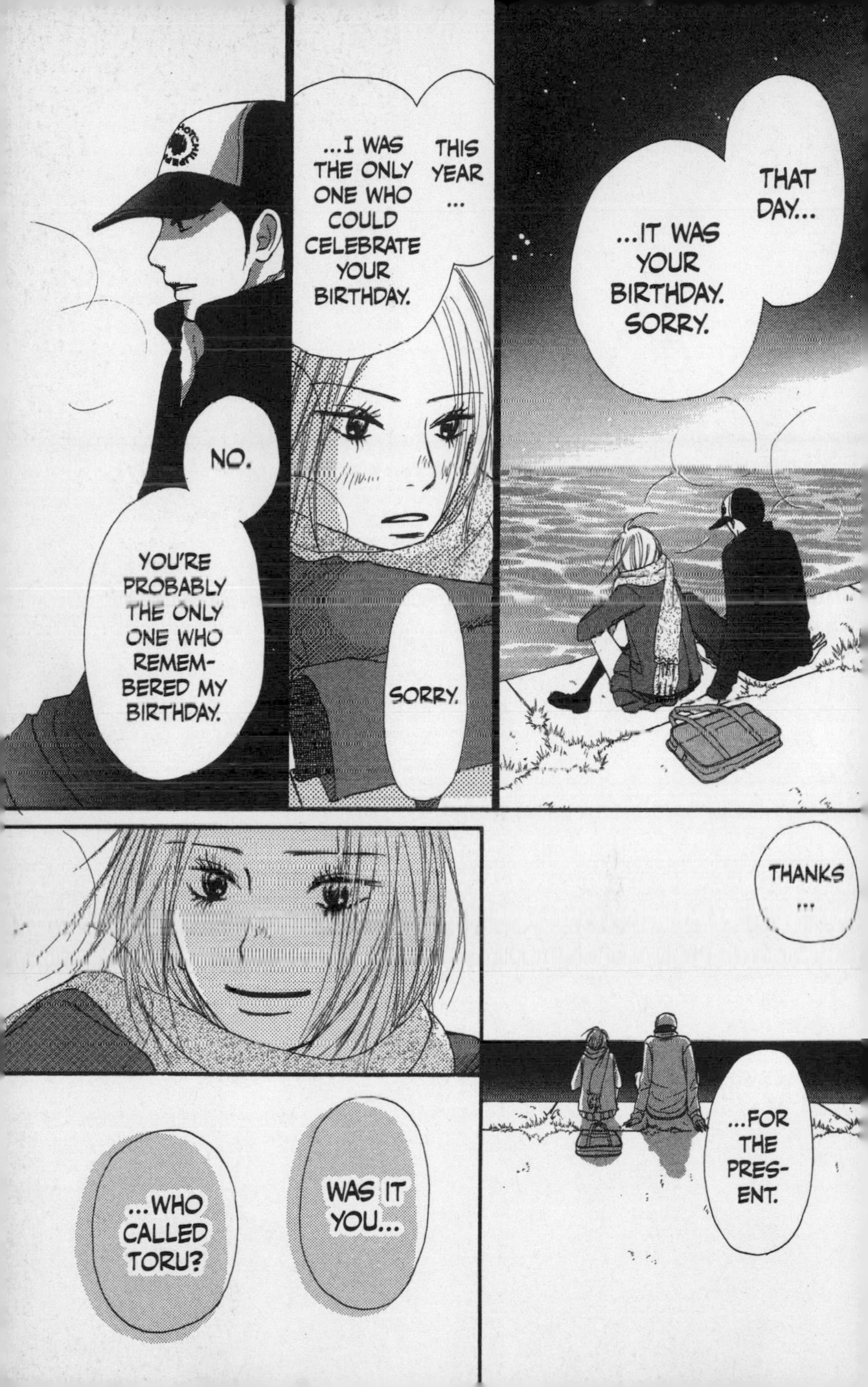
THAT DAY...
...IT WAS YOUR BIRTHDAY. SORRY.
THIS YEAR...
...I WAS THE ONLY ONE WHO COULD CELEBRATE YOUR BIRTHDAY.
SORRY.
NO.
YOU'RE PROBABLY THE ONLY ONE WHO REMEM-BERED MY BIRTHDAY.
THANKS...
...FOR THE PRES-ENT.
WAS IT YOU...
...WHO CALLED TORU?

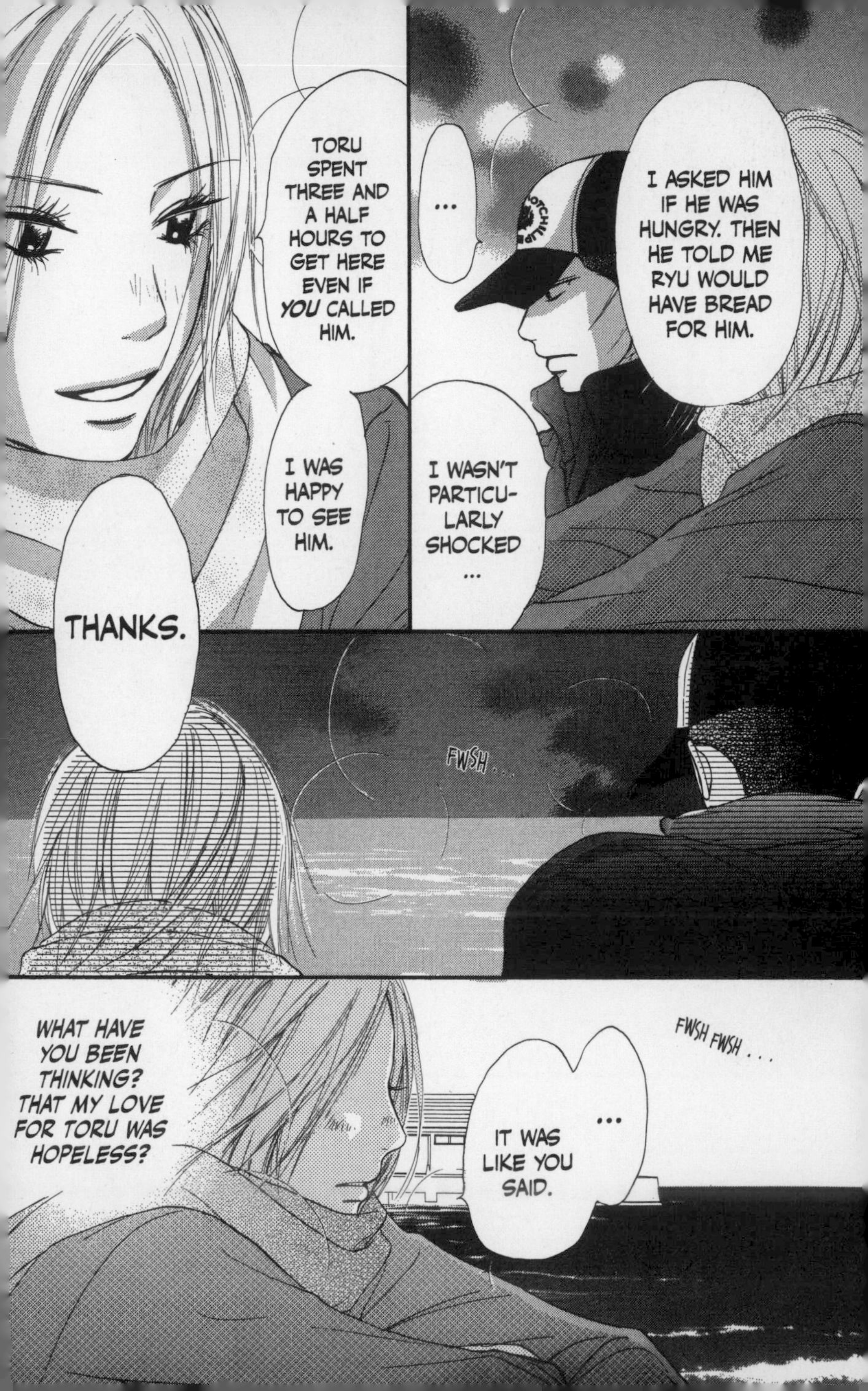
I ASKED HIM IF HE WAS HUNGRY. THEN HE TOLD ME RYU WOULD HAVE BREAD FOR HIM.
...
I WASN'T PARTICU-LARLY SHOCKED ...
TORU SPENT THREE AND A HALF HOURS TO GET HERE EVEN IF *YOU* CALLED HIM.
I WAS HAPPY TO SEE HIM.
THANKS.
FWSH . . .
FWSH FWSH . . .
...
IT WAS LIKE YOU SAID.
WHAT HAVE YOU BEEN THINKING? THAT MY LOVE FOR TORU WAS HOPELESS?

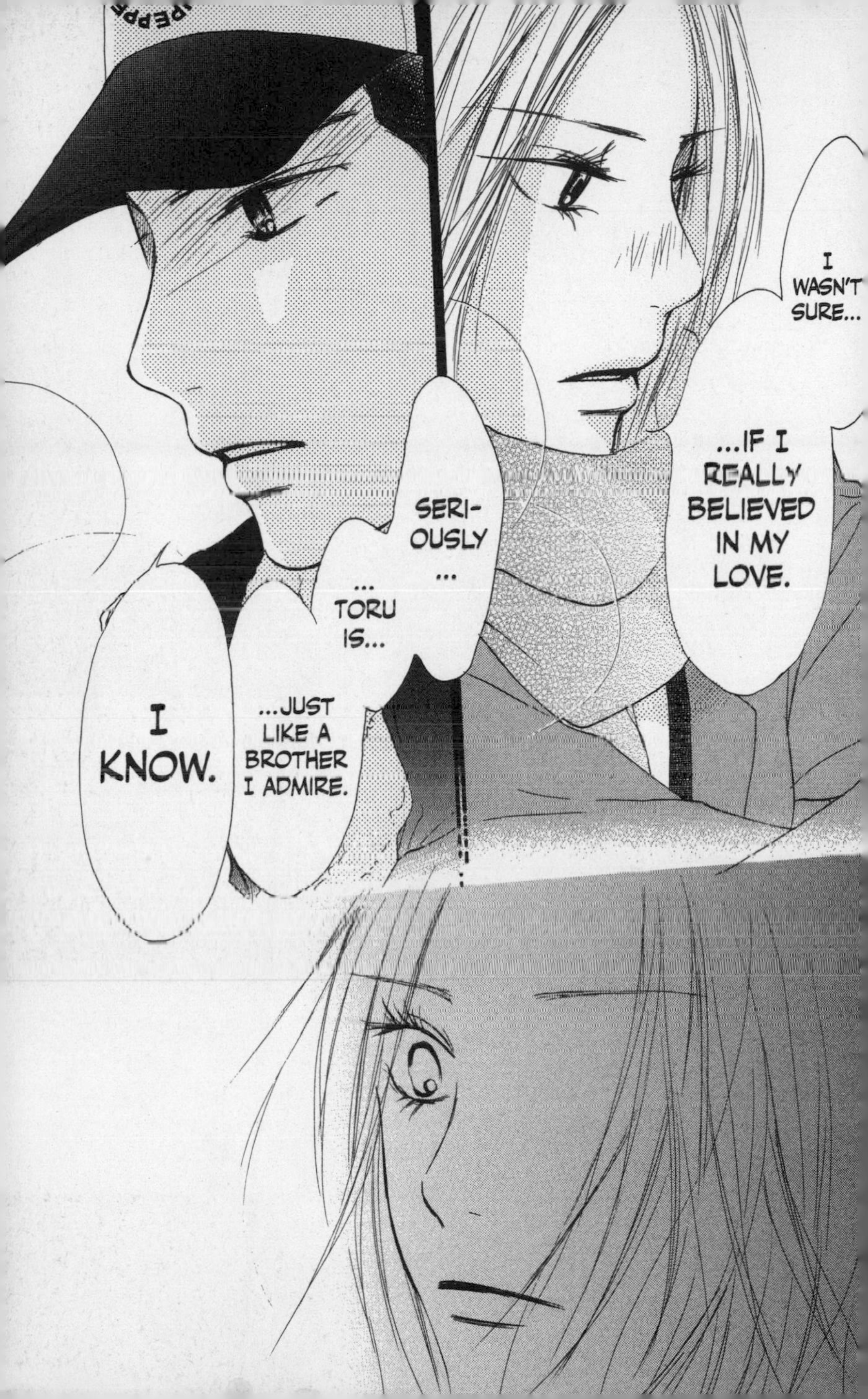
I WASN'T SURE...
...IF I REALLY BELIEVED IN MY LOVE.
SERI-OUSLY...
...TORU IS...
...JUST LIKE A BROTHER I ADMIRE.
I KNOW.

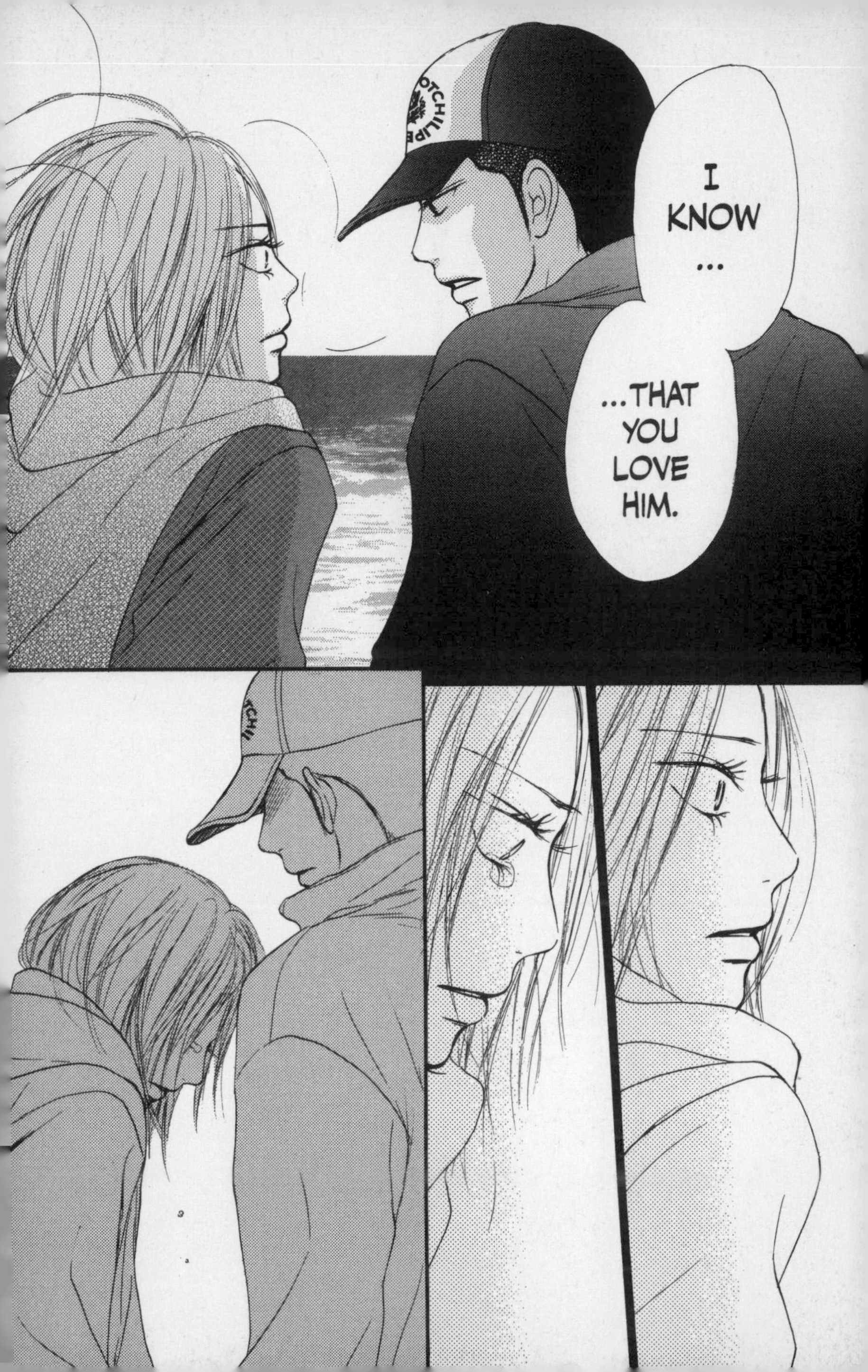
I KNOW ...
...THAT YOU LOVE HIM.

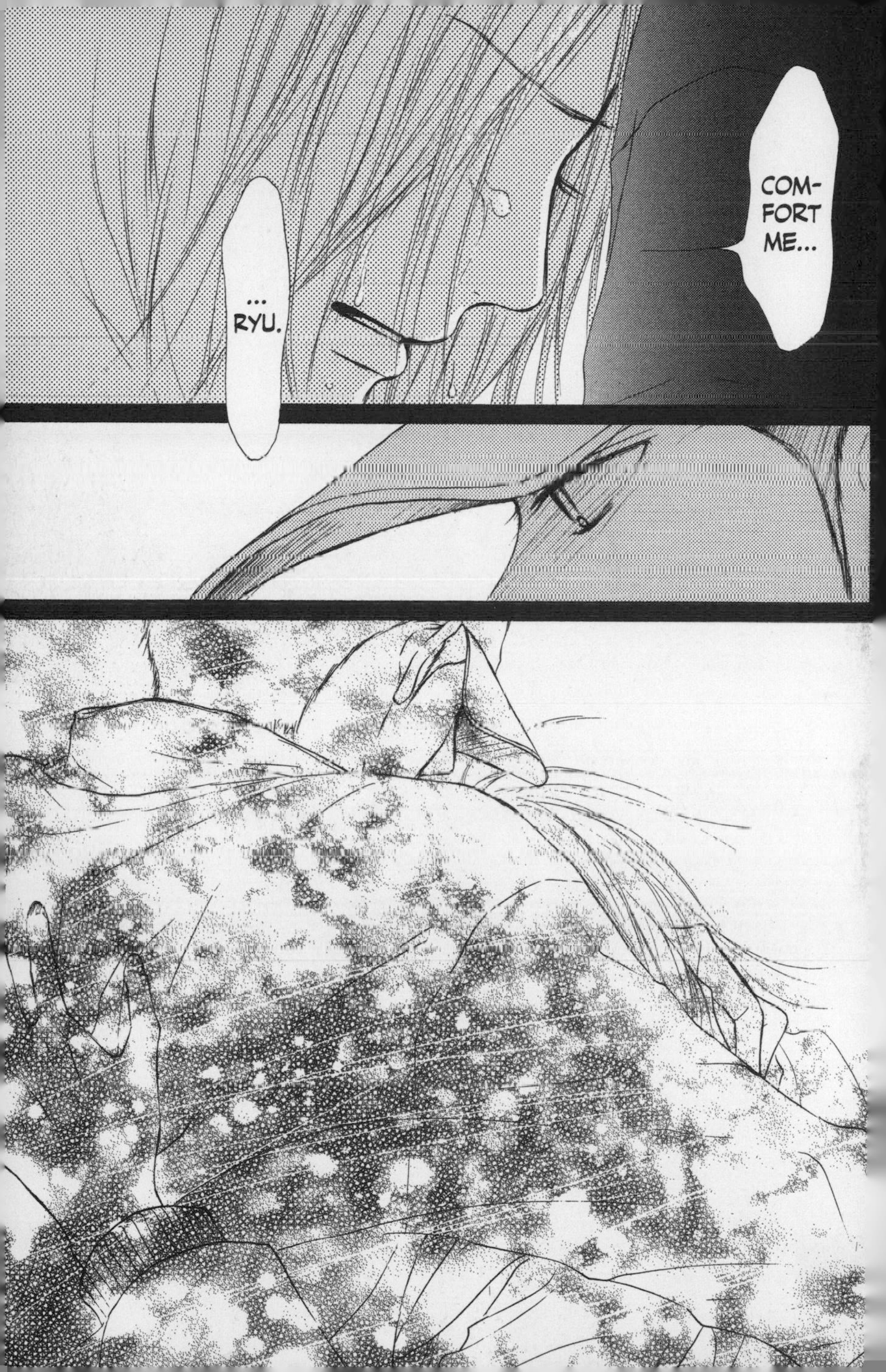
COM-FORT ME...
... RYU.

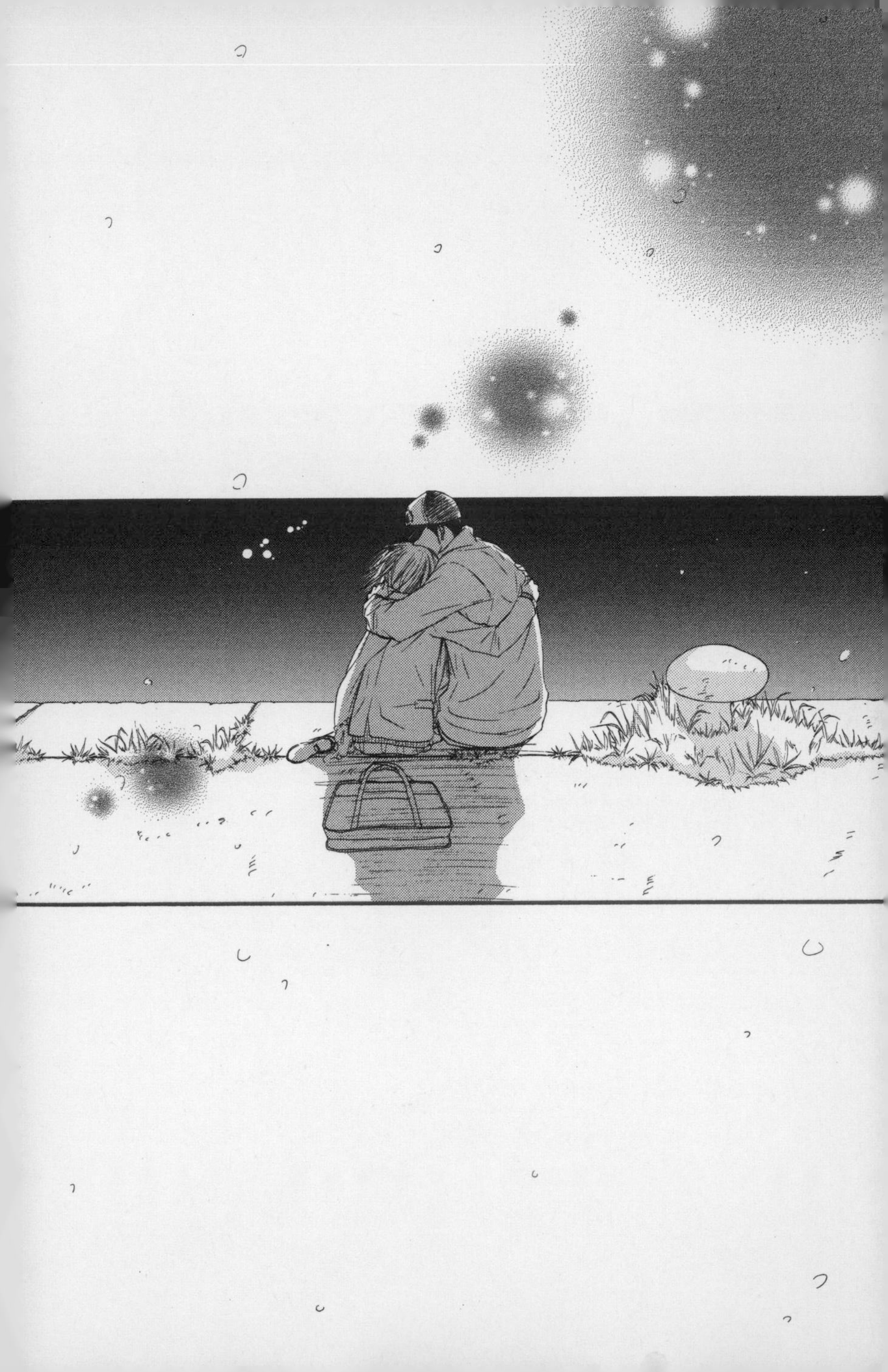

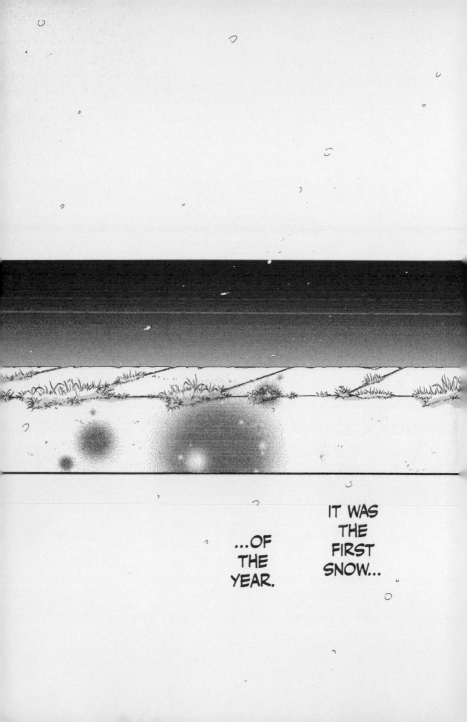

IT WAS
THE
FIRST
SNOW...

...OF
THE
YEAR.

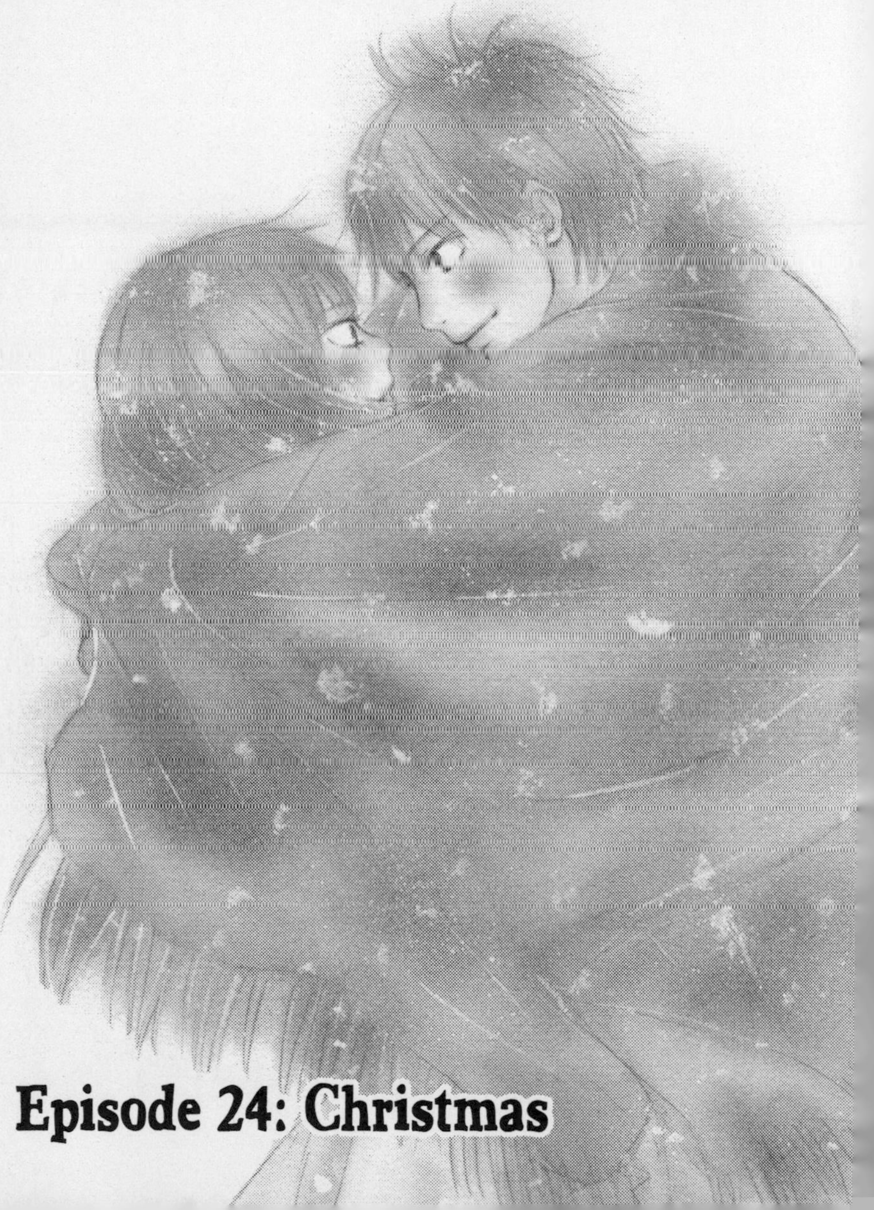

Episode 24: Christmas

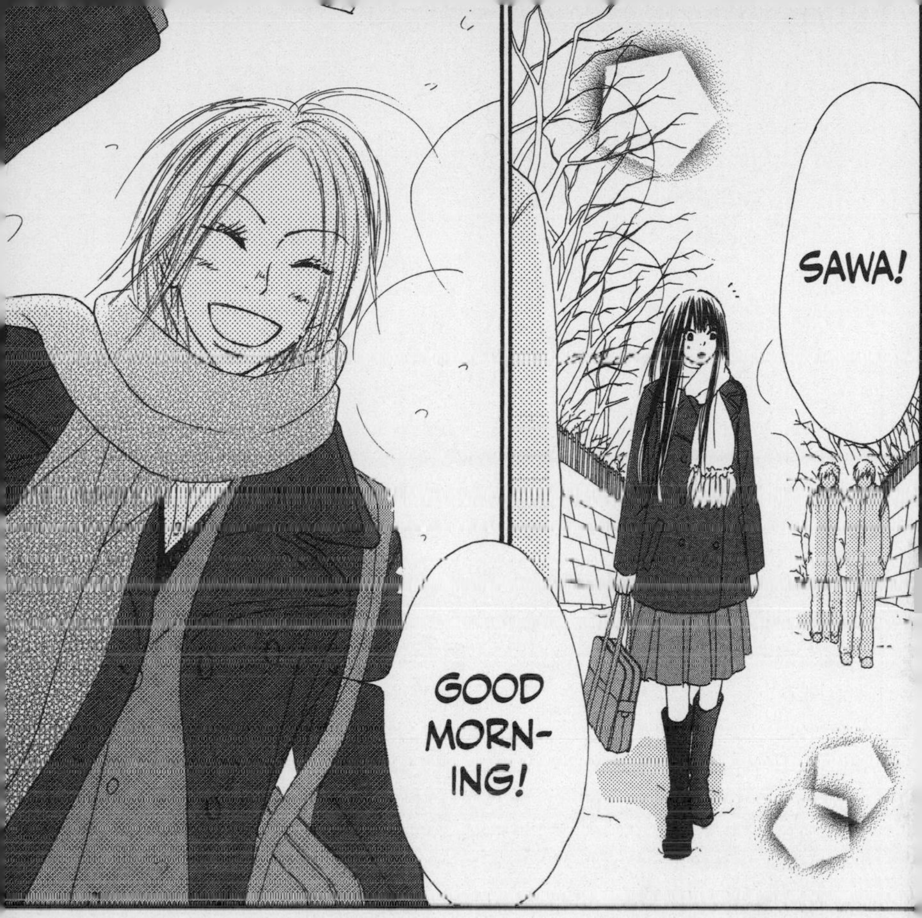
SAWA!
GOOD MORNING!

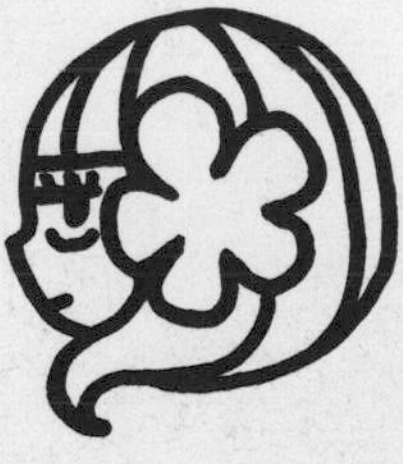

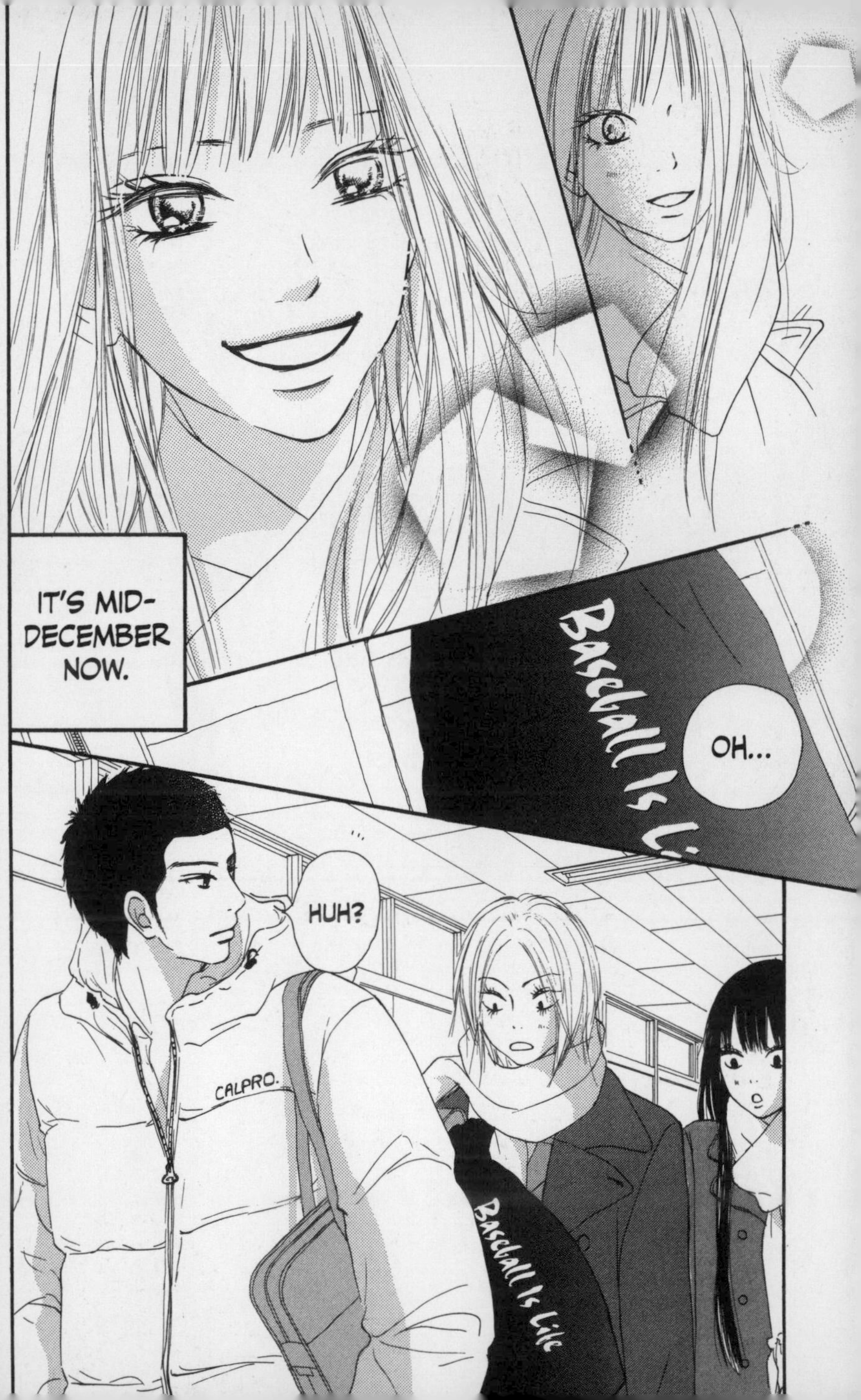
IT'S MID-DECEMBER NOW.
OH...
HUH?
CALPRO.
Baseball Is Life

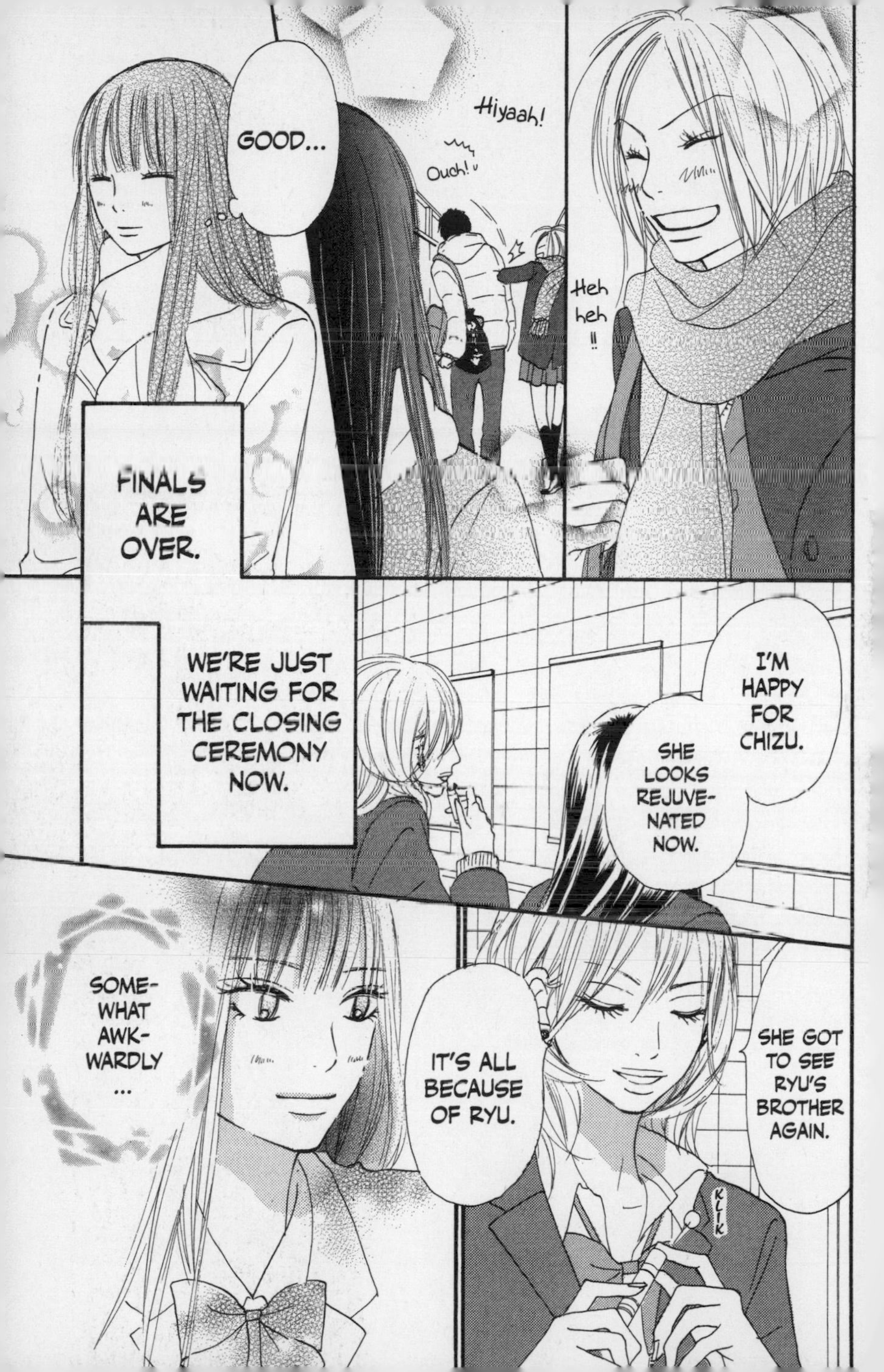
Heh heh !!
Hiyaah!
Ouch!
GOOD...
FINALS ARE OVER.
I'M HAPPY FOR CHIZU.
SHE LOOKS REJUVE-NATED NOW.
WE'RE JUST WAITING FOR THE CLOSING CEREMONY NOW.
SHE GOT TO SEE RYU'S BROTHER AGAIN.
KLIK
IT'S ALL BECAUSE OF RYU.
SOME-WHAT AWK-WARDLY ...

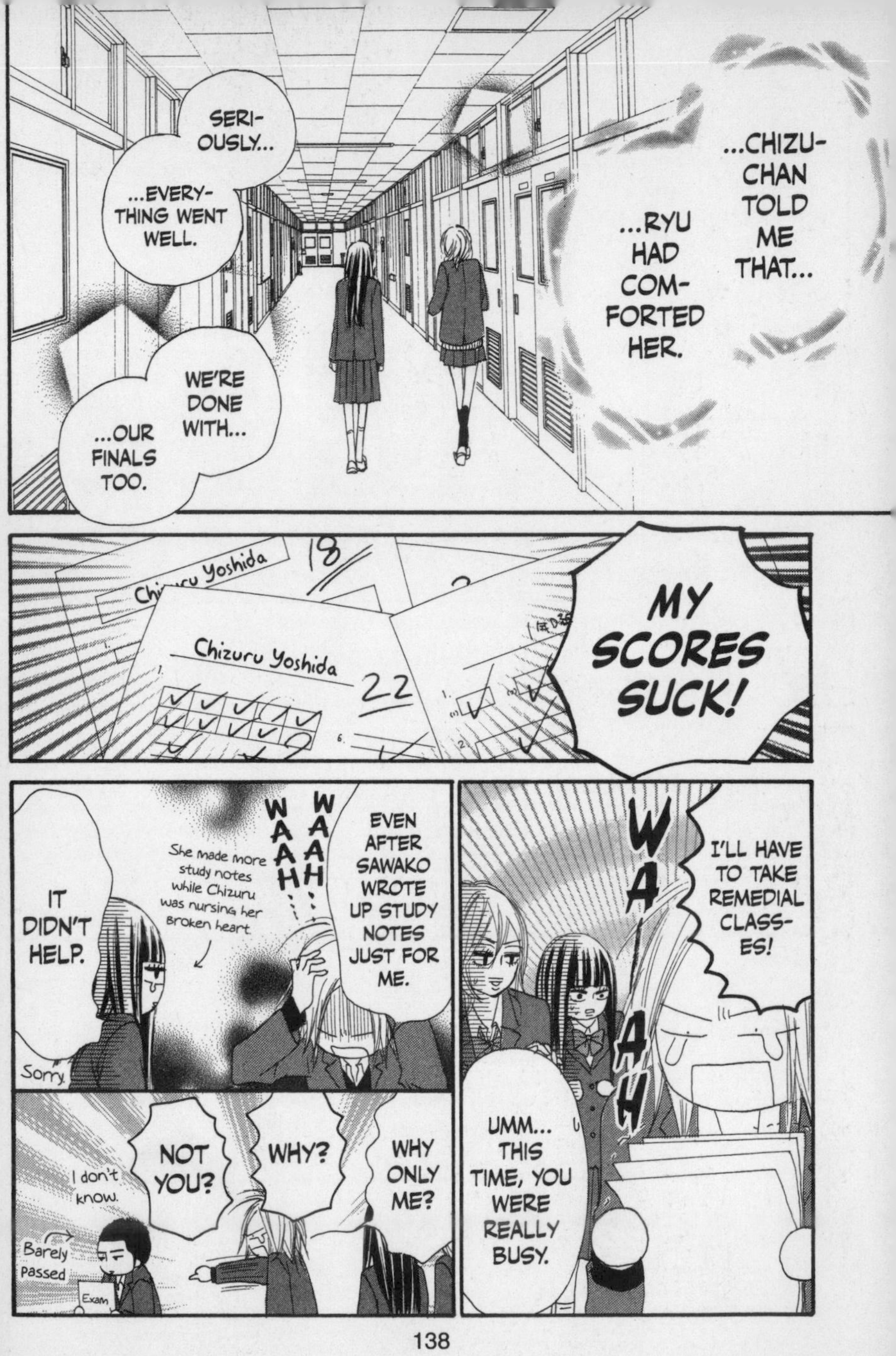
...CHIZU-CHAN TOLD ME THAT...
...RYU HAD COMFORTED HER.
SERIOUSLY...
...EVERYTHING WENT WELL.
WE'RE DONE WITH...
...OUR FINALS TOO.
MY SCORES SUCK!
Chizuru Yoshida
18
Chizuru Yoshida
22
WAAAH
I'LL HAVE TO TAKE REMEDIAL CLASSES!
UMM... THIS TIME, YOU WERE REALLY BUSY.
EVEN AFTER SAWAKO WROTE UP STUDY NOTES JUST FOR ME.
WAAH...
WAAH...
She made more study notes while Chizuru was nursing her broken heart.
IT DIDN'T HELP.
Sorry.
WHY ONLY ME?
WHY?
NOT YOU?
I don't know.
Barely passed
Exam

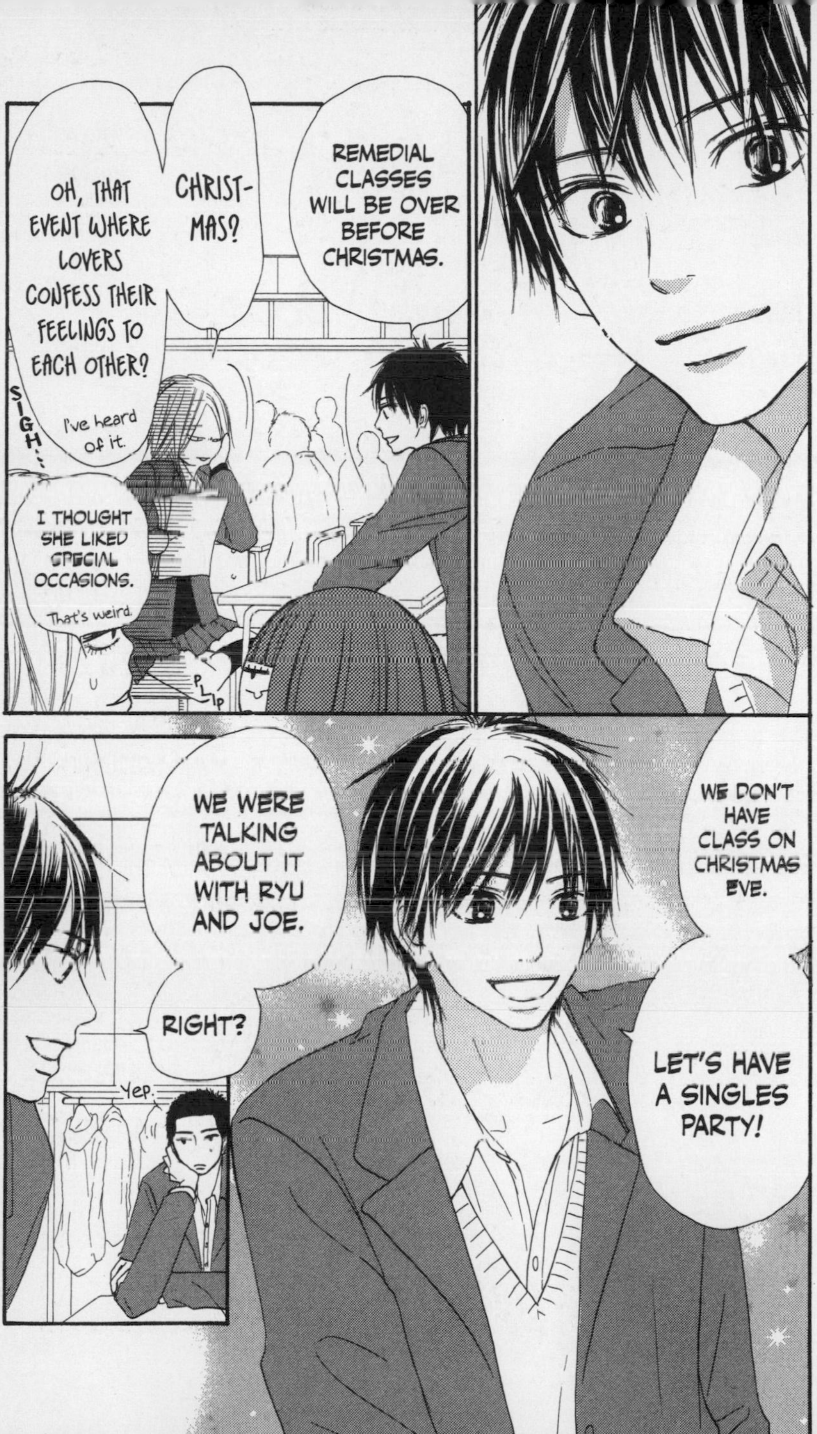
REMEDIAL CLASSES WILL BE OVER BEFORE CHRISTMAS.
CHRIST-MAS?
OH, THAT EVENT WHERE LOVERS CONFESS THEIR FEELINGS TO EACH OTHER?
SIGH...
I've heard of it.
I THOUGHT SHE LIKED SPECIAL OCCASIONS.
That's weird.
PLIP
WE DON'T HAVE CLASS ON CHRISTMAS EVE.
LET'S HAVE A SINGLES PARTY!
WE WERE TALKING ABOUT IT WITH RYU AND JOE.
RIGHT?
Yep.

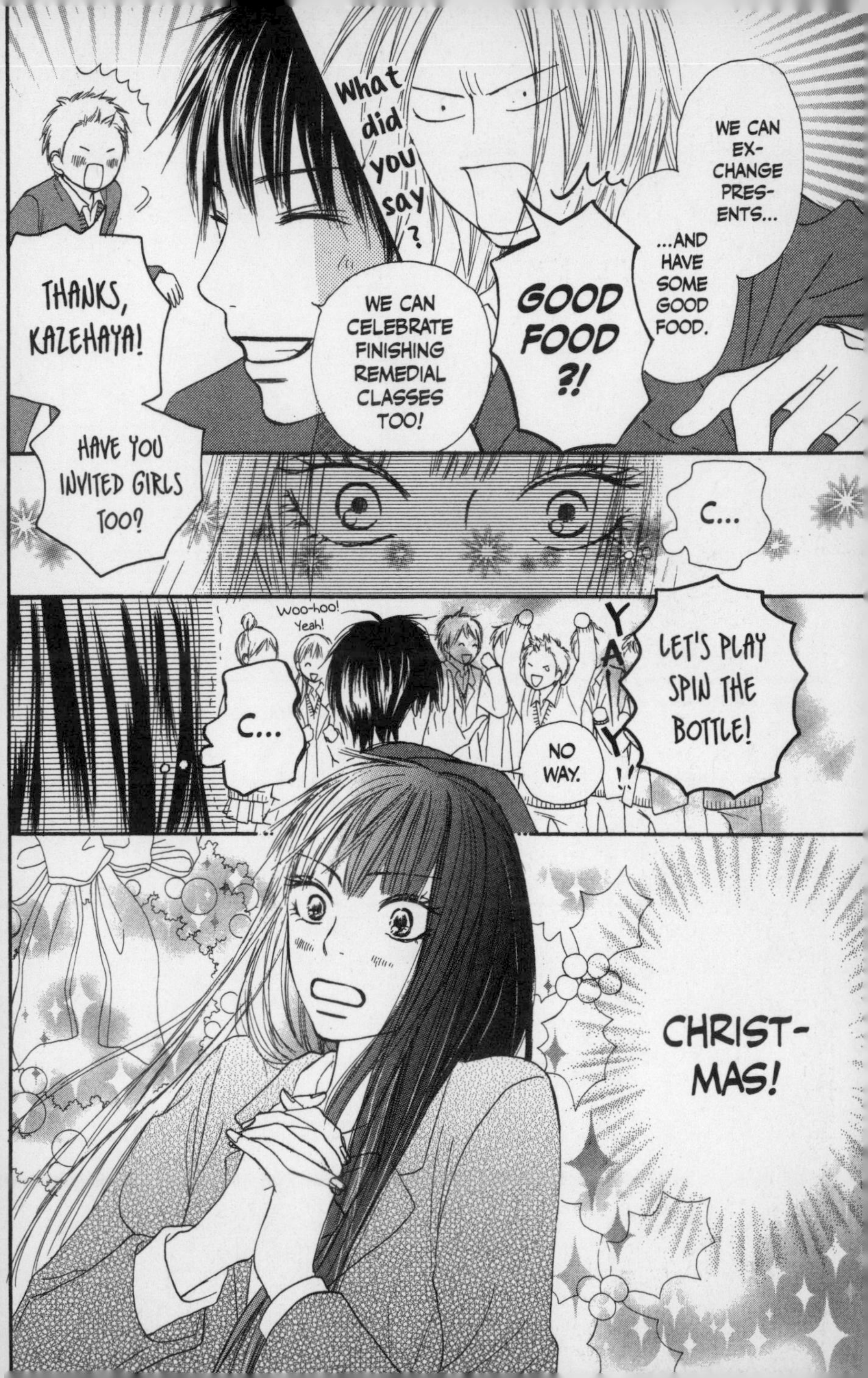
WE CAN EX-CHANGE PRES-ENTS...
...AND HAVE SOME GOOD FOOD.
GOOD FOOD ?!
What did you say?
WE CAN CELEBRATE FINISHING REMEDIAL CLASSES TOO!
THANKS, KAZEHAYA!
HAVE YOU INVITED GIRLS TOO?
C...
LET'S PLAY SPIN THE BOTTLE!
YAY!!
NO WAY.
Woo-hoo! Yeah!
C...
CHRIST-MAS!

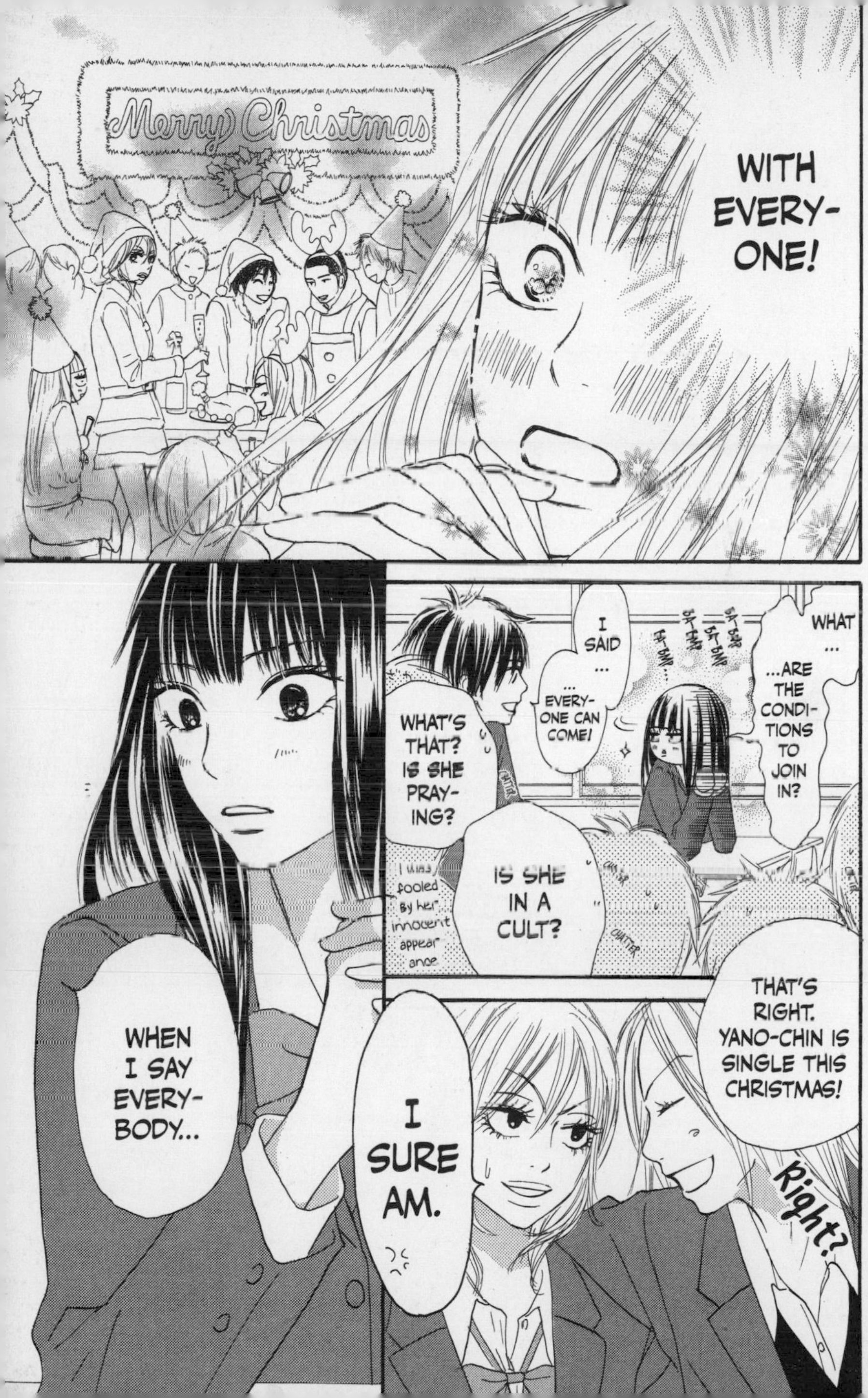
Merry Christmas
WITH EVERY-ONE!
WHAT ...
...ARE THE CONDI-TIONS TO JOIN IN?
BA-BMP BA-BMP BA-BMP...
I SAID ...
... EVERY-ONE CAN COME!
WHAT'S THAT? IS SHE PRAY-ING?
IS SHE IN A CULT?
I was fooled by her innocent appear-ance
CHATTER
THAT'S RIGHT. YANO-CHIN IS SINGLE THIS CHRISTMAS!
Right?
I SURE AM.
WHEN I SAY EVERY-BODY...

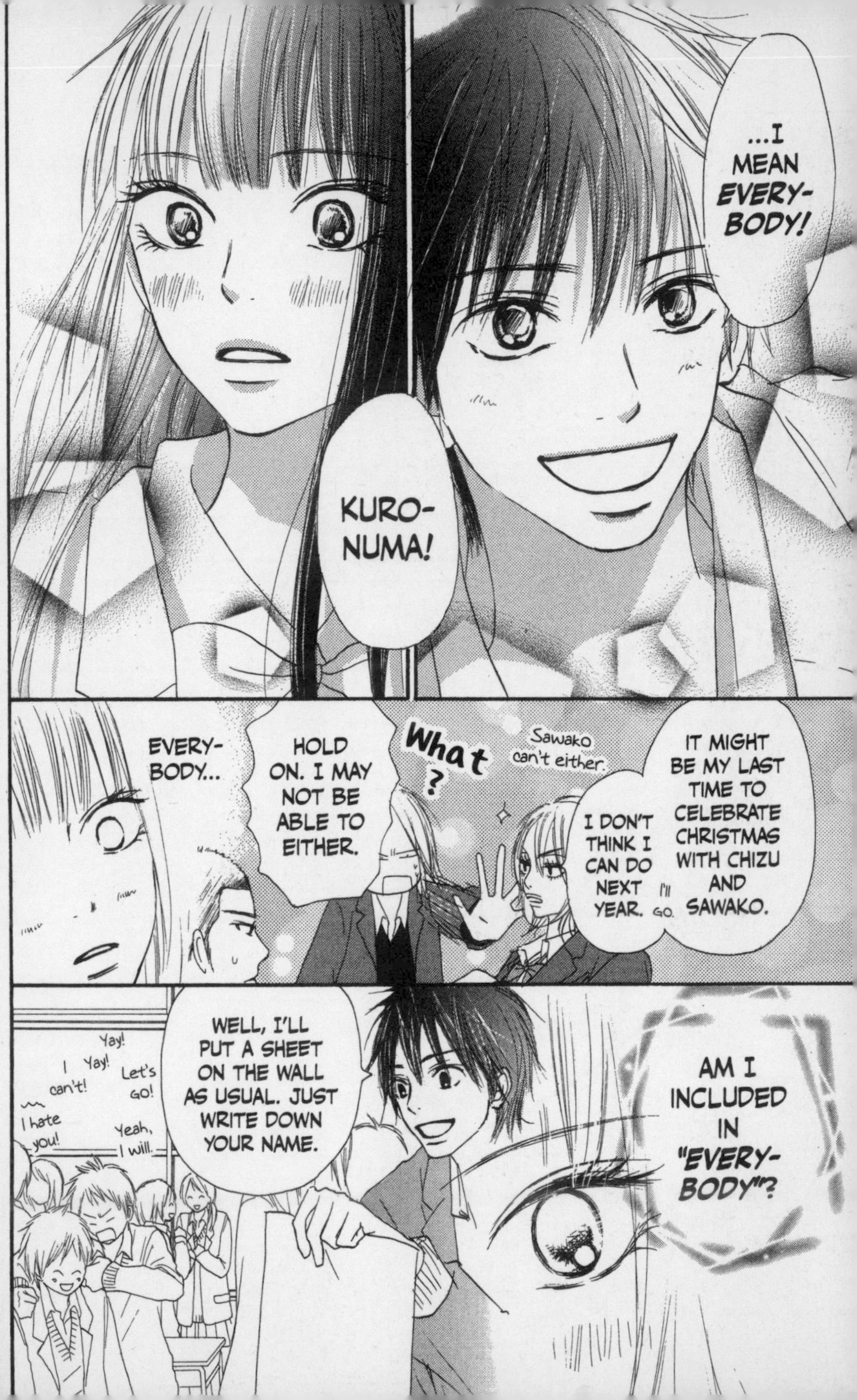
KURO-NUMA!
...I MEAN EVERY-BODY!
IT MIGHT BE MY LAST TIME TO CELEBRATE CHRISTMAS WITH CHIZU AND SAWAKO.
I'll GO.
I DON'T THINK I CAN DO NEXT YEAR.
Sawako can't either.
What?
HOLD ON. I MAY NOT BE ABLE TO EITHER.
EVERY-BODY...
AM I INCLUDED IN "EVERY-BODY"?
WELL, I'LL PUT A SHEET ON THE WALL AS USUAL. JUST WRITE DOWN YOUR NAME.
Let's go!
Yay!
Yay!
I can't!
Yeah, I will.
I hate you!

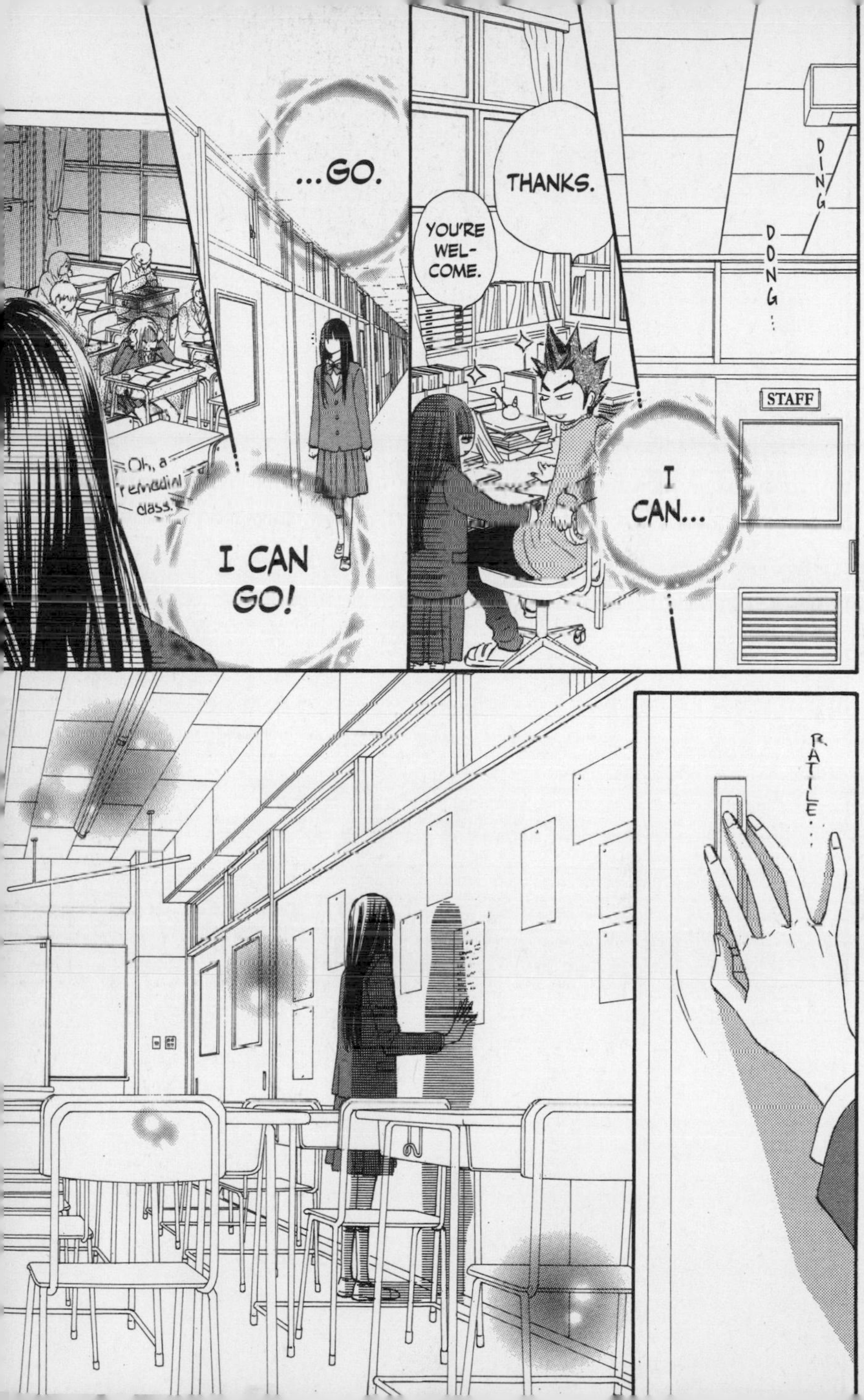
DING DONG...
THANKS.
YOU'RE WEL-COME.
I CAN...
...GO.
Oh, a remedial class.
I CAN GO!
RATTLE...

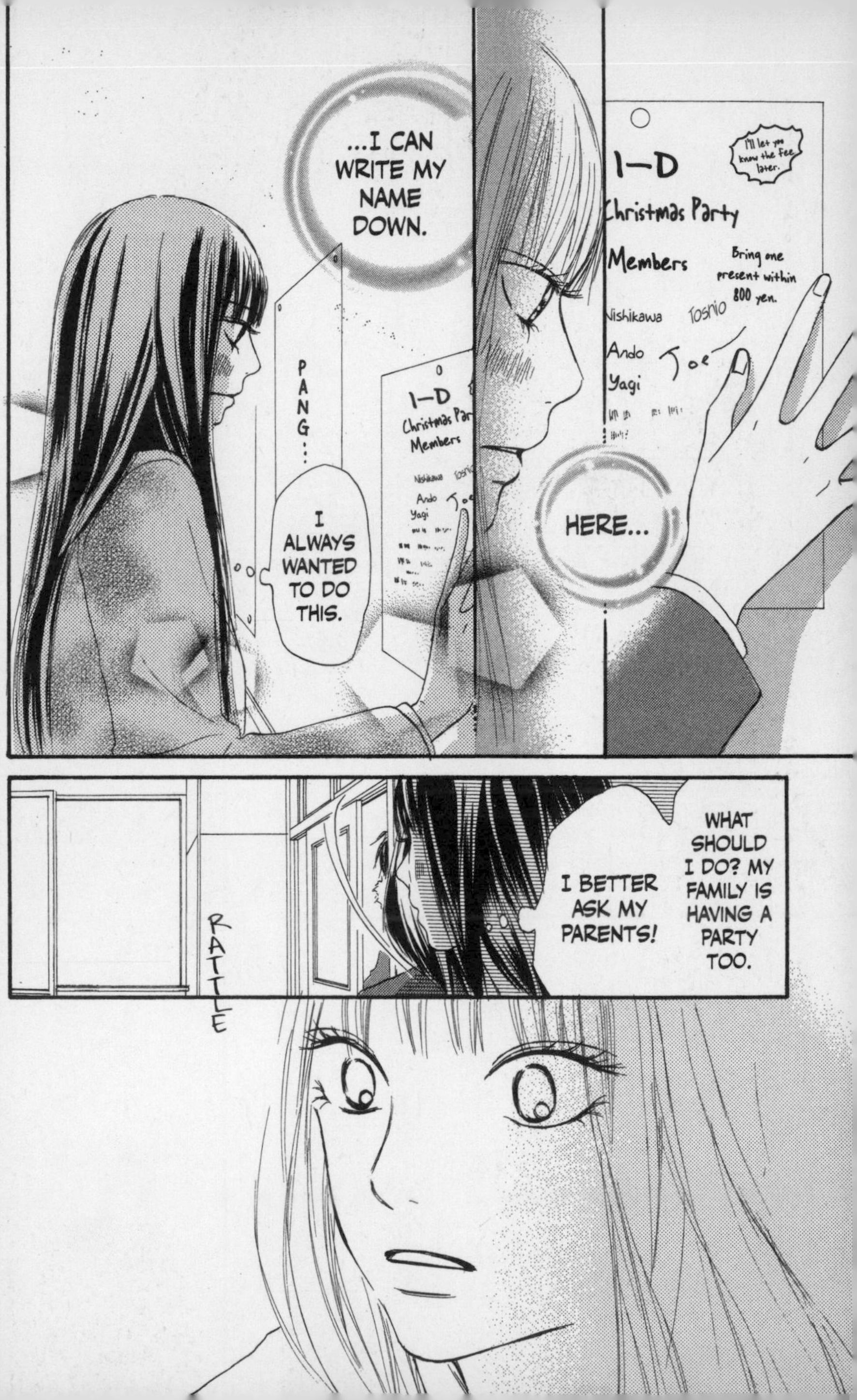

1-D
Christmas Party Members
I'll let you know the fee later.
Bring one present within 800 yen.
Nishikawa Toshio
Ando Joe
Yagi
HERE...
...I CAN WRITE MY NAME DOWN.
PANG...
I ALWAYS WANTED TO DO THIS.
WHAT SHOULD I DO? MY FAMILY IS HAVING A PARTY TOO.
I BETTER ASK MY PARENTS!
RATTLE

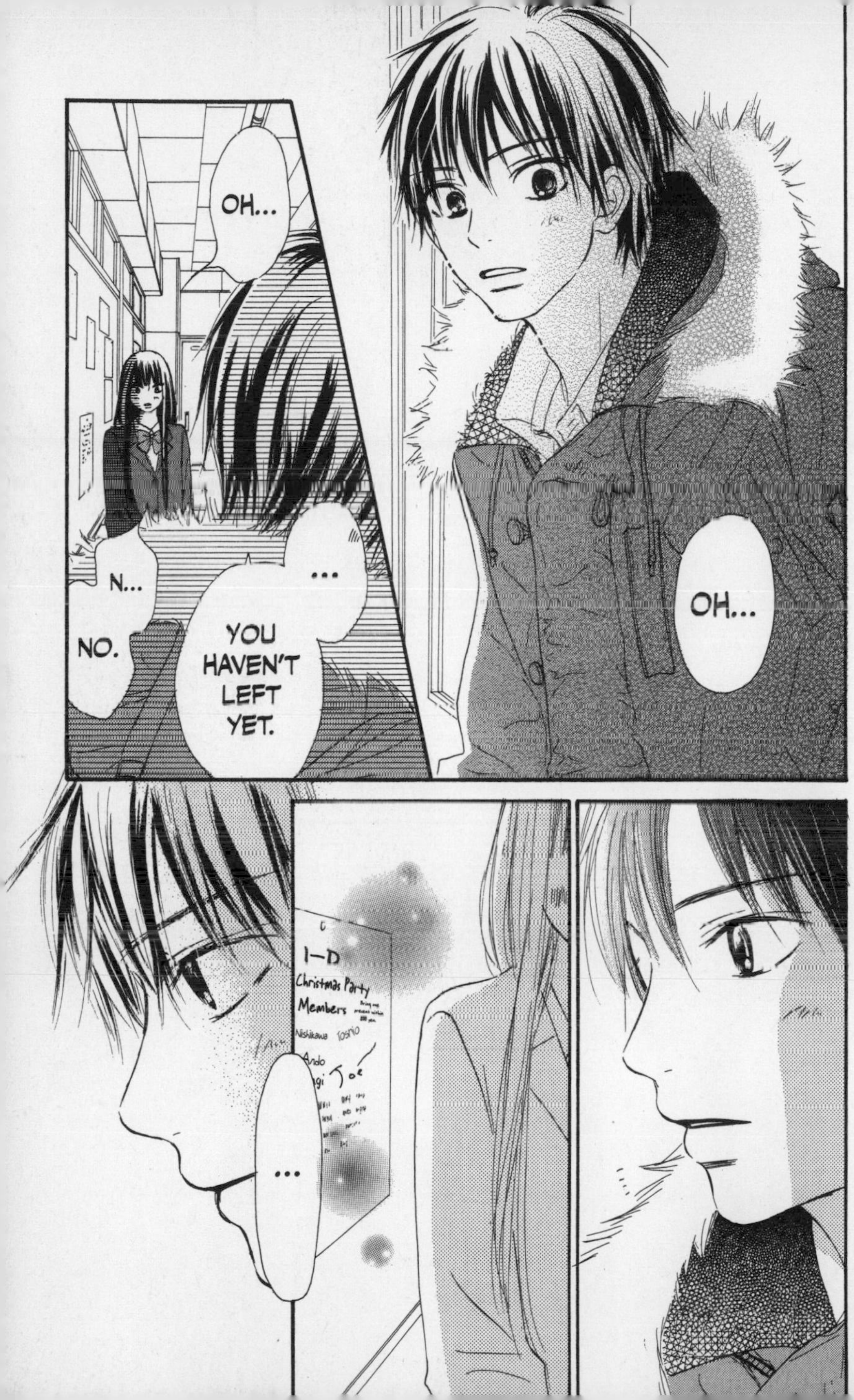
OH...
OH...
...
YOU HAVEN'T LEFT YET.
N...
NO.
...
1-D
Christmas Party
Members
Nishikawa
Ando

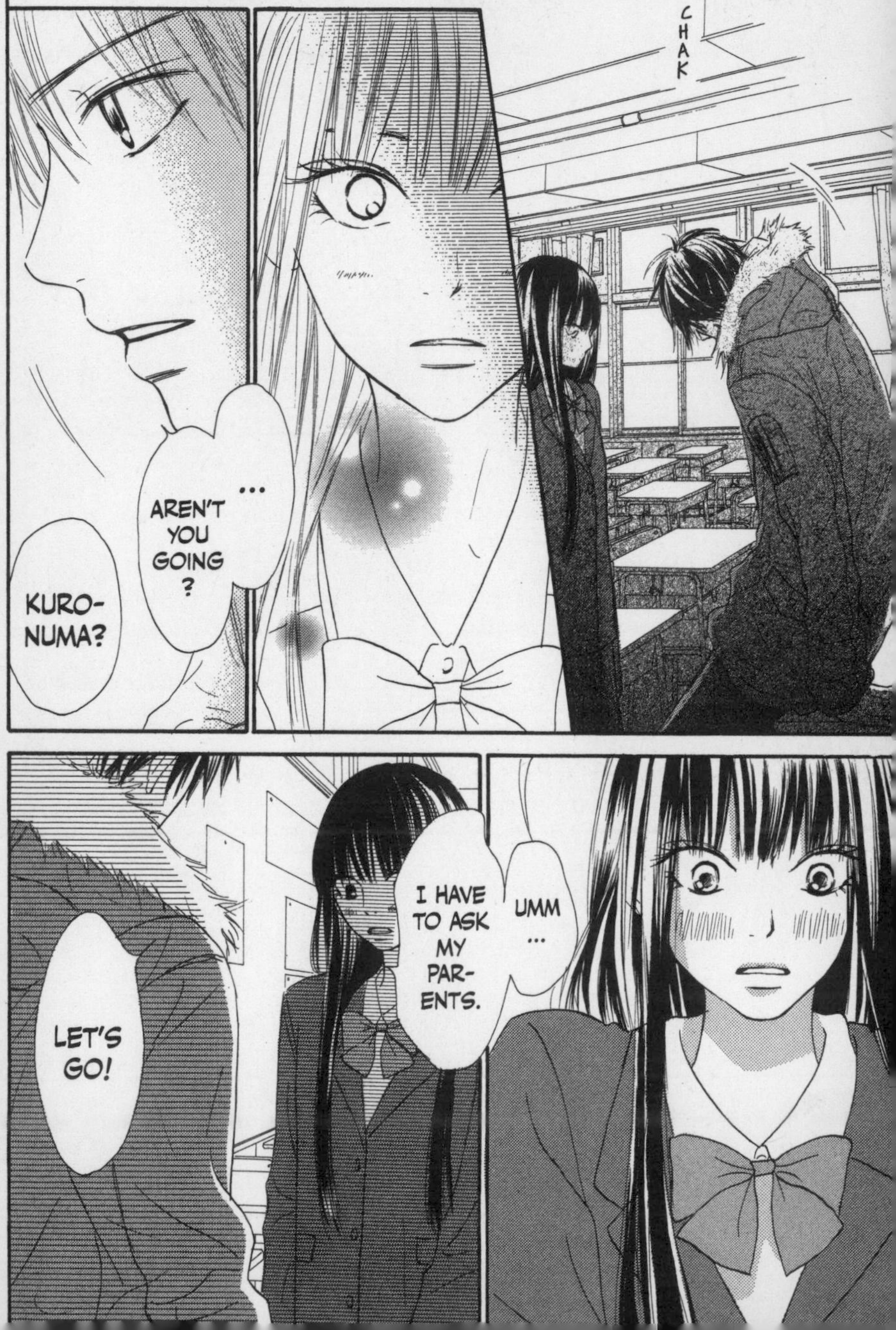
CHAK
...
AREN'T YOU GOING?
KURO-NUMA?
UMM ...
I HAVE TO ASK MY PAR-ENTS.
LET'S GO!

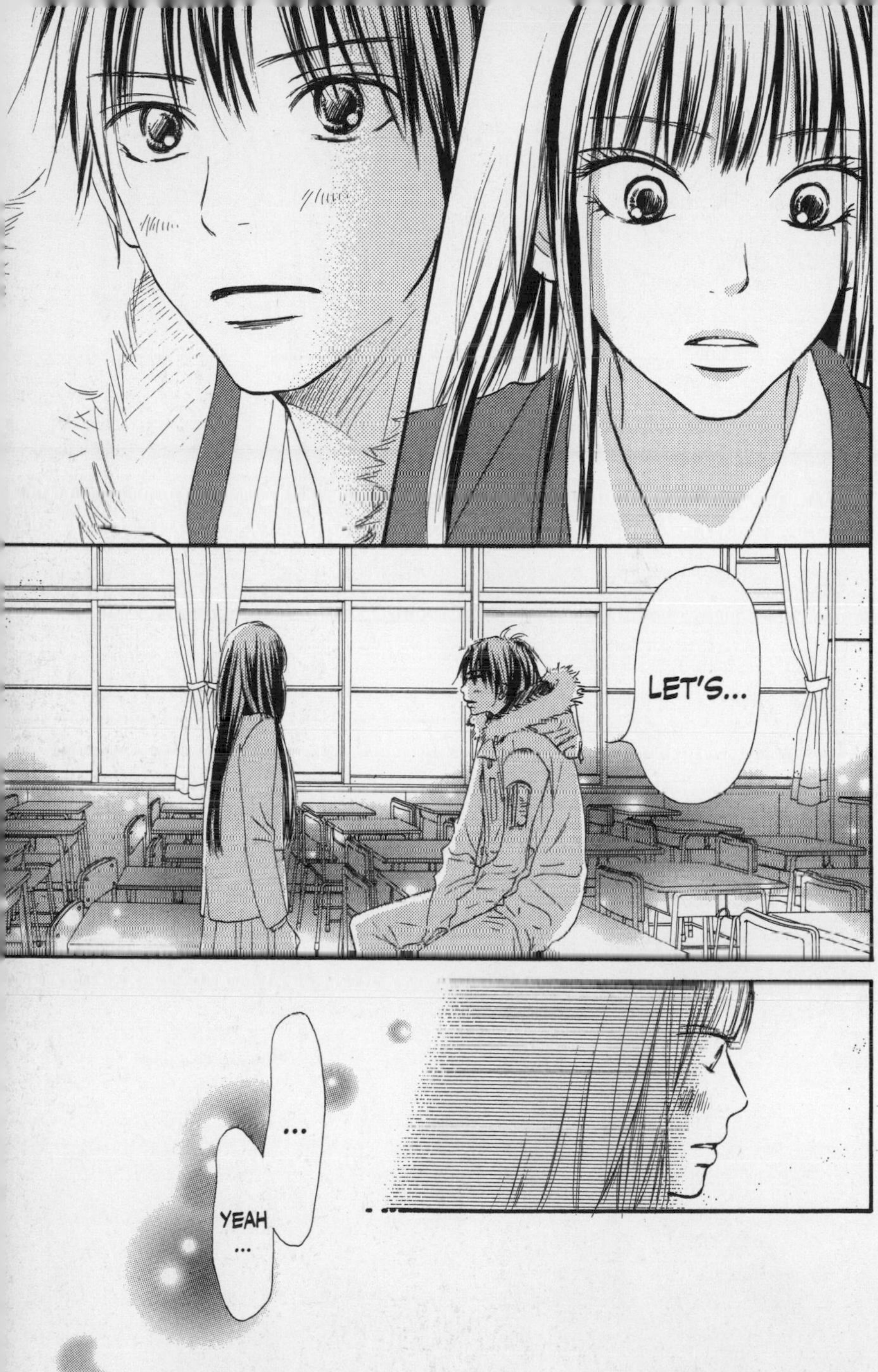
LET'S...
...
YEAH ...

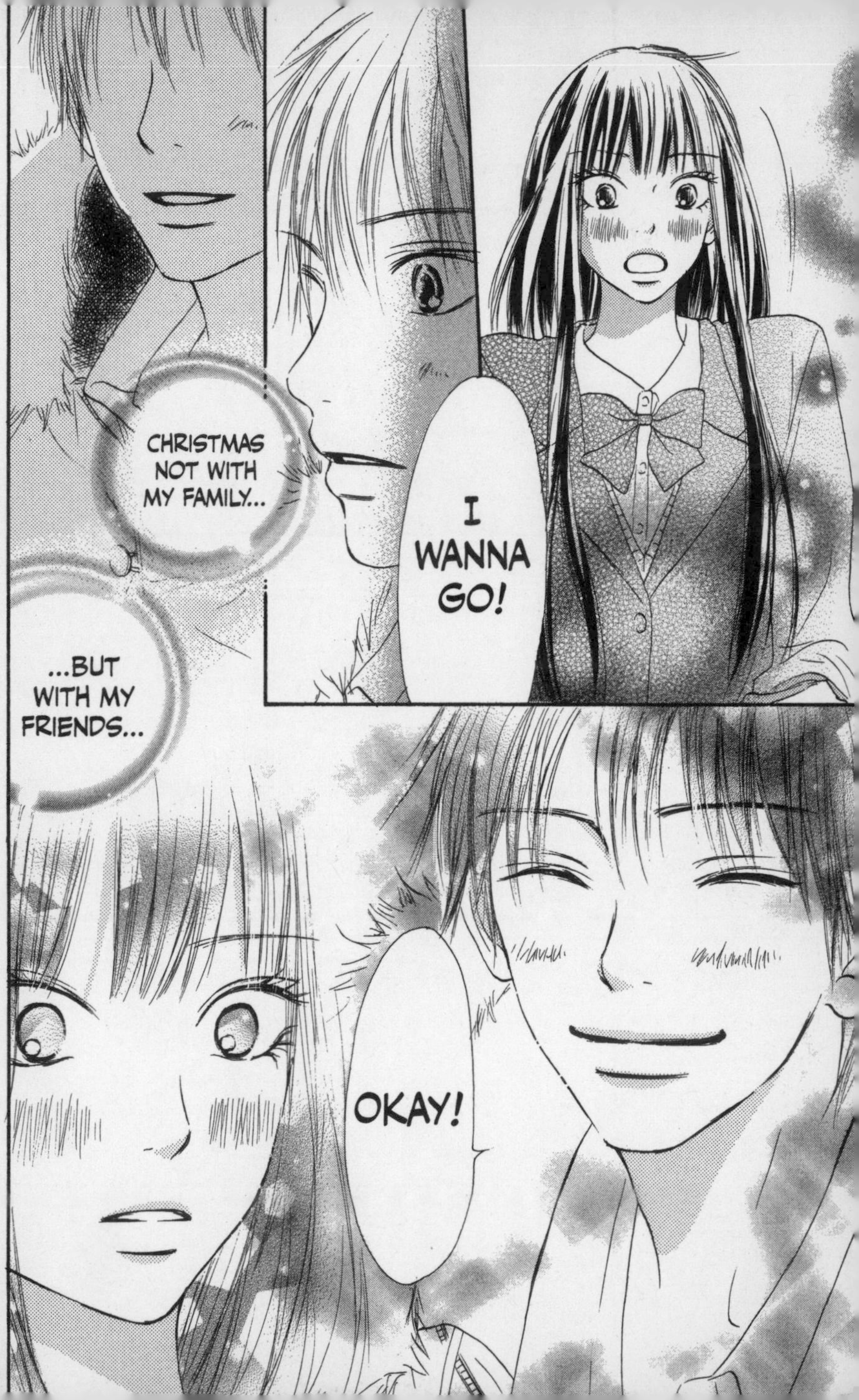
I WANNA GO!
CHRISTMAS NOT WITH MY FAMILY...
...BUT WITH MY FRIENDS...
OKAY!

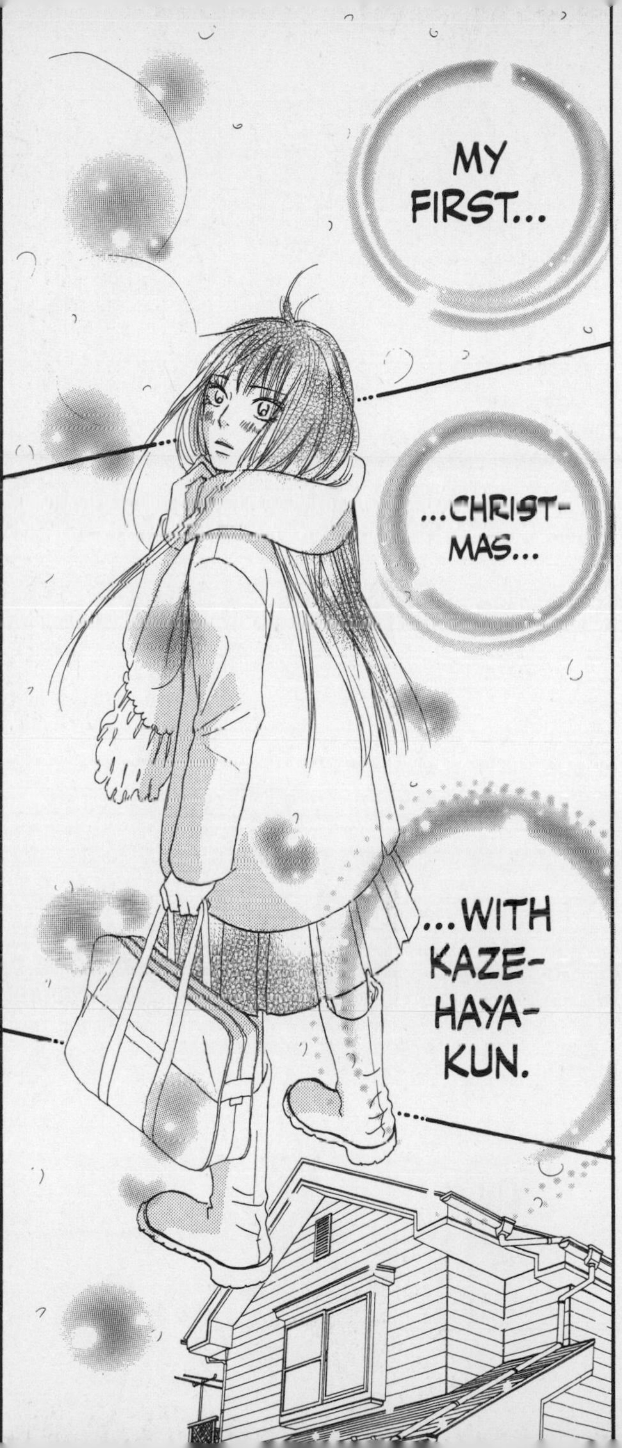
MY FIRST...
...CHRIST-MAS...
...WITH KAZE-HAYA-KUN.

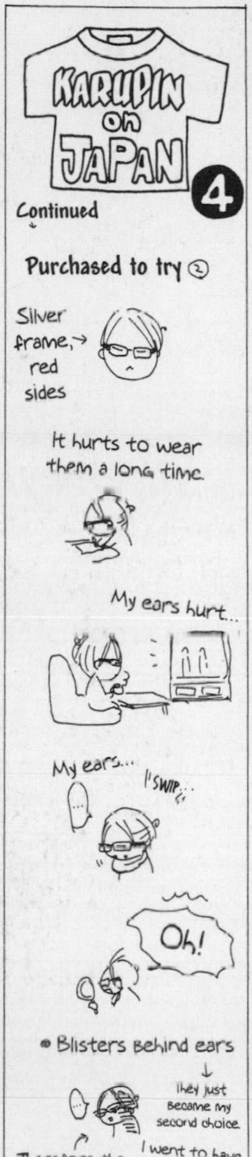
KARUPIN on JAPAN
4
Continued
Purchased to try ②
Silver frame, red sides
It hurts to wear them a long time.
My ears hurt...
My ears...
SWIP...
...
Oh!
• Blisters behind ears
They just became my second choice
...
Therefore the old ones are still my first choice.
I went to have them adjusted but they still hurt.

The last time I visited the optician, I found ones I kinda liked, but I haven't purchased them yet.

If they're gone the next time I go, it means those glasses were not meant for me to buy.

Will those glasses be the destined ones?! I'm a little nervous... Glasses are a part of your features! See you later! ✿

Shiina

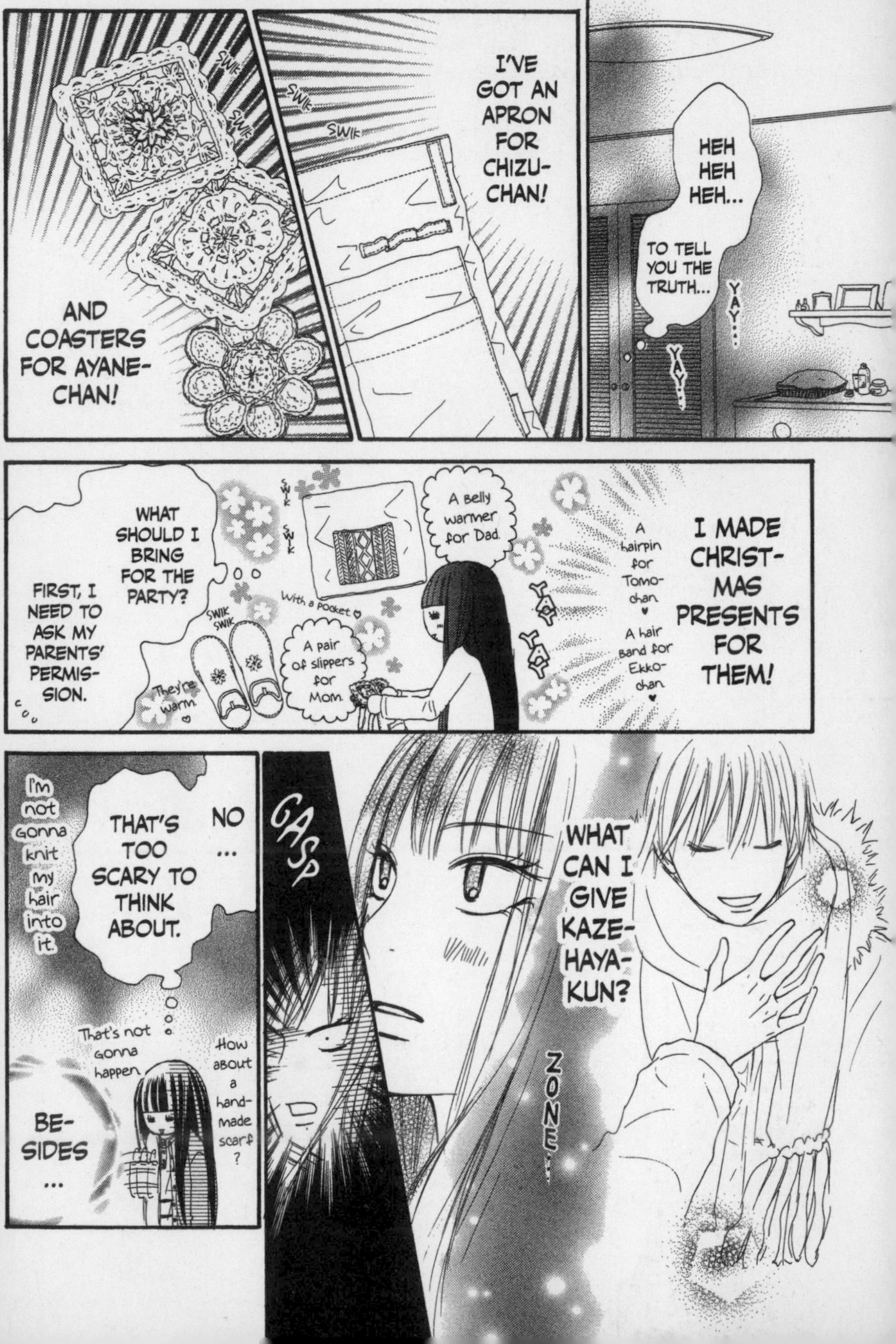
HEH HEH HEH...
TO TELL YOU THE TRUTH...
YAY...
YAY...
I'VE GOT AN APRON FOR CHIZU-CHAN!
SWIK
SWIK
SWIK
SWIK
SWIK
AND COASTERS FOR AYANE-CHAN!
I MADE CHRISTMAS PRESENTS FOR THEM!
A hairpin for Tomo-chan.
A hair band for Ekko-chan.
YAY
YAY
A belly warmer for Dad.
With a pocket.
SWIK SWIK
A pair of slippers for Mom.
SWIK SWIK
They're warm.
WHAT SHOULD I BRING FOR THE PARTY?
FIRST, I NEED TO ASK MY PARENTS' PERMISSION.
WHAT CAN I GIVE KAZE-HAYA-KUN?
ZONE...
GASP
NO...
THAT'S TOO SCARY TO THINK ABOUT.
I'm not gonna knit my hair into it.
How about a hand-made scarf?
That's not gonna happen.
BE-SIDES...

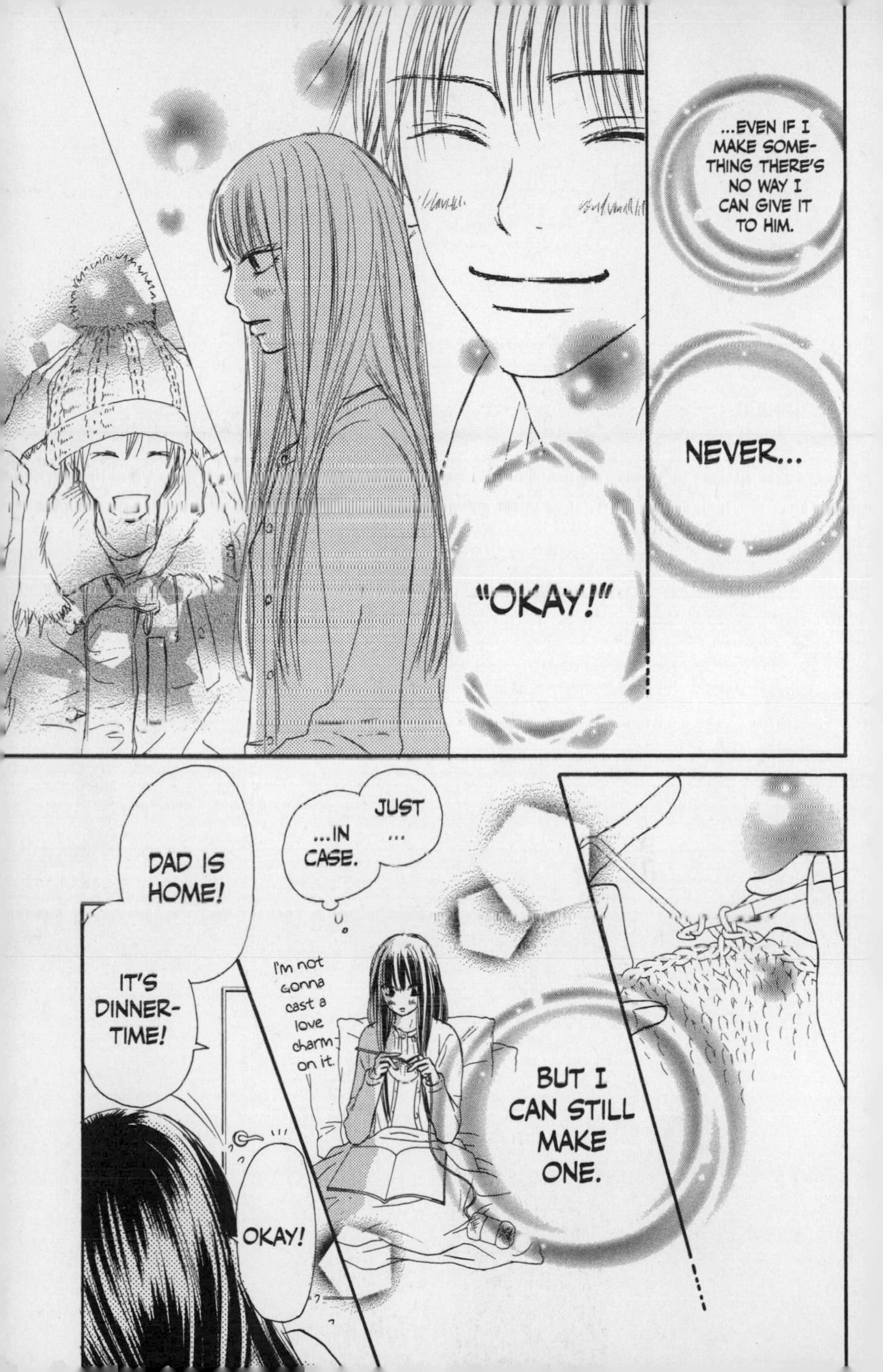
...EVEN IF I MAKE SOME-THING THERE'S NO WAY I CAN GIVE IT TO HIM.
NEVER...
"OKAY!"
BUT I CAN STILL MAKE ONE.
JUST ... ...IN CASE.
I'm not gonna cast a love charm on it.
DAD IS HOME!
IT'S DINNER-TIME!
OKAY!

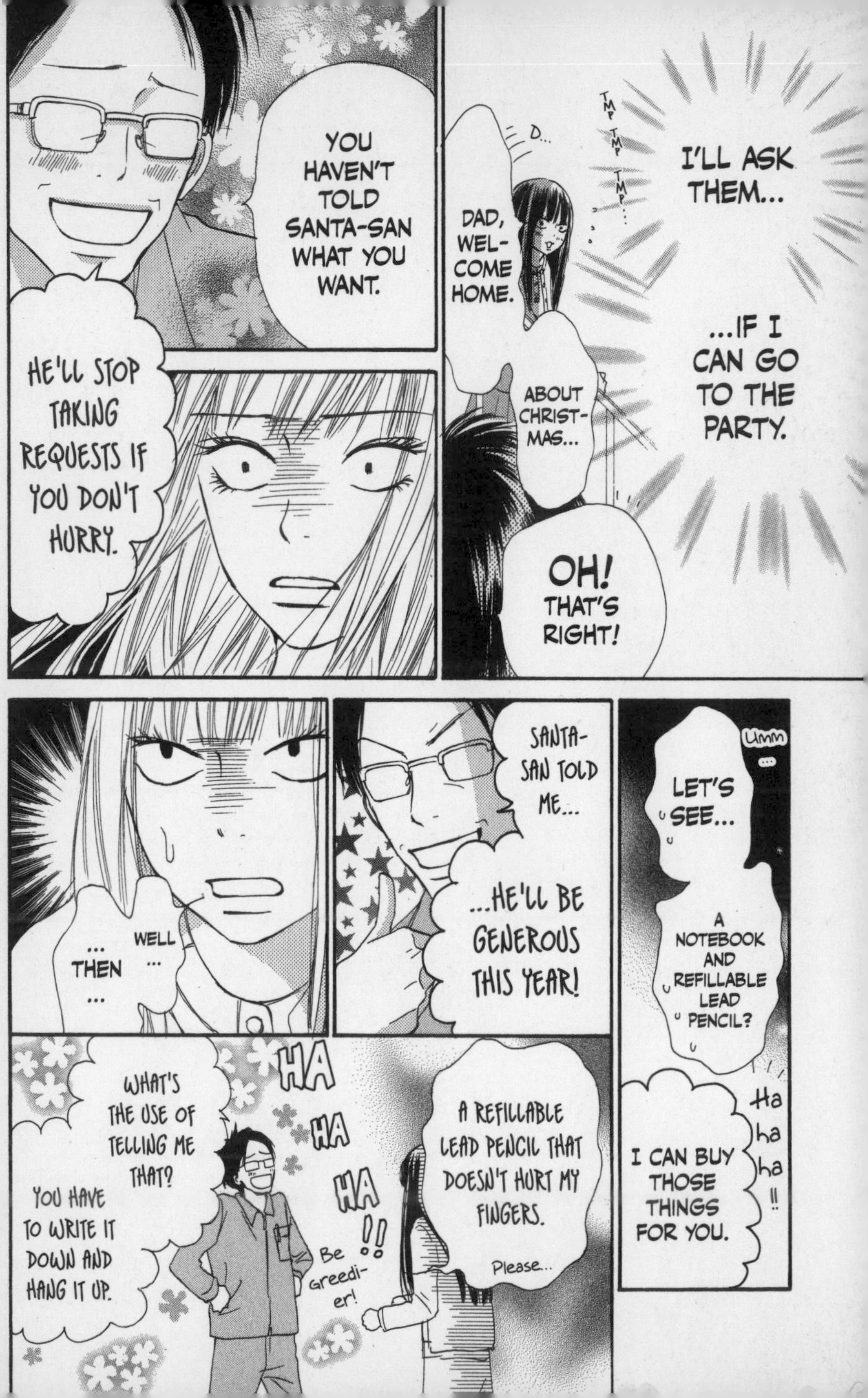
I'LL ASK THEM...
...IF I CAN GO TO THE PARTY.
TMP TMP TMP...
D...
DAD, WEL-COME HOME.
ABOUT CHRIST-MAS...
OH! THAT'S RIGHT!
YOU HAVEN'T TOLD SANTA-SAN WHAT YOU WANT.
HE'LL STOP TAKING REQUESTS IF YOU DON'T HURRY.
Umm...
LET'S SEE...
A NOTEBOOK AND REFILLABLE LEAD PENCIL?
Ha ha ha!!
I CAN BUY THOSE THINGS FOR YOU.
SANTA-SAN TOLD ME...
...HE'LL BE GENEROUS THIS YEAR!
WELL...
...THEN...
A REFILLABLE LEAD PENCIL THAT DOESN'T HURT MY FINGERS.
Please...
HA HA HA!!
Be greedi-er!
WHAT'S THE USE OF TELLING ME THAT?
YOU HAVE TO WRITE IT DOWN AND HANG IT UP.

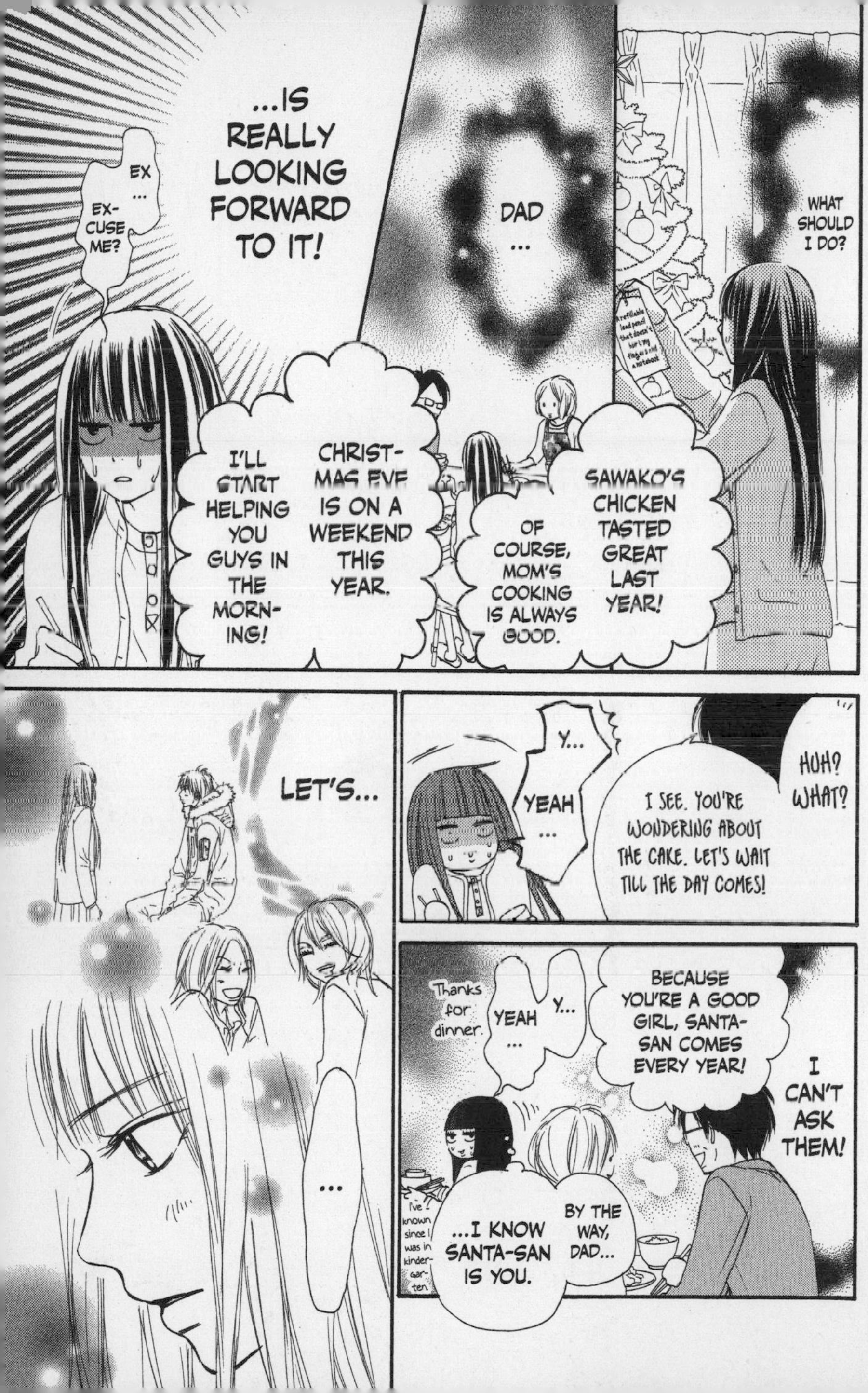
WHAT SHOULD I DO?
DAD ...
SAWAKO'S CHICKEN TASTED GREAT LAST YEAR!
OF COURSE, MOM'S COOKING IS ALWAYS GOOD.
CHRISTMAS EVE IS ON A WEEKEND THIS YEAR.
I'LL START HELPING YOU GUYS IN THE MORNING!
...IS REALLY LOOKING FORWARD TO IT!
EX ... EX-CUSE ME?
HUH? WHAT?
I SEE. YOU'RE WONDERING ABOUT THE CAKE. LET'S WAIT TILL THE DAY COMES!
Y... YEAH ...
I CAN'T ASK THEM!
BECAUSE YOU'RE A GOOD GIRL, SANTA-SAN COMES EVERY YEAR!
Y... YEAH ...
Thanks for dinner.
BY THE WAY, DAD...
...I KNOW SANTA-SAN IS YOU.
I've known since I was in kinder-gar-ten
LET'S...
...

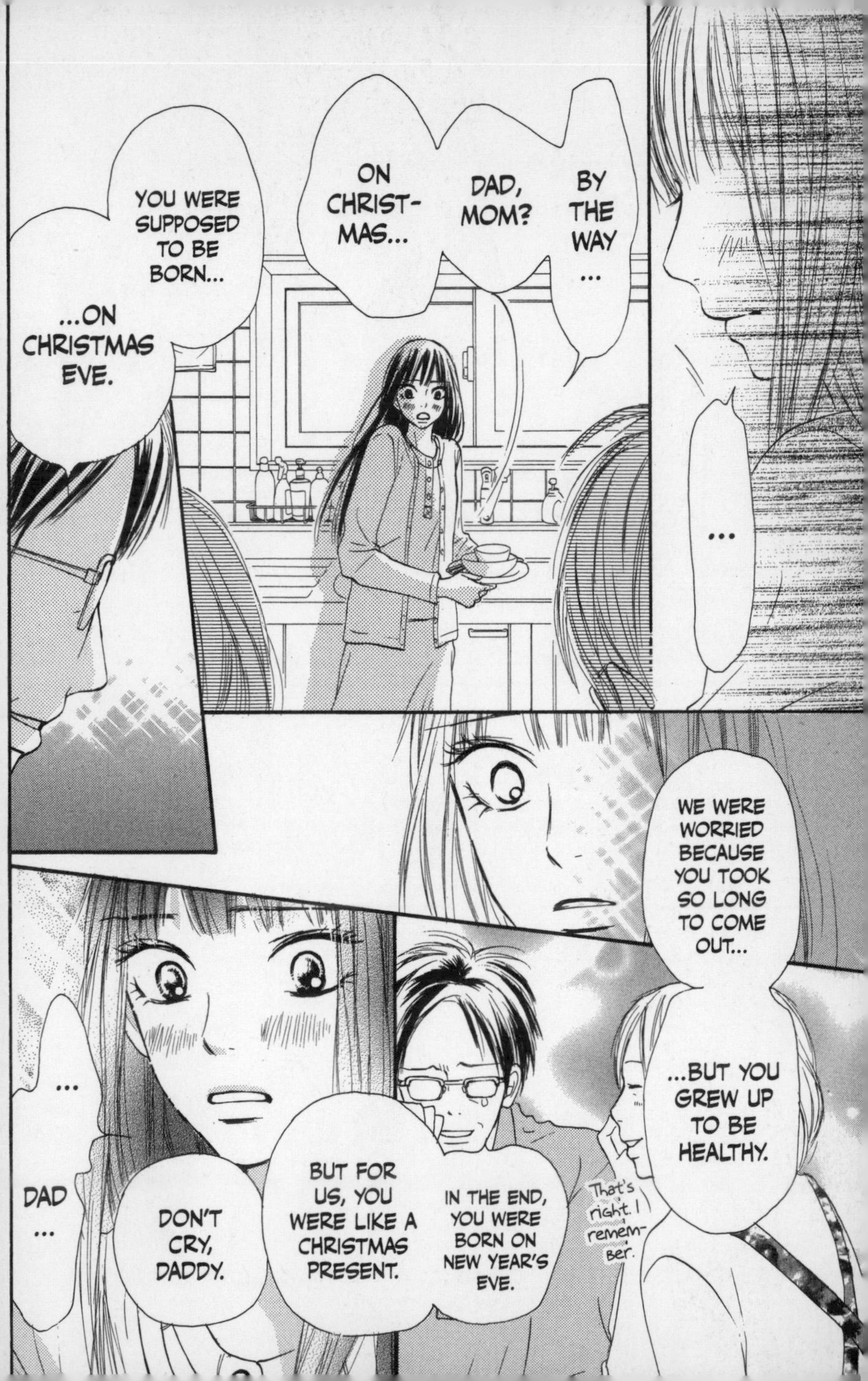
...
BY THE WAY ...
DAD, MOM?
ON CHRIST-MAS...
YOU WERE SUPPOSED TO BE BORN...
...ON CHRISTMAS EVE.
WE WERE WORRIED BECAUSE YOU TOOK SO LONG TO COME OUT...
...BUT YOU GREW UP TO BE HEALTHY.
That's right. I remem-ber.
IN THE END, YOU WERE BORN ON NEW YEAR'S EVE.
BUT FOR US, YOU WERE LIKE A CHRISTMAS PRESENT.
DON'T CRY, DADDY.
...
DAD ...

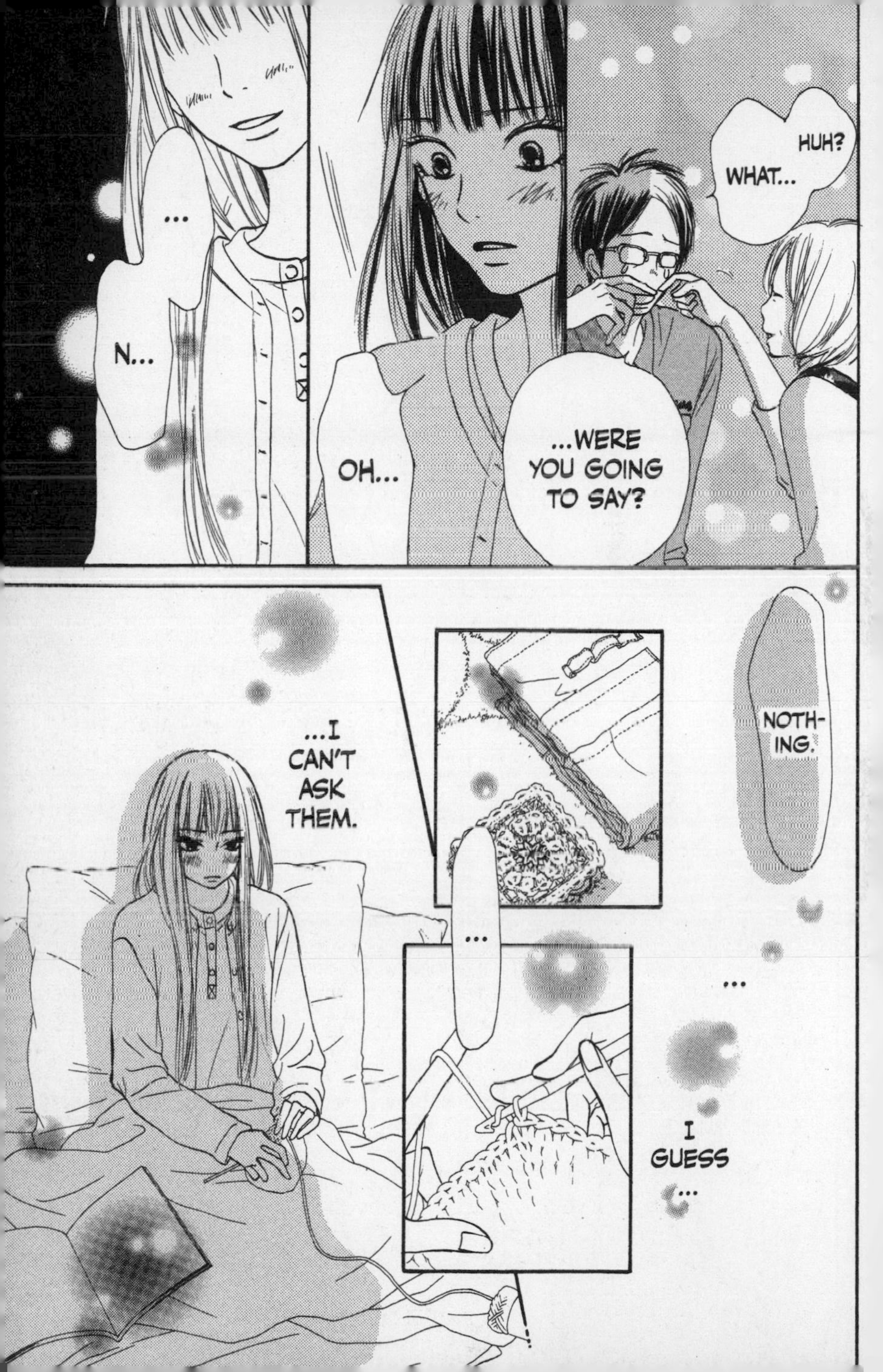
HUH?
WHAT...
...WERE YOU GOING TO SAY?
OH...
...
N...
NOTH-ING.
...
I GUESS...
...
...I CAN'T ASK THEM.

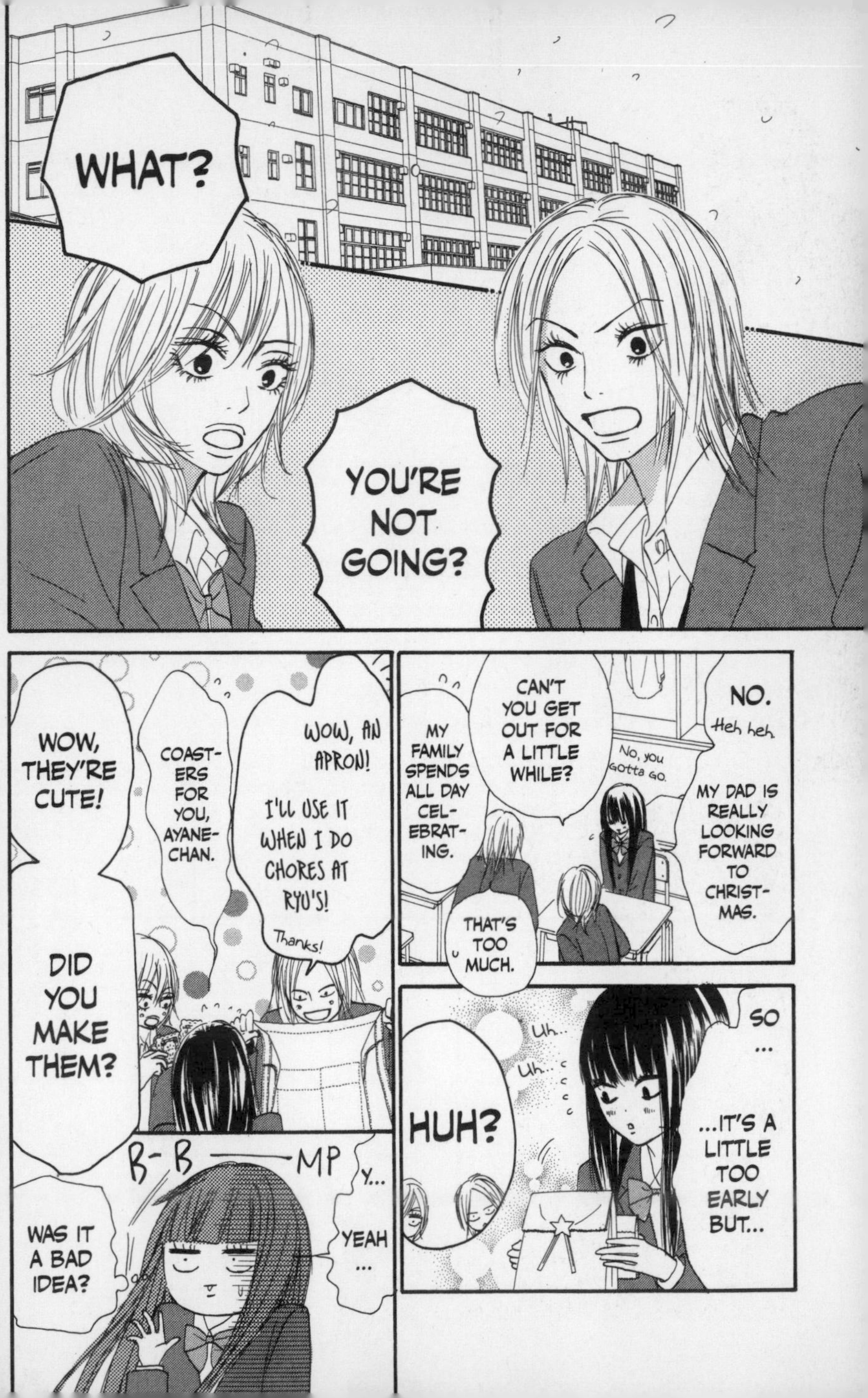
WHAT?
YOU'RE NOT GOING?
NO.
Heh heh.
MY DAD IS REALLY LOOKING FORWARD TO CHRISTMAS.
No, you gotta go.
CAN'T YOU GET OUT FOR A LITTLE WHILE?
MY FAMILY SPENDS ALL DAY CEL-EBRAT-ING.
THAT'S TOO MUCH.
SO...
...IT'S A LITTLE TOO EARLY BUT...
HUH?
Uh...
Uh...
WOW, AN APRON!
I'LL USE IT WHEN I DO CHORES AT RYU'S!
Thanks!
COAST-ERS FOR YOU, AYANE-CHAN.
WOW, THEY'RE CUTE!
DID YOU MAKE THEM?
Y...
YEAH...
B-B—MP
WAS IT A BAD IDEA?

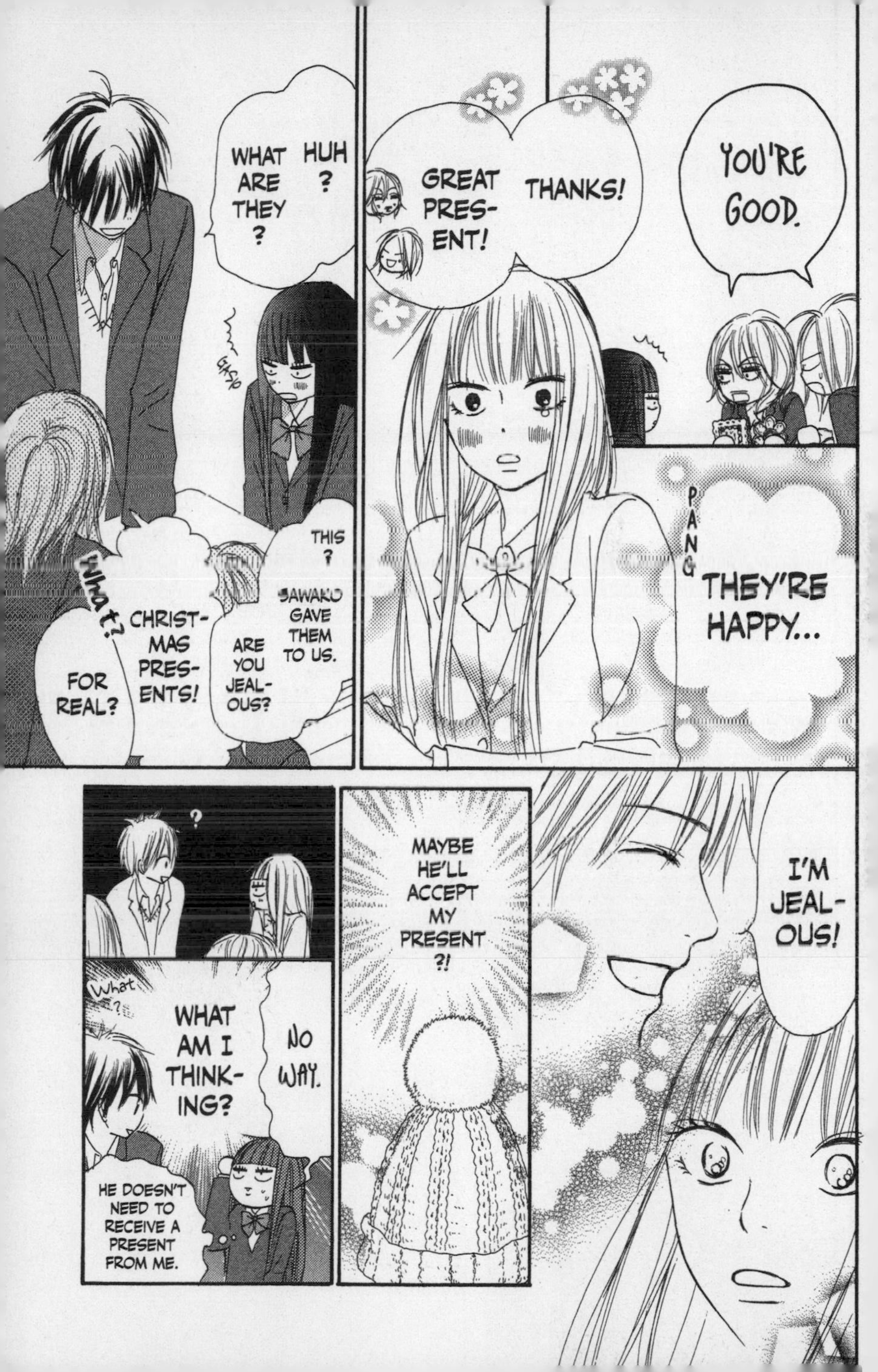
YOU'RE GOOD.
PANG
THEY'RE HAPPY...
THANKS!
GREAT PRESENT!
HUH?
WHAT ARE THEY?
GASP
THIS?
SAWAKO GAVE THEM TO US.
ARE YOU JEALOUS?
CHRISTMAS PRESENTS!
What?!
FOR REAL?
I'M JEALOUS!
MAYBE HE'LL ACCEPT MY PRESENT?!
?
NO WAY.
WHAT AM I THINKING?
What?
HE DOESN'T NEED TO RECEIVE A PRESENT FROM ME.

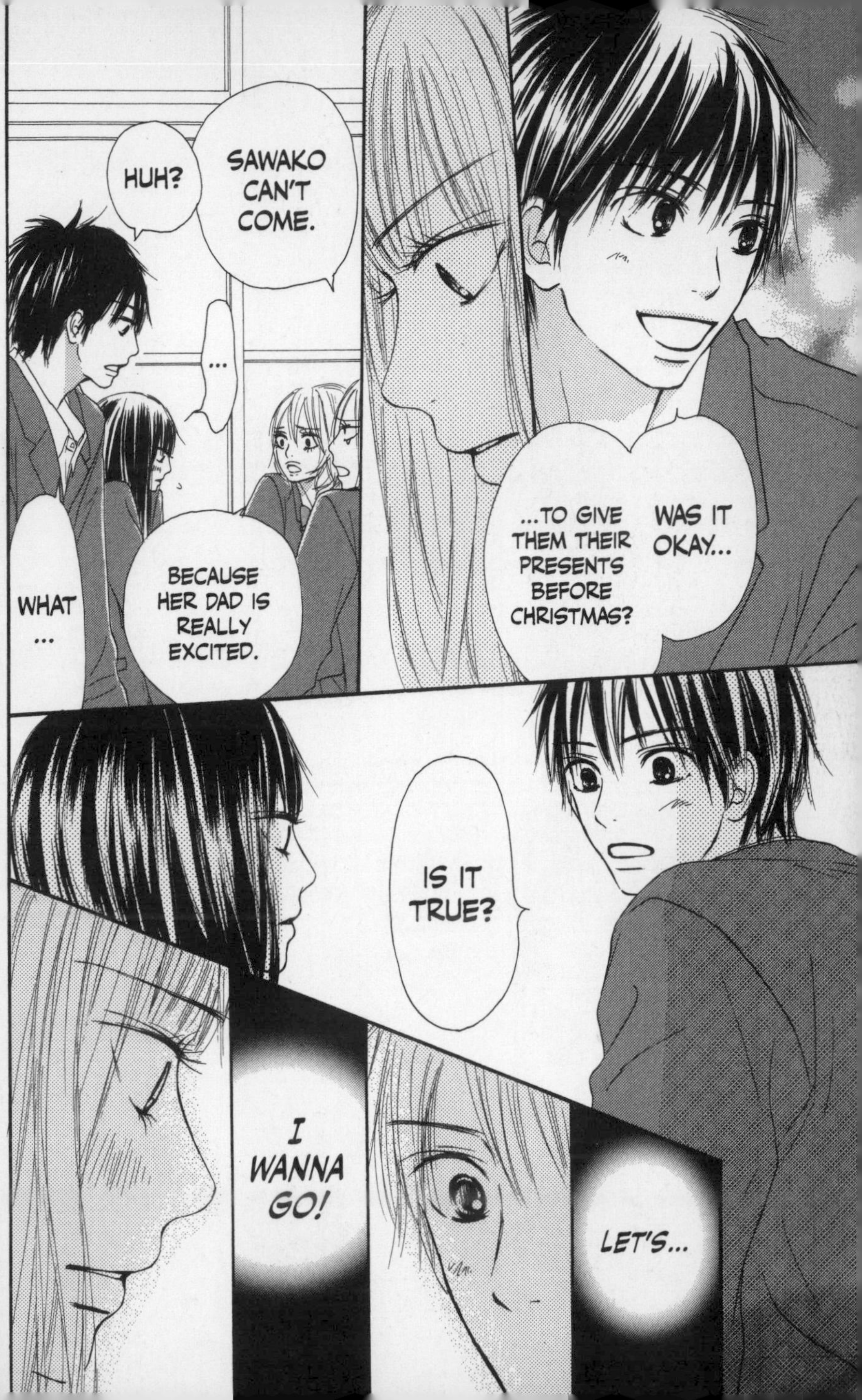
WAS IT OKAY...
...TO GIVE THEM THEIR PRESENTS BEFORE CHRISTMAS?
SAWAKO CAN'T COME.
HUH?
...
BECAUSE HER DAD IS REALLY EXCITED.
WHAT ...
IS IT TRUE?
LET'S...
I WANNA GO!

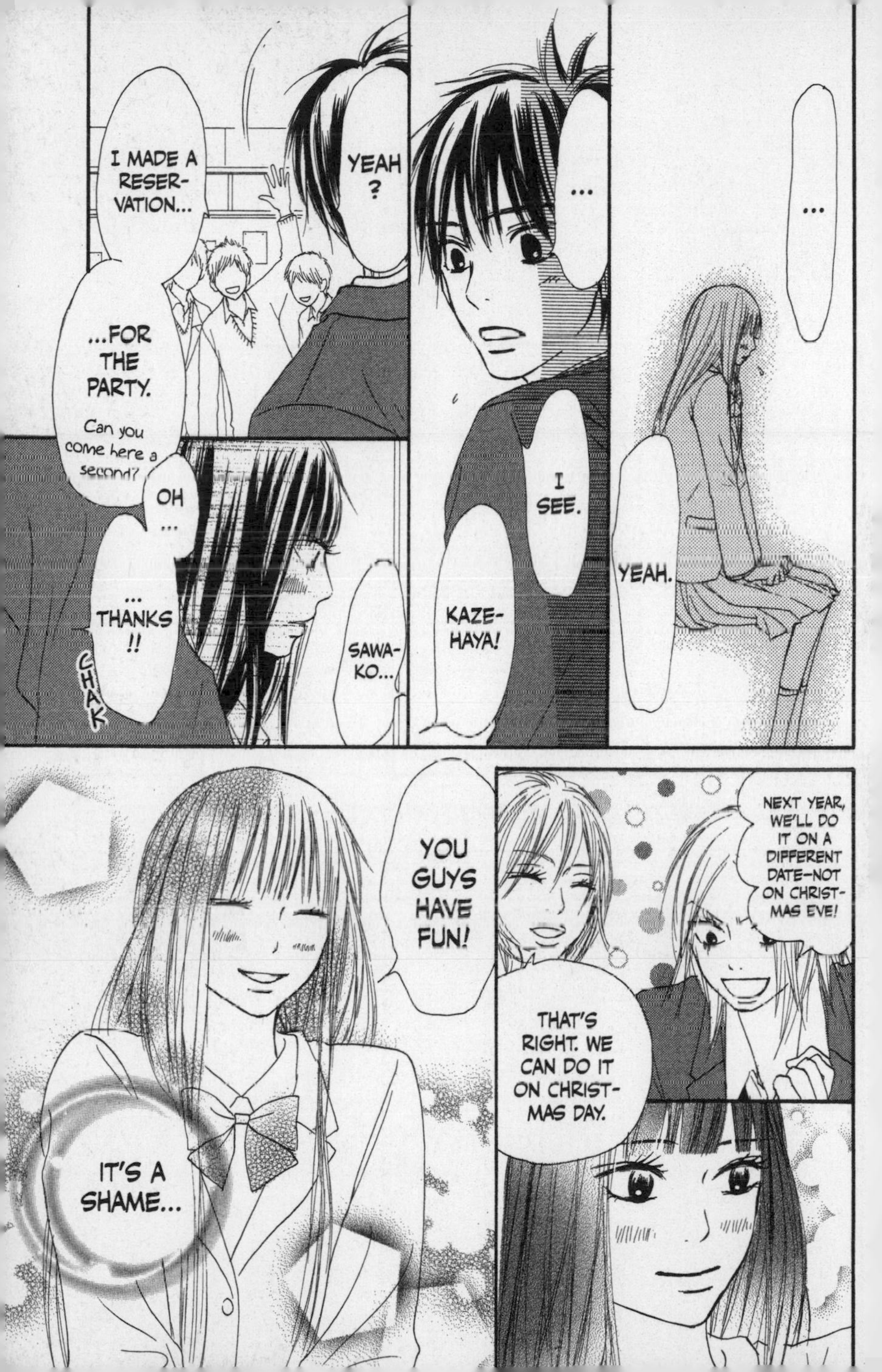
...
YEAH.
...
I SEE.
KAZE-HAYA!
YEAH ?
I MADE A RESER-VATION...
...FOR THE PARTY.
Can you come here a second?
SAWA-KO...
OH ...
... THANKS !!
CHAK
NEXT YEAR, WE'LL DO IT ON A DIFFERENT DATE—NOT ON CHRIST-MAS EVE!
THAT'S RIGHT. WE CAN DO IT ON CHRIST-MAS DAY.
YOU GUYS HAVE FUN!
IT'S A SHAME...

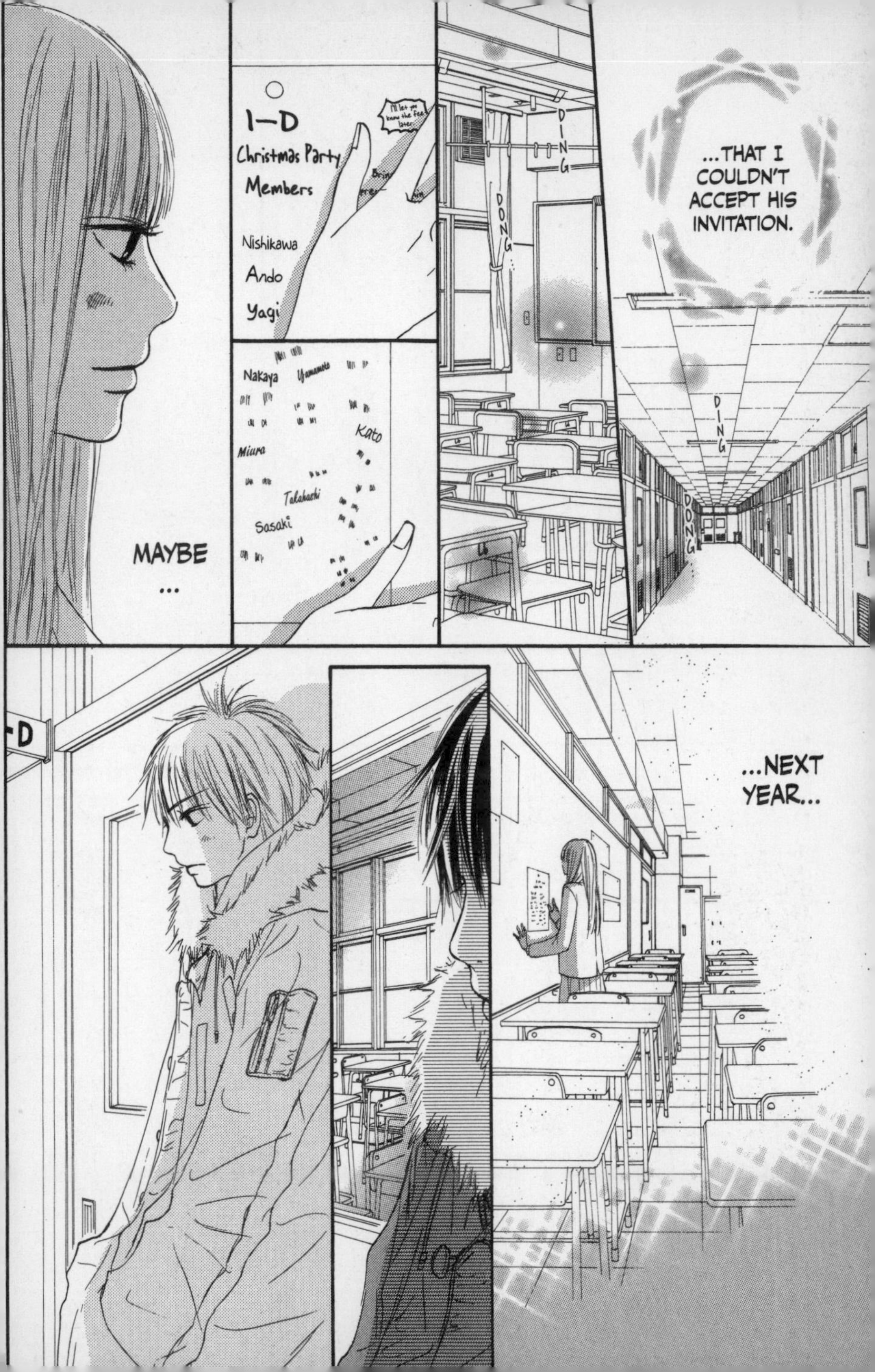
...THAT I COULDN'T ACCEPT HIS INVITATION.
DING
DONG
DING
DONG
I-D
Christmas Party
Members
I'll let you know the fee later.
Nishikawa
Ando
Yagi
Nakaya
Yamamoto
Kato
Miura
Takahashi
Sasaki
MAYBE
...
...NEXT YEAR...
I-D

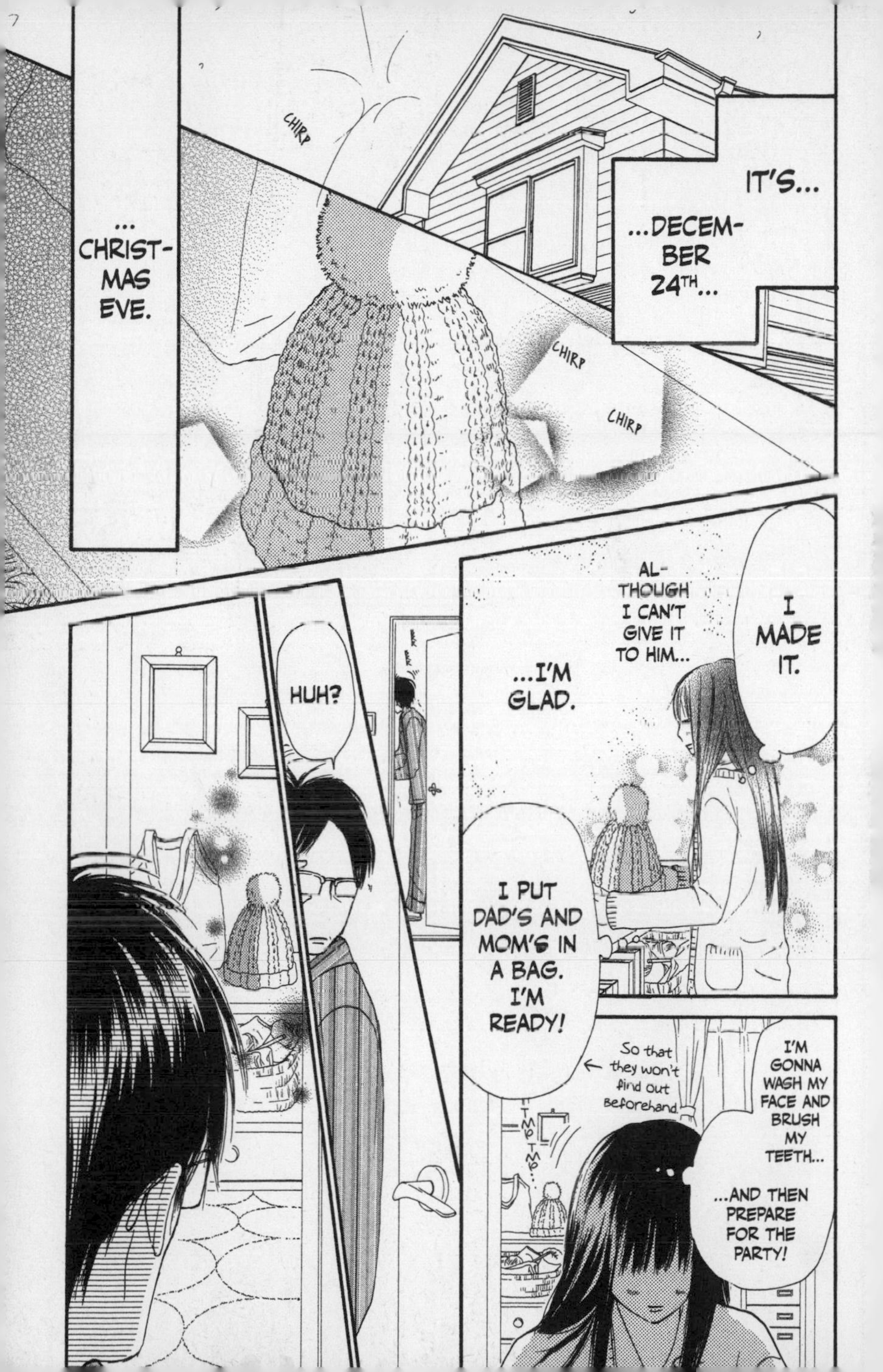
IT'S...
...DECEMBER 24TH...
CHIRP
CHIRP
CHIRP
...CHRISTMAS EVE.
I MADE IT.
ALTHOUGH I CAN'T GIVE IT TO HIM...
...I'M GLAD.
I PUT DAD'S AND MOM'S IN A BAG. I'M READY!
So that they won't find out beforehand.
I'M GONNA WASH MY FACE AND BRUSH MY TEETH...
...AND THEN PREPARE FOR THE PARTY!
TMP TMP
HUH?

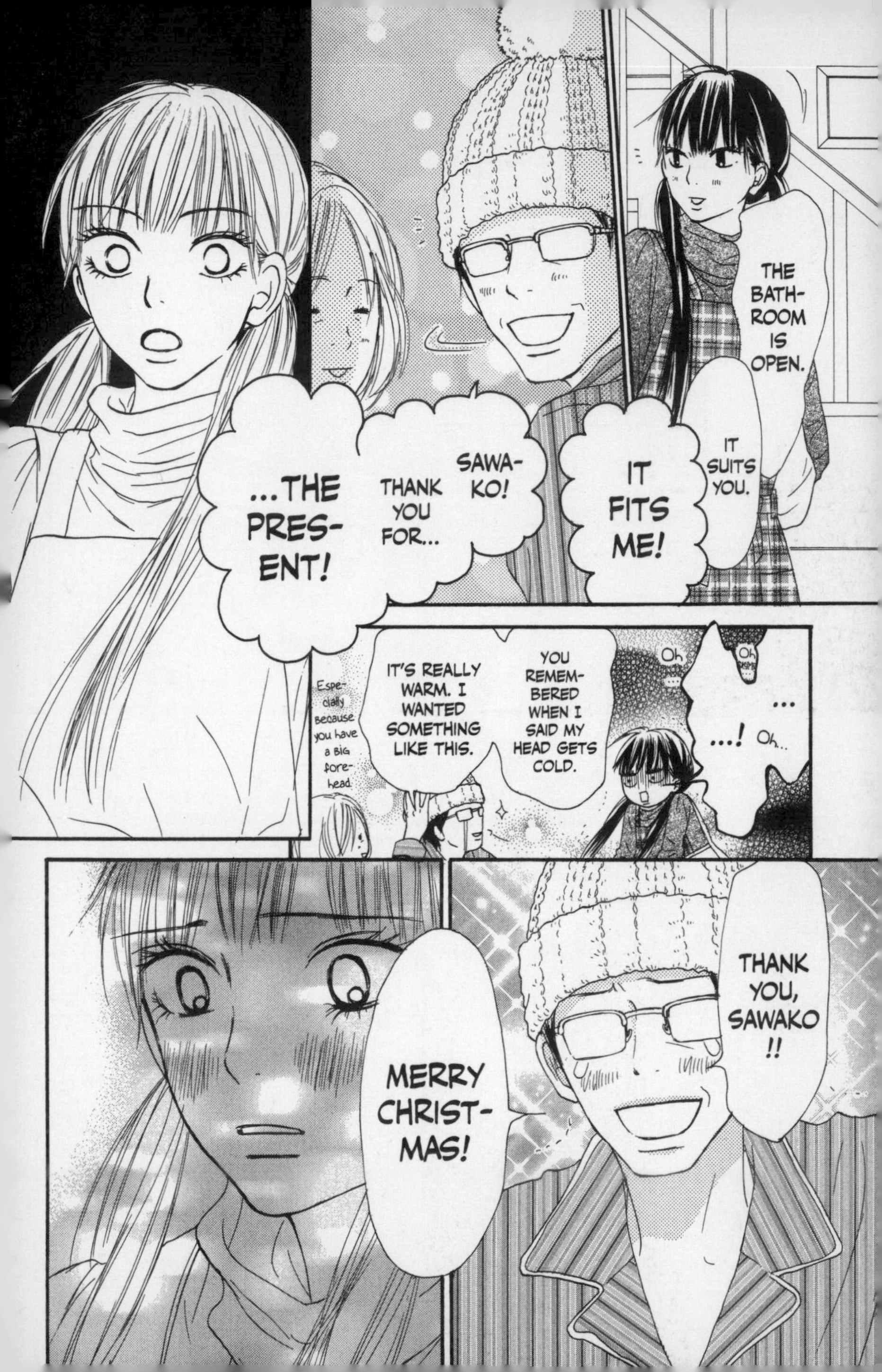
THE BATHROOM IS OPEN.
IT SUITS YOU.
IT FITS ME!
SAWAKO!
THANK YOU FOR...
...THE PRESENT!
Oh
Oh
...
...! Oh...
YOU REMEMBERED WHEN I SAID MY HEAD GETS COLD.
IT'S REALLY WARM. I WANTED SOMETHING LIKE THIS.
Especially because you have a big forehead.
THANK YOU, SAWAKO!!
MERRY CHRISTMAS!

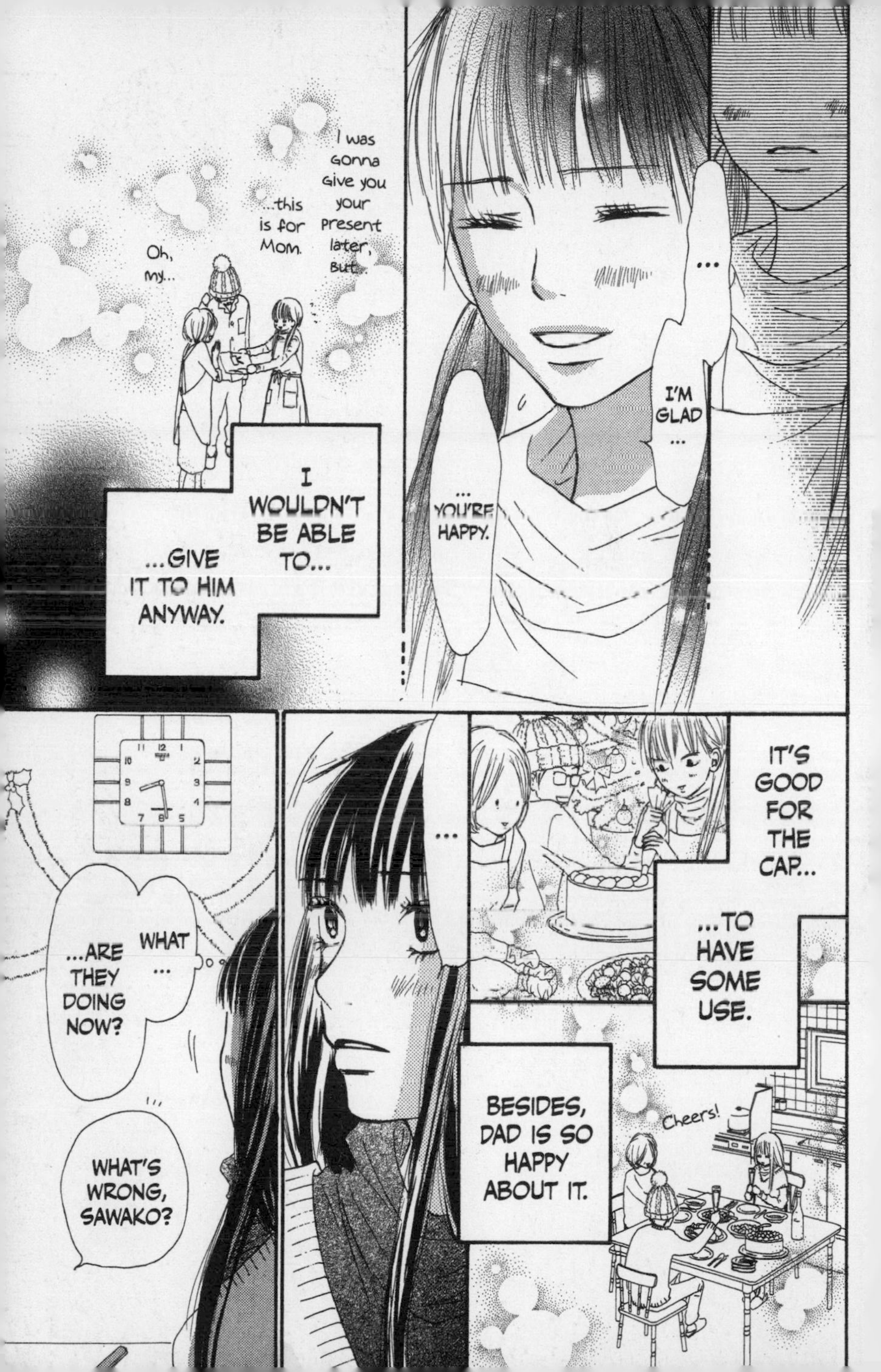
...
I'M GLAD ...
... YOU'RE HAPPY.
I was gonna give you your present later, but...
...this is for Mom.
Oh, my...
I WOULDN'T BE ABLE TO...
...GIVE IT TO HIM ANYWAY.
IT'S GOOD FOR THE CAP...
...TO HAVE SOME USE.
BESIDES, DAD IS SO HAPPY ABOUT IT.
Cheers!
...
WHAT ...
...ARE THEY DOING NOW?
WHAT'S WRONG, SAWAKO?

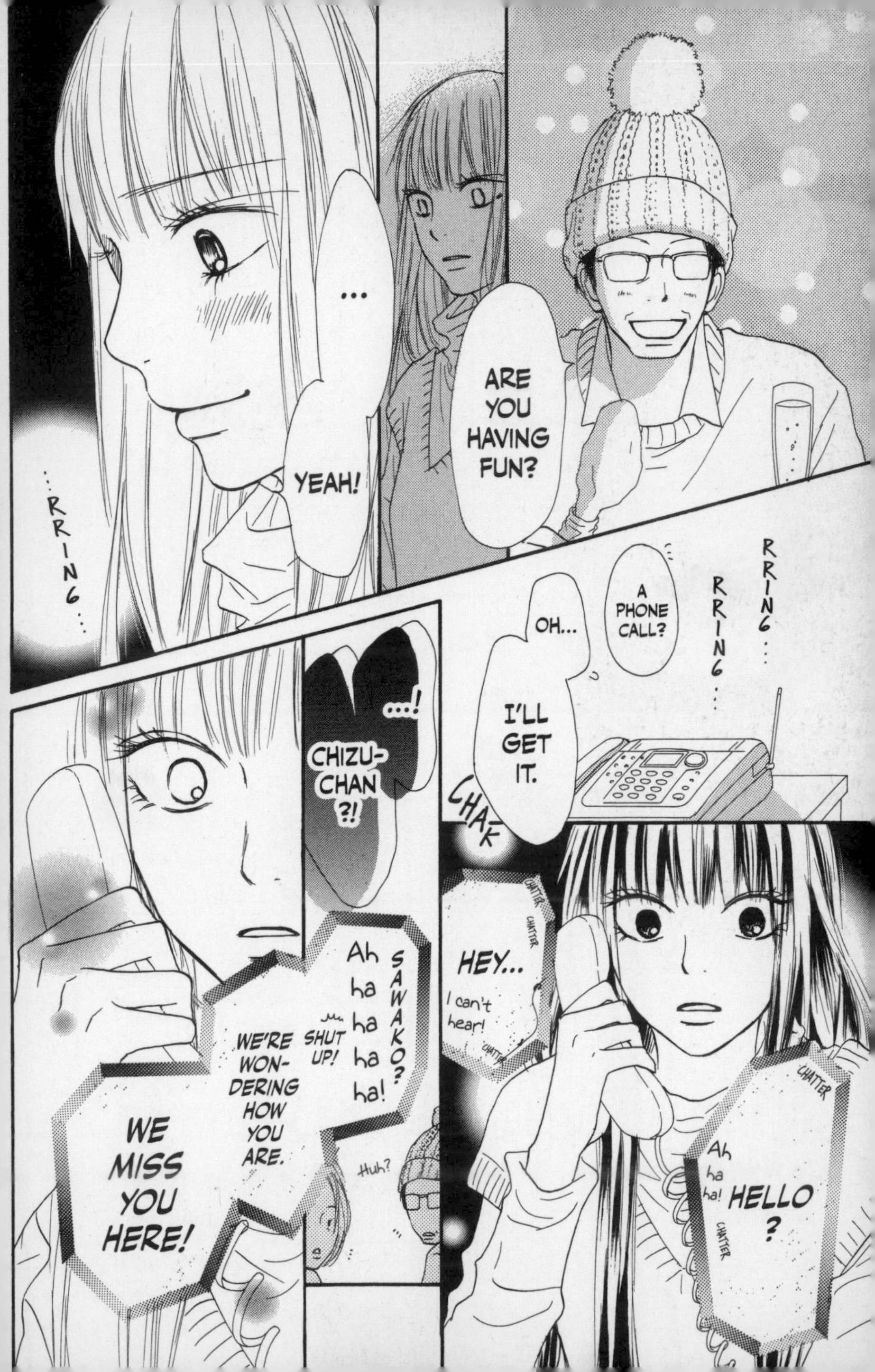
ARE YOU HAVING FUN?
...
YEAH!
...RRING...
RRING...
RRING...
A PHONE CALL?
OH...
I'LL GET IT.
CHAK
CHATTER
Ah ha ha!
HELLO?
CHATTER
CHATTER
CHATTER
HEY...
I can't hear!
CHATTER
...!
CHIZU-CHAN?!
SAWAKO?
Ah ha ha ha ha!
SHUT UP!
WE'RE WONDERING HOW YOU ARE.
Huh?
WE MISS YOU HERE!

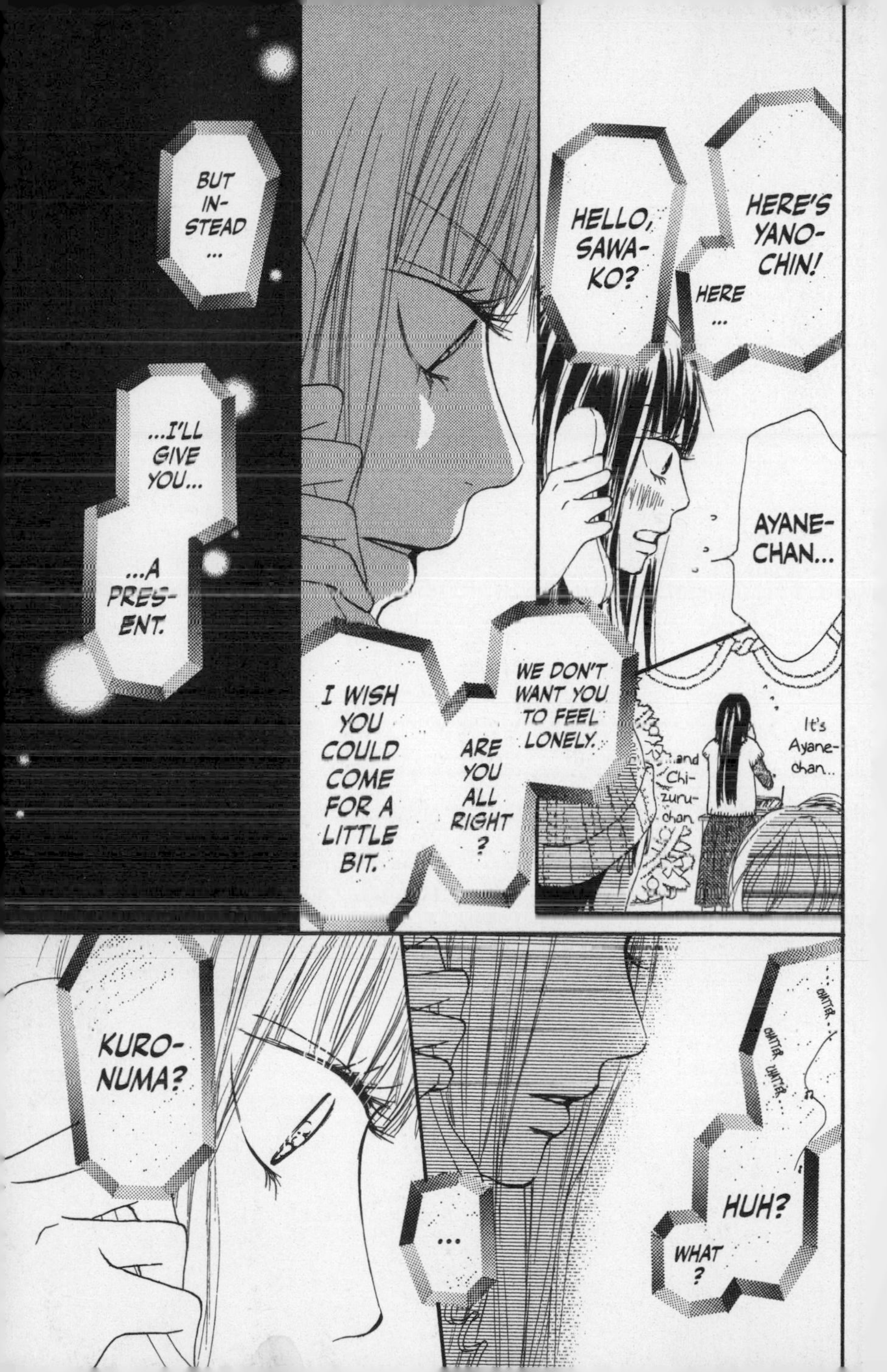
HERE'S YANO-CHIN!
HERE...
HELLO, SAWAKO?
AYANE-CHAN...
It's Ayane-chan...
...and Chi-zuru-chan.
WE DON'T WANT YOU TO FEEL LONELY.
ARE YOU ALL RIGHT?
I WISH YOU COULD COME FOR A LITTLE BIT.
BUT IN-STEAD...
...I'LL GIVE YOU...
...A PRES-ENT.
CHATTER...
CHATTER CHATTER...
HUH?
WHAT?
...
KURO-NUMA?

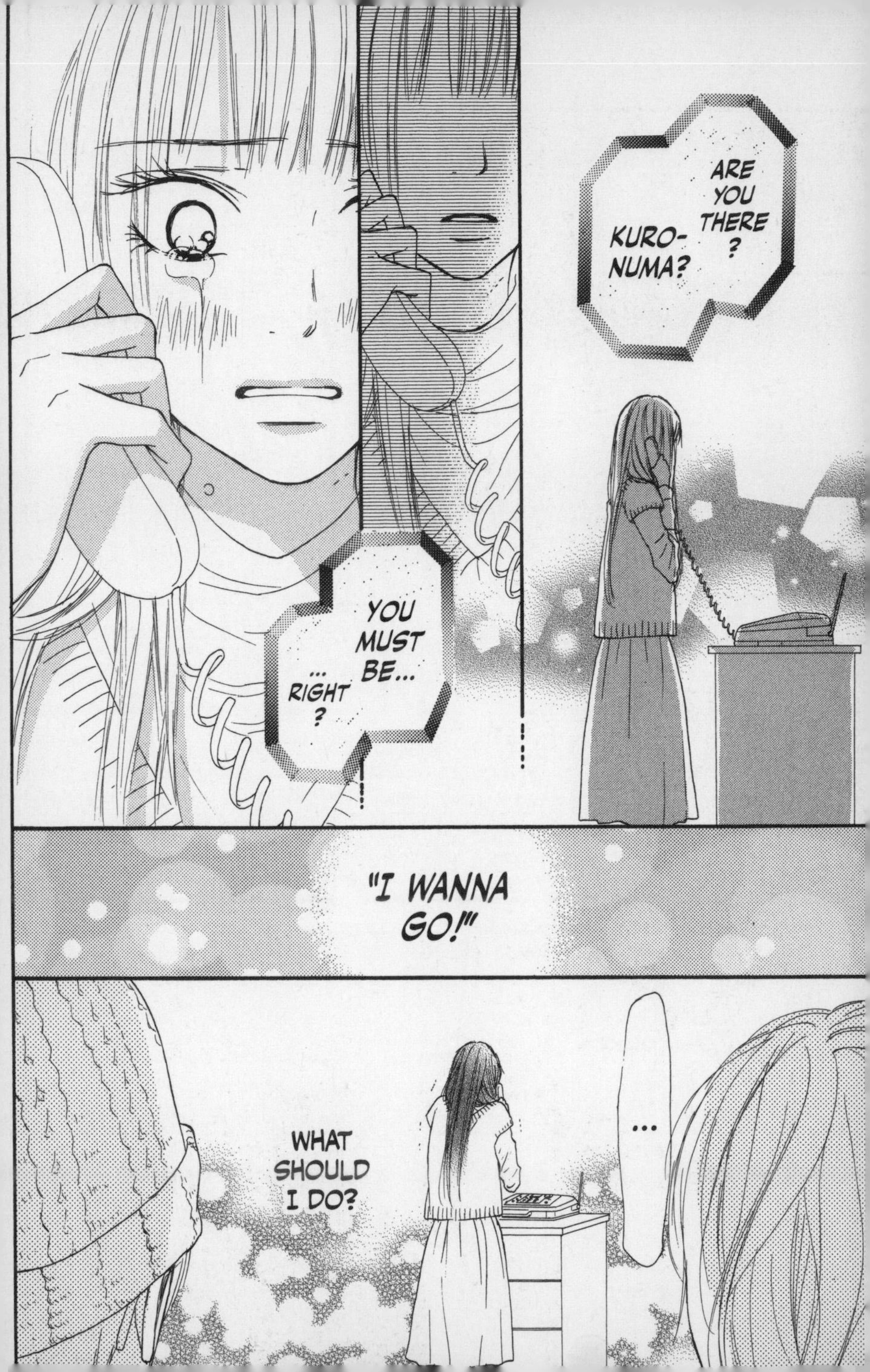
ARE YOU THERE? KURO-NUMA?
YOU MUST BE... ...RIGHT?
"I WANNA GO!"
...
WHAT SHOULD I DO?

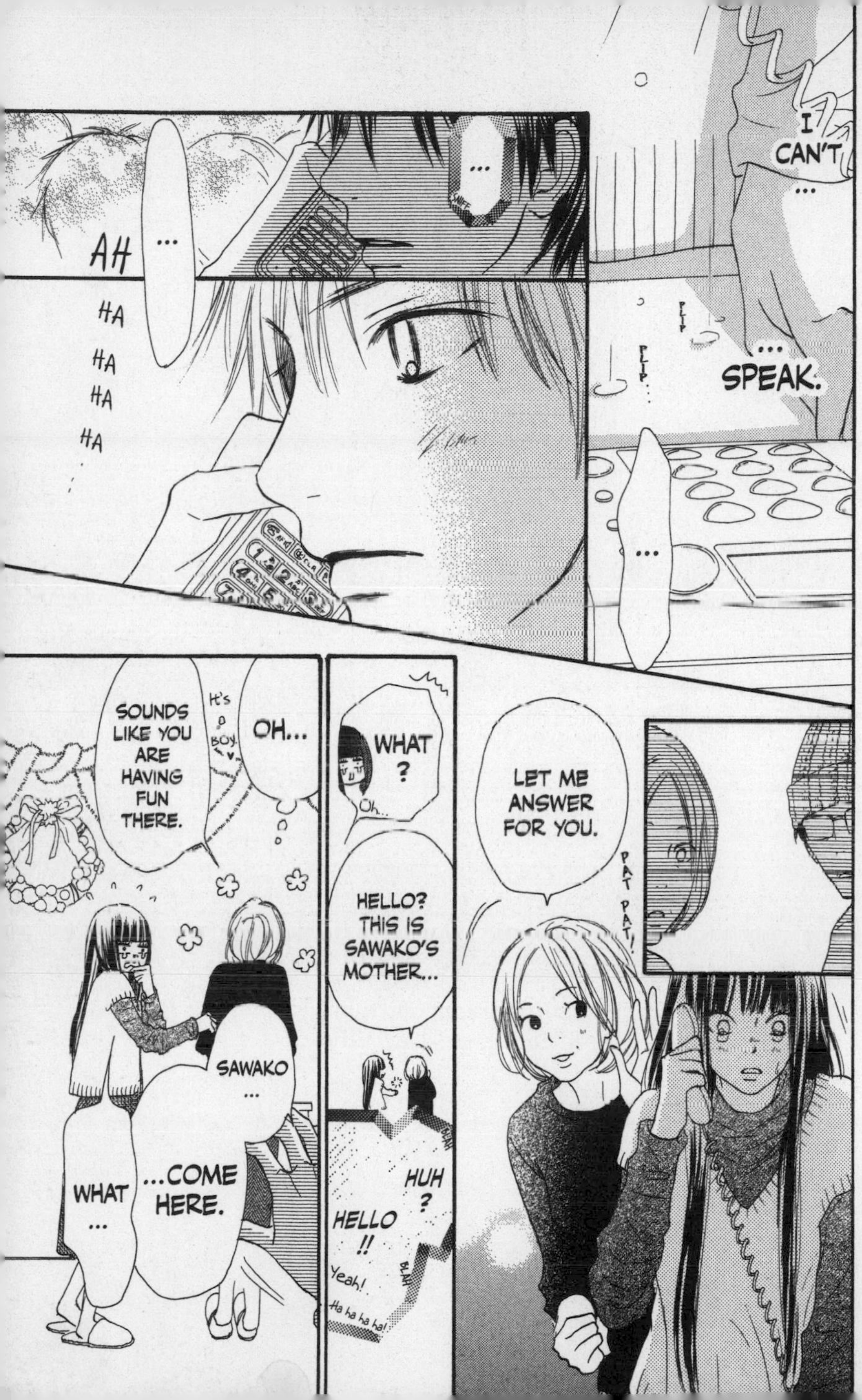
I CAN'T ...
... SPEAK.
PLIP PLIP...
...
...
AH
...
HA HA HA HA
LET ME ANSWER FOR YOU.
PAT PAT!
WHAT ?
Oh...
HELLO? THIS IS SAWAKO'S MOTHER...
HUH ?
HELLO !!
Yeah!
Ha ha ha ha!
OH...
It's a boy.
SOUNDS LIKE YOU ARE HAVING FUN THERE.
SAWAKO ...
...COME HERE.
WHAT ...

...
Ah ha ha ha ha!
Yay!
Woo-hoo!
YES, I AM.
BUT ...
...IF KURONUMA-SAN COULD COME, IT'D BE MORE FUN FOR EVERYBODY.
DAD ...
... CAN ...
...CAN I GO...
...FOR JUST A LITTLE BIT?
IF SHE COULD COME ...
...IT'D BE MORE FUN!
SWIP ...

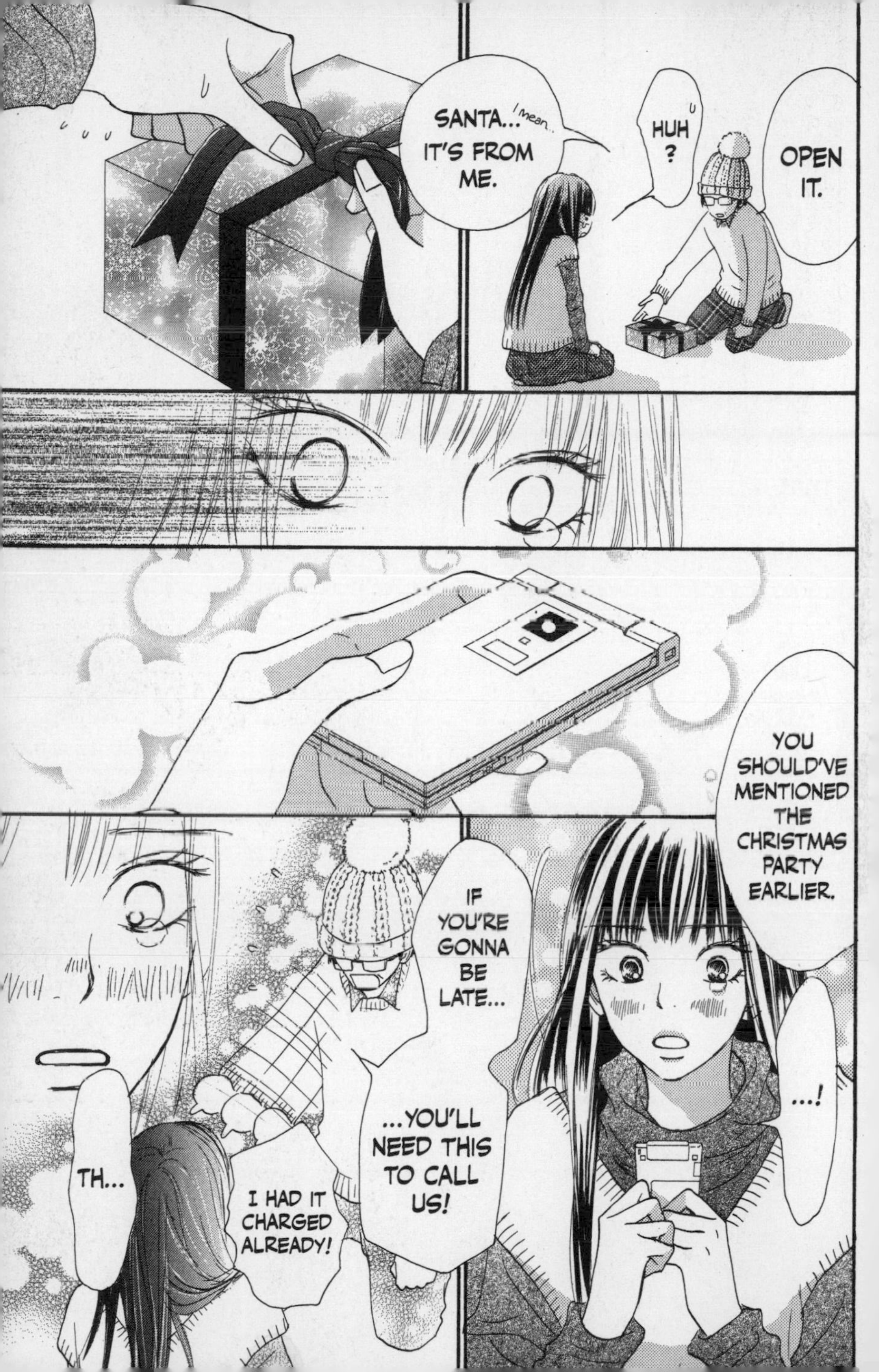
OPEN IT.
HUH ?
SANTA... I mean... IT'S FROM ME.
YOU SHOULD'VE MENTIONED THE CHRISTMAS PARTY EARLIER.
...!
IF YOU'RE GONNA BE LATE...
...YOU'LL NEED THIS TO CALL US!
I HAD IT CHARGED ALREADY!
TH...

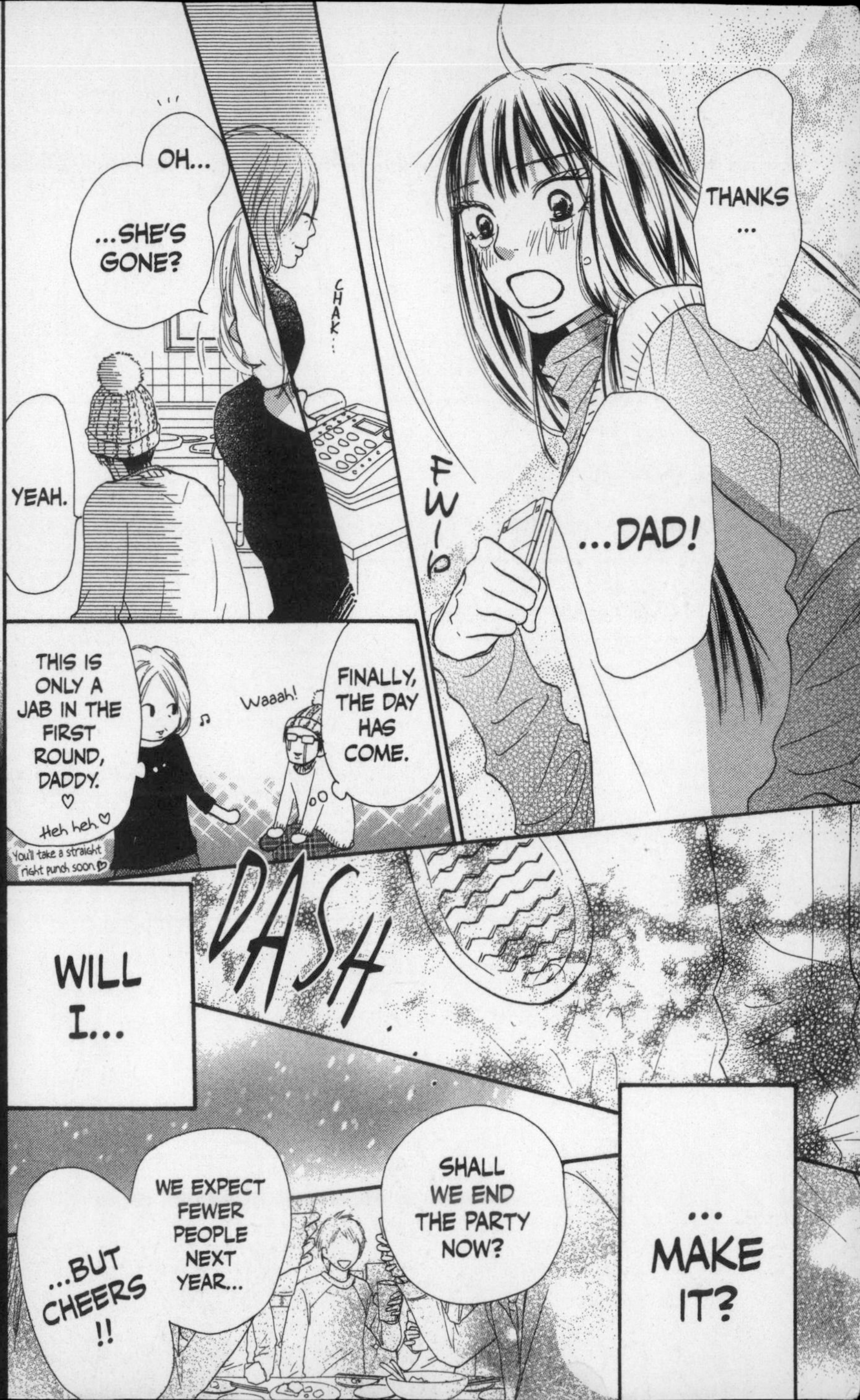
THANKS...
...DAD!
FWIP
OH...
...SHE'S GONE?
CHAK...
YEAH.
FINALLY, THE DAY HAS COME.
Waaah!
THIS IS ONLY A JAB IN THE FIRST ROUND, DADDY. ♡
Heh heh.♡
You'll take a straight right punch soon♡
DASH
WILL I...
...MAKE IT?
SHALL WE END THE PARTY NOW?
WE EXPECT FEWER PEOPLE NEXT YEAR...
...BUT CHEERS!!

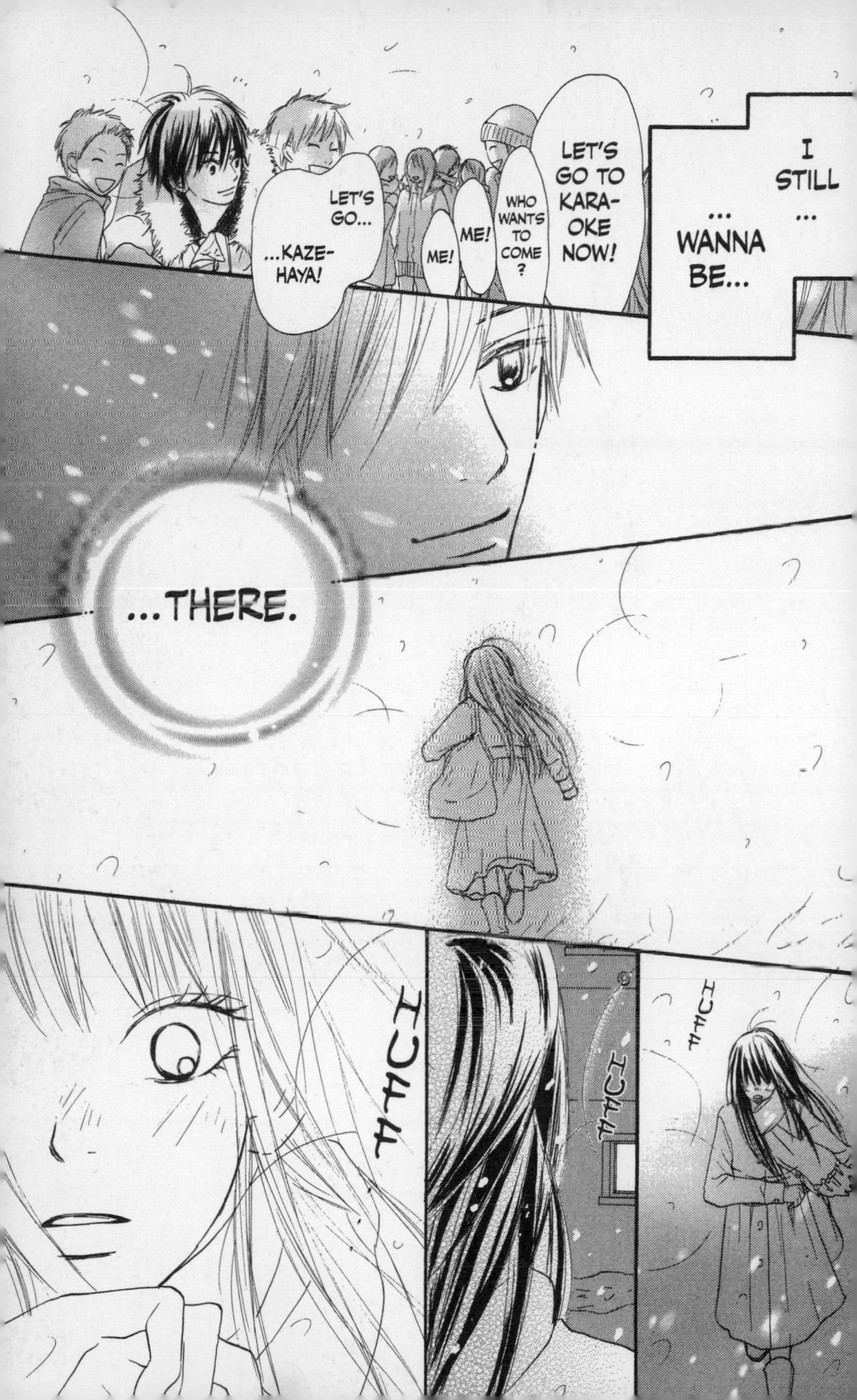
I STILL ...
... WANNA BE...
LET'S GO TO KARAOKE NOW!
WHO WANTS TO COME?
ME!
ME!
LET'S GO... ...KAZEHAYA!
...THERE.
HUFF
HUFF
HUFF

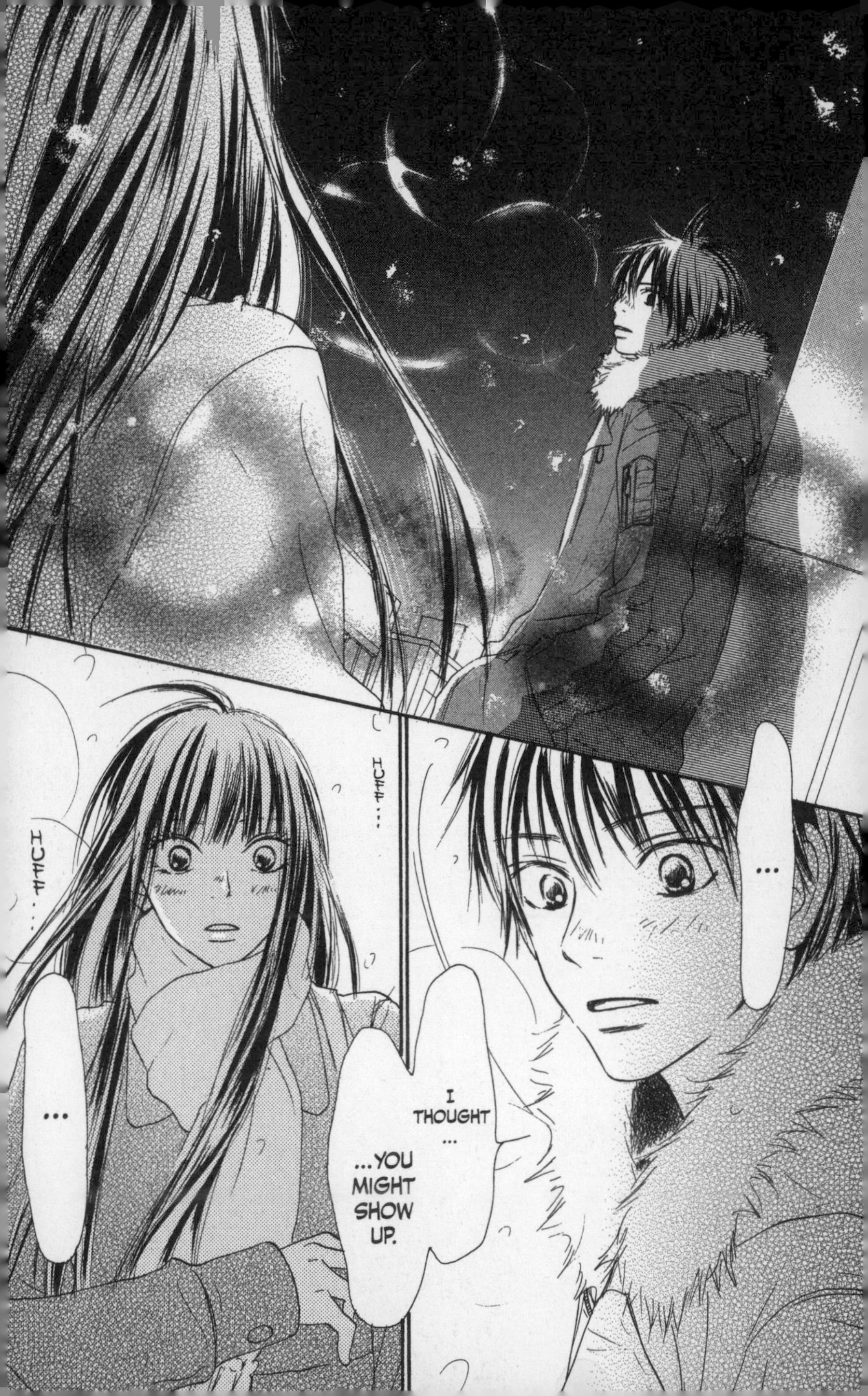
...
I THOUGHT ...
...YOU MIGHT SHOW UP.
HUFF...
HUFF...
...

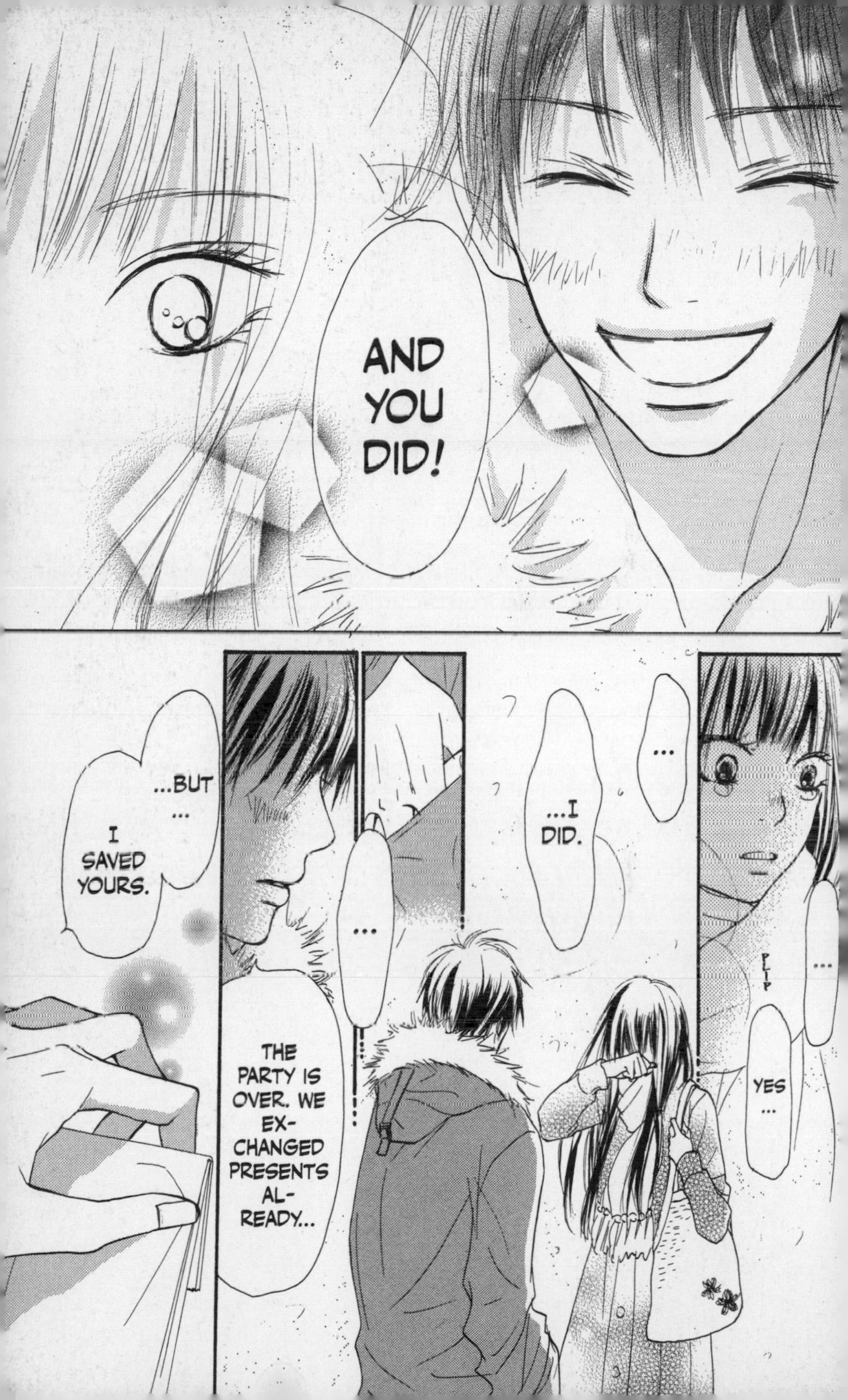
AND YOU DID!
...
...I DID.
PLIP
...
YES ...
...
...BUT ...
I SAVED YOURS.
THE PARTY IS OVER. WE EX- CHANGED PRESENTS AL- READY...

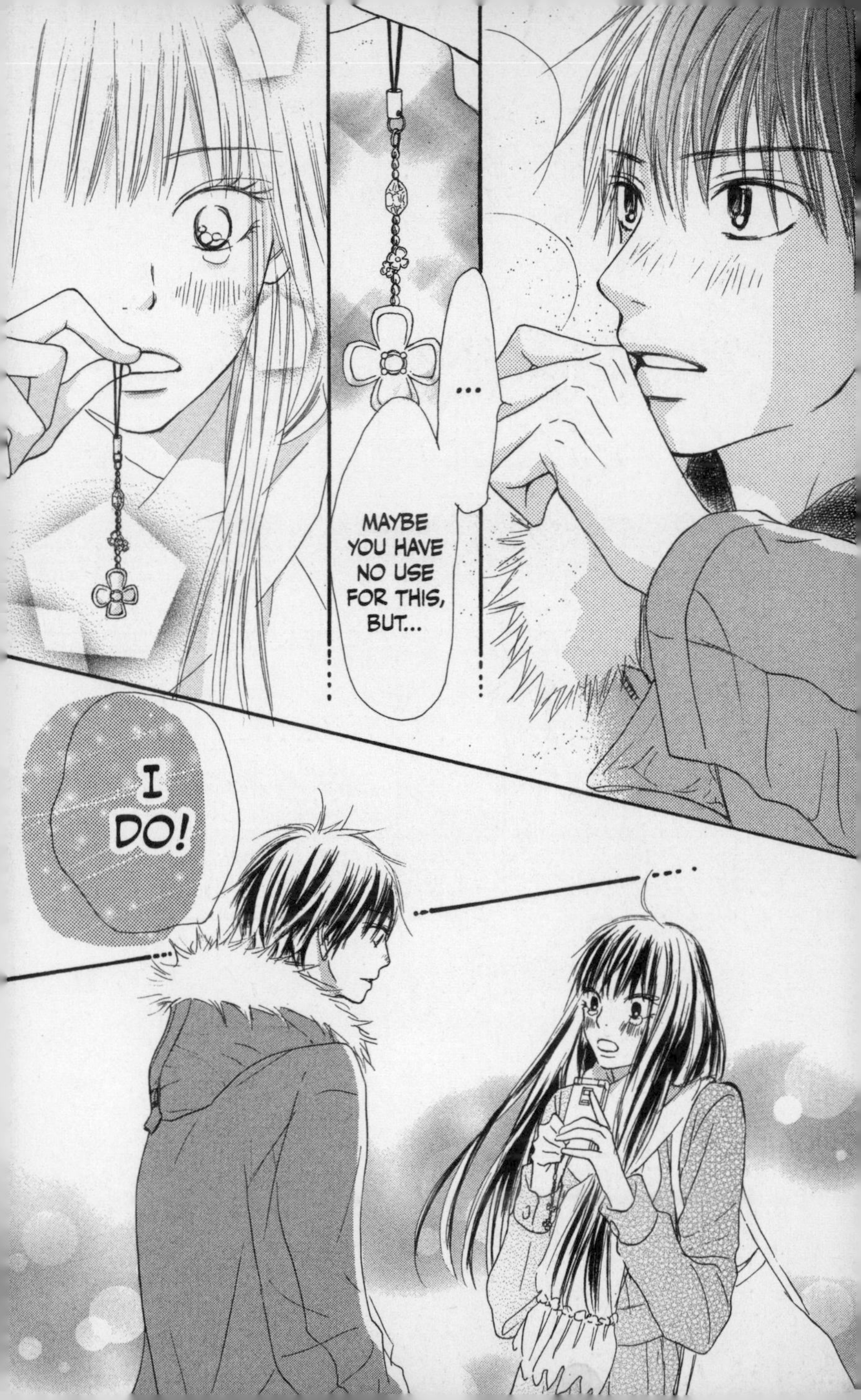
...
MAYBE YOU HAVE NO USE FOR THIS, BUT...
I DO!

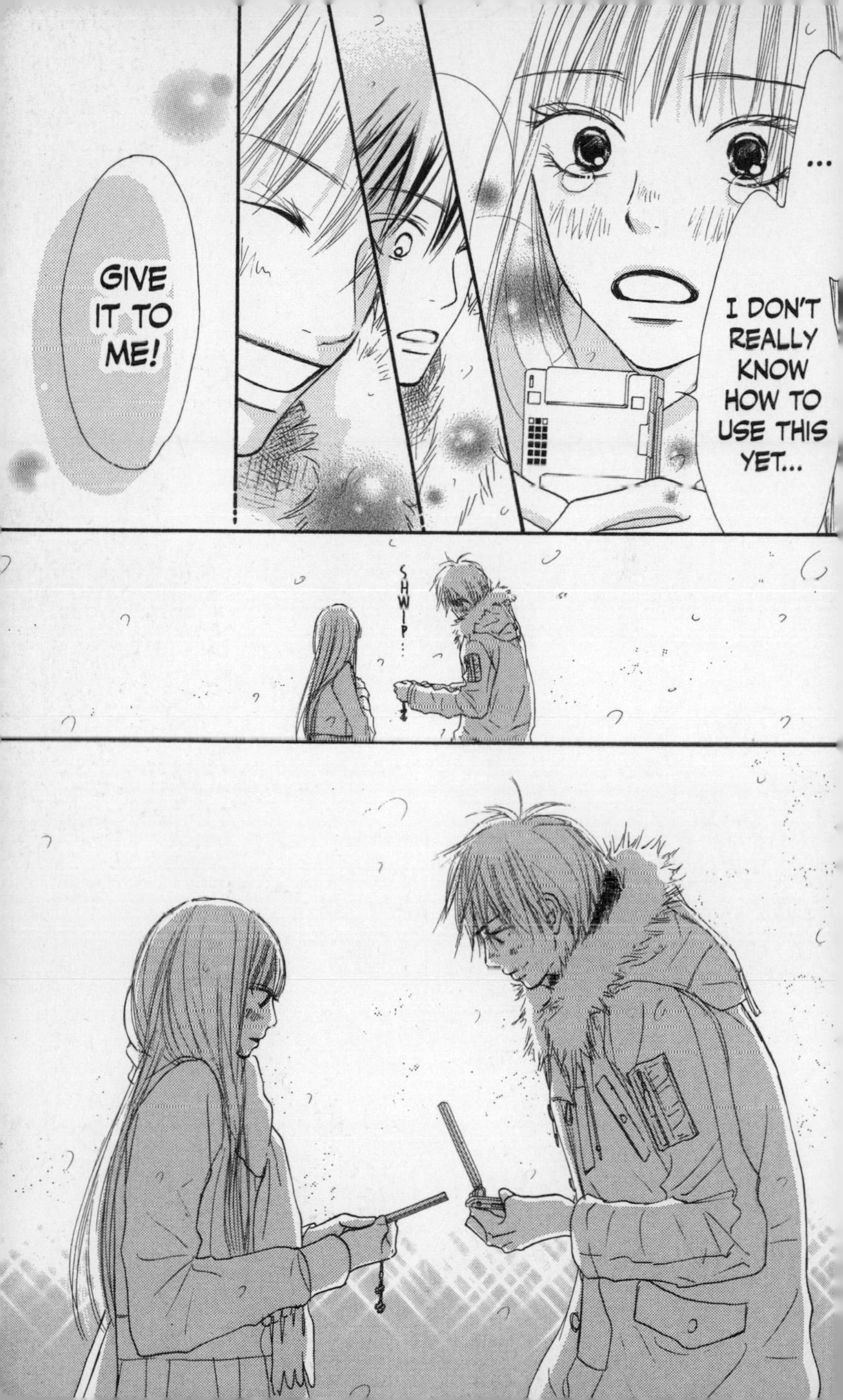
...
I DON'T REALLY KNOW HOW TO USE THIS YET...
GIVE IT TO ME!
SHWIP...

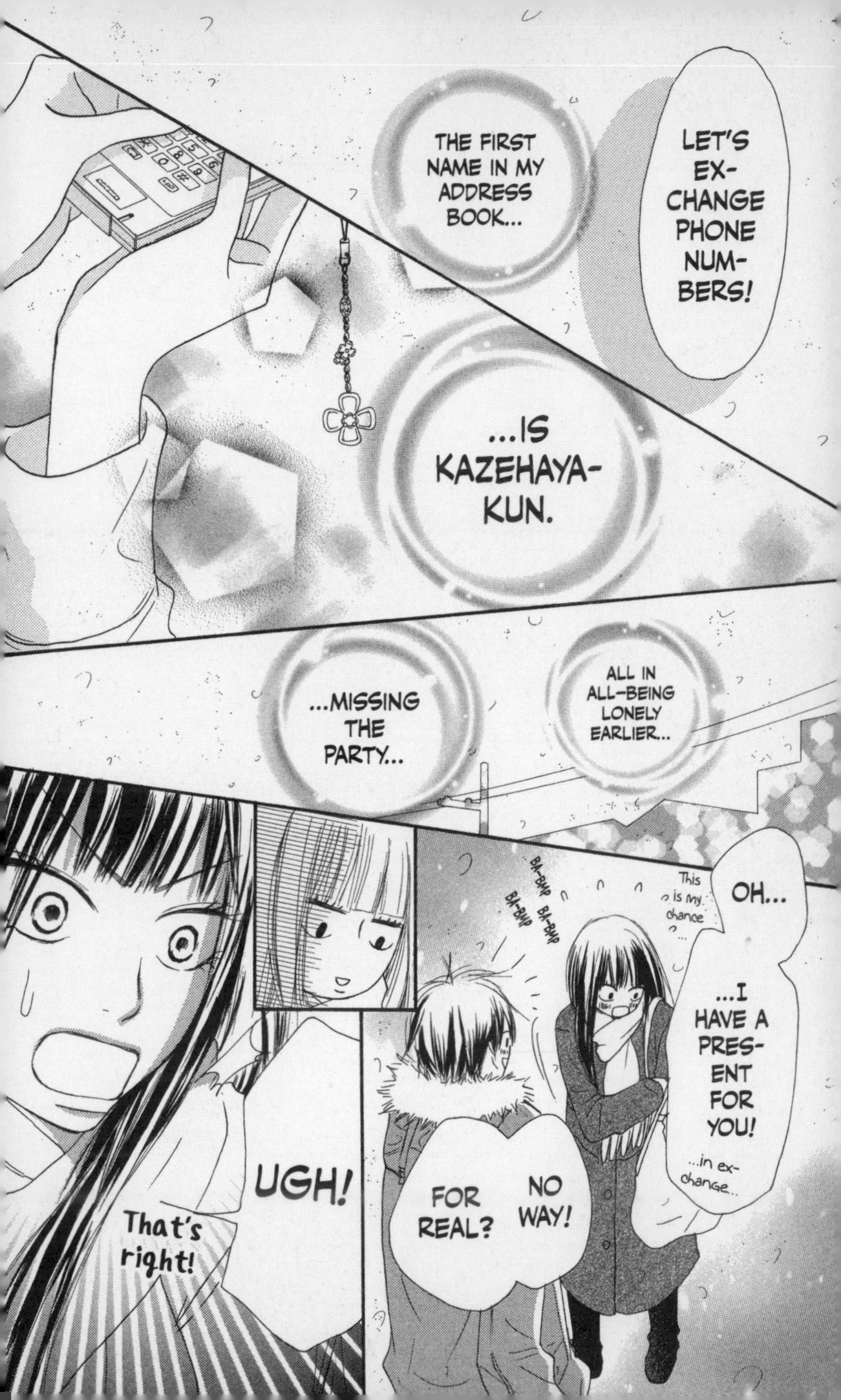
LET'S EX-CHANGE PHONE NUM-BERS!
THE FIRST NAME IN MY ADDRESS BOOK...
...IS KAZEHAYA-KUN.
ALL IN ALL—BEING LONELY EARLIER...
...MISSING THE PARTY...
OH...
This is my chance...
...I HAVE A PRESENT FOR YOU!
...in ex-change...
BA-BMP BA-BMP BA-BMP
NO WAY!
FOR REAL?
UGH!
That's right!

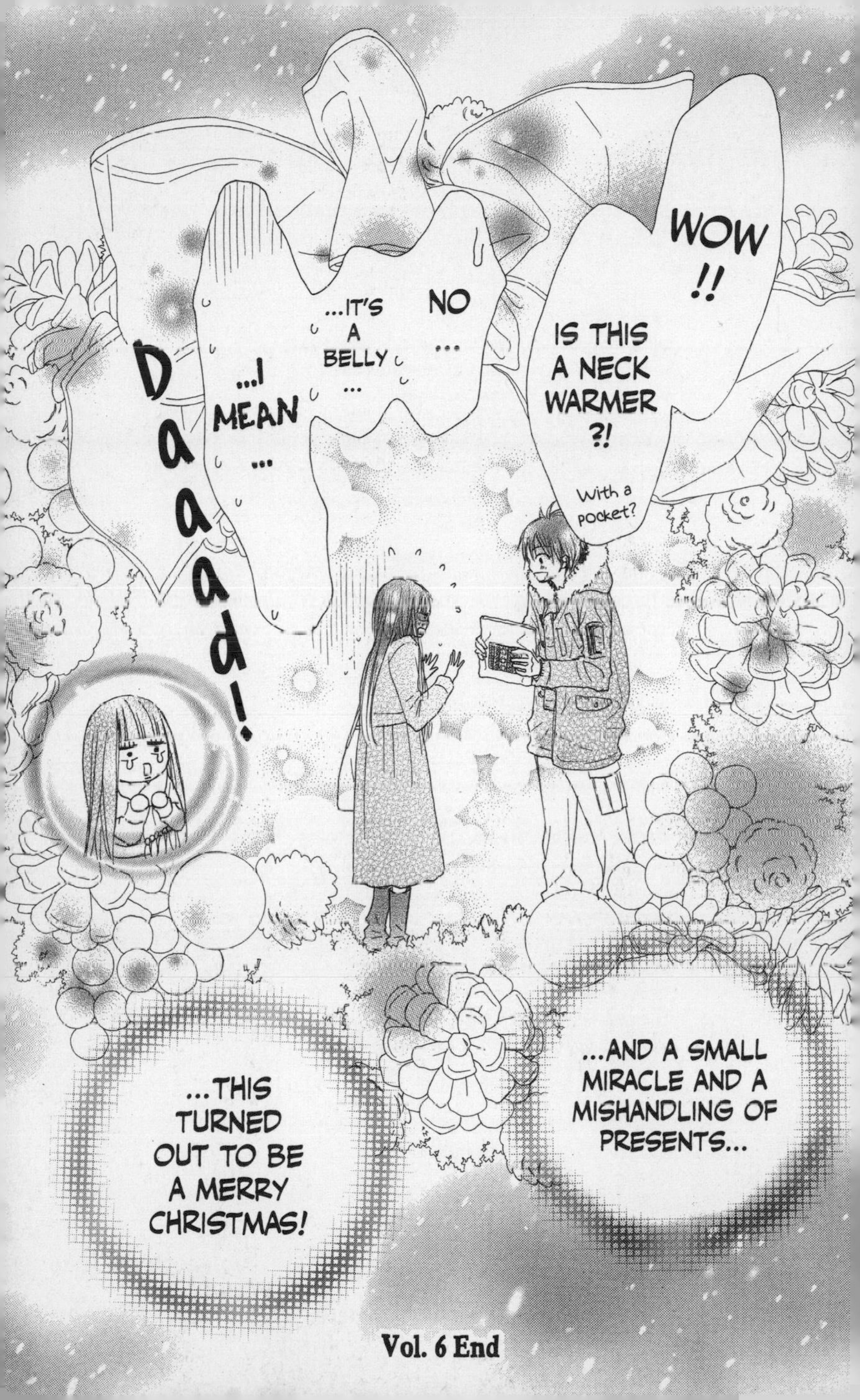
WOW!!
IS THIS A NECK WARMER?!
With a pocket?
NO...
...IT'S A BELLY...
...I MEAN...
Daaad!
...AND A SMALL MIRACLE AND A MISHANDLING OF PRESENTS...
...THIS TURNED OUT TO BE A MERRY CHRISTMAS!
Vol. 6 End

From me (the editor) to you (the reader).

Here are some Japanese culture explanations that will help you better understand the references in the *Kimi ni Todoke* world.

Honorifics:
When saying someone's name in Japanese, a suffix is often attached to indicate how familiar the speaker is with the person. Some are more polite and respectful, while others are endearing. Calling someone by just their first name is the most informal.
-kun is used for young men or boys, usually someone you are familiar with.
-chan is used for young women, girls or young children and can be used as a term of endearment.
-san is used for someone you respect or are not close to, or to be polite.

Page 13, Shogatsu:
Shogatsu, the New Year's Day holiday, is the most important holiday in Japan, traditionally spent with one's family.

Page 63, melon bread:
Melon bread, called *melon pan* in Japan, is a soft bread covered in a layer of crispy cookie dough.

Page 139, Christmas:
Christmas Eve is a popular night for couples to go out. Christmas day is not a national holiday, and unless it falls on a weekend, school and work are still in session.

Page 179, *yuzu*:
Yuzu is a fragrant citrus fruit with a tart flavor.

I like hot drinks. I always drink coffee, tea, and this and that. I often drink green tea, roasted green tea, brown rice tea, black tea, herb tea, flavored tea and coffee. I like my coffee black or with sugar only, or milk only or soy milk only—or sometimes with sugar and either milk or soy milk. I like to have some variety. If I think about it, I repeat the same drink for a while and then change to another drink for a while. Maybe I get tired of things easily. During the winter, I get yuzu and make yuzu tea. After drinking it for a few days, I totally forget about it. I guess I do get tired of things easily.

--Karuho Shiina

Karuho Shiina was born and raised in Hokkaido, Japan. Though *Kimi ni Todoke* is only her second series following many one-shot stories, it has already racked up accolades from various "Best Manga of the Year" lists. Winner of the 2008 Kodansha Manga Award for the shojo category, *Kimi ni Todoke* also placed fifth in the first-ever Manga Taisho (Cartoon Grand Prize) contest in 2008. An animated TV series debuted in October 2009 in Japan.

Kimi ni Todoke
VOL. 6

Shojo Beat Edition

STORY AND ART BY
KARUHO SHIINA

Translation/Ari Yasuda, HC Language Solutions, Inc.
Touch-up Art & Lettering/Vanessa Satone
Design/Yukiko Whitley
Editor/Carrie Shepherd

KIMI NI TODOKE © 2005 by Karuho Shiina
All rights reserved. First published in Japan in 2005 by SHUEISHA Inc.,
Tokyo. English translation rights arranged by SHUEISHA Inc.

Printed in the U.S.A.

Published by VIZ Media, LLC
P.O. Box 77010
San Francisco, CA 94107

10 9 8 7 6 5 4 3 2 1
First printing, November 2010

 www.viz.com

 www.shojobeat.com

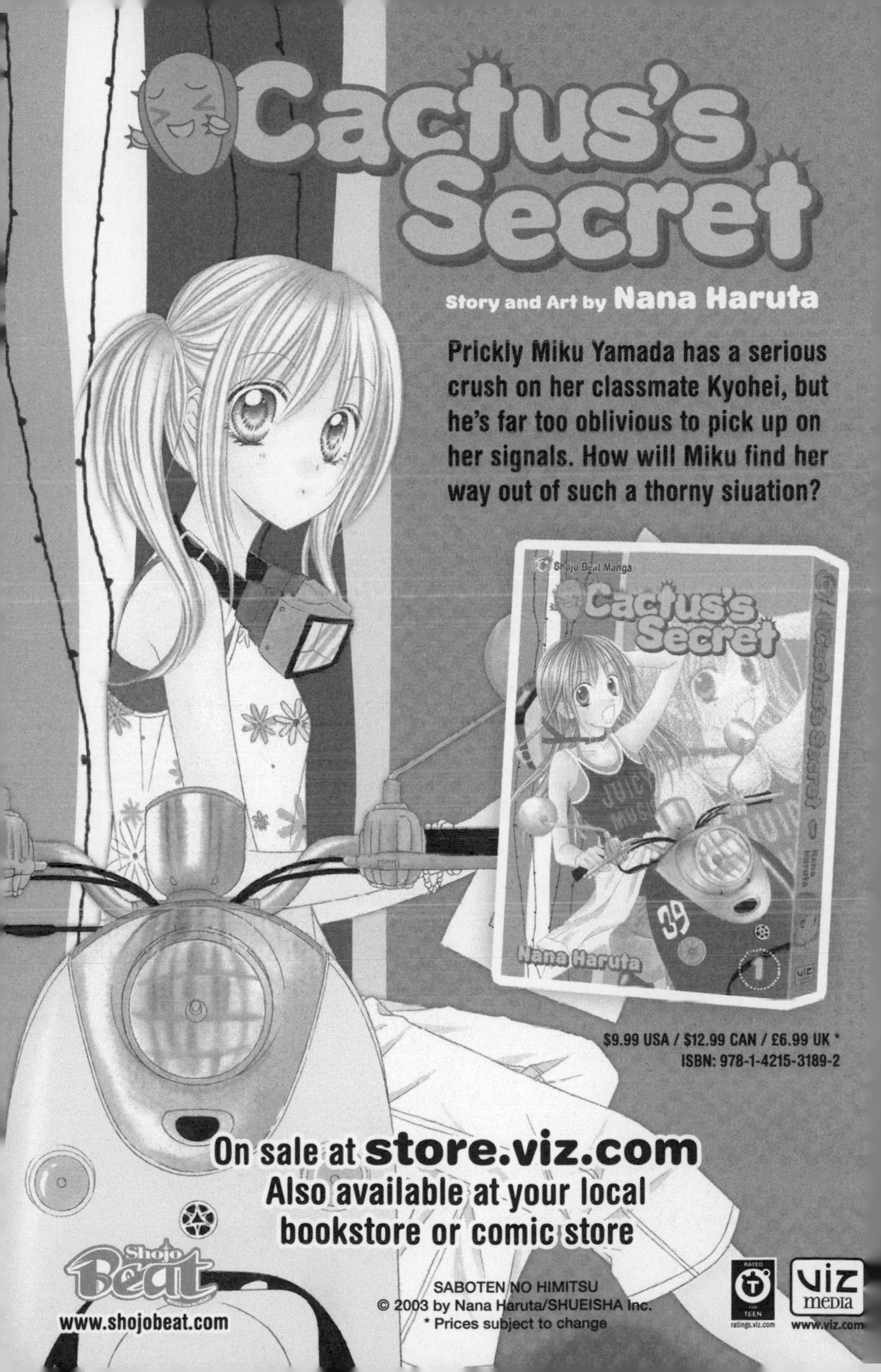
Cactus's Secret
Story and Art by Nana Haruta
Prickly Miku Yamada has a serious crush on her classmate Kyohei, but he's far too oblivious to pick up on her signals. How will Miku find her way out of such a thorny siuation?
Shojo Beat Manga
Cactus's Secret
Nana Haruta
1
$9.99 USA / $12.99 CAN / £6.99 UK *
ISBN: 978-1-4215-3189-2
On sale at store.viz.com
Also available at your local bookstore or comic store
Shojo Beat
www.shojobeat.com
SABOTEN NO HIMITSU
© 2003 by Nana Haruta/SHUEISHA Inc.
* Prices subject to change
RATED T FOR TEEN
ratings.viz.com
VIZ media
www.viz.com

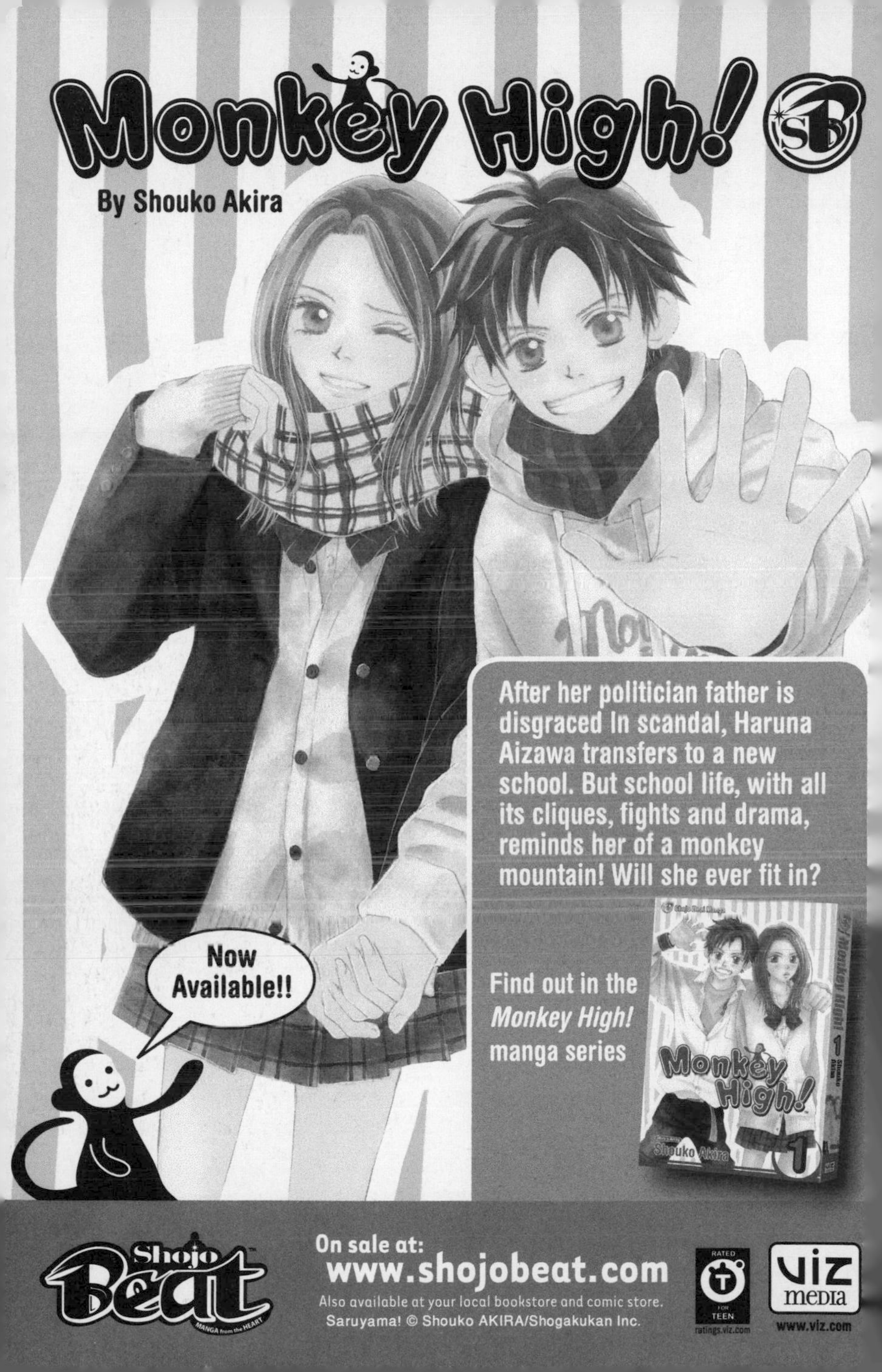
Monkey High!
By Shouko Akira
After her politician father is disgraced in scandal, Haruna Aizawa transfers to a new school. But school life, with all its cliques, fights and drama, reminds her of a monkey mountain! Will she ever fit in?
Now Available!!
Find out in the *Monkey High!* manga series
Monkey High! 1
Shouko Akira
Shojo Beat
MANGA from the HEART
On sale at:
www.shojobeat.com
Also available at your local bookstore and comic store.
Saruyama! © Shouko AKIRA/Shogakukan Inc.
RATED T FOR TEEN
ratings.viz.com
VIZ media
www.viz.com

Shojo Beat

MANGA from the HEART

MP

OTOMEN

STORY AND ART BY
AYA KANNO

VAMPIRE KNIGHT

STORY AND ART BY
MATSURI HINO

Natsume's
BOOK of FRIENDS

STORY AND ART BY
YUKI MIDORIKAWA

Want to see more of what you're looking for?

Let your voice be heard!

shojobeat.com/mangasurvey

Help us give you more manga from the heart!

RATED T TEEN

RATED T OLDER TEEN

VIZ MEDIA

www.viz.com